OXFORD STUDIES IN ANCIENT PHILOSOPHY

OXFORD STUDIES IN ANCIENT PHILOSOPHY

EDITOR: VICTOR CASTON

VOLUME LVIII

SUMMER 2020

OXFORD
UNIVERSITY PRESS

OXFORD
UNIVERSITY PRESS

Great Clarendon Street, Oxford, OX2 6DP,
United Kingdom

Oxford University Press is a department of the University of Oxford.
It furthers the University's objective of excellence in research, scholarship,
and education by publishing worldwide. Oxford is a registered trade mark of
Oxford University Press in the UK and in certain other countries

© the several contributors 2020

The moral rights of the authors have been asserted

First Edition published in 2020

Impression: 1

Published in the United States of America by Oxford University Press
198 Madison Avenue, New York, NY 10016, United States of America

British Library Cataloguing in Publication Data

Data available

Library of Congress Cataloging in Publication Data
Oxford studies in ancient philosophy.—
Vol. lviii (2020).—Oxford: Clarendon Press;
New York: Oxford University Press, 1983–
v.; 22 cm. Annual.
1. Philosophy, Ancient—Periodicals.
B1.O9 180.'5—c.19 84–45022
AACR 2 MARC-S

ISBN 978–0–19–885899–7 (hbk.)
ISBN 978–0–19–885901–7 (pbk.)

Printed and bound by
CPI Group (UK) Ltd, Croydon, CR0 4YY

ADVISORY BOARD

Contributions and books for review should be sent to the Editor, Professor Victor Caston, Department of Philosophy, University of Michigan, 435 South State Street, Ann Arbor, MI 48109-1003, USA (e-mail oxfordstudies@umich.edu).

Contributors are asked to observe the 'Notes for Contributors to Oxford Studies in Ancient Philosophy', printed at the end of this volume.

Up-to-date contact details, the latest version of Notes for Contributors, and publication schedules can be checked on the *Oxford Studies in Ancient Philosophy* website:

www.oup.com/academic/content/series/o/oxford-studies-in-ancient-philosophy-osap

CONTENTS

PLATO ON
THE UNITY OF THE POLITICAL ARTS
(*STATESMAN* 258 D–259 D)

ERIC BROWN

IN Plato's *Statesman*, the Eleatic Visitor argues that the four apparently distinct arts of politics (πολιτική), kingship (βασιλική), slaveholding (δεσποτική), and household-management (οἰκονομική) are in fact one and the same art (258 D–259 D).[1] Aristotle rejects this thesis in the second sentence of his *Politics* (1. 1, 1252ᵃ7–18), and spends the rest of Book 1 trying to substantiate the rejection.[2] Siding with Aristotle, recent commentators have judged Plato's argument 'more

---

[1] I cite Robinson's text in E. A. Duke et al. (eds.), *Platonis Opera*, vol. 1 ['OCT'] (Oxford, 1995), and translations are mine, with borrowings from C. J. Rowe (ed.), *Plato: Statesman* [*Statesman*] (Warminster, 1995) and J. Annas and R. Waterfield (eds.), *Plato: Statesman* [*Statesman*] (Cambridge, 1995). 'Kingship' might seem an inappropriately gendered rendering, but the interlocutors of the *Statesman* seem to have the patriarchal world around them firmly in view throughout. Note that the Visitor introduces their topic as a search for the 'political *man*' (πολιτικὸν ἄνδρα, 258 B 3) and saves 'monarchy' for limited use (291 D 1–5). Cf. P. Kleingeld, 'The Problematic Status of Gender-neutral Language in the History of Philosophy: The Case of Kant', *Philosophical Forum*, 25 (1993), 134–50.

[2] See also *Pol.* 3. 6, 1278ᵇ30–1279ᵃ21, *EN* 8. 10, 1160ᵇ22–1161ᵃ9, and *EE* 7. 9, 1241ᵇ27–40. There should be no doubt that Aristotle has our passage in his sights at *Pol.* 1. 1, 1252ᵃ7–9. Contrast P. L. P. Simpson, *A Philosophical Commentary on the Politics of Aristotle* (Chapel Hill, 1998), 16 n. 4. Simpson suggests that Aristotle might have had Xenophon's *Memorabilia* 3. 4 in mind, though Xenophon's Socrates compares the household-manager, chorus-leader, and general. (That the household-manager's knowledge is the same as the politician's is only implied at 3. 4. 6 and 3. 4. 12.) Simpson also points to passages in the *Politics* in which Aristotle opposes anonymous thinkers who identify politics and slaveholding or politics and money-making or kingship and slaveholding or household-management and slaveholding, though, of course, nothing suggests that any of these anonymous persons identified the four arts of politics, kingship, slaveholding, and household-management, which is what Aristotle targets at 1. 1, 1252ᵃ7–9. Simpson does not mention it, but Aristotle might have had the Platonic *Lovers* 137 B–139 A in mind. I am uncertain about the authorship of the *Lovers*, which is generally judged to be spurious but without any knockdown arguments in favour of that judgement. Cf. S. Peterson, 'Notes on *Lovers*', in A. Stavru and C. Moore (eds.), *Socrates and the Socratic Dialogue* (Leiden, 2017), 412–31. I am, however, confident that even if Aristotle had *Lovers* 137 B–139 A in mind, he was definitely responding to *Statesman* 258 D–259 D as well.

Eric Brown, *Plato on the Unity of the Political Arts* (Statesman *258 D–259 D*). In: Oxford Studies in Ancient Philosophy Volume LVIII. Edited by: Victor Caston, Oxford University Press (2020).
© Eric Brown.
DOI: 10.1093/oso/9780198858997.003.0001

persuasive than strict', 'extremely weak', or even 'flagrantly invalid'.³ I aim to offer a more charitable interpretation of Plato's argument. After I review the apparent problem in it and consider three inadequate responses, I reconsider Plato's purposes and reconstruct how the argument validly achieves them. My effort will not show that Plato was right and Aristotle wrong, but it will save Plato from failure and clarify what is at issue in their disagreement.

The argument in question comes early in the *Statesman*. The Visitor and young Socrates seek to define the expert citizen or statesman (hereafter, artificially, the 'politician'). They first place their target among the knowers (258 B 2–6), and then, to begin narrowing their search, they distinguish between practical (πρακτικήν) and theoretical (γνωστικήν) knowledge (ἐπιστήμας, 258 B 7–E 7). They agree that theoretical knowledge, such as arithmetic, is disengaged from action and dedicated to knowing, whereas practical knowledge, such as building, is naturally embedded in action, and brings a body into existence. This prompts an obvious question for their inquiry: is the politician a theoretical knower or a practical knower?⁴

But the Visitor does not ask the obvious question. Instead, he asks:

[T1] *Πότερον οὖν τὸν πολιτικὸν καὶ βασιλέα καὶ δεσπότην καὶ ἔτ' οἰκονόμον θήσομεν ὡς ἓν πάντα ταῦτα προσαγορεύοντες, ἢ τοσαύτας τέχνας αὐτὰς εἶναι φῶμεν ὅσαπερ ὀνόματα ἐρρήθη;* (258 E 8–11)

---

³ In order, Rowe, *Statesman*, ad 258 E 11; M. Schofield, *Plato: Political Philosophy* (Oxford, 2006), 167; and J. M. Cooper, 'Plato's *Statesman* and Politics' ['Politics'], in *Reason and Emotion* (Princeton, 1999), 165–91 at 169. There is not much discussion of this argument in M. H. Miller, Jr, *The Philosopher in Plato's* Statesman (The Hague, 1980); S. Rosen, *Plato's* Statesman: *The Web of Politics* [*Web*] (New Haven, 1995); M. S. Lane, *Method and Politics in Plato's* Statesman [*Method*] (Cambridge, 1998); or the many contributions in C. J. Rowe (ed.), *Reading the* Statesman: *Proceedings of the III Symposium Platonicum* [*Reading the* Statesman] (Sankt Augustin, 1995), although several contributors note the argument's anticipation of 292 E–293 A: see C. J. Rowe, 'Introduction', 11–28 at 14–15 with 25; M. Dixsaut, 'Une politique vraiment conforme à la nature', 253–73 at 257; U. Hirsch, 'Μιμεῖσθαι und verwandte Ausdrücke in Platons *Politikos*', 184–9 at 188; and P. Accattino, 'L'ἀρχή del *Politico*', 201–12 at 203.

⁴ It also prompts less obvious questions about the distinction itself. First, one might think that some arts are naturally embedded in actions but do not bring a body into existence. Medicine, for instance, brings health to a body, but does not bring a new body into existence. Is an art like this theoretical or practical? Second, one might wonder about expertise that combines an art of management with an art of manual activity, an expertise that a construction foreman might possess. I bracket these questions insofar as possible in this essay, and proceed with the rough distinction that the Visitor draws.

Shall we set the politician and king and slaveholder and also the household-manager down as a single thing though we call them all these things [*viz*., names], or should we say that the arts themselves are as many as the names they are called by?

So now the Visitor and young Socrates have two tasks. First, they need to determine whether 'politics', 'kingship', 'slaveholding', and 'household-management' name four arts or just one. Second, they need to determine whether politics is among the theoretical or practical arts.

They apparently try to discharge the first task with just three premises. The Visitor states the conclusion clearly:

[T2]   Οὐκοῦν, ὃ νυνδὴ διεσκοπούμεθα, φανερὸν ὡς ἐπιστήμη μία περὶ πάντ᾽ ἐστὶ ταῦτα· ταύτην δὲ εἴτε βασιλικὴν εἴτε πολιτικὴν εἴτε οἰκονομικήν τις ὀνομάζει, μηδὲν αὐτῷ διαφερώμεθα. (259 C 1–4)

Thus, with respect to what we were inquiring into just now, it is plain that there is one science concerning all these things; whether someone names it kingship or politics or household-management, let us not disagree with him at all.

Similarly clear are the second and third premises:

[T3]   Καὶ μὴν οἰκονόμος γε καὶ δεσπότης ταὐτόν. (259 B 7)

But a household-manager and a slaveholder are the same thing.

[T4]   Τί δέ; μεγάλης σχῆμα οἰκήσεως ἢ σμικρᾶς αὖ πόλεως ὄγκος μῶν τι πρὸς ἀρχὴν διοίσετον;

Οὐδέν. (259 B 9–11)

Well then, will the apparent character of a large household differ at all from the bulk of small city as far as rule is concerned?

Not at all.

There is room for quibbling about what exactly the Visitor and young Socrates agree to here, let alone whether they *should* so agree. But in light of the intended conclusion, it seems best to take these premises to be that the arts of household-management and slave-holding are the same and the arts of household-management and politics are the same. Then, if the first premise identifies the art of kingship with one of the others, the Visitor and young Socrates could draw their conclusion that all four arts are one and the same.

Unfortunately, the passage where the first premise should be does not identify kingship with one of the others. Instead, the Visitor and young Socrates say this:

[T5] εἴ τῳ τις τῶν δημοσιευόντων ἰατρῶν ἱκανὸς συμβουλεύειν ἰδιωτεύων αὐτός, ἆρ᾽ οὐκ ἀναγκαῖον αὐτῷ προσαγορεύεσθαι τοὔνομα τῆς τέχνης ταὐτὸν ὅπερ ᾧ συμβουλεύει;

Ναί.

Τί δ᾽; ὅστις βασιλεύοντι χώρας ἀνδρὶ παραινεῖν δεινὸς ἰδιώτης ὢν αὐτός, ἆρ᾽ οὐ φήσομεν ἔχειν αὐτὸν τὴν ἐπιστήμην ἣν ἔδει τὸν ἄρχοντα αὐτὸν κεκτῆσθαι;

Φήσομεν.

Ἀλλὰ μὴν ἥ γε ἀληθινοῦ βασιλέως βασιλική;

Ναί.

Ταύτην δὲ ὁ κεκτημένος οὐκ, ἄντε ἄρχων ἄντε ἰδιώτης ὢν τυγχάνῃ, πάντως κατά γε τὴν τέχνην αὐτὴν βασιλικὸς ὀρθῶς προσρηθήσεται;

Δίκαιον γοῦν. (259 A 1–B 6)

If someone who is himself private is able to advise one of the public doctors, mustn't the same name of the art be applied to him as to the one he advises?[5]

Yes.

Well, shall we not say that the one who is clever at helping the king of a country, though he is himself a private individual, has the knowledge which the ruler needed to have?

We shall say that.

But the knowledge that belongs to the true king is kingship?

Yes.

And the person who possesses this, whether he happens to rule or to be a private citizen, will be addressed with perfect correctness as an expert in kingship, on account of the art itself?

That is just.

In other words, just as whether one holds the office of public doctor is irrelevant to whether one has the public doctor's art, so too, whether one is actually a king is irrelevant to whether one has the art of kingship.

This is plainly not enough to deliver the conclusion of the argument. If we read very charitably, we have the following premises and conclusion:

---

[5] Two readings of this have been proposed. According to one, the advisor is a doctor in private practice and the advisee is a special public doctor appointed by the Athenian assembly (see Plato, *Gorg.* 455 B and Xenophon, *Mem.* 4. 2. 5, with E. R. Dodds (ed.), *Plato: Gorgias* (Oxford, 1959), ad 455 B 2 and J. B. Skemp, *Plato's Statesman* (New Haven, 1952), 124 n. 1). Alternatively, the advisor is an amateur who knows medicine and the advisee is a publicly recognized doctor (cf. *Gorg.* 514 D–E, with L. Campbell, *The* Sophistes *and* Politicus *of Plato* [*Politicus*] (Oxford, 1867), ad 259 B). I have tried to translate neutrally; for my purposes, either will do.

have is wisdom, and it should benefit the ruled. Of course, in the *Statesman*, the conversation is being led not by Socrates but by the Eleatic Visitor, and while we might be prepared for an intellectual from Elea to over-unify things, we cannot assume that he has Socratic thoughts in mind. Still, Socrates is hovering nearby, and the Visitor and young Socrates have quickly agreed to focus not on what actual statesmen or politicians do but on the expert.[12]

What Cooper dismisses as mere 'camouflage' is the harder part, of identifying the private with the public arts. In the *Phaedrus*, Socrates proposes that rhetoric is the same art whether it works in public, in the Assembly and law courts, or in private (261 A 7–B 5), and Phaedrus expresses surprise. In the *Statesman*, the Visitor might hint that this identification of public and private is more difficult when he first raises the question (at [T2]), since he uses 'also' (ἔτι) to emphasize whether household-management should be joined to the others. In any case, the only premises that the Visitor develops concern the possible distinction between private and public arts. Plainly, then, this is the objection that he is most concerned to fend off. A wider view begins to explain why, since there is in Greek political ideology a strong contrast between those who engage in politics and those who live a private or quiet life. The latter are ridiculed as 'useless', 'unmanly', 'fools', and 'nobodies to their friends'.[13] Plato's Meno gives voice to this ideology when he identifies the virtue of a man as 'being able to do the business of the city, and by doing this to benefit his friends and harm his enemies' (ἱκανὸν εἶναι τὰ τῆς πόλεως πράττειν, καὶ πράττοντα τοὺς μὲν φίλους εὖ ποιεῖν, τοὺς δ' ἐχθροὺς κακῶς) and then assigns 'managing the household well' (τὴν οἰκίαν εὖ οἰκεῖν) to the virtue of a woman (*Meno* 71 E 1–7). Later in the *Statesman*, the Visitor explains how hostility arises in a city between those committed to living the 'quiet life' and those who favour the vigorously engaged life (307 D–308 B). But the ideological conflict is not inevitable. Socrates challenges the ideology when he insists that he, a private citizen who has minimized his engagement in politics (*Ap.* 23 B, 31 D–32 A), is one of few Athenians, if not the only one, to try to practise the true

---

[12] See also R. Weiss, 'Statesman as ΕΠΙΣΤΗΜΩΝ: Caretaker, Physician, and Weaver', in C. J. Rowe (ed.), *Reading the* Statesman, 213–22.

[13] By, respectively, Pericles, in Thucydides' version of his funeral oration (Thuc. II. 40. 2), the philosophically withdrawn father's nagging wife in Plato's *Republic* (8, 549 D 6), those around that same man's son (8, 550 A 3), and Zethus, in the fragments of Euripides' *Antiope* (fr. 187 Kannicht, in *TGF* vol. 5.1).

political art (*Gorg.* 521 D 6–8).[14] It is similarly provocative to say that those who are expert household-managers and slaveholders have the same knowledge as those who are expert kings and statesmen.[15]

So let us consider a second response to the Visitor's argument. The argument lacks a premise identifying the arts of politics and kingship. Two scholars have independently proposed rectifying this by moving three lines of text.[16] In the manuscripts, the lines come at the very end of our passage, just before the Visitor suggests that they make a second division, between two kinds of theoretical knowledge. But the movers, and they include the editors of the most recent Oxford Classical Texts edition, propose to place these lines between the first two premises of the argument, [T5] and [T3]. Here they are:

[T6] Τὴν ἄρα πολιτικὴν καὶ πολιτικὸν καὶ βασιλικὴν καὶ βασιλικὸν εἰς ταὐτὸν ὡς ἓν πάντα ταῦτα συνθήσομεν;[17]

Δῆλον. (259 D 4–6)

---

[14] See J. C. Shaw, 'Socrates and the True Political Craft', *Classical Philology*, 106 (2011), 187–207.

[15] See E. Brown, 'False Idles: The Politics of the "Quiet Life" in Greek and Roman Antiquity', in R. Balot (ed.), *A Companion to Ancient Political Thought* (Oxford, 2009), 485–500.

[16] See F. H. Sandbach, 'Five Textual Notes' ['Notes'], *Illinois Classical Studies*, 2 (1977), 49–53, and D. Robinson, 'The New *Oxford Text* of Plato's *Statesman*: Editor's Comments' ['Comments'], in C. J. Rowe (ed.), *Reading the* Statesman, 37–46 at 41 with 37 n. 1. (Robinson's proposal is enshrined in Duke et al., *OCT*, and in Annas and Waterfield, *Statesman*.) Although Sandbach and Robinson propose moving three different lines, the difference is trivial. They both want to move the Visitor's sentence at 259 D 4–5 (using the lines numbers in Duke et al., *OCT*). Sandbach would additionally move the preceding response from young Socrates and locate 259 D 3–5 immediately after 259 B 5. Robinson also moves the following response from young Socrates and locates 259 D 4–6 immediately after 259 B 6. Sandbach ('Notes', 51) reasons that Δίκαιον γοῦν (at 259 B 6) is an unparalleled and infelicitous response to a question concerning whether something is said ὀρθῶς, since 'to say anything ὀρθῶς must be δίκαιον'. This seems to me to fear redundancy more than Plato in fact did, and above I consider Robinson's proposal. But nothing philosophically important hinges on this particular difference. Nor does much hinge on the emendations that Sandbach ('Notes', 51–2) proposes for the would-be-moved text (for which see the next note).

[17] Sandbach ('Notes', 51–2) suggests two emendations. First, he notes that manuscript T lacks καί before πολιτικόν and βασιλικόν, and suggests bracketing καί πολιτικόν and καί βασιλικόν, since if the archetype lacked καί πολιτικόν and καί βασιλικόν, πολιτικόν and βασιλικόν could have crept in from explanatory marginalia (explaining T) and then conjunctions would have been added to 'correct' the error in T (explaining B and W). Second, citing conversation with Richard Hackforth, he troubles about ὡς ἓν πάντα ταῦτα since 'even if four terms precede it there are in reality only two entities to be identified', and so he suggests that 'the phrase had been wrongly repeated' from [T1], 'as an explanation of εἰς ταὐτὸν συνθήσομεν'. This is more worrying than necessary, as I argue in what follows.

> So shall we place all these things—the political art, the expert politician, the kingly art, and the expert king—into the same thing [*viz.* category] as a single thing?
>
> Clearly.

Cooper calls the decision to move these lines 'a stunning example of editorial hubris and ignorance'.[18] I would not phrase it quite like that, but I tend to agree. There needs to be an outstanding reason to move text around: problems had better get solved. Unfortunately, this particular move solves no problem and creates a new one.

It creates a problem by depriving our passage of its effective conclusion. Recall that the Visitor and young Socrates have two tasks. They reach their conclusion for the first task in [T2], agreeing that the arts of politics, kingship, household-management, and slaveholding are the same, and then they take up the second task by considering whether this single political art is theoretical or practical (259 C 6–D 3). To do this, they agree that 'any king'— that is, anyone with the single political art that can be called the kingly art—has power that resides not in his (own) hands but in his mind (259 C 6–9), and so the art of kingship must be theoretical (259 C 10–D 3). This reasoning, even more than the reasoning for the first task, treats the agent who possesses the art as nothing but the art itself, embodied. That is why inferences can be made from what the artful king does to the nature of kingship (and vice versa).[19] The completion of the second task also sets up the double conclusion that the apparently various political arts are all one and the same art *and* that this one art belongs to the category of theoretical arts. The passage that some scholars want to move, [T6], states this double conclusion, concentrating on just politics and kingship: these arts belong to the same category—they are theoretical knowledge— as one art.[20] If [T6] is moved, there is no clear conclusion to the two

---

[18] Cooper, 'Politics', 168 n. 4.

[19] Sandbach's worries about [T6] (see n. 17) miss the way in which the argument before 259 D 5 licenses the identification of an artist with his art, in part because Sandbach has committed himself to moving the crucial question in [T6].

[20] Cooper ('Politics', 168 n. 4) sees the double conclusion clearly, and Waterfield (in Annas and Waterfield, *Statesman*) translates [T6] for the double conclusion but unfortunately misplaces it. Rowe, *Statesman*, under-translates εἰς ταὐτὸν . . . συνθήσομεν in [T6]: 'In that case shall we put all these things together—the states-man's knowledge and the statesman, the king's knowledge and the king—as one, and regard them as the same?' For εἰς ταὐτὸν . . . συνθήσομεν, Cooper ('Politics', 168 n. 4) aptly cites 276 E 2 and the related parallels at 260 E 6, 263 D 7–8, 266 E 9, 281 C 9–D 1. Julia Annas has insisted to me that these parallels are not relevant, since there is a difference between εἰς ταὐτὸν . . . συνθήσομεν and εἰς ταὐτὸν ὡς ἕν . . .

tasks the Visitor and young Socrates took up before the Visitor introduces a further division within theoretical knowledge.

But perhaps the more serious problem with moving [T6] is that it does not help the Visitor's argument. Notice that [T6] offers an inference (ἄρα). In its original location, it is clear how: [T6] completes the Visitor's two tasks by drawing together the two conclusions into one, validly inferring the claim (p & q) from the separate claims p and q. In its new home, however, what are the grounds in [T5], about a private individual having the same knowledge that a public doctor or king needs, for [T6]? Let us consider this dilemmatically. Either [T5] gives good grounds for [T6] or it does not. If it does not, then moving [T6] hardly helps the Visitor's cause. Yes, the Visitor now has a premise he needs to infer that the arts of politics, kingship, household-management, and slaveholding are the same, but unfortunately, he infers that premise invalidly. One invalidity has replaced another. What if, on the other hand, [T5] gives good grounds for [T6]? In this case, we do not need to move [T6] at all. If [T5] warrants the conclusion that the kingly and political arts are the same, then we can give the Visitor this as an *implicit* premise to get to his desired conclusion.

The possibility of an implicit premise offers a third approach to the argument. If we prefer not to call the argument flagrantly invalid for dubious gain and prefer not to shuffle the text for no gain, then perhaps we should try to extract from [T5] the grounds for an implicit claim that the kingly and political arts are the same. This would give the Visitor a valid argument:

(P1) Politics = kingship.   [assumed to be implicit in [T5]]

συνθήσομεν. On this view, which supports Rowe's rendering, εἰς ταὐτὸν ὡς ἕν . . . συνθήσομεν is just an especially elaborate way of saying that we will consider these arts to be the same. I think that this way of parsing the Greek is possible, but I do not see that it is mandatory. And Rowe's rendering makes [T6] repeat the conclusion in [T2] needlessly, as Cooper ('Politics', 168 n. 4) notes. Rowe (*Statesman*, ad 259 D 3–4) pretends otherwise, saying that [T2] established 'the identity of kingship and statesmanship' whereas [T6] 'confirms the identity of kingship and statesmanship with the knowledge which the true king/statesman will possess', since now it is clear that 'kingship/statesmanship is a matter of knowledge only'. But this defence misrepresents [T2] and confuses the issue of identifying the arts of kingship and statesmanship (done in [T2]) and identifying the single art of kingship or statesmanship as a theoretical art (only done in [T6], and only if we parse εἰς ταὐτὸν . . . συνθήσομεν and ὡς ἕν as making distinct points).

(P2) Household-management = slaveholding.   [T3]

(P3) Household-management = politics.   [T4]

Thus:

(C) Politics = kingship = household-management =
     slaveholding.   [T2]

The initial difficulty with this approach is that there is no explicit
mention in [T5] of the expert politician or the art of politics at
all.[21] But one might think that the implicit identity does not require
any explicit mention of the expert politician. The Visitor does ask,
'Well, shall we not say that the one who is clever at helping the king
of a country, though he is himself a private individual, has the
knowledge which the ruler [ἄρχοντα] needed to have?'[22] Here, the
word 'ruler' plainly refers to the same person that the word 'king'
does, but in other contexts, the same word easily refers to people
who are not kings but regular politicians, holding office in the city.
One might think that the Visitor's word choice reflects the casual
identification of the political art with the art of kingship. And if
[T5] casually assumes that the political art and the art of kingship
are the same, [T4] would too, with the use of 'rule' (ἀρχήν, 259 B 10).

There are two problems with this interpretation. First, it ren-
ders the argument valid but very weak. The first premise is not
articulated, and the second is *merely* articulated. Only the third
premise gets supported by reasoning (in [T4]). But if you were
inclined to doubt that the arts of politics, kingship, household-
management, and slaveholding were one and the same, you should
easily be able to continue doubting after learning in [T4] that the
largest households and smallest cities were similarly sized. Second,
there is a lot going on in [T5] beyond any implicit identification of
the arts of kingship and politics. The central point of [T5] is that
someone can possess the art of kingship without being a king.
A better interpretation of the Visitor's argument would explain this;
it would explain what the Visitor says in making the argument and
not merely what the Visitor assumes.

---

[21] I am thus confused by Sandbach's assertion ('Notes', 51) that 'the preceding
argument [that is, before 259 B 5 and so in [T5]] has shown that πολιτικός is equivalent to βασιλικός'. But I am grateful to an anonymous referee, Anne Baril, and Billy
Dunaway for encouraging me to take this reading more seriously.

[22] Τί δ'; ὅστις βασιλεύοντι χώρας ἀνδρὶ παραινεῖν δεινὸς ἰδιώτης ὢν αὐτός, ἆρ' οὐ
φήσομεν ἔχειν αὐτὸν τὴν ἐπιστήμην ἣν ἔδει τὸν ἄρχοντα αὐτὸν κεκτῆσθαι; (259 A 6–8).

So I turn now to a fourth approach to the argument. I propose
that we start by attending to the two points that the Visitor actually
develops, in [T5] and [T4]. In these passages, the Visitor addresses
reasons a person might have for distinguishing between the public
arts of politics and kingship and the private arts of household-
management and slavery. You might think, with Meno, that there
is a significant gulf between the manly sphere of the polis and the
womanly sphere of the household. Or you might think that what
politicians and kings do diverges sharply from what household-
managers and slaveholders do. In [T5], the Visitor focuses our
attention not on what these various agents do but on what they
know, and he insists that a person who is a private citizen can know
what a public doctor or king needs to know. A private citizen cannot do what a public doctor or king can do. Nor, one might worry,
can they have all the know-how that is embedded in what a public
doctor or king does. But they can nonetheless know things the public doctor or king needs to know, things that could be communi-
cated by an advisor to an advisee before any action. For the public
doctor or king needs to know what their goals are, and they must
know about how, broadly, to achieve those goals, quite apart from
any particular actions. Moreover, nothing prevents a private citizen from acquiring knowledge about how to promote health or
how to rule so as to promote the well-being of citizens. With this
reasoning, the Visitor has not established that an expert household-
manager and an expert politician share the same expertise. But he
has removed two reasons one might have for doubting this: both
Meno's about the difference between the manly polis and the
womanly household, and the appeal to divergent actions. Then,
with [T4], the Visitor removes a third reason for doubt. You might
think that the civic arts differ from the household ones because
cities are larger than households, but this, as the Visitor points out
in [T4], is false.

On this fourth approach to the argument, the Visitor is primarily
exercised to show that the public and private arts are the same. He
and his interlocutors nowhere doubt that the arts of politics and
kingship are the same, and they can take this identity for granted in
[T5] and especially [T4]. In [T3], he baldly claims that the arts of
household-management and slaveholding are the same. But in [T5]
and [T4], he does not merely assume or assert. He works to bridge
the gap between the pair of arts concerned with the business of the

polis and the pair concerned with the business of the household. Moreover, on this interpretation, the Visitor is primarily intent on bridging this gap by turning away from particular actions of ruling, on which the four arts differ, and towards some general knowledge of how to rule, on which the four arts might agree. This explains why he turns immediately from the implicit question of whether the expert statesman is a theoretical or practical knower to the explicit question of whether the arts of politics, kingship, slaveholding, and household-management are the same in [T1].[23] To answer the question about theoretical and practical knowledge, the Visitor needs to give greater content to his rough distinction between these kinds of knowledge, and to do that, the Visitor uses his argument for identity. This argument draws attention to the 'theoretical' knowledge shared by the political arts, knowledge not about particular actions but about what the goals of ruling human beings are and how, generally, to realize those goals. So understood, the Visitor is simultaneously preparing for the conclusion that the four arts are one and the conclusion that this one art is 'theoretical'.

But this interpretation faces an objection.[24] One might put the four premises I have attributed to the Visitor like this:

(P1) Whether a person is a public official or not is not significant to whether they know what an expert public official knows.　　[T5]

(P2) Household-management = slaveholding.　　[T3]

(P3) Whether the number of people managed is large or small is not significant to whether one has the art of managing people.　　[T4]

(P4) Politics = kingship.　　[assumed]

The problem is that these four premises are still quite far from the conclusion, in [T2], that the two private arts of household-management and slaveholding are the same as the two public arts of politics and kingship. The argument needs first to leap from (P1) and (P3) to:

(C*) There is no significant difference between a private political art such as household-management and slaveholding and a public political art such as politics and kingship.

---

[23] So, too, Campbell, *Politicus*, ad 258 E.

[24] For help with the objection, I'm indebted to Keith McPartland.

Then, the argument needs to leap again, from (C*), (P2), and (P4) to:

(C) Politics = kingship = household-management = slaveholding.[T2]

But both of these inferences seem to be problematic.[25]

The second inference, however, presents no real problem. The reasoning from (C*) to (C) moves from 'there is no significant difference between X and Y' to '$X = Y$'. This inference needs some premise or inference-rule according to which if X and Y differ only in insignificant ways, they are identical. This would be nonsense on some conceptions of identity. However, the Visitor is plainly not saying that the four political arts are identical in every particular, but only that they are essentially the same. For that, it will do to show that there are no essential differences among them. So there should be no difficulty in attributing to the Visitor the general premise or inference-rule he needs.

The first inference, from (P1) and (P3) to (C*), by contrast, looks like a hasty generalization. The Visitor has addressed three possible differences between private and public political arts.[26] It would be mad to attribute to him the premise that these are the *only* differences. So if we want the Visitor's argument to manifest textbook deductive validity, we must think him crazy. But this just shows the limited utility of deduction and the importance of other

---

[25] Cooper would lodge a third complaint, as he thinks the Visitor cannot assume the identity of expert kingship and politics without begging the question ('Politics', 168 n. 4). But whether an argument begs the question depends upon what question it is addressing. I have argued that the Visitor is not concerned to show that kingship and politics are identical. He is instead concerned to show that the public and private political arts are the same. He does not beg *that* question by assuming the identity of kingship and politics. Cooper would surely insist that the rest of the *Statesman* raises questions about whether kingship and politics really are identical. I doubt this. The Visitor takes care to characterize kingship correctly, swapping out the herdsman king in favour of the weaver king, and thus distinguishing kingship from tyranny. (See especially R. Blondell, 'From Fleece to Fabric: Weaving Culture in Plato's *Statesman*', *Oxford Studies in Ancient Philosophy*, 28 (2005), 23–75.) But the Visitor does not stop talking about kings and kingship, and he uses this talk interchangeably with talk of the politician and political art he is trying to define (e.g. 289 C 4–D 2, 291 C 3–7, 303 E 7–304 A 4, 305 C 10–D 5). It is clear enough why he does this: he continues to insist that knowledge alone makes someone an expert ruler (e.g. 292 E 9–293 A 1, 293 C 5–D 2) and that this knowledge is rare, limited to a few politicians or a single king (297 B 7–C 4).

[26] The first premise, recall, addresses two differences: one rooted in the shift from private to public and the other rooted in practical differences.

models of inferential validity. It is true that the Visitor is committed to all the differences between public and political arts being insignificant. But he cannot make good on this commitment exhaustively; he can, in his limited time, make good on it only for some obvious differences. Whether this suffices to show that (C*) is plausible *to us* depends upon whether *we* can think of other differences that are significant. Whether, that is, the argument succeeds as an argument depends upon what reasons we can adduce for doubting its conclusion.[27]

Exactly here, Aristotle shoulders the burden to register his disagreement with Plato. He argues that it is not the *number* of persons managed but the *kinds* of persons managed that matter to the distinction between household-management and city-management (*Politics* I *passim*). Plato has conceded that *the actions* in relation to a slave or child differ from those in relation to fellow-citizens, but he insists that the expert rulers of human beings—whether slaves or free, whether in the household or in the city—must know what the goal of ruling is and generally how to achieve those goals, which includes knowing what is good for human beings. So Plato is insisting that expert rulers of human beings, whether in the household or the city, must have the same knowledge of what is good for human beings. Aristotle, by contrast, thinks that what is good for a slave, a child, or a woman is not exhausted by considerations of what is good for a human being. He thinks that what is good for man, what is good for a woman, what is good for a slave, and what is good for a child differ. The Visitor does not make any case for his Socratic assumption, and this makes his argument vulnerable to Aristotle's rejoinder.

But the Visitor is not exactly undone by this rejoinder. Aristotle's distinctions are uncomfortably close to Meno's, including his sharp contrast between the manly world of politics and the womanly world of the household, and his appeals to the different natures of slaves and women are disappointing. The Visitor can agree with Aristotle that children are something different, but this difference does not underwrite a distinction between the public arts of ruling

---

[27] I am suggesting, then, that we treat the Visitor's argument as a case of nonmonotonic reasoning. He is adducing reasons for (C*) and thus for inferring (C), but the addition of further considerations could defeat (C*) and thus (C).

and the private ones, since nothing is more important to politics than the education of children (308 B–309 D; cf. *Rep.* 4, 423 D–E).

We might find a better way to resist the Visitor's argument by insisting that the knowledge of what ruling's goals are and how, generally, ruling can achieve those goals is not enough to character- ize what politics is, because the essence of politics is trapped in its practical particularities.[28] Later in the *Statesman*, the Visitor might even seem to support this case against himself. He favours the expert ruler who is not constrained by laws (293 C 5–E 6) and who always knows the right time to begin the most important things in cities (305 C 10–D 5). Such a person rules to the needs of particu- lars, and is not limited to general, systematic knowledge.

But this misses what really distinguishes expert politicians or kings from the pretenders to this title. What matters here is not knowledge embedded in action, learned by experience. Rather, it is wisdom about the goals of ruling.[29] This is a familiar Platonic les- son, very clear in Socrates' distinction between the art of politics and Gorgianic rhetoric (*Gorg.* 464 B–466 A). At least Socrates tries to do what expert politicians would do, to foster well-being in other citizens. Gorgias and his followers ignore what is good for human beings, but instead develop a knack to craft pleasing speeches so that they can manipulate audiences and satisfy their own desires for power and wealth.

Wisdom about the goals of ruling matters even when the Visitor is sharply distinguishing the fully expert ruler who rules without constraint from all the pretenders who live in cities without per- fectly expert rulers (291 A–303 D). In the midst of this discussion, the Visitor makes a case for the rule of law as an achievable second- best between the zenith of expert rule unconstrained by law and the nadir of inexpert rule unconstrained by law (297 D–300 C). He insists that it is disastrous to flout even the laws made on the advice of those who please and persuade the masses (300 B 1–6). But he does not deny that there are better and worse cities that lack fully expert rule, or even that there are laws that more and less closely imitate expertise (300 E–301 E). For better laws, we need better

---

[28] Cf. Rosen, *Web*, 21 and Lane, *Method*, 140.
[29] With my concluding reflections, cf. D. El Murr, 'Politics and Dialectic in Plato's *Statesman*', *Proceedings of the Boston Area Colloquium in Ancient Philosophy*, 25 (2009), 109–35, and *Savoir et gouverner: Essai sur la science politique platonicienne* (Paris, 2014).

advisors, who do not merely gratify those they seek to persuade. But these better advisors are better not by their practical knowledge of exactly what to do in particular circumstances, but by their general knowledge about what is good for human beings, and they are better whether they hold political office or are private citizens. To find progress in a world without perfectly expert rulers, we need to look for politics defined principally by the general knowledge of what benefits human beings, the politics which unifies the political arts at the start of the *Statesman*.[30]

Washington University in St. Louis

BIBLIOGRAPHY

Accattino, P., 'L'ἀρχή del *Politico*', in C. J. Rowe (ed.), *Reading the* Statesman, 201–12.

Annas, J., and R. Waterfield (eds.), *Plato:* Statesman [*Statesman*] (Cambridge, 1995).

Blondell, R., 'From Fleece to Fabric: Weaving Culture in Plato's *Statesman*', *Oxford Studies in Ancient Philosophy*, 28 (2005), 23–75.

Brown, E., 'False Idles: The Politics of the "Quiet Life" in Greek and Roman Antiquity', in R. Balot (ed.), *A Companion to Ancient Political Thought* (Oxford, 2009), 485–500.

Campbell, L., *The* Sophistes *and* Politicus *of Plato* [*Politicus*] (Oxford, 1867).

Cooper, J. M., 'Plato's *Statesman* and Politics' ['Politics'], in *Reason and Emotion* (Princeton, 1999), 165–191; reprinted from *Proceedings of the Boston Area Colloquium in Ancient Philosophy*, 13 (1997), 71–103.

Dixsaut, M., 'Une politique vraiment conforme à la nature', C. J. Rowe (ed.), *Reading the* Statesman, 253–73.

Dodds, E. R. (ed.), *Plato:* Gorgias (Oxford, 1959).

Duke, E. A. et al. (eds.), *Platonis Opera*, vol. 1 (Oxford, 1995).

---

[30] I thank the students in my Spring 2005 Plato course, and especially Amy and Don Goodman-Wilson, for their reactions to the first version of this material; I thank the conferees at the February 2009 Fourteenth Annual Arizona Colloquium in Ancient Philosophy, and especially my commentator Joel Martinez, for their comments on a second draft; I thank Dimitri El Murr for encouragement; I thank the members of Washington University's Workshop in Politics, Ethics, and Society, and especially my commentator Jason Gardner, for their feedback in September 2010; and I thank Anne Baril, Anne Margaret Baxley, Billy Dunaway, Eric Wiland, two anonymous referees, and Victor Caston for helpful criticisms of the penultimate draft.

El Murr, D., 'Politics and Dialectic in Plato's *Statesman*', *Proceedings of the Boston Area Colloquium in Ancient Philosophy*, 25 (2009), 109–35.

El Murr, D., *Savoir et gouverner: Essai sur la science politique platonicienne* (Paris, 2014).

Hirsch, U., '*Μιμεῖσθαι* und verwandte Ausdrücke in Platons *Politikos*', in C. J. Rowe (ed.), *Reading the* Statesman, 184–9.

Kleingeld, P., 'The Problematic Status of Gender-neutral Language in the History of Philosophy: The Case of Kant', *Philosophical Forum*, 25 (1993), 134–50.

Lane, M. S., *Method and Politics in Plato's* Statesman [*Method*] (Cambridge, 1998).

Miller, Jr, M. H., *The Philosopher in Plato's* Statesman (The Hague, 1980).

Peterson, Sandra. 2017. 'Notes on *Lovers*', in A. Stavru and C. Moore (eds.), *Socrates and the Socratic Dialogue* (Leiden: Brill), 412–31.

Robinson, D., 'The New *Oxford Text* of Plato's *Statesman*: Editor's Comments' ['Comments'], in C. J. Rowe (ed.), *Reading the* Statesman, 37–46.

Rosen, S., *Plato's* Statesman: *The Web of Politics* [*Web*] (New Haven, 1995).

Rowe, C. J. (ed.), *Plato:* Statesman [*Statesman*] (Warminster, 1995).

Rowe, C. J. (ed.), *Reading the* Statesman: *Proceedings of the III Symposium Platonicum* [*Reading the* Statesman] (Sankt Augustin, 1995).

Rowe, C. J., 'Introduction,' in C. J. Rowe (ed.), *Reading the* Statesman, 11–28.

Sandbach, F. H., 'Five Textual Notes' ['Notes'], *Illinois Classical Studies*, 2 (1977), 49–53.

Schofield, M., *Plato: Political Philosophy* (Oxford: 2006).

Shaw, J. C., 'Socrates and the True Political Craft', *Classical Philology*, 106 (2011), 187–207.

Simpson, P. L. P., *A Philosophical Commentary on the* Politics *of Aristotle* (Chapel Hill, 1998).

Skemp, J. B., *Plato's* Statesman (New Haven, 1952).

Weiss, R., 'Statesman as *ΕΠΙΣΤΗΜΩΝ*: Caretaker, Physician, and Weaver', in C. J. Rowe (ed.), *Reading the* Statesman, 213–22.

WHAT IS *EIKASIA*?

DAMIEN STOREY

In the *Republic*'s image of the Divided Line, Plato divides belief into two species: *pistis* and *eikasia*. *Pistis* is a direct grasp of sensible objects and *eikasia* is an indirect grasp of them through their 'images' or 'likenesses' (εἰκόνες), namely: 'shadows, then reflections, . . . and everything of that kind' (τὰς σκιάς, ἔπειτα τὰ ἐν τοῖς ὕδασι φαντάσματα καὶ . . . πᾶν τὸ τοιοῦτον; *Rep.* 6, 510 A 1–3). For what appears to be a fundamental epistemological distinction, this is puzzling: what is so significant about beliefs about shadows and reflections? While there is no consensus, something of a majority view has emerged, which I'll call the 'standard reading'. This reading makes two distinct claims. First, that *eikasia* with respect to shadows and reflections—sensory *eikasia*—is mistaking an image for that of which it is an image; for example, mistaking a shadow for the object that casts it. Second, it adds that what Plato is really interested in is an ethical kind of *eikasia*, and it offers a separate account of what this is: the error of unreflectively accepting popular or influential ethical opinions.

I am going to argue that the standard reading fails, primarily because there is no viable way to connect the two types of *eikasia* it introduces, sensory *eikasia* and ethical *eikasia*: the first says nothing about ethics; the second says nothing about images. I will argue for a more economical account of ethical *eikasia*: it is the same as *eikasia* with respect to sensible images like shadows and reflections; the only difference is that the relevant images include representations of value properties. This requires us to accept that the contents of perception extend as far as value properties, and that, I'll argue, is exactly Plato's view in the *Republic*. Once we take this step, we open the way for an account of *eikasia* that integrates far better with the *Republic* as a whole. The standard reading gives *eikasia* a comparatively minor role in the *Republic* and one that is largely detached from the dialogue's major theoretical themes. In contrast, I will argue that *eikasia* plays an essential role in explaining the origin and prevalence of ethical error—and, consequently,

Damien Storey, *What is* eikasia? In: Oxford Studies in Ancient Philosophy Volume LVIII. Edited by: Victor Caston, Oxford University Press (2020). © Damien Storey.
DOI: 10.1093/oso/9780198858997.003.0002

in explaining why there is a pressing need for knowledge of the Forms and a society ruled by philosophers—and that it does so in a way that draws on the full range of explanatory tools developed in the *Republic*, from its metaphysics to its psychology.

1. *Eikasia* and the Cave allegory

Before attempting an account of *eikasia*, one needs to decide whether or not it is represented in Plato's Cave allegory. I believe that it is, and in this I stand with the standard reading against its main rival, which sees *eikasia* as a way of studying an original through its image.[1] Importantly, the disagreement here is only derivatively about *eikasia*: the real disagreement concerns how the two readings interpret the Line and Cave, and especially the relationship between them. This makes it impossible to compare critically the two readings without defending an interpretation of the Line and Cave, which is a task that would require its own paper. Here, then, I will simply explain the assumptions behind each reading.

   Consider our most basic evidence. Plato first describes *eikasia* during his account of the two lower sections of his Line analogy:

---

[1] This reading was recently restated and defended by Y. H. Dominick, 'Seeing Through Images: The Bottom of Plato's Divided Line' ['Images'], *Journal of the History of Philosophy*, 48 (2010), 1–13. Other explicit defenders include J. L. Stocks, 'The Divided Line of Plato *Rep*. VI', *Classical Quarterly*, 5 (1911), 73–88; A. S. Ferguson, 'Plato's Simile of Light. Part II: The Allegory of the Cave (Continued)', *Classical Quarterly*, 16 (1922), 15–28, and 'Plato's Simile of Light Again' ['Simile'], *Classical Quarterly*, 28 (1934), 190–210; and J. Klein, *A Commentary on Plato's Meno* (Chapel Hill, 1965), 114, and the authors mentioned in n. 5 would have reason to be sympathetic. The remaining views of *eikasia*—those that cannot be identified with either rival—are more heterogeneous, but there is a rough third grouping, which includes the reading I'll defend. These readings assume, like the standard reading, that *eikasia* is represented in the Cave but they offer more phenomenal interpretations of 'images'. Some of its clearer members are H. J. Paton, 'Plato's Theory of EIKASIA' ['Eikasia'], *Proceedings of the Aristotelian Society*, 22 (1922), 69–104; J. R. Wilson, 'The Contents of the Cave', *Canadian Journal of Philosophy*, suppl. vol., 2 (1976), 117–27; J. S. Morrison, 'Two Unresolved Difficulties in the Line and Cave' ['Difficulties'], *Phronesis*, 22 (1977), 212–31; and most recently J. Moss, 'Plato's Appearance/Assent Account of Belief' ['Assent'], *Proceedings of the Aristotelian Society*, 114 (2014), 1–27, who in many ways revives and updates Paton's reading. Moss is an interesting contemporary contrast to my view. While we begin with substantial theoretical agreement, especially about images and their general role in cognition, we reach very different views about what *eikasia* is: see nn. 17, 32, and 52.

καί σοι ἔσται σαφηνείᾳ καὶ ἀσαφείᾳ πρὸς ἄλληλα ἐν μὲν τῷ ὁρωμένῳ τὸ μὲν ἕτερον
τμῆμα εἰκόνες, λέγω δὲ τὰς εἰκόνας πρῶτον μὲν τὰς σκιάς, ἔπειτα τὰ ἐν τοῖς ὕδασι
φαντάσματα καὶ ἐν τοῖς ὅσα πυκνά τε καὶ λεῖα καὶ φανὰ συνέστηκεν, καὶ πᾶν τὸ
τοιοῦτον, εἰ κατανοεῖς.... τὸ τοίνυν ἕτερον τίθει ᾧ τοῦτο ἔοικεν, τά τε περὶ ἡμᾶς
ζῷα καὶ πᾶν τὸ φυτευτὸν καὶ τὸ σκευαστὸν ὅλον γένος. (*Rep.* 6, 509 D 9–510 A 6)

In terms now of relative clarity and obscurity, you will have as one section
of the visible, images [εἰκόνας]. By images I mean, first, shadows, then
reflections in bodies of water and in all close-packed, smooth, and shiny
materials, and everything of that kind, if you understand.... In the other
section of the visible, put that which it [*sc.* an image] is like—that is, the
animals around us, every plant, and the whole class of manufactured
things.[2]

Visible objects[3] have different degrees of 'clarity', depending on
whether they are sensible 'images' or their originals. A few lines
later, we learn that this is a division in the 'opinable' (τὸ δοξαστόν,
6, 510 A 8–10), and it corresponds to a division between two kinds
of belief, *eikasia* and *pistis*:[4]

καί μοι ἐπὶ τοῖς τέτταρσι τμήμασι τέτταρα ταῦτα παθήματα ἐν τῇ ψυχῇ γιγνόμενα
λαβέ, νόησιν μὲν ἐπὶ τῷ ἀνωτάτω, διάνοιαν δὲ ἐπὶ τῷ δευτέρῳ, τῷ τρίτῳ δὲ πίστιν
ἀπόδος, καὶ τῷ τελευταίῳ εἰκασίαν...(6, 511 D 6–E 2)

Join me, then, in taking these four conditions in the soul as corresponding
to the four subsections of the line: *noēsis* for the highest, *dianoia* for the
second, *pistis* for the third, and *eikasia* for the last.[5]

---

[2] Unless otherwise noted, the text of the *Republic* is the OCT edition of Slings
(Oxford, 2003). Translations are adapted, at times significantly, from Reeve, *Plato:
Republic* (Hackett, 2004). Translations of other texts of Plato are adapted from
J. M. Cooper (ed.), *Plato: Complete Works* (Hackett, 1997).

[3] Standing for sensible objects generally. See *Rep.* 7, 524 C 13, in context, and
J. T. Bedu-Addo, 'Διάνοια and the Images of Forms in Plato's *Republic* VI–VII',
Platon, 31 (1979), 89–110 at 93, for discussion.

[4] Given the slight differences in their usages in English, I will sometimes use
'opinion' and sometimes 'belief' (and occasionally 'judgement'), without intending
to attribute any corresponding distinction to Plato. In all cases, they refer to that
which *eikasia* and *pistis* are kinds of, which Plato usually calls *doxa*.

[5] See also *Rep.* 7, 533 E 3–534 A 2, where *eikasia*'s status as a species of belief
(δόξα) is more explicit. The description of *eikasia* as an affection or condition (πάθημα)
has led some to argue that it is simply the *experience* of images, so that if one is
aware of an image, one is *ipso facto* in a state of *eikasia*. Dominick, 'Images', 2, cites
this as a reason to treat *eikasia* 'as something that one experiences rather than exercises'. Similarly, we might think that the four conditions relate to the two powers
(δυνάμεις) of belief and knowledge in Book 5 by being states of these powers (e.g.
N. Smith, 'Plato on Knowledge as a Power', *Journal of the History of Philosophy*, 38
(2000), 145–68 at 146 n. 3). But *dianoia* and *noēsis* are equally conditions, and
Socrates describes these as ways of reasoning about their objects. Even if one

This is the basic textual evidence—and it is not much. All it allows us to say with certainty is that *eikasia* is set over images (εἰκόνες) and that these are likenesses of the sensible originals that are the object of *pistis*. What we say beyond this depends on how (if at all) we think this minimal description is developed in the Cave allegory.

There are two main views. Some commentators believe that the Line's distinction between *eikasia* and *pistis* is introduced in order to illustrate the relationship between *dianoia* and *noēsis* (which also involves an image–original relationship). If that is right, *eikasia* is principally a way of illustrating *dianoia*, and not a significant kind of cognition in its own right.[6] From here, it is a small step to claim that *eikasia* has no place in the Cave allegory. The allegory represents 'the effect on our nature of education and lack of education' (τὴν ἡμετέραν φύσιν παιδείας τε πέρι καὶ ἀπαιδευσίας, 7, 514 A 1–2): if *eikasia* has little or no independent significance, it will hardly feature significantly in Plato's account of education. Other commentators, however, believe that the Line represents four *sui generis* kinds of cognition, each as literal as the other. After all, Socrates never says that *eikasia* or *pistis* have a special status—mere similes, expository tools, or the like—but simply calls them two kinds of belief (7, 533 E 3–534 A 2). Thus, they believe that Plato's account of all four kinds of cognition continues into the Cave allegory, where they feature as stages in the educational progression it represents. So understood, *eikasia* is represented by the first stage in

claimed that '*dianoia*' and '*noēsis*' only name states that are the *conclusions* of distinct ways of reasoning (though this would be hard to defend: e.g. 7, 533 D 4–7), this would make them cognitive states, but not passive ones, and the comparison would still suggest that *eikasia* is a cognitive attitude towards images that results from a particular way of thinking about them. See also G. Fine, 'Knowledge and Belief in *Republic* V–VII' ['*Republic* V–VII'], in ead., *Plato on Knowledge and Forms: Selected Essays* (Oxford, 2003), 85–116 at 102–3.

[6] See H. Jackson, 'On Plato's Republic VI 509 d sqq.', *Journal of Philology*, 10 (1881), 132–50; P. Shorey, 'The Idea of the Good in Plato's *Republic*', *Studies in Classical Philology*, 1 (1885), 188–239 at 229; A. S. Ferguson, 'Plato's Simile of Light. Part I', *Classical Quarterly*, 15 (1921), 131–52 and 'Simile'; R. Robinson, *Plato's Earlier Dialectic* [*Dialectic*] (Ithaca, 1941), 207; D. Ross, *Plato's Theory of Ideas* (Oxford, 1951), 77; J. E. Raven, 'Sun, Divided Line, and Cave' ['Sun, Line, Cave'], *Classical Quarterly*, 3 (1953), 22–32 at 25–6; C. Strang, 'Plato's Analogy of the Cave' ['Cave'], *Oxford Studies in Ancient Philosophy*, 4 (1986), 19–34; and Dominick, 'Images'. For a critical assessment of this reading, see R. C. Cross and A. D. Woozely, *Plato's Republic: A Philosophical Commentary* [*Republic*] (London, 1964), 209–13.

the Cave allegory: the condition of the prisoners who mistake reality for the play of shadows on the cave wall.[7]

This disagreement separates the two principal schools of thought on *eikasia*. For those who deny that the Line and Cave are parallel—who deny 'parallelism'—we learn most about *eikasia* by comparing it with *dianoia*. Since *dianoia* involves studying Forms through sensibles used as images, *eikasia* is understood to be studying sensible originals through images like shadows or reflections. For example, Yancy Dominick concludes that:

[E]ikasia is the state in which one can view an image [of a sensible] as an image—typically, it involves the attempt to learn about some object through consideration of an image of that object. This state, notably, does not usually involve any confusion of image and original.[8]

Parallelism, in contrast, leads us to the opposite conclusion. The prisoners *fail* to view the shadows as images and do indeed confuse image and original. It would also be at least misleading to say that the prisoners represent an 'attempt to learn' about sensibles. Thus, the standard reading, taking its cue from the condition of the prisoners, sees the essential feature of *eikasia* as mistaking image for original. This is combined with a view about the scope of the allegory: that by 'education and the lack of education', Socrates means the kind of upbringing that either succeeds or fails to make one a good person—one's ethical education, broadly construed.[9] This being so, the shadows on the cave wall do not represent any and all images, but images of the kind of value properties relevant to one's ethical education; thus, in Socrates' only direct reference to what the they represent, he describes 'shadows of justice' (αἱ τοῦ δικαίου σκιαί, 7, 517 D 8–9).[10] In short, the allegory tells us that just as the

---

[7] This has been a popular reading since the turn of the twentieth century. See J. P. Hardie, 'Plato's Early Theory of Ideas', *Mind*, 5 (1896), 167–85; R. L. Nettleship, *Lectures on Plato's* Republic [*Lectures*] (London, 1897); and, most influentially, J. Adam, *The* Republic *of Plato* [*Republic*], vol. 2 (Cambridge, 1902).

[8] Dominick, 'Images', 1.

[9] Arguably, this is not a special subject of education, but what education (παιδεία) means for Plato. See *Rep.* 4, 425 C 4–5; *Leg.* 1, 643 D 6–644 B 4; and J. Wilberding, 'Prisoners and Puppeteers in the Cave' ['Puppeteers'], *Oxford Studies in Ancient Philosophy*, 27 (2004), 117–39 at 133.

[10] There is an indirect reference at *Rep.* 7, 520 C 3–6. This form of parallelism has been influential since it was defended in the 1960s by J. Malcolm, 'The Line and the Cave', *Phronesis*, 7 (1962), 38–45, and shortly after by Cross and Woozley, *Republic*. Dominick challenges it, claiming that when he uses the phrase 'shadows of justice',

prisoners mistake shadows for real things, ordinary people mistake, for example, what appears good or just for what is good or just.

I am going to side with the standard reading insofar as I agree—and, for the purposes of this paper, simply assume—that the condition of the prisoners in the Cave allegory represents *eikasia* and that this is a specifically ethical form of *eikasia*. But I do not draw the same conclusions from the Cave allegory. In particular, I do not believe that *eikasia* is simply the error of mistaking image and original. To be sure, this is an error the prisoners make, but I will argue that it is not the best way to capture all the features, or even the essential features, of what is cognitively significant about their condition. A broader examination shows that *eikasia* is not merely a type of error, but rather a rudimentary form of cognition that we find (I argue) in many places in the *Republic*: the kind of appearance-sensitive, reason-insensitive cognition that seems to be crucially involved in Plato's explanation of both the cognition of the non-rational parts of the soul and ethical error.

2. The object of *eikasia*

The question 'What is *eikasia*?' can be divided into the questions 'What is the object of *eikasia*?' and 'What exactly is *eikasia* with respect to this object?'. Where possible, I will try to keep these questions separate, answering them in turn: the first in this section, the second in the following section. Here, then, my task is to offer an account of the 'likenesses' or 'images' (εἰκόνες) that are the object of *eikasia*. Socrates says that 'by images I mean, first, shadows, then reflections in bodies of water and in all close-packed,

---

'Socrates is not here describing the prisoners' contests, but rather the "evils of human life" . . . (517 D 5)' ('Images', 6–7). But Socrates is describing both: the prisoner's condition *represents* these evils of human life. Dominick fails to appreciate that the metaphor 'shadows of justice' has one foot in the allegory ('shadows . . .') and the other in what it represents ('. . . of justice'), as is common in Book 7. For example, the philosopher who turns to 'the evils of human life' is also said, in a clear reference to the cave, to be unaccustomed to the darkness around him (7, 517 D 6–7). The same mistake is behind Dominick's claim that the prisoners 'compete in identifying shadows not of justice, but of "people and other animals"': of course the prisoners do not see *literal* shadows of justice, whatever that would mean, but the shadows of people and animals that they do see are themselves metaphors that stand in need of interpretation, and the claim is that they *represent* ethical images, including those described (in a new metaphor) as 'shadows of justice'.

smooth, and shiny materials, and everything of that kind, if you understand' (6, 509 D 10–510 A 3). He goes on to tell us that ordinary sensibles—for example, 'the animals around us, every plant, and the whole class of manufactured things' (510 A 5–6, Greek text above)—are that of which they are images: ordinary sensibles are 'that which it [sc. an image] is like' (ᾧ τοῦτο ἔοικεν, A 5), and images and originals are related as 'likeness to that which it is like' (τὸ ὁμοιωθὲν πρὸς τὸ ᾧ ὡμοιώθη, A 10). So far, so clear: sensible 'images' are likenesses of ordinary sensibles (where 'ordinary' simply means sensibles that are not themselves images).

However, commentators have found it difficult to avoid introducing a further sense of 'image'. Specifically, they have found it difficult to accommodate the kind of 'shadows of justice' that seem to be the object of ethical *eikasia* without making the second of the two central claims of the standard reading, which by itself I'll label the 'second-hand belief reading': that the 'images' relevant to ethical *eikasia* are popular or influential ethical views that are taken over unreflectively. This has been the most popular view for over a century, a position helped by the fact that it has never received any direct critical assessment. But when so assessed, we find quite decisive reasons to reject it.

2.1. *The second-hand belief reading*

In one of the earliest and most influential accounts of *eikasia*, James Adam distinguished between two kinds of images: visible images and 'opinable' images.[11] The former are visible copies like shadows and reflections, and *eikasia* with respect to them would be, for example, mistaking a shadow of a man for the man himself. But these images, Adam thought, could not explain ethical errors. Thus, he introduced the second kind, opinable images, which includes what we grasp with our mind as well as what we grasp with our eyes. Among these images are 'popular canons or opinions' about what is good or just that are embodied in the works of culturally influential figures like sophists, poets, or politicians. Someone who suffers ethical *eikasia*, then, is someone who uncritically accepts these popular opinions and,

---

[11] Which Adam (*Republic*, 72, 157–8) calls ὁραταὶ εἰκόνες and δοξασταὶ εἰκόνες.

thus, fails to see that they are mere 'shadows' of what really is good or just. Many commentators since Adam have defended views along these lines, taking ethical *eikasia* to be the acquisition of beliefs that are in some sense 'second-hand', derived either directly from other people's beliefs or from ethical views embodied in more abstract cultural or political forces, like poems or laws.[12] This reading is seen as a solution to the putative problem posed by the move from sensory to evaluative images: from literal shadows to metaphorical 'shadows of justice'. On the one hand, it is thought that evaluative images cannot be sensory, on the grounds that we don't literally *see* value properties like goodness or justice. On the

[12] The following is by no means exhaustive, but it gives a sense of the range of readings that fall under this umbrella. Nettleship: '[when Plato speaks of] shadows and reflexions which are taken for realities we must think how many views there are which circulate in society and form a large part of what we call our knowledge, but which when we examine them are seen to be distorted, imperfect representations of fact, coming to us often through the media of several other men's minds, and the media of our own fancies and prejudices' (*Lectures*, 242–5). N. R. Murphy: visual *eikasia* illustrates how ordinary people 'owing to the vicious cycle in current education . . . receive their own opinions back again . . . as if reflected in a mirror' ('The "Simile of Light" in Plato's Republic', *Classical Quarterly*, 26 (1932), 93–102 at 101). Raven: while *eikasia* in the Line concerns strictly visual images, the corresponding imagery in the Cave presents 'a more comprehensive picture of second-hand impressions and opinions' ('Sun, Line, Cave', 27–8). Cross and Woozley: 'second-hand opinions purveyed by the rhetorician and politician, who put shadows or semblances between men's minds and the facts' (*Republic*, 220–1). J. Malcolm: the 'images' that the shadows represent are false ethical beliefs that are copies of true ethical beliefs (the objects of *pistis*) ('The Cave Revisited' ['Cave'], *Classical Quarterly*, 31 (1981), 60–8 at 61 and 68). J. Annas: 'for Plato relying on experience covers more than just assuming in an unthinking way that the things we see, like trees, are what is real. It also covers taking over beliefs, some of them important like our beliefs about justice, which are second-hand, picked up from society in the way the prisoners see the shadow-pictures on the wall of the Cave' ('Plato, *Republic* V–VII' ['*Rep.* V–VII'], *Royal Institute of Philosophy Lecture Series*, 20 (1986), 3–18 at 15; see also 'Understanding and the Good: Sun, Line, and Cave', in R. Kraut (ed.), *Plato's Republic: Critical Essays* (Lanham, Md, 1997), 143–68 at 155). T. H. Irwin: ethical *eikasia* occurs when we 'accept, without question or criticism, the views we have been brought up with or have absorbed from our social environment' (*Plato's Ethics* (Oxford, 1995), 276; cf. *Plato's Moral Theory* (Oxford, 1977), 221). Fine: 'Plato speaks about contending "about the shadows of justice"—about, that is, ordinary, unreflective beliefs about justice' ('*Republic* V–VII', 103). N. Pappas: 'the prisoners who squint at and squabble over shadows represent all those citizens who believe what politicians and artists tell them' (*Routledge Philosophy Guidebook to Plato and the Republic* [*Republic*], 2nd ed. (London, 2003), 110). Wilberding: the conjectures of sophists, poets, and politicians about what the many believe (the latter beliefs being *pistis*) ('Puppeteers', 129–32). M. Schofield: 'the shadow in their minds left by the culture in which they have been raised' ('Metaspeleology', in D. Scott (ed.), *Maieusis: Essays on Ancient Philosophy in Honour of Myles Burnyeat* (Oxford, 2007), 216–31 at 225).

other hand, Plato says elsewhere that people typically do unreflectively accept the prevailing opinion of what is good or just. The
proposed solution, then, is to broaden our understanding of 'image'
to include this latter phenomenon. Difficulties begin, however, as
soon as we compare second-hand opinions with Plato's actual
examples of images: shadows, reflections, 'and everything of that
kind' (καὶ πᾶν τὸ τοιοῦτον, 6, 510 A 3). Some commentators claim
that shadows and reflections are just metaphors for the real objects
of *eikasia*.[13] But this is difficult to reconcile with the text. The Line
itself is an analogy, but the four states it illustrates, and Socrates'
description of them, are literal. This is obviously true of *noēsis*,
dianoia, and *pistis*, and it is unlikely that Socrates silently switches
to symbolism only when he describes *eikasia*. For one thing, doing
so would lead to highly convoluted imagery, with the lowest section
of the Line representing (as Socrates tells us) shadows and reflections that in turn represent (as he fails to tells us) the real object of
eikasia—a real object never explicitly identified in the dialogue.
Notice also that Socrates defines the proposed metaphors, shadows
and reflections, by their relationship to the entirely literal object of
pistis, sensible originals. Finally and crucially: what is the metaphor? At least in a philosophical context, to warrant being called a
'metaphor', there should be some demonstrable analogical similarity between taking images for originals and unreflectively accepting popular opinions. As far as I'm aware, no one has spelt out how
the metaphor is supposed to work, and no obvious answer suggests
itself.[14]

---

[13] See Wilberding, 'Puppeteers', 131–2; Pappas, *Republic*, 110; V. Karasmanis,
'Plato's *Republic*: The Line and the Cave', *Apeiron*, 21 (1988), 147–71 at 159–60;
and Morrison, 'Difficulties', 222; C. P. Sze, '*Eikasia* and *pistis* in Plato's Allegory of
the Cave', *Classical Quarterly*, 27 (1977), 127–38; and Nettleship, *Lectures*, 242–5.

[14] On one side, a person bases (*a*) their belief on (*b*) a shadow or reflection that is
a likeness of (*c*) some original. On the other, a person bases (1) their belief on (2)
another influential belief. One suggestion is (*a*) : (*b*) :: (1) : (2). Perhaps the idea is
that both beliefs are based on something 'shadowy' in the sense of unclear or less
than true. But this drops the essential likeness relationship between (*b*) and (*c*).
Alternatively, perhaps (*b*), the shadows, are analogous to (1), the unreflective beliefs,
so: (*b*) : (*c*) :: (1) : (2). The idea might be: as shadows are passive copies of what casts
them, ordinary ethical beliefs are passive copies of others' beliefs. But images are
supposed to *fall short* of their original, and these two beliefs seem equally inadequate. Moreover, if the shadows and reflections of the Line represent the *beliefs* of
eikasia, do the statues of animals and plants represent the beliefs of *pistis*? Or in the
Cave, are the prisoners' beliefs represented not by their beliefs but by the shadows
themselves?

The second-hand belief reading must, then, find a place for popular ethical opinions within the scope of 'everything of that kind', alongside shadows and reflections. To do so, these opinions need to meet two criteria. First, (*a*) they must actually be images (εἰκόνες) in some relevant sense. The word εἰκών, a cognate of ἐοικέναι, 'to be like', refers to something that is an image or likeness of something else, and in this context we know that it refers to images of the object of *pistis*, ordinary sensibles. A shadow of a man is *like* a man, but not a man; an image of an *F* thing (a sensible original) is something that is like an *F* thing, but not really *F*. The relevant sense of 'likeness' here is not faithful resemblance but persuasive verisimilitude: it seems or appears *F*, without actually being so.[15] Second, (*b*) they must, as images, play the right kind of explanatory role in *eikasia*. That is, their nature as images must explain why a person at the level of *eikasia* acquires the beliefs that they acquire. This should include explaining the prisoners' basic error: believing that an image of an *F* thing is an *F* thing because, first, it appears to be an *F* thing and, second, they fail to recognize that it *merely* appears so. These criteria do little more than demand of any account of images that it describe something that is recognizably the same thing that Plato describes when he talks about images in Books 6 and 7.

The second-hand belief reading struggles with both criteria. With respect to criterion (*a*), how can popular beliefs (or prevalent cultural norms, folk wisdoms, or the like) *themselves* be images in the relevant sense? For example, if we believe that all pleasure is good, the idea would need to be not that all *pleasure* seems good, but that our *belief* itself is a likeness in some relevant sense. After all, if it is pleasure that seems good to me, what others believe about it is in this respect irrelevant: pleasure's appearance would give me a reason to believe it is good whether or not the poets tell me so—it even gives me a reason to *dis*believe them if they claimed the opposite.[16] In fact, few defenders of the second-hand belief

---

[15] See e.g. the context of Socrates' reference to 'shadows of justice' at 7, 517 D 8–9, where it is clear that he means what appears just but does not in fact have any substantial resemblance to real justice.

[16] There have been some attempts to make beliefs *bona fide* images. Malcolm, 'Cave', argues that the images are false beliefs that are copies of true beliefs with 'distortions and misrepresentations', though even he admits that 'it is not obvious in what sense falsities are ' "copies" of truths' (68). N. Smith, 'How the Prisoners in

reading make a serious attempt to meet criterion (*a*). A little reflection makes it clear why: images are theoretically important only if the fact that they *are* images is playing an explanatory role. In fact, despite their prominence in Plato's own account, the second-hand belief reading makes no theoretical use of images at all.

Instead, it has its own independent account of why people adopt their ethical beliefs. The central claim of the second-hand belief reading is that ethical *eikasia* is an uncritical acceptance of the dominant ethical beliefs in one's society, beliefs that gain apparent credibility by being enshrined in laws, eulogized in poems, taught by supposedly wise sophists, or simply widely believed. The error is to trust implicitly the testimony of these apparent authorities, rather than examine their claims for oneself. This is the sense in which a person's belief is 'second-hand': they adopt it as their belief because it is a certain other's belief. Thus, insofar as a belief is genuinely second-hand, it is acquired not because of the content of the 'copied' belief, but because of the trust placed in the other believer. Whether the belief is 'ϕ-ing is just' or 'ϕ-ing is unjust', the person's reason for believing it will be the same: that it is, for example, what the poets say. So *even if* popular ethical beliefs were images of the right kind, somehow likenesses of the object of *pistis*, for the second-hand belief reading this would still not be *why* ordinary people uncritically accept them. Thus, against criterion (*b*), this reading suggests that there is no theoretical connection between images and *eikasia*.

We find, then, that the second-hand belief reading presents something that has very little relation (metaphorical or otherwise) to what Plato describes: it introduces both a new sense of 'image' and a new error for these images to cause, neither of which are present in the text. So what reason *do* people have to think that it is what Plato is talking about? I believe much of the explanation is the conviction (perhaps implicit) that value properties are just not the sort of things to be seen and, therefore, that we are forced to introduce *something* different from the sensory images that we find in the text. Consider, for example, Julia Annas's complaint that:

Plato's Cave are "Like Us" ', *Proceedings of the Boston Area Colloquium in Ancient Philosophy*, 13 (1997), 187–204, argues that the images are false accounts, like the definitions of justice found in Book 1, which approximate true definitions.

In these passages too much has got lumped together on the side of experience. Relying on the senses is taken to involve a passive and uncritical attitude, and accepting the reality of what the senses report is run together with accepting second-hand opinions about values. Plato is so eager to downgrade the senses because he has not bothered to analyse very carefully what 'the senses' covers.[17]

It is interesting that, despite attributing this view to Plato, Annas criticizes it for much the same reason that I do: second-hand beliefs do not have enough in common with the sensory images that Plato describes. Yet she still finds this interpretation unavoidable, presumably because she finds it difficult to imagine what evaluative images might be, if not second-hand beliefs. What I hope to show in the next few pages is that it is *we*, not Plato, who need 'to analyse very carefully what "the senses" covers'. If we are to reconcile the *Republic*'s appeals to evaluative and sensory images, we need to ask: how narrow or broad are the contents of perception for Plato and, in particular, do they extend to value properties? Many commentators have simply assumed the answer is no. I will argue that the answer is yes.

2.2. *Evaluative images are sensory*

I will argue that the evaluative images that are the object of ethical *eikasia* are the same in kind as the shadows or reflections that are the object of perceptual *eikasia*. In other words, ethical *eikasia* is just a subset of perceptual *eikasia*, and there is no need to posit an additional non-perceptual kind of *eikasia*.[18]

---

[17] J. Annas, '*Rep.* V–VII', 16; see also 'Good', 155.

[18] This should be distinguished from the claim that *all* perceptual experience is *eikasia*. Paton, 'Eikasia', argues that *eikasia* is perceptual experience as such (including imagination, memory, dreams, etc.), before its content has been affirmed or denied. Moss, 'Assent', defends a similar view. Consider Plato's claim that perception is sufficient by itself to tell us what a finger is, without any help from understanding (7, 523 A 1–525 A 14, discussed further below). For Paton, since this is just perception—without reflection or active affirmation—it is *eikasia*. On my account, since it allows us to grasp an ordinary sensible—to grasp what a finger is—it is *pistis*. The accuracy of the perception matters: perception can adequately grasp some properties, like 'being a finger', but not others, like 'being just', so only perceptual experiences of the latter properties—insofar as they are misleading and, thus, prevent us from grasping a sensible original—are the object of *eikasia*. As H. W. B. Joseph, *Knowledge and the Good in Plato's Republic* (London, 1948), 40, said in response to Paton: 'it is surely strange that when Plato named as objects of

I think most people would agree that *if* other things were equal, we should treat all the examples of images in Books 6 and 7 as equally sensory. After all, images are sensory in Plato's explicit descriptions of them, and he never invites us to modify this description: instead, he moves seamlessly from images like shadows and reflections to images like 'shadows of justice', as if they are all, *qua* images, the same. But many commentators believe that other things are unequal, because they believe that the idea of sensible images of goodness or justice is intrinsically problematic and, thus, an idea from which Plato must be rescued. The usual rescue strategy is, as we saw, to interpolate a change in the meaning of 'image'. So understood, this reading is motivated almost entirely by a putative need for interpretive charity.

The problem is that, implicitly, this takes a dogmatic stance in a debate about the contents of perception, effectively failing to appreciate that it is a debate with *two* sides. On one side, it is sometimes argued that perception only has 'low level' content: simple and uncontroversially perceptible properties like colours, shapes, smells, or tones. From this perspective, the idea of sensory evaluative appearances is almost a category error. An alphabet of colours and smells could never spell something like 'good' or 'just'—after all, goodness and justice don't have a colour or smell. But on the other side, there are those who argue that perception can also have 'high level' content. A proponent of this view will believe, for example, that I can see the books on my shelf, and see them *as* books, even though 'being a book' is not a property that is reducible to colours and shapes. Similarly, they might believe that I can see that the books are on the shelf; that three lie horizontally; or that some are damaged. Arguably, this is closer to a commonsense view of perception, since it fits both ordinary language (we say 'I see books' not 'I see a mosaic of colours and shapes and infer there are books') and our experience (try looking at a bookshelf

---

eikasia the shadows and reflections of things, he meant to include the sensible appearances of things as we perceive them and not their shadows and reflections.' One source of the problem is an argument (10, 598 A 1–B 8) that is sometimes thought to imply that *veridical* perceptual experiences are included in the appearances that Plato is concerned with in Book 10 (see Paton, 85–6; Moss, 223–4); I think a closer reading of the passage shows that the argument's conclusion is that even in many ordinary perceptions there are properties that are *not* veridically represented.

and seeing shapes and colours rather than coloured books). Within
such a theory, there is space for disagreement about exactly which
properties can be represented in perception—can we see that something is fragile, dangerous, hot, disgusting, tasty, angry, or good?—
but there is nothing in principle against including value properties.[19]

I will argue that Plato holds this second view of perception and
includes value properties among its contents. Indeed, we already
have one argument in favour of this: now that we have shown that
the putative need for interpretive charity was misguided, the 'problem' that we started with—that Plato *seems* to treat evaluative
images as another type of sensory image—becomes instead a *prima
facie* reason to think that his view of perception includes value
properties among its content. On investigation, the *Republic* gives
us plenty of reasons to think this is right.

In the *Republic*, Plato says most about perception in the so-called
'finger' passage, where Socrates describes the different faculties the
soul must use to understand different types of properties (7, 523 A
1–525 A 14). We learn that 'the judgements of perception are themselves sufficient' (ἱκανῶς ὑπὸ τῆς αἰσθήσεως κρινόμενα, 523 B 1–2) to
tell us what a finger is, and it presents information, albeit less fully
or reliably, about relational properties like thickness, lightness, and
smallness. By 'sufficient', Plato means that the soul can use perception to grasp the property without help from another cognitive
ability: 'an ordinary soul isn't compelled to ask the understanding
what a finger is, since sight doesn't indicate to it that a finger is at
the same time the opposite of a finger' (οὐκ ἀναγκάζεται τῶν πολλῶν
ἡ ψυχὴ τὴν νόησιν ἐπερέσθαι τί ποτ' ἐστὶ δάκτυλος· οὐδαμοῦ γὰρ ἡ ὄψις

---

[19] For a modern discussion of these two positions, and a defence of the latter, see
S. Siegel, *The Contents of Visual Experience* (Oxford, 2010). Among those who
explicitly include value properties in perception's high-level content, Plato would
be a less controversial example. The view I attribute to him is that we can have a
perceptual experience of something *as good* or *as just* where this requires no direct
or even reliable link between a perceiver and actual instantiations of goodness or
justice. This can be contrasted with those who appeal to 'moral perception' as a way
to ground a realist moral epistemology (e.g. R. Audi, 'Moral Perception Defended',
Argumenta, 1 (2015), 5–28). Such a view requires the possibility that we veridically
perceive moral properties and do so in a way that is not grounded in, for example,
prior moral judgements. It is hard to imagine anyone who could disagree with this
view more than Plato. He believes that moral knowledge requires intelligible Forms
of moral properties precisely because perception is insufficient. He is interested in
the *mis*representation of value properties by perception, since this helps him to
explain why perception *fails* to ground a realist moral epistemology.

αὐτῇ ἅμα ἐσήμηνεν τὸν δάκτυλον τοὐναντίον ἢ δάκτυλον εἶναι, 523 D
3–6). Thus, perception has a significant share of the work of representing the world and it represents high-level properties, like
'being a finger'. Consonantly, in the same passage, perception is
described as an interpretive faculty that is not limited to the role of
passively recording what strikes the senses, but actively presents us
with representations of the world: it 'gives reports to the soul'
(παραγγέλλειν τῇ ψυχῇ, 524 A 2–3), 'says' (λέγει) something to us
(524 A 7), and offers 'interpretations' (ἑρμηνεῖαι, 524 B 1). There is
more than one way to flesh out this view of perception, but this is
enough to show that it is a view that is highly amenable to the possibility of higher-level perceptual content.

Further evidence that this high-level content includes value
properties comes from the role that images play in Plato's tripartite
psychology.[20] Consider the following argument:

1. The cognitive resources available to the non-rational parts of
   the soul are sensory.
2. The non-rational parts are able to cognize evaluative images.

Therefore:

3. Evaluative images are sensory.

The two premises here are substantial claims, but they are not
especially controversial. Both have been discussed and defended at
length elsewhere, and I will not add to their defence here.[21] But in
order to make clear the motivation behind them, it will be useful to
outline briefly Book 10's move from sensory to evaluative images,
which is a striking parallel of the move from sensory to evaluative
images in Books 6 and 7.[22]

---

[20] We might also consider the discussion of belief in Book 5, where the 'sight
lovers' (φιλοθεάμονες) have beliefs about the *sights* of not only beauty, but even justice
(479 A 3–5 and D 10–E 4). This is certainly suggestive, although the passage does not
make it easy to pin down exactly how the lovers of sights get from sensible instances
(or putative instances) of beauty and justice to their beliefs about beauty and
justice.

[21] See e.g. H. Lorenz, *The Brute Within: Appetitive Desire in Plato and Aristotle*
[*Brute*] (Oxford, 2006), and J. Moss, 'Appearances and Calculation: Plato's Division
of the Soul' ['Calculation'], *Oxford Studies in Ancient Philosophy*, 34 (2008), 35–68.
Note, however, that neither Lorenz nor Moss endorse (explicitly, at least) my
conclusion (3).

[22] The images discussed in Book 10 are the same as those that are the object of
eikasia. Both are introduced as—very nearly defined as—sensory copies of ordinary

The first step is an argument that appeals to optical illusions to show that sensory images 'exert their power' on the non-rational parts of the soul (10, 602 C 4–603 A 8). It does so by arguing that even after our rational part has used reason to conclude that an optical illusion is false, there is still a non-rational part of us that continues to believe it. While the mechanics of the argument are tricky, it gives a clear picture of what the non-rational parts can and cannot do.[23] They are aware of sensory images and can form a belief[24] that assents to them. But they don't have access to higher, non-sensory cognitive abilities: they cannot themselves use reason to figure out that an image is illusory (they are *alogiston*: non-rational or unreasoning) and they cannot correct their error in response to the conclusions reached by the rational part.

Plato then moves from these sensory images to evaluative images. The example of optical illusions is introduced simply to illustrate how the non-rational parts will be affected by the real object of Plato's concern: the 'images of virtue' (εἴδωλα ἀρετῆς; 10, 600 E 5) that imitative poetry produces. He gives the example of a non-rational part's inability to question, and thus automatic acceptance of, misleading theatrical appearances of how one ought to grieve. In short, the story seems to be that the non-rational parts' sensory

sensibles, with reflections being illustrative examples in both cases. Many commentators over the years have made the connection between the Line and Cave and Book 10; recent examples are Moss, 'Assent', and Dominick, 'Images' (Dominick cites Book 10 as evidence *against* the idea that *eikasia* typically involves error, though he focuses exclusively on paintings and reflections, and does not discuss the images of imitative poetry that certainly are error-inducing, albeit in a complex psychological way: see Section 3.3 below). S. Halliwell, *The Aesthetics of Mimesis* (Princeton, 2002), 57–8, denies there is a connection, citing, first, the fact that paintings lack a one-to-one relationship with their originals (unlike reflections and shadows)—though he does not explain why this is significant—and, second, a lack of shared vocabulary between the two passages. Yet the images of both passages are variously described as semblances (φαντάσματα), images (εἴδωλα), and even imitations (sensible originals are 'that which was imitated', τοῖς μιμηθεῖσιν, by images, 6, 510 B 4). And although the most common word for images in Books 6 and 7, εἰκόνες, is not used in Book 10, it had already been used to describe imitations in Book 3 (e.g. 401 B 2). Plato generally eschews the use of technical vocabulary, and various words can, as here, be used to describe the same thing. See also C. Belfiore, 'A Theory of Imitation in Plato's Republic', *Transactions of the American Philological Association*, 144 (1984), 121–46 at 129 n. 26.

[23] For a full reading of the argument, see my 'Appearance, Perception, and Non-rational Belief: *Republic* 602 c–603 A', *Oxford Studies in Ancient Philosophy*, 47 (2014), 81–118.

[24] The non-rational part of the soul believes (δοξάζει) something (10, 602 E 8–603 A 2) and the two parts form opposite beliefs (δόξαι, 603 D 1–2).

but non-rational access to the world explains their recalcitrant acceptance of sensory images, whether these are optical illusions or evaluative images.[25] This, then, is the second time in the *Republic* that Plato shifts from sensory to evaluative images without comment, as if there is no significant difference in kind between them. But this time we have two further reasons to think that there is indeed no significant difference. One is that the shift occurs within an explicit argument that would be invalidated by a change in the meaning of 'images'.[26] The second is that this passage invites a version of the aforementioned argument: it argues that the non-rational parts are both (1) unable to reason yet able to grasp sensory information and (2) able to grasp evaluative images, which entails that (3) these evaluative images are sensory.

I conclude that in the *Republic* Plato recognizes, and makes significant theoretical use of, sensory evaluative images. Nonetheless, we might still wonder what exactly they are for Plato. For a range of simple value properties, like goodness or pleasure, the idea is simple, assuming we accept the tenability of high-level perceptible properties: just as a column of a certain sort can look like—i.e. be represented in perception as—a *doric* column, armour of a certain sort can look like *fine* armour. And if the armour *merely* appears fine—perhaps it is impressively ornate, but poorly constructed—then it is a fitting example of the kind of misleading evaluative images that are the object of *eikasia*.[27] It is more challenging to understand how Plato thinks perception represents the thick value properties that are mentioned in the *Republic*'s two key discussions of images: 'shadows of *justice*', 'images of *virtue*'. One clue is that in Book 10 the normative force of 'images of virtue' comes from how they represent behaviour as pleasant or painful.[28] A plausible

---

[25] For a detailed defence of this reading, see Moss, 'Calculation'.

[26] A number of key conclusions about sensory images are required in his account of evaluative images: that they are 'third in relation to the truth' (10, 595 C 8–597 E 10); that they are epistemically inferior (598 A 1–602 C 3); and that they affect the non-rational part of the soul (602 C 4–603 A 8).

[27] See J. Moss 'What is Imitative Poetry and Why is it Bad?', in G. R. F. Ferrari (ed.), *The Cambridge Companion to Plato's Republic* (Cambridge, 2007), 415–44 for more discussion of the properties that might make something appear e.g. fine or excellent.

[28] Pleasure and pain constantly attend imitative poetry's images of people and their actions (10, 603 C 5–9), and Socrates' example of poetic images—apparently praiseworthy responses to grief—clearly compels its audience by the way various behaviour is represented as pleasant or painful.

proposal, then, is that for Plato representations of more complex value properties are grounded in representations of pleasure or pain, perhaps in a way that is, in turn, grounded in memories of and associations between previous perceptual experiences (the kind of empirical cognitive activity I will associate with *eikasia* in Section 3.2). According to this view, 'images of virtue' will be pleasure- and pain-tinted images of how one ought to behave or of what sort of person one ought to be. Since this does not require a direct grasp of concepts like 'justice' or 'courage', it is easier to see how they are accessible to the non-rational parts of the soul (which are the primary target of poetry's 'images of virtue'). At the same time, someone familiar with the relevant concepts could identify such an image of how we ought to behave as just behaviour, and in that sense perceive the behaviour as just.

2.3. *Eikasia as an explanation of ethical error*

Now that a view of *eikasia* is beginning to emerge, I want to take a step back and make some general observations about the role *eikasia* plays in the *Republic*. It is important to recognize that *eikasia* is introduced as a fundamental part of images that illustrate Plato's basic epistemology and metaphysics and his account of the effect of education. Given this setting, we should expect *eikasia* to describe a fact about the human condition that is intimately related to Plato's epistemology and metaphysics. We should also expect it to be something important: the elaborate imagery of the Cave allegory is designed primarily to represent the prisoners' strange life and the surprising fact that they are, with respect to education, 'like us'. With this in mind, the second-hand belief reading again looks out of place: that most people are content with second-hand ethical opinions is a fairly unremarkable psychological or sociological fact, with no particular relevance to Plato's epistemology and metaphysics, and it does not seem to warrant the dismal appraisal implied by comparing us to the cave dwellers.

My proposal is that Plato is offering a general account of ethical error based on a view about value properties. Plato believes that evaluative facts are especially difficult to grasp accurately. This is a fundamental premise of the *Republic*'s project, since ordinary people's failure to understand goodness or justice is what explains the need for philosophy and philosopher rulers. The point is not simply that ethical knowledge requires grasping Forms, but that knowledge, rather than true belief, is necessary in ethics to a much greater extent than it is elsewhere. With respect to most properties, we have the less error-prone *pistis* (see Section 3.1), and even in other practical areas there doesn't seem to be the same need for knowledge: a farmer or carpenter, for example, can do just fine with a useful set of true beliefs. In contrast, people's beliefs about goodness or justice are often greatly mistaken and Plato is, consequently, pessimistic about our ability to live happy and virtuous lives: truly living well requires achieving, or being ruled by those who have already achieved, a formidable philosophical education that is well beyond most people's reach and confined to a very specific political setting. Plato goes so far as to say that 'there can be no happiness, either public or private, in any other city [than one ruled by philosophers]' (χαλεπὸν γὰρ ἰδεῖν ὅτι οὐκ ἂν ἄλλῃ τις εὐδαιμονήσειεν οὔτε ἰδίᾳ οὔτε δημοσίᾳ, 5, 473 E 3–4). Even allowing for hyperbole, this calls for explanation.

My point, in short, is that we will not find this explanation if we look only at the upper regions of Plato's metaphysics and epistemology, such as the austere requirements on the acquisition of knowledge. The essential other half of the explanation is his account of the sensible world, the two kinds of belief it produces, and why everyday ethical beliefs are of the lower kind, *eikasia*. By explaining why *eikasia* is not an adequate practical guide, Plato thereby justifies his pessimistic assessment of ordinary people's state of ethical education. Note that this pessimism is not about ordinary people per se, but about the world that ordinary people live in: the problem is not widespread foolishness, but the obscurity of evaluative facts. When it comes to value properties like goodness or justice, we don't have easy access to self-explanatory sensible examples and, thus, most of us rely on images or likenesses of goodness or justice.[29] Unfortunately, mere images of goodness or justice are usually false or misleading, so in the absence of knowledge, or a knowledgeable guide, we are likely to acquire false beliefs. Rather than the prisoners themselves—who are, after

---

[29] The implication is that not all properties are equal: e.g. we can identify large and small things accurately, yet not just and unjust things. See *Polit.* 285 D 9–286 A 4 and *Phaedr.* 250 B 1–5, which both N. Cooper, 'The Importance of διάνοια in Plato's Theory of Forms', *Classical Quarterly*, 16 (1966), 65–9, and Strang, 'Cave', 23–4, discuss in this context.

all, *prisoners*, compelled to face the shadows because their legs and necks are manacled (7, 514 A 5–B 1)—we should blame their imprisoned condition: the cave and the shadow-show that is the world they are compelled to live in, which represents the sensible world that we live in. The condition of the prisoners represents Plato's belief that when it comes to questions of value, we live in an inherently misleading world: what appears good or just is often not so, and what is good or just often doesn't appear so. That this mis-alignment of appearance and reality is an unalterable feature of the world is illustrated by the fact that the cave itself is not something that even philosopher rulers can change or truly escape, just as we cannot get rid of the sensible world and the faults inherent in it. Those who are made to return to the cave with knowledge of the outside world do not dismantle the shadow-show or lead the pris-oners outside; the best they can do is recognize the shadows for what they are (520 C 1–5) and educate and rule the prisoners accordingly.[30]

3. Eikastic cognition

The forgoing highlights the importance of understanding how *eikasia* is represented by the condition of the prisoners in the Cave allegory. Examining the prisoners' condition will allow me to address the second of the two basic questions about *eikasia*: I have so far concluded that *eikasia*'s object is sensory images, but what exactly is *eikasia* with respect to this object? I will begin by exam-ining the prisoners' error of confusing shadows for real things, which is commonly identified with *eikasia*. I will argue that this identification is a mistake and that it has prevented commentators from noticing the more successful, if still rudimentary, features of the prisoners' thinking that allow them to function despite being confined to a stream of shadows.

---

[30] By blaming the limitations of the sensible world, not ordinary people, I am not suggesting that human nature has no role. It seems likely, for example, that mislead-ing appearances are, for Plato, tied to how human motivation works, and in particu-lar how we represent something as pleasant or painful. My claim is just that the conditions that explain *eikasia*'s prevalence are not a fault of a person or group of people, but a result of inescapable features of the human condition.

3.1. *The basic error*

Drawing on the Cave, it is common to identify *eikasia* with the error of mistaking an image for that of which it is an image, like mistaking a shadow for what casts it. Though I will argue that it is wrong to identify *eikasia* with this error, as if the word just labels a type of fallacy, I think it is indeed true that it is a kind of cognition in which something related to this error is fundamental. But a number of clarifications are necessary.

First, some formulations of the error associated with *eikasia* have a slight but significant difference. Gail Fine, for example, defines *eikasia* as a failure to 'systematically discriminate between images and their objects'.[31] Notice that this formulation remains neutral about whether *eikasia* is an encounter with images or with originals. This is because Fine believes that experiencing an image is not only insufficient (which I think is right) but also *unnecessary* for *eikasia*. As I understand it, her point is that if you have only experienced apparent justice, you will fail to recognize a genuinely just act when you see it; thus, you can have *eikasia* even while experiencing the original of something, not just its image. But in this example, is the relevant object of *eikasia* really the just act? The idea is that the person fails to recognize the action *as* a just action, so it will not *appear* like something just to them, but something, for example, unjust or foolish. Thus, since it is the appearance that matters in *eikasia*, the object of cognition is still an image, such as a mere image of injustice or foolishness.

The second clarification is subtle but important. The prisoners are introduced to explain the ethical mindset of ordinary people. This being so, they do not represent ethical *eikasia*, exactly, but ordinary people's ethical *eikasia*, and this leaves open the possibility that there could be unordinary kinds of *eikasia*. In particular, while the prisoners' ignorance represents something typical of *eikasia*, it is not obvious that it is essential. Consider the following (unlikely) possibility. Imagine I recognize ethical images as images, but have no experience of or information about their originals. I might (mistakenly) think: 'Though these are just images, they're probably pretty close to reality, and they're all I have to go on, so

---

[31] Fine, '*Republic* V–VII', 102. A similar definition is given by Wilberding, 'Puppeteers', 129.

I'm going to base my beliefs on them.' Following this line of thinking, I would acquire all the same ethical beliefs as any ordinary person and *do so for the same reason*: I've based my beliefs on mere images.
Is this still *eikasia*? How one answers depends on what one takes to be
essential to *eikasia*: mistaking image for original or the cognitive condition that *results* from this mistake, namely, a condition in which a
person derives their judgements entirely from sensible images,
taken largely at face value. Since the Line primarily concerns kinds
of cognition, not kinds of error, I take the latter to be what *eikasia*
names, and the former to be its typical cause. So understood, *eikasia* is defined by what one in fact derives one's beliefs from—sensible
images, rather than sensible originals or Forms—not what has led
one to do so.[32] Note that even though, strictly speaking, this entails
that the standard view of *eikasia* as mistaking image and original is
false, it remains a moderately benign falsehood. For the most part,
it conveys a fairly accurate picture of *eikasia*, since it is true of most
occurrences of *eikasia* and it entails what *is* the essential characteristic of all *eikasia*: that one forms one's judgements on the basis of
mere images alone.[33]

---

[32] Thus, I agree with I. M. Crombie, *An Examination of Plato's Doctrines*, vol. ii:
Plato on Knowledge and Reality (London, 1963), 76, that '*eikasia* seems to mean
"having only an image to go on"'. A parallel point can be made about Socrates'
inference, in Book 5, from his claim that, with respect to sensible and intelligible
beauty, the cognitive state of the lovers of sights and sounds is a result of their error
of thinking 'that a likeness is not a likeness, but the thing itself that it is like' (τὸ
ὅμοιόν τῳ μὴ ὅμοιον ἀλλ' αὐτὸ ἡγῆται εἶναι ᾧ ἔοικεν, 476 C 4–5)—i.e. mistaking sensibles for Forms—to the conclusion that they only have belief, not knowledge. While
making this error is sufficient to restrict a person to belief, we should not assume
that it is also a necessary condition of belief. Many would agree, for example, that
although philosophers are immune to this mistake, at least some of their judgements about the sensible world are beliefs.

[33] This brings out the sharpest difference between my view and the view defended
by Moss, 'Assent'. Rather than simply being limited to their respective objects,
Moss makes certain internalist criteria essential to *pistis* and *eikasia*: *pistis* is active
affirmation, typically after reflection, about how things are; *eikasia* is passive 'yielding to' appearances, without affirmation or denial. I think this misidentifies certain
cases. For Moss, if one brings the apparent/real distinction to bear on a question,
and affirms something as one or the other, this is, *ipso facto*, *pistis*. But ordinary
people do, in general, grasp the difference between real and apparent, and if asked,
they presumably would assert that (e.g.) pleasure really is, just as it appears, good.
This leads to the strange result that *pistis* sometimes differs from *eikasia* simply by
being a more brazen error: not just 'pleasure is good' (*eikasia*) but 'pleasure really *is*,
as it appears, good' (*pistis*). A second problem is that Plato characterizes *pistis* solely
by pointing us to its object: 'that which it is like—that is, the animals around us,
every plant . . .' (6, 510 A 5–6). There is no suggestion that it requires a special

Two further clarifications are invited by the two occasions when Socrates explicitly describes the errors in the prisoners' attitude to the shadows. Notably, on neither occasion does he say that they are simply mistaking them for the statues that cast them. The first is the following:

οὐ ταῦτα ἡγεῖ ἂν τὰ παριόντα αὐτοὺς νομίζειν ὀνομάζειν ἅπερ ὁρῷεν; (7, 515 B 4–5)

Don't you think they would assume that the names they used applied to the things [*sc.* the shadows] they see passing in front of them?[34]

For example, if a puppeteer carries a statue of a wolf along the wall, and a prisoner points at its shadow and says 'a wolf is running past', he is misapplying the name 'wolf' to the shadow. But notice that the name 'wolf' most properly refers not to statues of wolves, but to the real wolves running around outside the cave, which represent Forms.[35] So we might think that they do not mistake images for *sensible* originals, but rather images for Forms. At this point, it is especially important to appreciate that *eikasia* is not any old error, but a fundamental epistemological concept defined in relation to Plato's ontology. It is one of the four measures in the Line and Cave of how well or badly we grasp the relevant Form, the principal determinant of which is whether we grasp the Form directly or indirectly through its instantiations. In this respect, *eikasia* is twice removed from the Form. The shadow of a wolf is

---

attitude to animals and plants, like reflection or affirmation. Yet for Moss, many beliefs about animals and plants will be *eikasia* rather that *pistis*, since for her *pistis* is a kind of *active* affirmation, which usually—she suspects always—follows explicit reflection (225–6). She recognizes that this means *pistis* will be rarer than we might think, but to make it so rare that it excludes many beliefs about sensible originals seems to contradict Socrates' explicit characterization of *pistis* (see n. 17 above).

[34] For a compelling discussion of the meaning and implications of this line, see V. Harte, 'Language in the Cave', in D. Scott (ed.), *Maieusis: Essays on Ancient Philosophy in Honour of Myles Burnyeat* (Oxford, 2007), 195–215. I follow Harte—and presumably Reeve in his translation—in using Adam's text over Slings's; nonetheless, I think much the same point results from Slings's text (cf. 515 B 7–9).

[35] Compare the second error (which I will discuss shortly) of thinking that 'reality is nothing other than the shadows'. Just like the prisoner's error about names, this is, so to speak, two errors deep. Their error is to suppose that, for example, sensible images of justice are the only candidates for what justice really is. But it would also be an error to suppose that just sensible *originals*—i.e. real sensible instances of justice—are what justice really is, since this fails to acknowledge properly the Form of justice (this latter error is the one that, in Book 5, the lovers of sights make about beauty).

an image of a statue of a wolf that is itself an image of a real wolf: *eikasia*'s object is a mere image of a sensible that is itself an image of a Form. As Plato will describe them in Book 10, such images are 'third place from the what is' (τριττὰ ἀπέχοντα τοῦ ὄντος, 599 A 2). What is unique to *eikasia* is still the last step, mistaking mere images for their sensible originals, so we are not wrong to associate it with this. But we need also to recognize that *eikasia* is a way of relating to the type of fundamental facts that can only be properly understood through knowledge of Forms: facts concerning the nature of things (like what piety is) and not, except perhaps derivatively, isolated empirical facts (like who mutilated the Hermai).

The second description of the error is the following:

παντάπασι δή, ἦν δ' ἐγώ, οἱ τοιοῦτοι οὐκ ἂν ἄλλο τι νομίζοιεν τὸ ἀληθὲς ἢ τὰς τῶν σκευαστῶν σκιάς. (7, 515 C 1–2)

In every way, then, what the prisoners would take for reality is nothing other than the shadows of the artefacts.

Everyone will occasionally mistake image and original, perhaps mistaking someone for their reflection in a hall of mirrors. But even if these are brief episodes of *eikasia*, they bear little similarity to the prisoners' condition. If I confuse someone with their reflection, I still know the difference between a person and a reflection; it is not, then, a mistake that affects my basic understanding of the world. In contrast, the condition of the prisoners leads them to make a general ontological error over and above any individual errors: believing that 'reality is nothing other than the shadows'. Here the scope of the Cave allegory matters a great deal.[36] Since the prisoners' condition represents ordinary people's ethical *eikasia*, the lesson to draw is, adapting the sentence, that ordinary people 'in every way believe that *ethical* reality is nothing other than the mere appearances of sensible ethical properties'. Not *de dicto* of course: typically a person will not think that they are dealing with mere appearances any more than the prisoners think they are

---

[36] If there is no limit to the Cave's scope, then 515 C 1–2 would support D. W. Hamlyn's claim that *eikasia* is 'the state of mind of him who holds that sense-data or appearances are all that there is, who is unaware that or does not acknowledge that there are also material objects', 'Eikasia in Plato's *Republic*' ['*Eikasia*'], *Philosophical Quarterly*, 8 (1958), 12–23 at 23.

dealing with shadows.[37] Rather, the implication is that, with respect to value properties, they do not recognize a distinction between what appears F and what is F. In other words, they assume that, as is indeed the case with many ordinary sensibles, what seems so is so: what seems good or just is good or just.

Finally, a note on error and truth. It is important not to confuse the distinction between *pistis* and *eikasia* with the distinction between true and false belief. Only some false beliefs result from the error of treating images as originals, and there is no reason to think that there are not some true beliefs about sensible images (whether recognized as such or not). Similarly, there are many false things that can be believed about sensible originals, even when recognizing them as such. The temptation to identify *eikasia* with false belief comes from its strong association with error. All belief—both *pistis* and *eikasia*—is open to error (only knowledge is infallible (ἀναμαρτήτῳ, 5, 477 E 7–8)). But *eikasia* makes a person especially prone to error, for at least two reasons. A general reason is that images of F things represent F-ness even less completely and accurately than sensible F things, which already have their flaws. A particular reason is that widespread ethical error is caused by the especially sharp disparity between appearance and reality in the evaluative domain (as I emphasized in Section 2.3), which makes *pistis* considerably more accurate in this domain.

3.2. *The shadow-spotting competition*

One lesson from the preceding is that the prisoners' error is not a departure from the norms that govern their everyday cognition, but an error that shapes those norms. This leads me to the second major claim of this paper: *eikasia* should not be identified with the isolated error of mistaking an image for an original, but with a kind of cognitive activity that someone is compelled to engage in when

---

[37] The exception would be the 'enlightened' *eikasia* mentioned earlier, where one recognizes that one is limited to images but trusts them anyway. Such a person could be compared to someone who knows that a reflection of a person is different from a person, yet who does not know *how* it differs, since they have only experienced people-reflections. Notice that even someone with enlightened *eikasia* would believe and act *as if* 'reality is nothing other than the shadows' and, crucially, since they assume images are accurate, they would make the same general error: they assume that when it comes to value properties, what seems so is so.

they only have a perceptual, image-confined access to the world. In particular, I propose that it is the kind of cognition that we get a glimpse of in the following passage, in which Socrates describes the returning philosopher's attitude to a sort of shadow-spotting competition that preoccupies the prisoners:

τιμαὶ δὲ καὶ ἔπαινοι εἴ τινες αὐτοῖς ἦσαν τότε παρ' ἀλλήλων καὶ γέρα, τῷ ὀξύτατα καθορῶντι τὰ παριόντα καὶ μνημονεύοντι μάλιστα ὅσα τε πρότερα αὐτῶν καὶ ὕστερα εἰώθει καὶ ἅμα πορεύεσθαι, καὶ ἐκ τούτων δὴ δυνατώτατα ἀπομαντευομένῳ τὸ μέλλον ἥξειν, δοκεῖς ἂν αὐτὸν ἐπιθυμητικῶς αὐτῶν ἔχειν καὶ ζηλοῦν τοὺς παρ' ἐκείνοις τιμωμένους τε καὶ ἐνδυναστεύοντας . . . ; (7, 516 c 8–d 4)

If there had been any honours, praises, or prizes among them for the one who was sharpest at identifying the shadows as they passed by and who best remembered which usually came earlier, which later, and which simultaneously, and who could thus best divine what's going to happen, do you think that our man would desire these rewards or envy those among the prisoners who were honoured and held power?

My claim is that we should identify this cognitive activity with *eikasia*. An obvious and compelling reason to do so is that it is the cognitive activity of people in a condition that is typically thought to represent *eikasia*.[38] If that is right, then mistaking shadows for originals is only a small part of what is distinctive about the prisoners' cognition. This is, on reflection, unsurprising. The prisoners conduct their whole lives in the cave. Plato describes them holding court cases, debating justice, competing for positions of power, and condemning people to death—and doing all these ethical charged activities through the medium of shadows. This suggests a kind of ethical thinking that is comprehensively shaped by the fact that they are limited to images, and the shadow-spotting competition is our best insight into what this might be. However, while Plato is clearly describing something specific and distinctive, it is not obvious

---

[38] I assume that this is a cognitive activity practised by all prisoners. It might be objected that the reference to 'those among the prisoners who were honoured and held power' suggests a narrower application, perhaps to something unique to politicians and poets. I have two reasons for a broader application. First, the honours go to those among the whole group of prisoners (the subject is still the 'fellow-prisoners'; συνδεσμῶται, 516 c 5) who are sharp*est* at shadow-spotting (ὀξύτατα καθορᾶν, 516 c 9), which implies that the others engage in shadow-spotting, but with less laudable sharpness. Second, the skills described seem to be essential life skills for anyone confined to shadows: it is hard to imagine a prisoner functioning without *some* capacity for identifying, remembering, and anticipating the only objects they know.

what it is. We can see that it involves identifying and anticipating shadows by making guesses that are based on what we remember, and we can also see that it is analogous to some activity or activities for which people receive honours, rewards, and power. But where can we go from here?

Consider first the word itself, *eikasia*. In the Line analogy, Plato mostly uses existing words as placeholders for the new kinds of cognition he is describing: *pistis*, *dianoia*, and *noēsis*.[39] But *eikasia* is the exception, being much rarer and possibly a Platonic neologism.[40] So Plato presumably chose '*eikasia*' because he thought it was apt. A little reflection makes it clear why. The objects of the lowest section of the Line are *eikones*, 'images' or 'likenesses', and Plato wishes to name a kind of cognition relating to these. The natural place to look is the cognate verb, *eikazein*: if *eikones* are the object of cognition, *eikazein* is a good place to look for the manner in which they are cognized. *Eikazein* has a variety of related meanings: to represent by an image (thus, to paint: 2, 377 E 1); to compare or liken (as when Meno likens Socrates to a torpedo fish, *Meno* 80 C 4); or to infer, imagine, or guess something (*Meno* 89 E 2; *Sym.* 190 A 4). If there is an active side to *eikasia*—something it does with images—activities such as likening, imagining, and guessing are excellent candidates. They also do a good job of describing what is happening in the shadow-spotting competition: the prisoners identify passing shadows and make guesses or conjectures about what is or will be the case (they 'divine what's going to happen') by likening them with memories of previous correlations they've seen ('which usually came earlier, which later, and which simultaneously').[41]

---

[39] He even warns us against placing any weight on the specific words he has chosen: 7, 533 D 6–9.

[40] I find two near-contemporary uses, though neither is free from Plato's sphere of influence. In the spurious Platonic dialogue *Sisyphus*, it is used to describe a certain bad type of practical deliberation; Gallop translates 'guesswork' (390 C 7). In Xenophon's *Memorabilia*, Socrates describes painting as 'representation of the visible' (εἰκασία τῶν ὁρωμένων, 3. 10. 1. 5). An example of later uses is Plutarch's *Themistocles*, 29. 3, where it has a clear meaning of likeness or comparison and, consonantly, in Demetrius, *On Style*, a manual on rhetoric, it is used in an apparently technical sense for 'simile' (2. 80. 5).

[41] For similar views of the connection between *eikasia* and *eikazein* (though not necessarily similar conclusions), see Nettleship, *Lectures*, 241; Robinson, *Dialectic*, 203; Hamlyn, '*Eikasia*', 19–20, who also connects it to the prisoners' shadow-spotting; and Wilberding, 'Puppeteers', 130. Adam, *Republic* (in contrast to his editor,

This is satisfying, but speculative. For firmer ground, we need to look at what the prisoners are actually doing. Clearly a central skill in the shadow-spotting is the ability to draw conjectural judgements from comparisons with previously experienced shadows: identifying present shadows and predicting future ones. A natural hypothesis, then, is that it represents a kind of cognition that draws conclusions about images by some purely empirical means, such as comparison and inductive conjecture. Though if it is a *bona fide* kind of reasoning, it must be one about which Plato has (like his returning prisoner) a low opinion: we are not thinking of reliable, scientific induction, but something more haphazard and conjectural.

I think that we can make best sense of this passage if we consider it alongside a number of other passages in which Plato draws a contrast between, on the one hand, reason and art, and, on the other, 'mere experience' (ἐμπειρία).[42] The two most striking passages are in the *Gorgias* and *Philebus*. Although they appear in quite different philosophical contexts, from the *Republic* and each other, they have a relevance that speaks for itself, not least because all three appear to be attempts to describe the same thing: the lowest kind of cognitive activity in which humans typically engage.[43]

In the *Gorgias*, Socrates describes a low class of activities—including rhetoric, sophistry, pastry baking, and cosmetics—that fall short of being genuine arts:

κομιδῇ ἀτέχνως ἐπ' αὐτὴν ἔρχεται, οὔτε τι τὴν φύσιν σκεψαμένη τῆς ἡδονῆς οὔτε τὴν αἰτίαν, ἀλόγως τε παντάπασιν ὡς ἔπος εἰπεῖν οὐδὲν διαριθμησαμένη, τριβῇ

Rees: xxxvii) believes that 'the translation "conjecture" is misleading, for conjecture implies conscious doubt or hesitation, and doubt is foreign to *eikasia* in Plato's sense'. It is true that *eikasia* is closely related to a failure to doubt specifically that what appears to be the case is the case—but not to a failure to doubt *as such*.

[42] The 'mere' is important: it is experience *on its own* that Plato is discussing here. It is easy to caricature Plato, especially if used as a foil to Aristotle, as an arch rationalist who hubristically ignored the role of experience in practical knowledge. But that is inaccurate. The importance of experience, as a supplement to reason and understanding, is a major theme in the *Republic*. A sufficient (though far from the only) example is the role experience plays at both ends of the Guardians' education: their early education in music, poetry, and gymnastics and the fifteen years of practical experience—more than is devoted to either mathematics or dialectic—that they must do so that 'they won't be inferior with respect to ἐμπειρία' (7, 539 E 3–6).

[43] The *Gorgias* and *Philebus* passages often come up in discussions of Plato's view of *empeiria*, though not *Rep.* 7, 516 C 8–D 4. A notable exception is C. Balla, 'Early Forerunners of Medical Empiricism' ['Medical Empiricism'], Φιλοσοφία, 48 (2018), 253–80, who draws on all three passages, though in the context of a reading very different from my own.

καὶ ἐμπειρίᾳ μνήμην μόνον σῳζομένη τοῦ εἰωθότος γίγνεσθαι, ᾧ δὴ καὶ πορίζεται τὰς ἡδονάς. (501 A 4–B 1)

It proceeds towards its object in an entirely artless way, without having at all examined either the nature or cause of pleasure. It does so completely non-rationally [ἀλόγως], with virtually no discrimination. Through habit and experience [τριβῇ καὶ ἐμπειρίᾳ] it merely preserves the memory of what usually happens and that is how it procures pleasures.

In the *Philebus*, Socrates presents a hierarchy remarkably reminiscent of the Divided Line (*Phileb.* 55 C–59 D): he ranks kinds of arts in order of purity (τὸ καθαρόν) or clarity (τὸ σαφές), where the lowest includes rhetoric, music, and poetry; the highest is the philosophical art of dialectic; and mathematical arts lie in between. We are interested in his description of the lowest:

ΣΩ. Οἷον πασῶν που τεχνῶν ἄν τις ἀριθμητικὴν χωρίζῃ καὶ μετρητικὴν καὶ στατικήν, ὡς ἔπος εἰπεῖν φαῦλον τὸ καταλειπόμενον ἑκάστης ἂν γίγνοιτο.

ΠΡΩ. Φαῦλον μὲν δή.

ΣΩ. Τὸ γοῦν μετὰ ταῦτ᾽ εἰκάζειν λείποιτ᾽ ἂν καὶ τὰς αἰσθήσεις καταμελετᾶν ἐμπειρίᾳ καί τινι τριβῇ, ταῖς τῆς στοχαστικῆς προσχρωμένους δυνάμεσιν ἃς πολλοὶ τέχνας ἐπονομάζουσι, μελέτῃ καὶ πόνῳ τὴν ῥώμην ἀπειργασμένας. (*Phileb.* 55 E 1–56 A 1)

SOC: If someone were to take away all counting, measuring, and weighing from the arts, the rest might be said to be worthless.

PHIL: Worthless, indeed!

SOC: All we would have left would be conjecture [εἰκάζειν] and the training of our perceptions through experience and habit [ἐμπειρίᾳ καί τινι τριβῇ]. We would have to rely on the ability to make guesses that many people call art, once it has acquired strength through exercise and toil.

All three passages describe a similar kind of cognition. First, it is empirical: at least at its most rudimentary, it seems to be the ability to repeat what is remembered, in particular a remembered pleasure. (While memory is not explicitly mentioned in the *Philebus* passage, it was earlier defined as the 'preservation of perception' (σωτηρία αἰσθήσεως, *Phileb.* 34 A 10–11), so it can reasonably be assumed to be involved in the 'training of our perceptions'.) Second, it is 'non-rational' in the sense that it does not use reasoning (like 'counting, measuring, and weighing') or seek understanding (it doesn't examine 'the nature or cause of pleasure'). Thus, it appears to be a kind of empirical, non-rational ability we have when we rely solely on 'habit' and 'experience', τριβή and ἐμπειρία:

a combination that we find often in Plato, almost always as a contrast to a genuine *technē*.[44] If there is any difference between them, perhaps τριβή, 'habit', emphasizes repetition (literally it means rubbing) and ἐμπειρία, 'experience', emphasizes a previous acquaintance, both of which capture aspects of what we mean when we talk about 'learning by experience'.

It is worth examining Plato's view of memory more closely. Something that stands out in the passages from the *Republic* and *Gorgias* is that they talk about using a memory of what 'usually' or 'typically' happens. We can't literally have *a* memory of what typically happens, since nothing is typical of a single occasion. So the relevant 'memory' must be either a series of memories or, more likely, some kind of synthesis of such memories: a series of memories of glass breaking, for example, seems to fall short of remembering that glass is fragile. (I take it that it is for reasons such as this that Aristotle introduces what he calls 'experience' as a separate kind of cognition in this role: 'in human beings experience comes about from memory; for many memories of the same thing bring about the power of one experience.')[45]

But even if we say that he is describing a kind of cognition drawn from a series of memories, this still leaves open a wide range of possibilities. At its most sophisticated, it could be a judgement that is the conclusion of an explicit inductive inference, perhaps even with accurate estimates of the probabilities involved. At its most rudimentary, it might be a mere disposition to act in a certain way born from a habituated response to the repetition of similar experiences. So far, then, the possibilities range over everything from the work of an empirical scientist to a lion salivating when it sees a deer. Which of these is representative of Plato's view?

I believe the answer is, in a way, both. We might think that the decisive evidence is Plato's description of what he is referring to as something 'non-rational' (ἄλογος), and a result of mere habit and the 'training of our perception'. This certainly seems to favour the salivating lion over the empirical scientist. But we need to be cautious here. We should not assume that Plato's experience/reason

---

[44] E.g. *Gorg.* 463 B 3–4 (οὐκ ἔστιν τέχνη ἀλλ' ἐμπειρία καὶ τριβή), *Phaedo* 270 B 6–7 (μὴ τριβῇ μόνον καὶ ἐμπειρίᾳ ἀλλὰ τέχνῃ), and *Leg.* 11, 936 A 4 (εἴτ' οὖν τέχνη εἴτε ἄτεχνός ἐστίν τις ἐμπειρία καὶ τριβή).

[45] *Metaph.* 1. 1, 980 B 28–981 A 1: γίγνεται δ' ἐκ τῆς μνήμης ἐμπειρία τοῖς ἀνθρώποις· αἱ γὰρ πολλαὶ μνῆμαι τοῦ αὐτοῦ πράγματος μιᾶς ἐμπειρίας δύναμιν ἀποτελοῦσιν. See also *Post. An.* 2. 19, 100 A 3–9.

dichotomy aligns with our own. In particular, his attitude to induct-ive reasoning seems very far from ours. It is not even clear that Plato recognized inductive inference as a *bona fide* kind of reasoning at all.[46] He might, then, consider mere experience to be non-rational and yet include in it activities that *we* would characterize as reason-ing. Certainly judging on the basis of which things 'usually came earlier, which later, and which simultaneously' brings to mind something like inductive reasoning, and this impression is strength-ened by the fact that it is said to be the experiential method of cer-tain arts, especially if these include, as is claimed in the *Philebus*, arts like 'medicine, agriculture, navigation, and strategy' (56 B 1–2).

Medicine gives us some further clues. There was to be, and to a limited extent may already have been, a debate about whether medicine can rely on experience alone (as Plato implies in the *Philebus*) or also needs theoretical accounts that go beyond experi-ence.[47] However, those who came to be called the 'Empiricists' (ἐμπειρικοί) in this debate describe a form of empirical thought very different from our own: not only do they embrace a descrip-tion of medicine's method centred on memorizing and associating experiences, but they combined it with a conception of reason that is as narrow as Plato's seems to be, and crucially doesn't leave space for any kind of inductive reasoning. Michael Frede, for example, describes them as follows:

They defend the view that we can account for our technical beliefs and even for our technical knowledge solely in terms of the senses and mem-ory...To claim this seems to presuppose a particular conception of reason which is different from ours, a conception on which it is not true by definition that anything we would call 'inference' or 'reasoning' will be a function of

---

[46] The best candidate for a counter-example is the Socratic *epagōgē*, though many doubt that this involves inductive inference. M. L. McPherran, 'Socratic *epagōgē* and Socratic Induction', *Journal of the History of Philosophy*, 45 (2007), 347–64, gives an excellent survey of the debate, himself concluding that many are indeed probabilistic inferences. Without suggesting that it addresses McPherran's many careful arguments, I think it is important to recognize that the *epagōgē* can be per-suasive (rather than purely explanatory) even if it is not an inductive inference. It strikes me that Socrates often appeals to sets of examples neither for empirical sup-port nor purely for illustration. The aim is often to make a common property in a set of examples salient to an interlocutor, as a step towards persuading them of a general claim that involves this property (I think something like this is also going on in McPherran's example of *Polit.* 277 C–278 C).

[47] The debate is Hellenistic, but for a discussion of its antecedents and how they might have interacted with Plato's and Aristotle's views, see Balla, 'Medical Empiricism'.

reason. It rather seems to be a view which attributes some or all functions of reason, to the extent that it recognises them, to memory.[48]

Frede sees the ancestors of this view in the fifth and fourth century BCE, where we find, on the one hand, a narrow and austere conception of the work of reason, and, on the other, a correspondingly broad conception of the work of perception, memory, and other perceptual abilities.[49] With respect to the latter, it might be thought that Plato is less generous to our perceptual abilities than this, since he clearly thinks of experience as a low kind of cognition, typical of lower or even pseudo-arts, and even as a source of error in ethical thought. But if we set aside his critical tone, we can see that he is also allowing experience considerable achievements: the pastry chef makes tasty pastries and the farmer's crops grow (sometimes ancient doctors even healed). This is more than the kind of mindless or animalistic activities that we might expect from pure memory and perception.

We find, then, that Plato has a consistent story to tell about the lowest kind of human cognition, one that makes it, from a modern perspective, a mixture of primitive and sophisticated: it relies only on the kind of perceptual abilities that we can imagine sharing with animals, and yet involves something that is at least a close cousin of inductive reasoning. With this in mind, it seems highly likely that when Plato describes the prisoners' identifying, remembering patterns between, and predicting shadows, he is representing the manner in which anyone confined to images forms more complex judgements, beyond simple assent to images. This makes it especially clear that *eikasia* represents not an isolated error, but a comprehensive way of cognitively engaging with images, just as *dianoia* and *noēsis* are comprehensive ways of reasoning about their objects.

3.3. Eikasia *without reason*

Eikasia has turned out to be a perceptual and—in a specific Platonic sense—unreasoning kind of cognition that plays a key role in explaining ethical error. It should not come as too much of a

---

[48] M. Frede, 'An Empiricist View of Knowledge: Memorism', in S. Everson (ed.), *Epistemology*, Companions to Ancient Thought, vol. i (Cambridge, 1990), 225–50 at 226.

[49] Lorenz presents his book *The Brute Within* as a study of the antecedents of the Hellenistic Empiricist/Rationalist debate in Plato and Aristotle, and in this respect it largely corroborates the distinction drawn here.

surprise, then, that my final claim is that *eikasia* is a kind of cognition available to (not exclusive to) the non-rational parts of the soul.[50] One reason to think that this is so, and possibly a sufficient reason, is simply that *eikasia* has turned out to be extremely similar to what we would expect non-rational cognition to look like for Plato, at least according to some recent interpretations of the latter.[51] But we see a further and more direct reason when we look again at the passage described briefly earlier (Section 2.2) in which Socrates examines a putative opposition in the soul that arises when we use reasoning to see through an optical illusion.

As we saw earlier, there are close connections between the *Republic*'s discussion of *eikasia* and its discussion of imitation in Book 10. Both are discussions of 'images' or 'appearances' that emphasize their low place in Plato's ontological hierarchy: they are mere images of sensibles that are, in turn, mere images of Forms. Equally, both emphasize how appearances are epistemologically unreliable in a way that has serious consequences in ethics: images give us incomplete and distorted views of the world, yet they are sufficiently persuasive to fool the ordinary person who assumes that what appears so, is so. Consequently, most people's ethical beliefs are deeply flawed. Unlike Books 6 and 7, however, Book 10 adds an explicit account of the psychological effect of images, beginning in the argument from optical illusions. The argument aims to show that images exert their power on the non-rational parts of our soul. Socrates asserts that when we reason our way out of an optical illusion, there remains a cognitive conflict in the soul: we have one belief agreeing with the sensory image (e.g. that a partially immersed stick is bent) and another belief that results from reasoning, which recognizes that the image is false (e.g. that in reality the stick is straight). Thus, the first belief confuses image for reality and the other reaches the real state of affairs behind the image—one is set over a sensible image, the other over a sensible original. If it were not for the unusual context, with both beliefs occurring at the same time in the same soul, we would hardly need

---

[50] Others who have made this claim include C. D. C. Reeve, *Philosopher-Kings: The Argument of Plato's Republic* (Princeton, NJ, 1988), 139, and Moss, 'Assent' and 'Pleasure and Illusion in Plato', *Philosophy and Phenomenological Research*, 72 (2006), 503–35 at 522.

[51] For example, Lorenz, *Brute*.

a second glance to see that the first is an example of *eikasia* and the second of *pistis*.[52]

But this is surely the right reading. Notice that the belief attributed to a non-rational part doesn't obey the norms that usually govern beliefs, but is instead so firmly rooted in appearances that it fails to update even when the believer has decisive evidence that the appearance is false, and it persists even while being overtly contradicted by another belief that does follow this evidence. Plato is not simply pointing out two token beliefs, but marking a distinction between two kinds of belief, where the uniquely non-rational kind is defined by its inability to listen to reason and, thus, its reliance on, and implicit trust in, the evidence of images. So both this argument and the Line divide belief into two kinds, and they make essentially the same point: one kind of belief goes beyond mere images, but the other invariably takes them at face value, and is in this way trapped—imprisoned—by them. The only significant difference is that in Book 10, the lower kind of belief is held by a non-rational part of the soul.[53]

While Books 6 and 7, in contrast, do not explicitly attempt to integrate the *Republic*'s psychology, we do get a telling glimpse of Plato's position. During his commentary on the Cave allegory, Socrates tells us that education can turn the intellect in the right direction only if it turns it 'together with the whole soul' (σὺν ὅλῃ τῇ ψυχῇ, 7, 518 C 4–D 1)—that is, together with the non-rational parts of the soul. Thus, as a prerequisite for intellectual education, a person must possess the non-intellectual virtues that are acquired

---

[52] There is also an interesting similarity to our *Philebus* passage, 55 E 1–56 A 1: there, the lowest cognition was what was left when we 'take away all counting, measuring, and weighing'; here it is what we get when a part of us is unable to use 'measuring, counting, and weighing' (τὸ μετρεῖν καὶ ἀριθμεῖν καὶ ἱστάναι; *Rep.* 10, 602 D 6).

[53] Moss, 'Assent', 222–7, uses this argument, 602 C 4–603 A 8, as the primary source in her account of *eikasia* and *pistis*. See also Paton, 'Eikasia', 86. My use of this passage differs in two ways. First, I do not take it to be paradigmatic. Plato's goal is not to describe *eikasia* or *pistis*, but to establish a conclusion about imitative art, so it is not always possible to generalize. For example, I think *pistis* is rarely either a result of explicit reasoning or a response to a problematic perception (see n. 32 above). Second, as I interpret it, 602 C–603 A does not support the conclusion that *eikasia* involves no affirmation or denial. Since this is not asserted in the passage, it would have to be implicit in the argument it makes. But in fact the argument appeals to beliefs that are strongly opposed to each other in the way required for the principle of opposites to apply (602 E 8–9), and as such we would expect them to be symmetrical: that is, not an active and a passive attitude, but opposing attitudes of the *same* kind, such as affirming (or denying) both *p* and not-*p*.

though 'habit and practices' (ἔθεσι καὶ ἀσκήσεσιν, 518 D 11).[54] A purely intellectual education would produce a character who is vicious, but clever (519 A 2), about whom Socrates tells us:

τοῦτο μέντοι, ἦν δ' ἐγώ, τὸ τῆς τοιαύτης φύσεως εἰ ἐκ παιδὸς εὐθὺς κοπτόμενον περιεκόπη τὰς τῆς γενέσεως συγγενεῖς ὥσπερ μολυβδίδας, αἳ δὴ ἐδωδαῖς τε καὶ τοιούτων ἡδοναῖς τε καὶ λιχνείαις προσφυεῖς γιγνόμεναι περικάτω στρέφουσι τὴν τῆς ψυχῆς ὄψιν, ὧν εἰ ἀπαλλαγὲν περιεστρέφετο εἰς τὰ ἀληθῆ, καὶ ἐκεῖνα ἂν τὸ αὐτὸ τοῦτο τῶν αὐτῶν ἀνθρώπων ὀξύτατα ἑώρα, ὥσπερ καὶ ἐφ' ἃ νῦν τέτραπται. (7, 519 A 7–B 5)

If a nature of this sort had been hammered straight from childhood and freed from the leaden weights of kinship with becoming, *which have been fastened to it by feasting, greed, and other such pleasures* and which turn the soul's vision downwards—if, being rid of these weights, it turned to look at the true things, then I say that the same soul of the same person would see these most sharply, just as it does the things it is now turned towards. (Emphasis mine)

This is a remarkable yet often unnoticed passage: it is the only place where Plato tells us what the prisoners' chains symbolize, and it strongly suggests that they represent an intellectual constraint imposed by intemperate non-rational passions. It is well recognized that for Plato, undisciplined non-rational parts can distort a person's rational cognition—for example, by inclining them towards false beliefs that conform with their intemperate passions.[55] Exactly how this should be spelt out is a complex interpretive question, but we can at least say that it makes sense to expect that what explains why the non-rational passions are themselves misled—they are passions of parts of the soul confined to *eikasia*, and, thus, to unreliable images—will help explain how they, in turn, cause a person to have false beliefs. A plausible explanation is that intemperate passions, guided by certain images, incline a person to take at face value those same images, and, correspondingly, make denying those images painful and difficult, since it entails denying the satisfaction of the passions. For example, the decent person in Book 10, after a loss, tries to resist his non-rational desire to grieve dramatically, since despite the fact that it appears satisfying

---

[54] I argue that this is the right way to read this difficult passage in my 'The Soul-Turning Metaphor in *Republic* Book 7' (in progress).

[55] See e.g. D. Scott, 'Platonic Pessimism and Moral Education', *Oxford Studies in Ancient Philosophy*, 17 (1999), 15–36.

and cathartic, he trusts the arguments that tell him it would do more harm than good; but if the passion is very strong, and resisting it requires great effort, this can cause him to give up his earlier arguments and assent to the false image of grief. Thus, his existing non-rational acceptance of the false image leads his rational part to endorse it. Or, in other words, the *eikasia* of the non-rational parts of his soul leads him to lapse into a more widespread *eikasia*. For most people who are, in contrast to the decent person, more fully ruled by one of their non-rational parts, this effect will be more comprehensive and will face less, if any, resistance. This gives us a way to interpret the prisoners' chains: their intemperate passions keep their cognition to the low level of *eikasia*, which accords with the passions' continued satisfaction.

Plato's account of *eikasia* has turned out to be thoroughly integrated into the connected theoretical concerns of the *Republic*, including its epistemology, metaphysics, and psychology. This is important not only because integration is intrinsically desirable, but also because it does justice to its presentation in the Line and the Cave, which are images that in all other respects present a remarkably comprehensive and unified vision of the *Republic*'s project. This is especially clear when we look at the prisoners of the Cave allegory. It is true that ordinary people may lack ethical knowledge and often uncritically accept what they are told—claims hardly unique to Plato—but this does not explain the very specific situation of the prisoners or the deep pessimism it embodies. In contrast, the reading I've defended shows that the Cave allegory carries a concrete message that explains, as the allegory appears to promise it will, why it is necessary for some of us to 'leave the cave' and acquire knowledge: when it comes to ethical questions, ordinary people are constrained—in part, as we just saw, by non-rational pressures—to a rudimentary empirical kind of thought, called *eikasia*, that cannot reach beyond how things sensibly appear; since this leads to inadequate beliefs about such all-important things as goodness and justice, untutored ethical beliefs are insufficient, and ethical knowledge is necessary.[56]

Koç University

[56] I am grateful to Elena Cagnoli Fieeconi, Robert Howton, Jessica Moss, Henry Shevlin, and Nicholas Smith for helpful discussions and/or comments on earlier drafts of this paper. I would also like to thank Victor Caston and the anonymous readers of this paper for their many constructive suggestions.

BIBLIOGRAPHY

Adam, J., *The* Republic *of Plato*, vol. 2 [*Republic*] (Cambridge, 1902).

Annas, J., 'Plato, *Republic* V–VII' ['*Rep.* V–VII'], *Royal Institute of Philosophy Lecture Series*, 20 (1986), 3–18.

Annas, J., 'Understanding and the Good: Sun, Line, and Cave', in R. Kraut (ed.), *Plato's Republic: Critical Essays* (Lanham, 1997), 143–68.

Audi, R., 'Moral Perception Defended', *Argumenta*, 1 (2015), 5–28.

Balla, C., 'Early Forerunners of Medical Empiricism' ['Medical Empiricism'], Φιλοσοφία, 48 (2018), 253–80.

Bedu-Addo, J. T., 'Διάνοια and the Images of Forms in Plato's *Republic* VI–VII', *Platon*, 31 (1979), 89–110.

Belfiore, E., 'A Theory of Imitation in Plato's *Republic*', *Transactions of the American Philological Association*, 144 (1984), 121–46.

Cooper. J. M. (ed.), *Plato: Complete Works* (Hackett, 1997).

Cooper, N., 'The Importance of διάνοια in Plato's Theory of Forms', *Classical Quarterly*, 16 (1966), 65–9.

Crombie, I. M., *An Examination of Plato's Doctrines*, vol. ii: Plato on Knowledge and Reality (London, 1963).

Cross, R. C., and Woozley, A. D., *Plato's Republic: A Philosophical Commentary* [*Republic*] (London, 1964).

Dominick, Y. H., 'Seeing Through Images: The Bottom of Plato's Divided Line' ['Images'], *Journal of the History of Philosophy*, 48 (2010), 1–13.

Ferguson, A. S., 'Plato's Simile of Light. Part I', *Classical Quarterly*, 15 (1921), 131–52.

Ferguson, A. S., 'Plato's Simile of Light. Part II: The Allegory of the Cave (Continued)', *Classical Quarterly*, 16 (1922), 15–28.

Ferguson, A. S., 'Plato's Simile of Light Again' ['Simile'], *Classical Quarterly*, 28 (1934), 190–210.

Fine, G., 'Knowledge and Belief in *Republic* V–VII' ['*Republic* V–VII'], in ead., *Plato on Knowledge and Forms: Selected Essays* (Oxford, 2003), 85–116.

Frede, M., 'An Empiricist View of Knowledge: Memorism', in S. Everson (ed.), *Epistemology*, Companions to Ancient Thought, vol. i (Cambridge, 1990), 225–50.

Halliwell, S., *The Aesthetics of Mimesis* (Princeton, 2002).

Hamlyn, D. W., '*Eikasia* in Plato's *Republic*' ['*Eikasia*'], *Philosophical Quarterly*, 8 (1958), 12–23.

Hardie, J. P., 'Plato's Early Theory of Ideas', *Mind*, 5 (1896), 167–85.

Harte, V., 'Language in the Cave', in D. Scott (ed.), *Maieusis: Essays on Ancient Philosophy in Honour of Myles Burnyeat* (Oxford, 2007), 195–215.

Irwin, T., *Plato's Moral Theory* (Oxford, 1977).

Irwin, T., *Plato's Ethics* (Oxford, 1995).

Jackson, H., 'On Plato's *Republic* VI 509 d sqq.', *Journal of Philology*, 10 (1881), 132–50.

Joseph, H. W. B., *Knowledge and the Good in Plato's Republic* (London, 1948).

Karasmanis, V., 'Plato's *Republic*: The Line and the Cave', *Apeiron*, 21 (1988), 147–71.

Klein, J., *A Commentary on Plato's* Meno (Chapel Hill, 1965).

Lorenz, H., *The Brute Within: Appetitive Desire in Plato and Aristotle* [*Brute*] (Oxford, 2006).

Malcolm, J., 'The Line and the Cave' ['Cave'], *Phronesis*, 7 (1962), 38–45.

Malcolm, J., 'The Cave Revisited', *Classical Quarterly*, 31 (1981), 60–8.

McPherran, M. L., 'Socratic *epagōgē* and Socratic Induction', *Journal of the History of Philosophy*, 45 (2007), 347–64.

Morrison, J. S., 'Two Unresolved Difficulties in the Line and Cave' ['Difficulties'], *Phronesis*, 22 (1977), 212–31.

Moss, J., 'Pleasure and Illusion in Plato', *Philosophy and Phenomenological Research*, 72 (2006), 503–35.

Moss, J., 'What is Imitative Poetry and Why is it Bad?', in Ferrari, G. R. F. (ed.), *The Cambridge Companion to Plato's Republic* (Cambridge, 2007), 415–44.

Moss, J., 'Appearances and Calculation: Plato's Division of the Soul' ['Calculation'], *Oxford Studies in Ancient Philosophy*, 34 (2008), 35–68.

Moss, J., 'Plato's Appearance/Assent Account of Belief' ['Assent'], *Proceedings of the Aristotelian Society*, 114 (2014), 1–27.

Murphy, N. R., 'The "Simile of Light" in Plato's *Republic*', *Classical Quarterly*, 26 (1932), 93–102.

Nettleship, R. L., *Lectures on Plato's* Republic [*Lectures*] (London, 1897).

Pappas, N., *Routledge Philosophy Guidebook to Plato and the Republic* [*Republic*], 2nd ed. (London, 2003).

Paton, H. J., 'Plato's Theory of EIKASIA' ['Eikasia'], *Proceedings of the Aristotelian Society*, 22 (1922), 69–104.

Raven, J. E., 'Sun, Divided Line, and Cave' ['Sun, Line, Cave'], *Classical Quarterly*, 3 (1953), 22–32.

Reeve, C. D. C., *Philosopher-Kings: The Argument of Plato's Republic* (Princeton, NJ, 1988).

Robinson, R., *Plato's Earlier Dialectic* [*Dialectic*] (Ithaca, 1941).

Ross, D., *Plato's Theory of Ideas* (Oxford, 1951).

Schofield, M., 'Metaspeleology', in D. Scott (ed.), *Maieusis: Essays on Ancient Philosophy in Honour of Myles Burnyeat* (Oxford, 2007), 216–31.

Scott, D., 'Platonic Pessimism and Moral Education', *Oxford Studies in Ancient Philosophy*, 17 (1999), 15–36.

Shorey, P. 'The Idea of the Good in Plato's *Republic*', *Studies in Classical Philology*, 1 (1885), 188–239.

Siegel, S., *The Contents of Visual Experience* (Oxford, 2010).

Smith, N. D., 'How the Prisoners in Plato's Cave are "Like Us"', *Proceedings of the Boston Area Colloquium in Ancient Philosophy*, 13 (1997), 187–204.

Smith, N. D., 'Plato on Knowledge as a Power', *Journal of the History of Philosophy*, 38 (2000), 145–68.

Stocks, J. L., 'The Divided Line of Plato *Rep.* VI', *Classical Quarterly*, 5 (1911), 73–88.

Storey, D., 'Appearance, Perception, and Non-rational Belief: *Republic* 602c–603a', *Oxford Studies in Ancient Philosophy*, 47 (2014), 81–118.

Strang, C., 'Plato's Analogy of the Cave' ['Cave'], *Oxford Studies in Ancient Philosophy*, 4 (1986), 19–34.

Sze, C. P., '*Eikasia* and *pistis* in Plato's Allegory of the Cave', *Classical Quarterly*, 27 (1977), 127–38.

Wilberding, J., 'Prisoners and Puppeteers in the Cave' ['Puppeteers'], *Oxford Studies in Ancient Philosophy*, 27 (2004), 117–39.

Wilson, J. R. S., 'The Contents of the Cave', *Canadian Journal of Philosophy*, suppl. vol., 2 (1976), 117–27.

ATTRIBUTING BELIEFS AND JUDGEMENTS IN PLATO'S *GORGIAS*, *MENO*, AND *THEAETETUS*

ALEX LONG

WHAT are the criteria in Plato's dialogues for attributing beliefs and judgements? If people believe something, must they have given it their assent and asserted it internally? This paper is about three Platonic passages, and their closest parallels in other dialogues, that seem to present conflicting criteria for belief-attribution and judgement-attribution.

In the *Theaetetus*, Socrates suggests that a belief or judgement (*doxa*, plural *doxai*; translators do not agree on which English word is more apt) develops when, and only when, the subject has given a question thought, taken a position on it, and asserts his or her answer internally. Without internal affirmation, or internal denial, there is no judgement or belief. By contrast, Socrates has been interpreted as suggesting in the *Gorgias* that a subject 'believes' (ἡγεῖσθαι) a proposition *p* if he or she believes other propositions that entail *p*.[1] From this it sounds as if people's beliefs are often vastly more numerous than they suppose, and that assent and internal assertion are unnecessary for belief. The third dialogue is the *Meno*, where Socrates attributes true *doxai* to the recollecting slave on the strength of what the slave is disposed to affirm sincerely when questioned. They include *doxai* of which the slave was not aware, at least for some of the time when he had them. This too suggests that people often contain more *doxai* than they recognize, and that internal statement is unnecessary for the possession of a *doxa*.

The relationship and ostensible disagreement between the *Theaetetus* and the other two texts will be my principal concern: does Socrates in the *Theaetetus* have criteria for the attribution of *doxa* that are incompatible with what he says about belief in the *Gorgias* and *doxa* in the *Meno*, respectively? I will have less to say by way

---

[1] R. Woolf, 'Socratic Authority' ['Authority'], *Archiv für Geschichte der Philosophie*, 90 (2008), 1–38 at 29.

Alex Long, *Attributing Beliefs and Judgements in Plato's* Gorgias, Meno, *and* Theaetetus. In: Oxford Studies in Ancient Philosophy Volume LVIII. Edited by: Victor Caston, Oxford University Press (2020).
© Alex Long.
DOI: 10.1093/oso/9780198858997.003.0003

of comparison between the *Gorgias* and *Meno* themselves. So my
first step will be to consider the passage from the *Theaetetus*, and
its most direct parallels, and defend the interpretation outlined
above. As what precedes should already make clear, my starting
question is not 'Which attitude(s) or cognitive state(s) are these
passages about?', but 'What are the criteria for attribution?',
although, as I outline at the end, exploring criteria for attribution
sheds light on what is and is not being attributed.

Doxa as internal affirmation and denial

In the *Theaetetus* and *Sophist*, Socrates discusses false 'belief' or
'judgement' (*doxa*). As there is no agreement about whether 'belief'
or 'judgement' is the more appropriate translation, I will keep the
noun in transliterated Greek, except when providing a translation of
a passage.[2] To begin with the *Theaetetus*, Socrates represents thought
as an internal dialogue, and *doxa* as an internal statement. At first the
soul hesitates between options, sometimes briefly, sometimes for a
long time; if it reaches a verdict, it forms at that moment a *doxa*.

[T1]   ΣΩ. Κάλλιστα. τὸ δὲ διανοεῖσθαι ἆρ' ὅπερ ἐγὼ καλεῖς;
       ΘΕΑΙ. Τί καλῶν;

       ΣΩ. Λόγον ὃν αὐτὴ πρὸς αὑτὴν ἡ ψυχὴ διεξέρχεται περὶ ὧν ἂν σκοπῇ, ὥς
       γε μὴ εἰδώς σοι ἀποφαίνομαι.[3] τοῦτο γάρ μοι ἰνδάλλεται διανοουμένη

---

[2] In what follows all translations are my own, unless noted otherwise. For the Greek,
I have used the most recent OCT editions, except for the *Republic*, for which I used
Burnet's edition. C. Rowe, *Plato: Theaetetus and Sophist* (Cambridge, 2015) has 'belief',
whereas it is translated 'judgement' in M. Burnyeat, *The Theaetetus of Plato* [*Theaetetus*],
with a translation by M. J. Levett (Indianapolis and Cambridge, 1990). For defence of
the translation 'judgement', see Burnyeat, *Theaetetus*, 69–70 and S. Broadie, 'The
Knowledge Unacknowledged in the *Theaetetus*', *Oxford Studies in Ancient Philosophy*,
51 (2016), 87–117 at 92–3, 95–6, 101–4. Compare the more tentative discussion in
J. Moss, 'Plato's Appearance-assent Account of Belief' ['Belief'], *Proceedings of the
Aristotelian Society*, 114 (2014), 213–38, especially 217, 219–20, 236. According to
W. Schwab, true *doxa* in the *Meno* includes states that would typically be called 'knowledge' today ('Explanation in the Epistemology of the *Meno*', *Oxford Studies in Ancient
Philosophy*, 48 (2015), 1–36 at 28 n. 44). Even if the requirements of *doxa* (prior thought,
internal affirmation and denial) are more demanding than those of belief, *doxa* need not
be about something philosophical or, more generally, intellectual. Examples of *doxa*
include identifying an animal as a horse (*Theaet.* 190 C 1–3) or a distant object as a statue
or human being (*Phileb.* 38 D 5 –E 4).

[3] For the punctuation here, see D. N. Sedley, *The Midwife of Platonism: Text and
Subtext in Plato's Theaetetus* [*Midwife*] (Oxford, 2004), 129 n. 16. Chapter 6 of my
Conversation and Self-Sufficiency in Plato (Oxford, 2013) explores the conception of
thought as dialogue but says less about the outcome, *doxa*.

οὐκ ἄλλο τι ἢ διαλέγεσθαι, αὐτὴ ἑαυτὴν ἐρωτῶσα καὶ ἀποκρινομένη, καὶ φάσκουσα καὶ οὐ φάσκουσα. ὅταν δὲ ὁρίσασα, εἴτε βραδύτερον εἴτε καὶ ὀξύτερον ἐπάξασα, τὸ αὐτὸ ἤδη φῇ καὶ μὴ διστάζῃ, δόξαν ταύτην τίθεμεν αὐτῆς. ὥστ' ἔγωγε τὸ δοξάζειν λέγειν καλῶ καὶ τὴν δόξαν λόγον εἰρημένον, οὐ μέντοι πρὸς ἄλλον οὐδὲ φωνῇ, ἀλλὰ σιγῇ πρὸς αὑτόν· σὺ δὲ τί; ΘΕΑΙ. Κἀγώ.

ΣΩ. Ὅταν ἄρα τις τὸ ἕτερον ἕτερον δοξάζῃ, καὶ φησίν, ὡς ἔοικε, τὸ ἕτερον ἕτερον εἶναι πρὸς ἑαυτόν.

ΘΕΑΙ. Τί μήν; (*Theaet*. 189 E 4–190 B 1)

SOC. Very good. But do you call thinking what I call it?

THEAET. What do you call it?

SOC. Discourse that the soul goes through, addressing itself, about whatever it is investigating, at least on the account I'm giving you without knowing about it. The picture I have is that the soul, when it thinks, is precisely engaged in dialogue, asking itself and answering questions on its own, saying yes and no. When it is decided, whether quite slowly or in a quite rapid leap, and it is now saying the same thing without wavering, that is what we set down as its judgement. So for my part I call judging *saying*, and I call judgement discourse addressed not to someone else, or out loud, but in silence to oneself. What about you?

THEAET. I do too.

SOC. In that case, whenever someone judges one of two things to be the other, he also, it seems, *says* to himself that the one is the other.

THEAET. Of course.

This account of *doxa* and thought is then used against one explanation of false *doxa*. It is taken up again in the *Sophist* (263 D 6–264 B 9) and *Philebus* (38 B 12–39 A 7). Thought is internal dialogue, and *doxa* arises when the soul settles on a verdict: as the visitor puts it in the *Sophist*, when affirmation, or denial, comes about silently in the soul because of thought, that is *doxa* (263 E 10–264 A 2).[4]

Does [T1] outline (1) necessary conditions for *doxa* or merely (2) one way for *doxa* to come about? If *doxa* is translated as 'belief', we may be inclined to favour interpretation (2). Arguably there are

---

[4] Compare Arist. *NE* 6. 9, 1142b13–14: 'judgement is not inquiry, but already a kind of affirmation' (καὶ γὰρ ἡ δόξα οὐ ζήτησις ἀλλὰ φάσις τις ἤδη). See M. Duncombe, 'Thought as Internal Speech in Plato and Aristotle' ['Thought'], *Logical Analysis and History of Philosophy*, 19 (2016), 105–25 for both the similarities and the differences between the accounts of thought in Plato and Aristotle.

lots of things that people believe without going through this process, or without articulating the belief internally. So on interpretation
(1), the conditions for *doxa* may seem implausibly demanding, and
the passage should, we might say, allow for other ways of coming
to believe things. On the other hand, Socrates acknowledges that
the prior stage of thinking may be short and superficial, when the
soul reaches a decision with a 'rapid leap'. We might compare the
account of recollection in the *Phaedo*, where Socrates says that
whenever similarity causes us, on seeing A, to recall B, it is necessary to think whether A falls short of B in respect of similarity
(74 A 5–7). Here again, we may think, the requirement is too
demanding. But evidently Socrates supposes that this thought is
necessary or inevitable whenever similarity triggers recollection,
and (although he does not say as much) he may allow that the
thought is so rapid that it barely registers with the subject. If A and
B are human beings, the following may count as recollection: the
subject sees A, is put in mind of B but quickly realizes that A is not
identical with B, as they differ in one or two respects, and then,
instead of greeting A as if A were B, immediately becomes
absorbed with thoughts about B.

In any case, there is strong textual evidence for interpretation
(1).[5] First, in the context of [T1] the objective is to understand
doxa and thereby to understand false *doxa*. So Socrates should not
describe only one kind of *doxa*, or one kind of origin for it, without
explicit indication that his account is incomplete. Secondly, in [T1]
Socrates offers what looks very much like a definition of *doxa*: 'I
call judging [the cognate verb: δοξάζειν] saying, and I call judgement [δόξα] discourse addressed not to someone else, or out loud,
but in silence to oneself.' He does not say that some *doxai* are like
this, and others are different. Thirdly, according to Socrates' last
sentence in [T1], *whenever* people believe or judge, they say the
proposition to themselves. Internal statement thus looks essential.
Furthermore, the *Sophist* suggests that the prior process of thinking is essential if there is to be *doxa*: the visitor says that *doxa* 'is
the completion of thought' (διανοίας ἀποτελεύτησις, 264 B 1).

According to these passages, then, asserting the proposition
internally, after giving it thought, is necessary for there to be *doxa*

---

[5] Compare Moss' account of [T1] ('Belief', 233): 'on the view here developed
doxai are always assents.'

at all. There are thus claims about what *doxa* is, namely internal affirmation or denial; about the manner in which it comes to be—thinking about something and then deciding to give a verdict on one side; and finally about the time of origin. A *doxa* comes to be at a specific time: when the soul approves an answer to the question it has posed.[6]

When I turn to the relevant part of the *Gorgias*, I will put some emphasis on the passage's context and argue that the comments on belief there are not representative of Socrates' treatment of belief in the rest of the dialogue. So, before we turn to the *Gorgias*, I should consider whether the significance of [T1] is somehow reduced by its context. In its immediate context, the account of *doxa* in [T1] compounds the difficulties about false judgement. Socrates will observe that nobody would say to himself or herself, 'The odd is even', or 'The cow is a horse' (*Theaet.* 190 B 2–D 2), and yet, according to [T1], that is what it would be to have those false judgements. But it would be a mistake to limit the function of this conception of *doxa* to making Theaetetus yet more puzzled about falsehoods, for it plays an indispensable role in the explanation of false *doxa* that Plato eventually provides in the *Sophist*. In that dialogue the visitor first explains how there can be false discourse or statement (*logos*), by which he means false oral utterances, although in explaining them he also provides an explanation of false writing. The challenge at this stage is to show how something could *both* be a genuine *logos and* be false. The visitor's answer depends on there being a certain structure in any *logos*: saying something of or about something (262 E 6–263 B 13), as in the false *logos* 'Theaetetus flies'. A false *logos* is of or about something (if it were not, it would not be a *logos* at all) and yet says about it something different from what really 'is' concerning it. The visitor immediately extends his explanation of false *logos* to false *doxa*, and

---

[6] There is a further question about what becomes of a *doxa* some time *after* it has come to be, when it is no longer occurrent: should we speak of the subject as 'believing/judging' (δοξάζειν) or merely as containing the *doxa*? (A similar question arises when I consider below the discussion of recollection in the *Meno*.) The most promising passage is the *Philebus*, where the soul is famously compared to a book in which *doxai* are stored (38 E 12–39 A 7), but even that passage is less informative than we might wish. Socrates says merely that *doxai* 'come to be in us' (ἐν ἡμῖν γιγνόμενοι, 39 A 3–6). He later speaks of a person 'believing' or 'judging' (δοξάζειν, 40 C 8–D 2), but this may refer to the time when the *doxa* first comes about and is said to oneself. So it is not clear whether at a later time, during the absence of an occurrent belief or judgement, the subject should still be said to believe or judge.

he can do so only if *doxa* shares the structure of *logos*.[7] Otherwise the visitor would need a brand new explanation of false *doxa*. In the visitor's own words, 'as they [perceptual impression and *doxa*] are akin to *logos*, some of them too, some of the time, must be false' (ἀνάγκη δὴ καὶ τούτων τῷ λόγῳ συγγενῶν ὄντων ψευδῆ γε αὐτῶν ἔνια καὶ ἐνίοτε εἶναι, 264 B 3–4). Plato's explanation of false *doxa* thus depends on the isomorphism of *doxa* and *logos*.

If we are to measure the level of commitment to the account of *doxa* in [T1], we should also consider how Socrates behaves as midwife in the rest of the *Theaetetus*. After all, part of Socratic midwifery is drawing out his interlocutor's 'belief' or 'judgement' (δόγμα, 157 D 2).[8] So it is worth seeing what he does and does not count as grounds for attributing a belief or judgement to Theaetetus. In the first part of the *Theaetetus*, Socrates examines theories that are, at least on one interpretation, entailed by Theaetetus' definition of knowledge.[9] Theaetetus defines knowledge as perception; Socrates then clearly associates (to use a neutral verb) that definition with Protagoras' relativism and then with the secret doctrine of flux and relativity. According to this interpretation, both Protagoreanism and the secret doctrine are relevant because Theaetetus' definition of knowledge entails them. And yet Theaetetus is not told that, simply by virtue of his definition and that logical relationship, he has the belief or judgement that Protagoreanism and the secret doctrine are true.

Instead, Socrates outlines the theories and their attractions, and then asks Theaetetus whether he accepts them. Concerning

---

[7] 'This allows the visitor to import to the cognitive realm the semantic account of falsehood he established earlier' (Duncombe, 'Thought', 108).

[8] In Plato, *dogma* is often equivalent to *doxa*. See *Rep.* 3, 412 E 5–8 (δόγματος . . . δόξαν); 6, 493 A 8 (δόγματα, ἃ δοξάζουσιν); 6, 506 B 8–C 9; *Phileb.* 41 B 4–5 (κατά γε τὴν ἐμήν [sc. δόξαν]. τοῦτο δὲ τὸ δόγμα . . .). In oral discussion of the paper, it was suggested to me that the reason for choosing *dogma* in the *Theaetetus* passage is that Socrates and Theaetetus have just asked each other what 'seems true' (δοκεῖ, 157 C 1–6), but that verb can also be associated with *doxa*, as in *Gorg.* 469 C 5–D 5. For the examination of *doxa* in Socratic midwifery, see also *Theaet.* 161 E 4–162 A 3.

[9] See above all M. Burnyeat, 'Idealism and Greek Philosophy: What Descartes Saw and Berkeley Missed', *Philosophical Review*, 90 (1982), 3–40 and *Theaetetus*, 9–10. According to Sedley (*Midwife*, especially 40, 44, 48), Theaetetus' definition is assimilated to Protagoreanism and can be true only if the world is in total flux. For an opposed interpretation, see M.-K. Lee, *Epistemology after Protagoras: Responses to Relativism in Plato, Aristotle, and Democritus* (Oxford, 2004), especially 79, 88, 90–1, and 117.

Protagoras' theory, Theaetetus is asked whether he and Socrates will 'be persuaded by' (πεισόμεθα) Protagoras and agree that the wind is cold for one person and not cold for another person (152 B 6–7). The introduction of the secret doctrine is more complicated. Socrates first shows Theaetetus the doctrine's intrinsic credibility. For example, he is shown that the doctrine can resolve puzzles about growing and shrinking: we can accept without hesitation that an item is now larger, now smaller, without worrying about what size it has independently of the comparisons an observer might make. There is nothing to say about that, for nothing has intrinsic size. Socrates then asks Theaetetus for his belief or judgement: 'tell me if you are satisfied with this claim: nothing *is* good, beautiful, or any of the things we were going through just now, but things always *come to be* good and so on' (λέγε τοίνυν πάλιν εἴ σοι ἀρέσκει τὸ μή τι εἶναι ἀλλὰ γίγνεσθαι ἀεὶ ἀγαθὸν καὶ καλὸν καὶ πάντα ἃ ἄρτι διῆμεν, 157 D 7–9).[10] Theaetetus then says simply that the thesis should be accepted, not that he is committed to it by his definition: 'when I hear you expounding the theory like this, it appears wonderfully reasonable to me; we must suppose that things are as you have set them out' (ἐπειδὴ σοῦ ἀκούω οὕτω διεξιόντος, θαυμασίως φαίνεται ὡς ἔχειν λόγον καὶ ὑποληπτέον ᾗπερ διελήλυθας, 157 D 10–12).[11]

This is not the place to show whether or not the secret doctrine does follow, or is thought by Socrates or Plato to follow, from Theaetetus' definition. What we should note is that the logical relationship between the definition and the secret doctrine is not used as grounds for attributing to Theaetetus belief in the latter before he has explicitly endorsed it. Scholars who think that the definition does not imply the secret doctrine, and is not treated in the dialogue as implying it, will have a ready explanation: as there is no entailment in that direction, we should not expect Socrates to use it in order to attribute beliefs or judgements. But if the secret doctrine does (and, in the dialogue, is supposed to) follow from Theaetetus' definition, as other scholars argue, the account of *doxa* in [T1] explains Socrates' quietness about that point. That logical

---

[10] The expression σοι ἀρέσκει should be translated 'you are satisfied with', 'you are convinced that', or something similar, rather than 'you are pleased with'. The Greek verb can be used of the decisions or opinions of a public group (compare the consciously political language in *Rep.* 380 C 4–5), and in later Greek will be used of a philosopher's doctrines—not of what 'pleases' the philosopher.

[11] Compare Theaetetus' endorsement at 160 C 3 (παντάπασι μὲν οὖν, ὦ Σώκρατες).

relationship, together with Theaetetus' statement of the definition, does not permit him to attribute to Theaetetus the *doxa* that the doctrine is true. Indeed, it would scarcely be an exaggeration to say that the conversation of the *Theaetetus* is built on the assumption that a *doxa* must be asserted—to oneself and then, in interpersonal dialogue, to the interlocutor.

Polus and injustice in the *Gorgias*

In Plato's *Gorgias*, Socrates has a debate with Polus about which is worse: acting unjustly or being the victim of injustice. According to Socrates, committing injustice is worse than being its victim, a thesis I will abbreviate to CIW. By contrast, Polus believes that being the victim is worse. Or at least that is what Polus says he believes: at the start of the debate, Socrates says that Polus shares Socrates' own belief, and even that everyone else shares it as well.[12]

[T2] ΣΩ. ἐγὼ γὰρ δὴ οἶμαι καὶ ἐμὲ καὶ σὲ καὶ τοὺς ἄλλους ἀνθρώπους τὸ ἀδικεῖν τοῦ ἀδικεῖσθαι κάκιον ἡγεῖσθαι καὶ τὸ μὴ διδόναι δίκην τοῦ διδόναι.

ΠΩΛ. Ἐγὼ δέ γε οὔτ' ἐμὲ οὔτ' ἄλλον ἀνθρώπων οὐδένα. ἐπεὶ σὺ δέξαι' ἂν μᾶλλον ἀδικεῖσθαι ἢ ἀδικεῖν;

ΣΩ. Καὶ σύ γ' ἂν καὶ οἱ ἄλλοι πάντες.

ΠΩΛ. Πολλοῦ γε δεῖ, ἀλλ' οὔτ' ἐγὼ οὔτε σὺ οὔτ' ἄλλος οὐδείς. (*Gorg.* 474 B 2–10)

SOC. You see, I think that I, you and the rest of humankind believe that committing injustice is worse than having injustice done to you, and that not being punished is worse than being punished.[13]

POL. But for my part I think that neither I nor any other person believes that. Just think: would you choose to have injustice done to you rather than commit it?

---

[12] As Woolf, 'Authority', 28 n. 52 observes, Socrates does not deny that Polus also believes what he (Polus) professes. Socrates may think that Polus holds contradictory beliefs. Woolf's valuable discussion of [T2] ('Authority', 27–31) says much less than my own account about (*a*) Socrates' attribution of a belief to 'the rest of humankind', and (*b*) the immediate context of [T2] in the *Gorgias*.

[13] In what follows directly, I focus on CIW, not the question of punishment. In [T2], Polus challenges Socrates on CIW specifically, and later in the dialogue, Socrates takes himself to have shown that everyone, Polus included, would make the same choice as he would between committing injustice and being its victim (475 E 3–6). But in the subsequent discussion of punishment (476 A 3–481 B 5), he does not return to the point about Polus' belief or choice, as I observe below.

soc. Yes. So would you and everyone else.

pol. Far from it! I wouldn't, you wouldn't, and nobody else would.

What lies behind this claim about Polus' belief?[14] We might suppose that Socrates is looking forward to the later point in the dialogue where Polus endorses CIW (475 D 3–E 6). But that fails to explain Socrates' claim that the rest of humankind share the belief: at no point in the conversation will there be an expression of agreement from all of them or some other evidence that they assent, or have assented, to CIW. Moreover, the verb translated 'believe' (ἡγεῖσθαι) is the present infinitive, not the future. So in [T2] Socrates is not saying that Polus will believe CIW after he has heard Socrates' argument for it, but that Polus, like everyone else, believes it now, despite what he professes, and before he has heard Socrates' argument.

[T2] contains a disagreement about choice as well as about belief: Polus asks whether Socrates would really choose to be treated unjustly in order to avoid acting unjustly, and Socrates, saying that he would, denies that the choice makes him unlike other people. The shift from belief to choice is first made in Polus' challenge ('would you choose...?'), and so we might suppose that Socrates himself would prefer to speak of Polus' belief, not what he would choose. But, if it is a concession to Polus, it is not merely a short-term concession, for later Socrates expresses the conclusion of his argument in terms of choice:

[T3] ΣΩ. Ἀληθῆ ἄρα ἐγὼ ἔλεγον, ὅτι οὔτ' ἂν ἐγὼ οὔτ' ἂν σὺ οὔτ' ἄλλος οὐδεὶς ἀνθρώπων δέξαιτ' ἂν μᾶλλον ἀδικεῖν ἢ ἀδικεῖσθαι· κάκιον γὰρ τυγχάνει ὄν. (475 E 3–6)

soc. Then I said the truth when I said that neither I nor you nor any other person would choose to commit injustice rather than be its victim. For committing injustice is in fact worse.

---

[14] The Greek verb is now ἡγεῖσθαι. It can be used in Plato as an equivalent of having a *doxa* (*Theaet.* 170 A 6–8; compare 171 A 6–9). At times, we may wonder whether apparently cognitive nouns refer to cognitive states or merely to their contents (see n. 45 below). But within the *Gorgias*, the verb ἡγεῖσθαι consistently refers to the speaker's or interlocutor's cognitive state (see e.g. 453 A 1, 472 D 2, 477 B 6), and the translation 'believe' or 'think' is appropriate. At 474 C 5–D 2, there seems to be no difference between ἡγῇ σύ and δοκεῖ σοι—one of Polus' beliefs, for which the second locution is used, points, when put together with his other answers, to another belief, concerning which Socrates says ἡγῇ σύ—and δοκεῖ σοι can be the equivalent of having a *doxa* (469 C 5–7, *Theaet.* 170 A 3–7). Compare *Gorg.* 471 E 3–4 (ἡγούμενοι ... δοκοῦσιν).

Polus' challenge in [T2] presupposes a direct connection between people's choices and their beliefs about goodness and evil: if people really did believe CIW, they would choose to be the victim of injustice if that were the only way to avoid committing it. Polus is putting pressure on Socrates to concede that, faced with such a choice, he would not choose victimhood; and Polus thinks that this concession would confirm that people, including even Socrates himself, do not believe CIW. That, I think, is the connection marked by ἐπεί (loosely translated 'just think' above) in the Greek of [T2]. In [T2], Socrates does not deny the connection between choice and belief, but uncompromisingly swaps Polus' *modus tollens* for the following *modus ponens*: people do believe CIW, and so they would choose victimhood if committing injustice were the only other possibility. Socrates thus has no reason to resist talking about choice, even though at first he speaks in terms of belief. But when at the end of the argument ([T3] above) Socrates establishes his point about Polus' choice, he must take himself to have established that Polus holds the corresponding belief (that is, the belief that CIW). Otherwise the dialogue would offer nothing to defend Socrates' claim about belief in [T2].[15]

The confirmation for Socrates' claim about Polus' belief—and indeed the belief of everyone else—must therefore lie in the argument between [T2] and [T3] (474 C 4–475 E 6). That argument relies on an account of the fine or beautiful (καλός) as either pleasurable or beneficial, and of its opposite, the repellent (αἰσχρός),[16] as either painful or bad. Polus needs no convincing that committing

---

[15] On the other hand, the Greek of [T3] suggests that the basis for Socrates' claim there about choice is that one of the two items really is worse, not that it is *believed* to be worse. Compare the discussion of what people want in R. Kamtekar, *Plato's Moral Psychology: Intellectualism, the Divided Soul, and the Desire for Good* [*Psychology*] (Oxford, 2017), 72–3, 87–91. In [T3], as often in Plato, τυγχάνω with the participle marks not chance or coincidence but reality.

[16] The Greek word is not easy to translate. In T. Griffith and M. Schofield, *Plato: Gorgias, Menexenus, Protagoras* [*Gorgias*] (Cambridge, 2010), the translation is 'disgraceful', which has the disadvantage of suggesting that the pain and harm flow from the disapproval of others, or from the expectation of their disapproval. Socrates' point is easier to understand when he speaks about its opposite, the fine or beautiful: a fine body (474 D 3–E 1) is so called either because it brings pleasure to the viewer or because it benefits by enabling one (primarily, I suppose, the person whose body it is, but also, say, the owner of a 'fine'-bodied animal) to do what he or she wants. A body that is 'repellent' is either painful to look at or a hindrance to its users; I admit that my translation 'repellent' has a poor fit with the body's being a hindrance.

injustice is more repellent than being its victim; he accepts that as soon as it is put to him (474 C 4–8, 475 D 1–3). Let us abbreviate it to CIR. According to Socrates, ordinary people too agree to CIR, and Polus agrees that they do (475 D 1–3).[17] The task now is to get from CIR to CIW. Socrates argues that if one item is more repellent than another, the former must have either (*a*) more pain, or (*b*) more badness, or (*c*) both. When spelling out the implications of CIR, the first—committing injustice exceeds in pain—is eliminated quickly, which of course rules out (*c*) as well. So committing injustice must exceed in badness. And that, Socrates says, is CIW, the thesis he set out to show.

It is this argument that Socrates later describes as having the firmness of adamant and iron (508 E 6–509 A 4). However, what concerns us here is not the strength or persuasiveness of the argument but its bearing on the belief-attribution in [T2].[18] As I have said, the support for Socrates' belief-attribution must come from this argument; there is no other support for it in the dialogue. When Socrates says, before delivering the argument, that Polus and other people believe CIW, his statement derives partly from confidence that Polus and other people believe CIR, but also from confidence in the connection between CIR and CIW. We should notice that near the start of the argument Socrates asks Polus, in effect, whether CIW follows from CIR, and Polus says 'no' (474 C 7–D 2). But Polus then endorses the account of the fine and the repellent that enables Socrates to derive CIW from CIR (475 A 2–5). Concerning Polus, then, we can say the following against his having the belief that CIW at the time of [T2]: (i) he denies CIW at [T2]; and (ii) directly after [T2] he denies that CIW follows from CIR. What tells in favour of his believing CIW at [T2] is (iii) he believes CIR, probably already in [T2]; and *either* (iv) soon after the time of [T2], he will accept from Socrates the account of the repellent that connects CIR to CIW, and so at [T2] he is already disposed to accept that account, *or* (v) CIW follows, in point of fact, from CIR. Socrates treats (iii) and (v), or (iii) and (iv), as outweighing (i) and (ii).

---

[17] The point is repeated in the debate with Callicles (489 A 2–4).

[18] For assessment of the argument, see E. R. Dodds, *Plato: Gorgias* (Oxford, 1959), 249; T. Irwin, *Plato: Gorgias* (Oxford, 1979), 157–8; Griffith and Schofield, *Gorgias*, 46 n. 47.

Concerning the 'rest of humankind', to quote Socrates in [T2], things are clearer. There is no equivalent of (iv) in their case. So the belief-attribution to them must rest on (v) and their counterpart to (iii): CIW follows from CIR, given the real nature of the fine and the repellent, and these other people believe or 'have agreed to' CIR (ὡμολογεῖτο, 475 D 1–3). So when Socrates says in [T2] that other people too believe CIW, he must be leaning partly on their belief in CIR, and partly on the real connection, as he sees it, between CIR and CIW, a connection that is independent of these people's beliefs on the matter. He is simply silent on whether these other people believe, or could come to agree, that CIW follows from CIR. Socrates moves directly from his conclusion about Polus' choice to the equivalent conclusion about that of other people (475 E 1–3, followed by [T3] above), with no hint of a contrast between the arguments used for Polus and for them. So, given what we have found about the argument concerning other people, it is most natural to take his argument about Polus' choice—and, implicitly, his belief—to rest on (iii) and (v), not (iii) and (iv).

These belief-attributions, to Polus and all humankind, obviously fail to meet the conditions for *doxa* set down in the passage from the *Theaetetus*, [T1] above. Unless Polus is lying, he has not considered CIW and given it his approval—and of course it would be extremely implausible to say that every human being had done this. In the *Theaetetus*, Socrates has a temporal requirement as well, and this too has not been satisfied: from a Theaetetan perspective, until such a time as Polus and everyone else do give their approval to Socrates' claims, they do not have the relevant *doxa*. Logical connections, even of adamantine strength, do not warrant a *doxa*-attribution.

At this point, we must try to understand the rationale for speaking about belief at all in [T2], and then examine the status of [T2] within the *Gorgias* as a whole. We might agree with Socrates that there is a sense in which someone competent in logic may know more about our beliefs than we ourselves do, if we either lack the competence or fail to self-apply it thoroughly. It may be common knowledge that we believe *p* and *q*, but we ourselves may fail to know or consider what follows from them; considering or being shown what follows will be startling when the previously unrecognized consequence has a poor fit with our self-image—as in contemporary tests for implicit bias. But we may protest that this is better expressed as a point about commitment, not beliefs: it is better to say that our beliefs commit us to what they, or more strictly their contents, entail than that that consequence is itself believed.[19]

Here, it seems to me, recent discussions have paid insufficient attention to the immediate context.[20] Before the debate, Polus says that Socrates is refuted by the fact that nobody else shares his position: 'don't you think you have been utterly refuted, Socrates, when you say the kinds of things no one in the world would say?' (οὐκ οἴει ἐξεληλέγχθαι, ὦ Σώκρατες, ὅταν τοιαῦτα λέγῃς ἃ οὐδεὶς ἂν φήσειεν ἀνθρώπων; 473 E 4–5). Socrates says in reply that, for the kind of proof he favours, the statements of other people are irrelevant: what matters is making his interlocutor—Polus, in this case—speak in favour of Socrates' own position and 'testify' for it (474 A 2–B 1).[21] This is the immediate context of [T2]. And directly after [T3] Socrates repeats this point about his own kind of proof: he dismisses other people and says that he is concerned only with what his interlocutor says (475 E 7–476 A 2). So even though Socrates discusses in the argument what other people believe and would choose, he wants to make Polus shift to a different model of proof and refutation, where only the beliefs and statements of the two participants matter. The startling claim about belief must be understood in this context. Socrates is not trying to use, as support for his own position, the belief of 'the rest of humankind' ([T2] again); on the contrary, he is trying to make Polus attach *less* importance to what other people believe and say. To that end, Socrates shows that the balance of opinion is more complicated than Polus assumes: whatever people would initially say, if we asked them about injustice, they have another belief (in CIR) that commits them to Socrates' own position. Socrates is thus destabilizing the apparent consensus against him, and this can be done more effectively if he allows himself to treat a consequence what is believed as itself believed.

---

[19] Compare L. J. Cohen, 'Belief and Acceptance', *Mind*, 98 (1989), 367–89 at 372–3. Alternatively, we might say that the relationship of entailment is not enough: the entailment must be obvious, or immediate, or the consequence must be, in some way, relevant to the believed proposition from which it follows. See R. Audi, 'Dispositional Beliefs and Dispositions to Believe' ['Dispositions'], *Noûs*, 28 (1994), 419–34 at 429 for the first of these ('obviously entails'), although the discussion there is of being disposed to believe, not of beliefs themselves.

[20] Woolf, 'Authority' and Kamtekar, *Psychology*, 93–6.

[21] Compare *Gorg.* 471 E 2–472 D 4.

But, to repeat, his aim in saying that is not to draw support for his own side from his claim about other people, but to unsettle Polus' initial confidence in a consensus.

If we look beyond the passage's immediate context to the rest of the *Gorgias*, we find elsewhere an ostensibly similar willingness on Socrates' part to contradict his interlocutors about what their position is. But only in [T2] is this inflected as a point about the interlocutor's current 'belief', and in the other passages there is a reference to previous statements by the interlocutor that support Socrates' account of their position. In an earlier part of the *Gorgias*, Socrates and Polus disagree about what Polus is 'claiming' (φησιν, 466 E 4–5): according to Socrates, Polus denies that doing whatever you please is having great power.[22] Polus is baffled. Socrates' point is as follows: Polus has *already said* that having great power is good for the possessor (466 B 6–8), but doing as you please, at least without understanding, is not good but bad for you—as Polus himself thinks and admits (466 E 9–12, 467 A 4–7). Unlike in [T2], Socrates's attribution is supported by what Polus has already said (as Socrates himself points out, 466 E 6–7, 467 A 4). Socrates does not say that Polus *believes* the conclusion, namely that doing whatever you please is not to have great power, before he hears the argument for it; and the beliefs of other people are not mentioned at all.[23] Later in the *Gorgias*, Socrates asserts that Callicles 'claims' or 'is saying'[24] what he, Socrates, says (516 D 4–5). Here again, unlike in [T2], Socrates is looking back to what has already been said: Callicles has agreed that Pericles made the Athenians more savage and more unjust, whereas a good statesman should make citizens more just, and so Callicles, like Socrates, 'claims' that Pericles was not a good statesman. Elsewhere, then, Socrates puts together, and draws inferences from, his interlocutors' previous statements to show them what they are 'claiming'. But only in [T2] does he attribute to

---

[22] The Greek verb can be used to introduce an account of someone's meaning, thought, or point rather than a precise quotation. See J. Kerschensteiner, *Kosmos: Quellenkritische Untersuchungen zu den Vorsokratikern* (Munich, 1962), 76 n. 4.

[23] I am less confident than Woolf ('Authority', 28 n. 52) that Socrates' point at 466 E 4–5 about what Polus claims should be reworded as a point about Polus' belief, particularly as it comes in a dialogue so obviously alive to the possibility of insincerity (see e.g. n. 25 below). At *Gorg.* 470 A 9–12 (cited in Kamtekar, *Psychology*, 93), Socrates says what 'appears' to Polus, but, unlike in [T2], he is summarizing what Polus has just agreed to in the conversation (469 E 6–470 A 8).

[24] The verb φῄς needs to be supplied from the context.

an interlocutor prior belief in his conclusion, and it is only in [T2] that the support in the conversation for the attribution lies exclusively in what comes next, not in previous admissions.[25]

The lack of a parallel concerning belief reinforces the sense that in [T2], where Socrates does speak of Polus' belief, he is addressing a failing in Polus that has just come to light: being excessively impressed by other people's beliefs, particularly when they converge. By contrast, Callicles, who appeals to nature as his authority, is obviously free from that failing, whatever else we may dislike in him. Indeed, his complaint that Socrates is a 'demagogue' ($\delta\eta\mu\eta\gamma\delta\rho\sigma\varsigma$, 482 C 4–5, E 2–5, 494 D 1) may take aim at Socrates' appealing and deferring, in Callicles' view, to popular beliefs.[26] Early in Callicles' intervention he rejects CIR (482 D 7–8), which ordinary people were said to accept (475 D 1–3): according to Callicles, committing injustice is more repellent only by convention, whereas by nature being the victim of injustice is more repellent (483 A 7–8). Unlike Polus, Callicles sees no dialectical cost in contradicting the views of ordinary people—although, as we later learn (481 D 1–482 A 2), in politics Callicles himself has to be more circumspect and defer to the Athenian people. But in a private conversation there is little point in using against Callicles the kind of belief-attribution found in [T2].[27] On the contrary, Socrates says that most people agree not with him but with Callicles, although they do not express their real views as openly as Callicles does (492 D 1–3). The attribution to other people of belief in Socrates' position is used only against Polus, whose confidence in a consensus on his own side needs to be shaken.

---

[25] See also 495 E 1–2, but there (as in Griffith and Schofield, *Gorgias*) a future verb should be supplied: Callicles *will* not agree with what he has said. Finally, see Callicles' self-contradiction in 482 B 4–6. Callicles may deny now that committing injustice, without punishment, is the worst evil, but, whenever the Athenian people say that it is, he will change his tune (481 D 1–482 A 2). The point is that Callicles will *say* something different in order to ingratiate himself with the people and so will contradict himself ($\dot{\epsilon}\nu\alpha\nu\tau\dot{\iota}\alpha$ $\lambda\dot{\epsilon}\gamma\epsilon\iota\nu$, 482 C 1–2), not that he shares Socrates' belief. Given that Callicles' intention will be to curry favour with the people, there is little reason to expect all his statements to them to express his own beliefs.

[26] This is the interpretation suggested by Griffith's translation of 482 E 3–4: 'dragging the discussion down to commonplace appeals to public opinion'.

[27] For discussion of the dialectic between Callicles and Socrates, see, among other studies, J. Doyle, 'The Fundamental Conflict in Plato's *Gorgias*', *Oxford Studies in Ancient Philosophy*, 30 (2006), 87–100 and M. Schofield, 'Callicles' Return: *Gorgias* 509–22 Reconsidered', *Philosophie Antique*, 17 (2017), 7–30.

Even within the discussion with Polus, Socrates does not sustain the paradoxical belief-attribution of [T2]. At [T2], Socrates says that Polus believes not only CIW but also that 'not being punished is worse than being punished'. But when Socrates actually turns to the subject of punishment (476 A 3–481 B 5) and argues that not being punished is the worse of the two fates, he does not suggest again that Polus already, at the time of [T2] or earlier, shared Socrates' belief. On the contrary, he now puts himself and Polus on opposed sides of the debate: Polus, unlike Socrates, 'thought' ($o\check{\iota}\epsilon\sigma\theta a\iota$) it worse to be punished, and the two of them were disagreeing about, or disputing ($\dot{a}\mu\phi\iota\sigma\beta\eta\tau\epsilon\hat{\iota}\nu$), the value of punishment (476 A 2–6, 479 D 7–E 6). This is, strictly speaking, compatible with Polus' already believing Socrates' conclusion about punishment, for Polus may of course have inconsistent beliefs.[28] But we must not leave unexplained why Socrates first (in [T2]) attributes to Polus belief in the Socratic conclusion concerning punishment, and then, when arguing for that conclusion, mentions only Polus' previous opposition to it. The most plausible explanation, I submit, is that the belief-attribution has already served its purpose when Socrates turns to the subject of punishment at 476 A 2: Socrates has shown Polus, by means of a parallel between Polus himself and other people, an unexpected complexity in other people's views about injustice, and thus the difficulty for Polus of using an apparent consensus on that subject to belittle Socrates' position and reinforce his own.

A similarly *ad hominem* interpretation is most appropriate in the closest parallel to [T2] in Plato: the discussion of Love with Diotima in the *Symposium*. Here it is Socrates' own confidence that needs to be unsettled. According to Socrates, *everyone agrees* that Love is a great god (202 B 6–9). Diotima replies that Socrates, like her, claims that Love is not a god at all (202 B 1–C 4). As in [T2] from the *Gorgias*, the conclusion is attributed to the interlocutor before the argument is delivered and while the interlocutor still puts himself on the other side of the debate. Although Diotima speaks at first of what Socrates 'claims'—he is one of those who 'claim' ($\phi a\sigma\iota\nu$, 202 C 1) that Love is not a god—at the end of the argument she moves to a belief-attribution: 'you see that you too believe that Love is not

---

[28] Compare n. 12 above.

a god' (ὁρᾷς οὖν... ὅτι καὶ σὺ Ἔρωτα οὐ θεὸν νομίζεις; 202 D 7).[29] When Diotima attributes this belief, she takes herself to have vindicated her statement that Socrates 'claims' Love not to be a god; that statement of hers was made at the start of the argument, and in opposition to Socrates' account of himself. So it is reasonable to take her to mean that Socrates believed all along (including at the time when he expressed the opposed view) that Love is not a god. Like Socrates in the conversation with Polus, Diotima thinks herself qualified to gainsay Socrates' self-description. And the context is of course similar to that of [T2]: Socrates has just said that there is universal agreement that Love is a god, which suggests that one of Diotima's goals in the apparently premature attribution is to shake his confidence in that agreement.[30] Once this aspect of the context is recognized, the similarity between the two passages shows that we are dealing not with a single Socratic doctrine about belief and its requirements so much as with a Socratic (or Socratic-Diotimean) strategy for addressing an apparently straightforward consensus on the other side.

The *Symposium* is the closest Platonic parallel, inasmuch as there too (if my interpretation is right) belief in the conclusion is

---

[29] I prefer this translation of the Greek to 'do not believe that Love is a god', as in M. C. Howatson, and F. C. C. Sheffield, *Plato: The Symposium* (Cambridge, 2008), which leaves open the possibility that Socrates has no belief at all about Love's divinity. On Diotima's account, Socrates claims Love not to be a god (202 C 1–2) and so has a position on the subject. In Greek, οὐ νομίζεις can mean 'you believe that . . . not', rather than 'you do not believe that . . .', and it is this wording that is used for the allegation of atheism against Socrates (Pl. *Ap.* 26 C 1–8, 35 D 6). See H. W. Smyth, *Greek Grammar*, rev. Messing (Cambridge, MA, 1956), 610 (2691–2). For discussion of the Greek verb in ancient discussions of religion and atheism, see H. S. Versnel, *Coping with the Gods: Wayward Readings in Greek Theology* (Leiden 2011), Appendix IV, 541 n. 10, 542–4, 554–9.

[30] Some readers may be surprised to see Socrates of all people placing confidence in this consensus. Two explanations: (1) in the *Symposium* he is speaking about what is and is not a god, and—strange as this may seem to us—a consensus on that subject may have been thought to carry special importance. In the *Apology* (26 D 1–3), Socrates himself appeals to the fact that everyone believes the sun and moon to be gods. (2) Socrates is attributing to himself, in the conversation with Diotima, an error of Agathon and the others that he wishes to expose and correct. Ever since the subject was introduced (177 A 8) Love has been treated by Agathon, Phaedrus, and the others as a god, and so Socrates has reason to undermine trust in their agreement on Love's godhead. He achieves this by representing *himself* as putting trust in that agreement and then being refuted by his teacher.

attributed to the interlocutor before he hears the argument for it.[31] The discussion in the *Apology* of Socrates' alleged atheism may constitute another parallel. Socrates asks how he could both believe in spirits or lesser deities, as his accuser Meletus says, and be an atheist:

[T4] εἰ δ' αὖ οἱ δαίμονες θεῶν παῖδές εἰσιν νόθοι τινὲς ἢ ἐκ νυμφῶν ἢ ἔκ τινων ἄλλων ὧν δὴ καὶ λέγονται, τίς ἂν ἀνθρώπων θεῶν μὲν παῖδας ἡγοῖτο εἶναι, θεοὺς δὲ μή; ὁμοίως γὰρ ἂν ἄτοπον εἴη ὥσπερ ἂν εἴ τις ἵππων μὲν παῖδας ἡγοῖτο ἢ καὶ ὄνων, τοὺς ἡμιόνους, ἵππους δὲ καὶ ὄνους μὴ ἡγοῖτο εἶναι. (*Ap.* 27 D 8–E 3)

If spirits are illegitimate children of gods, born from nymphs or from some others, as the stories actually go, what person could believe that there are children of gods but no gods? It would be as absurd as if one believed in mules, the offspring of horses and donkeys, but not in horses and donkeys.

On one interpretation, Socrates means that the existence of spirits, and their being the children of gods, together entail the existence of gods, and that this logical connection absolves him of atheism.[32] But equally Socrates could mean that, as a psychological and cultural fact, belief in spirits inevitably involves some thought about their origin—and so anyone who believes in spirits and regards them as the offspring of gods will inevitably come to believe (if he or she has not already done so) that gods exist. Nobody could believe in an offspring of a god and fail to see the connection to the gods' existence, particularly given that Greeks tell detailed stories about the origins of gods and lesser deities, as Socrates points out ('as the stories actually go', in my translation). The text seems to me indeterminate between these two interpretations.

---

[31] We might expect a parallel in the *Euthydemus*, where Euthydemus and his brother know in advance where their arguments will lead and sometimes cannot resist showing this off. But on inspection, the brothers turn out to use less startling language than Socrates does in the *Gorgias*: the brothers say, at the start of an argument, that their interlocutor will be refuted, or that he may deny what he now says, or will be made to accept bizarre claims (275 E 3–6, 295 A 4–5). The brothers never start an argument with the claim that their interlocutor already asserts or believes its conclusion, let alone that everyone believes it.

[32] Strictly speaking, the *current* existence of the gods does not follow (gods could have produced offspring and then all perished), but it would be uncontroversial to assume that gods cannot exist without being everlasting. Woolf, 'Authority', 29 n. 53 says that the passage contains a 'hint' that beliefs should be attributed on the strength of other beliefs and logical connections.

I have tried to articulate precisely what supports the belief-attribution in [T2], but, as we have seen, it would be exaggerating to describe what has emerged as 'the Socratic conception of belief', or even the conception of belief defended or assumed by him throughout the *Gorgias*, or, more narrowly still, a conception of belief sustained throughout the conversation with Polus. The belief-attribution is made in response to Polus' treating a consensus on his own side as authoritative proof that Socrates is wrong, and it belongs firmly to that context. Elsewhere in the *Gorgias* (466 E 4–5, 516 D 4–5), Socrates gainsays his interlocutors about what they are 'claiming', not about their beliefs, and in those other passages he draws support not only from an argument that he is about to deliver but also from what the interlocutors have already said to him.

Recollection and true *doxa* in the *Meno*

Of Plato's three discussions of recollection (*Meno*, *Phaedo*, *Phaedrus*), only the *Meno* mentions the presence of *doxai* in the recollecting subject. To see how *doxa* comes to be relevant, we must start with the dialogue's famous challenge about inquiry.

The challenge comes within a twofold attack by Meno on Socrates that is partly about Socrates' habit of causing puzzlement, partly about his ability to inquire. The latter, the challenge about inquiry, asks how people who do not know can pursue an inquiry and complete it successfully.[33] By this point in the discussion, both Meno and Socrates have described themselves as puzzled, but the challenge about inquiry, as Meno formulates it (80 D 5–8), applies to people by virtue not of their feeling puzzled or perplexed, but of their lack of knowledge. Meno seems to have Socrates himself in mind: 'how will *you* search for something, Socrates, if you don't know at all what it is?' (καὶ τίνα τρόπον ζητήσεις, ὦ Σώκρατες, τοῦτο ὃ μὴ οἶσθα τὸ παράπαν ὅτι ἐστίν;, 80 D 5–6).[34] It is Socrates' lack of knowledge, not his puzzlement, that

---

[33] For the importance of success in the inquiry, see G. Fine, *The Possibility of Inquiry: Meno's Paradox from Socrates to Sextus* [*Inquiry*] (Oxford, 2014), 109–10 and the response there to D. Scott, *Plato's* Meno [*Meno*] (Cambridge, 2006).

[34] See especially R. M. Dancy, *Plato's Introduction of Forms* [*Forms*] (Cambridge, 2004), 221, who emphasizes the importance for Meno of Socrates' claim not to

(the challenge suggests) makes successful inquiry impossible.[35] But Meno has also complained, with the vivid image of an electric ray, about Socrates' habit of causing others to be puzzled (79 E 7–80 B 7). And the examples in the dialogue of the knowledge-less position all involve puzzlement as well. The first is Meno's own condition after his attempt to define virtue, where he is, by his own description, 'full of puzzlement' (μεστὸν ἀπορίας, 80 A 3–4) and out of answers (B 1–2). Socrates himself, puzzled and lacking knowledge of what virtue is (C 9, D 1), is the second. The third example is the slave,[36] who, after two unsuccessful attempts to answer Socrates' question in geometry, admits that he lacks the knowledge and, as Socrates puts it, realizes that he is puzzled (84 A 1–B 1).

Socrates needs to respond both to Meno's complaint about puzzlement and to his challenge about inquiring without knowledge. His response is to show, through the conversation with a slave, that (1) puzzlement is beneficial, not harmful, for the purpose of inquiring, and (2) people who do not know can inquire successfully. *Doxai* become relevant in the discussion of (2). According to Socrates, when the slave endorses the correct answer to the geometrical question, he shows the presence inside himself of true *doxai*. That, Socrates suggests, is how the discussion of geometry shows that the absence of knowledge is not a barrier to inquiry.

[T5] ΣΩ. Τῷ οὐκ εἰδότι ἄρα περὶ ὧν ἂν μὴ εἰδῇ ἔνεισιν ἀληθεῖς δόξαι περὶ τούτων ὧν οὐκ οἶδε;

MEN. Φαίνεται. (85 C 6–8)

SOC. So in someone who doesn't know—whatever the things may be which he doesn't know—there are true beliefs about the very things he doesn't know?

MEN. Evidently so.

know 'at all' (71 B 3). Compare G. Fine, *Plato on Knowledge and Forms: Selected Essays* [*Knowledge*] (Oxford, 2003), 50–1; D. N. Sedley and A. G. Long, *Plato: Meno and Phaedo* (Cambridge, 2010), xvi; Fine, *Inquiry*, 82.

[35] Socrates broadens the scope of the problem beyond himself—'impossible for a human being to inquire . . .' (οὐκ ἄρα ἔστιν ζητεῖν ἀνθρώπῳ)—and reformulates it so as to include those who have knowledge (80 E 1–5). See Scott, *Meno*, 78; Fine, *Inquiry*, 84–5. But in Socrates' formulation too, the problem is about knowledge and its absence, not the feeling of puzzlement.

[36] Slave, not slave boy: the noun παῖς does not show his age. See LSJ s.v. III; E. Dickey, *Greek Forms of Address: From Herodotus to Lucian* (Oxford 1996), 232, 234; R. Benitez, 'Boy! What Boy? (A Plea for Meno's Slave)', *Ancient Philosophy*, 36 (2016), 107–14.

Meno's reply may give strong, not weak, endorsement—'so we have seen', or 'evidently so'—as it is the presence of true *doxai* that is supposed to be shown empirically by the slave's answers. By contrast, there are not similar empirical grounds for accepting Socrates' next claim (85 C 9–D 1), that the slave would eventually *know*, not merely have the *doxa*, to which Meno replies with a probably weaker 'so it seems' (ἔοικεν, 85 D 2).

As we have seen, Meno's challenge, so far as it concerns inquiry, is about the absence of knowledge, but it is brought into focus by three examples (Meno, Socrates, and in Socrates' response the slave) involving puzzlement as well. Socrates' response in [T5] should speak directly to these examples. After all, Socrates' objective is to show that he and Meno should continue discussing virtue and try to find out what it is, even at the point where both he and Meno are in *aporia*. So Socrates' wording at [T5] should describe not only the slave's current condition in geometry, when the correct answer has been endorsed by him, but also the slave's condition back at the time when he felt perplexed and unable to answer.[37] [T5] should also describe Socrates' own condition and Meno's concerning virtue, even at the time when Meno has despaired of finding the correct definition of it and says that he has no answers left (80 B 1–2). Otherwise the passage would fail to show that they should not, at that time and in that condition, abandon the inquiry into virtue.

The application of [T5] to this time is confirmed when Socrates goes on to argue that the slave 'has in him' (ἐνέσονται αὐτῷ) true *doxai* both when he was a human being and when he was not a human being, and takes this to mean that they are in the slave 'for all time' (τὸν ἀεὶ χρόνον, 86 A 6–9). If the *doxai* are present for all time, then obviously they were present when the slave (and, in the parallel case, Meno) felt perplexed and out of answers. But I have defended my interpretation independently of that slightly later

---

[37] Further evidence in the text: (1) Socrates says that the *doxai* 'were present' in the slave (ἐνῆσαν, 85 C 4), and in the context this means at the same time as when they said that the slave did not know (see 85 C 2), which is either 82 E 8–9 or 84 A 1–B 10. On either alternative, the true *doxai* are already present in 84 A–B, when the slave despairs of giving the right answer. (2) Directly after [T5], Socrates notes that the *doxai* have 'now' been 'stirred up' in the slave (νῦν . . . ἀνακεκίνηνται, 85 C 9). This suggests that the immediately preceding exchange, where the correct answer is endorsed, is the time when the *doxai* were 'stirred up', not the time when they first came to be inside the slave.

passage, where Socrates uses his attribution of *doxai* to argue for the soul's immortality. Socrates has a distinct reason to defend the soul's immortality that does not have to do with Meno's challenge about inquiry or complaint about puzzlement: Meno is not waiting to take part in the Eleusinian Mysteries (76 E 8–9), which suggests an alarming indifference to the fate of his soul after death.[38] The part of the 'recollection' passage concerned with immortality, and the consequent need to live 'as piously as possible' (ὡς ὁσιώτατα, 81 B 6), may address this indifference in Meno, not the challenge in 80 D 5–8 about inquiry and knowledge.

What exactly is Socrates attributing in [T5] to the slave—and, in the parallel discussion of virtue, to Meno and himself? More specifically, do the true *doxai* mentioned there, or their content, include the solution to the geometrical problem, as well as the more elementary answers used to reach it? When the slave gives the solution, Socrates insistently attributes it to the slave ('on your account, slave of Meno . . .', 85 B 5–6). He then asks Meno whether the slave failed at any point to give his own *doxa* as his reply (85 B 8–9), to which the answer is 'no'—the slave expressed his own *doxai* throughout. It is in this context that Socrates and Meno agree (85 C 4–5) that 'these *doxai*' were in the slave, and [T5] follows directly. So it seems certain that in [T5] Socrates is including every *doxa* expressed by the slave, including the solution.[39] That implies

---

[38] For the connection of the Mysteries to the afterlife, see e.g. the Homeric *Hymn to Demeter* 478–82; Sophocles fr. 753 Nauck (Plut. *Aud. poet.* 21 F); Isocrates 4. 28. In their commentaries, R. S. Bluck, *Plato's* Meno (Cambridge, 1961) and R. W. Sharples, *Plato:* Meno (Warminster, 1991) note that 'initiation' can be used to describe philosophical enlightenment, but they do not note the connection between Meno's non-participation in the literal Mysteries and Socrates' argument for the soul's immortality. Meno has told Socrates, 'I have to go away before the Mysteries' (ὥσπερ χθὲς ἔλεγες, ἀναγκαῖόν σοι ἀπιέναι πρὸ τῶν μυστηρίων, 76 E 8–9); is it really likely that Meno was alluding to philosophy? Moreover, Socrates has only just committed himself to speaking in a way intelligible to Meno (75 D 2–7), and there is no reason to expect Meno to interpret Socrates' talk of the Mysteries as a reference to philosophy. In my view, scholars have assumed too quickly that there is no reference at all to the literal Mysteries, and this has caused them to miss the relevance of this passage for the later discussion of reincarnation and immortality.

[39] So L. Brown, 'Connaissance et réminiscence dans le "Ménon"', *Revue philosophique de la France et de l'étranger*, 181 (1991), 603–19 at 612–13; J. Gentzler, 'Recollection and "The Problem of the Socratic Elenchus"' ['Recollection'], *Proceedings of the Boston Area Colloquium in Ancient Philosophy*, 10 (1994), 257–95 at 281; Dancy, *Forms*, 231. Contrast Fine, *Knowledge*, 4 n. 8 and Fine, *Inquiry*, 121 (during the exchange, the slave acquires 'new' beliefs), 128 ('these beliefs need not be about what the answer is'), 132, 134, 160–1.

that, in the parallel case, the correct *doxa* about the definition of virtue 'is in' Meno and himself. There is no paradox in saying that the slave believes the solution to the geometrical problem at the time when he has endorsed it, but, as I have argued, Socrates must intend the attribution in [T5] to obtain even before that, when the slave has no answer for Socrates. Similarly, [T5] should describe Meno's condition at 80 A 2–B 7, when he 'is numb' (ναρκᾶν) with perplexity. As in our examination of the *Gorgias*, the contrast with the discussion of *doxa* in the *Theaetetus*, [T1] above, should be evident. When the slave is in the grip of perplexity, he has not yet endorsed internally, at least during his current life, the correct solution to the problem Socrates has set him. And yet he is said to contain already the *doxa* concerning it.

It now becomes essential to examine Socrates' wording in [T5] and in particular to see whether, in Plato's Greek, saying that (*a*) the *doxa* that some proposition *p* is true 'is inside' a subject necessarily implies that (*b*) the subject 'believes' or 'judges' that *p*, in the sense that he or she has the relevant cognitive attitude towards it.[40] In the *Theaetetus* ([T1] above), Socrates puts it beyond doubt that he has in mind 'judging' or 'believing', the possession of a cognitive state or attitude: he is giving an account not only of *doxa* but also of the cognate verb, *doxazein* (190 A 4–10). By contrast, [T5] says not that the slave 'judges' or 'believes', *doxazein*, but that the true *doxai* 'are inside' the slave (ἔνεισιν, 85 C 6; compare 85 C 4, 86 A 7). There has been comparatively little discussion of the use of the second verb in recent scholarship on the passage.[41] Elsewhere in Plato it is very unusual to say that a *doxa* 'is inside' (ἔνεστι or some other form of the verb) people or their souls. Much more common is to say that a virtue (such as justice) or a vice 'is inside' them.[42] Outside the *Meno* I can find only one passage where a *doxa*

---

[40] As I observe later (n. 45), on one interpretation the *doxa* is itself a 'truth' or proposition. Adherents of this view would spell out or reword (*a*), in their own account of the *Meno*, as something like the following: 'the *doxa* consisting of the proposition that *p* . . .'

[41] Gentzler and Dancy accurately reproduce Plato's wording (e.g. the true belief 'was in the slave', Gentzler, 'Recollection', 281; 'the belief that the side of the double square was a belief in him', Dancy, *Forms*, 231, emphasis added), but they do not discuss his choice of it.

[42] Notice especially the change of wording at *Chrm.* 159 A 1–3: if the virtue of moderation (σωφροσύνη) 'is in' (ἐνοῦσαν) Charmides, he 'would have a belief about it' (δόξα ἄν τίς σοι περὶ αὐτῆς εἴη). Socrates does not say that the belief would 'be in'

is said to 'be inside' people, and even this passage is in fact about the virtues:

[T6] Καὶ μὴν εἴπερ αὖ ἐν ἄλλῃ πόλει ἡ αὐτὴ δόξα ἔνεστι τοῖς τε ἄρχουσι καὶ ἀρχομένοις περὶ τοῦ οὗστινας δεῖ ἄρχειν, καὶ ἐν ταύτῃ ἂν εἴη τοῦτο ἐνόν. ἢ οὐ δοκεῖ; (*Rep.* 4, 431 D 9–E 2)

And if there is any city where the *same belief is in* both the rulers and the subjects about who should rule, it will be in this one. Don't you think so?

The passage comes from the discussion of the city's virtues in *Republic* Book 4. Socrates and Glaucon ask not only what the virtues are, but 'in whom' they are (428 D 5–7, E 7–9, 429 A 8)—that is, the group or groups of citizens that we should look to when calling the entire city brave, wise, and so on. In [T6], Socrates has turned to moderation or self-discipline (σωφροσύνη), which he will define as agreement or unanimity between better and worse about which should be in command (432 A 6–B 1). He and Glaucon are about to agree that this particular virtue, when it is a property of a city, 'is in' both the rulers and their subjects (431 E 4–6)—we cannot decide whether rulers and subjects are in agreement without looking to them both. This, I suggest, is what causes him to speak of the *doxa* as 'being in' both groups: he is on the point of suggesting that the *virtue* 'is in' both groups, in the sense outlined above. So the passage from the *Republic* should not be used as evidence that in other contexts, such as the *Meno*, where Socrates does not have special reason to use of *doxa* a verb used more commonly of virtue, 'the *doxa* is in *X*' necessarily implies '*X* believes or judges'.[43]

Charmides. For virtue and vice 'being in' people, see also *Rep.* 1, 352 A 6, C 4; 2, 358 B 5–6; 3, 402 C 5, 409 B 6. Intelligence (νοῦς) can also be said to 'be in', or not to 'be in', people (*Ion* 534 B 6); if S. Menn is right in interpreting intelligence as a virtue (*Plato on God as Nous* (Carbondale, 1995), 14–18), this is not surprising. For the sake of completeness, I note that according to the Seventh Letter, *doxa*, together with knowledge and intelligence, 'is in' souls (ἐνόν, 342 C 4–6). For the question of the letter's inauthenticity, see M. Burnyeat and M. Frede, *The Pseudo-Platonic Seventh Letter*, ed. by D. Scott (Oxford 2015).

[43] The point is only strengthened if we look for uses of the same wording about knowledge. In the *Meno*, knowledge is not said to 'be in' people or souls, and so we have to look to the *Phaedo*. There knowledge is said to 'be in' people before recollection (ἐνοῦσα, 73 A 9), and yet it is denied that 'we know throughout our lives' (ἐπιστάμεθα διὰ βίου, 76 A 5; see 76 B 10–C 4 for the denial). So knowledge of an item can 'be in' people without their 'knowing' that item. (I use 'item' so as not to exclude either propositions or objects.) My interpretation of the *Meno* has been anticipated by Dancy: 'the boy has in him beliefs to the effect that so-and-so and

So far I have argued only that we are not required to interpret Socrates in [T5] as saying that the person without knowledge believes correctly. More significantly, a later part of the *Meno* gives us reason not to suppose that Meno, the slave, and Socrates already believe or judge correctly at the time when they experience perplexity. The conception of true *doxa* introduced in [T5] will become crucial to the final round of the discussion of virtue. Socrates and Meno will agree there that someone believing truly—not someone 'in whom there are true *doxai*', but someone 'believing correctly' (ὀρθῶς... δοξάζων, 97 B 1)—is just as reliable a guide as someone with the relevant knowledge. The example is someone who, because he believes truly, leads others correctly to Larisa. Indeed, Socrates says, *whenever* someone 'has correct *doxa*' (ἔχων ὀρθὴν δόξαν, 97 C 9–10), he or she acts correctly.[44] But Meno is not a reliable guide on the subject of virtue, or the slave (during his perplexity) in geometry. True answers can be elicited from the slave, and presumably Socrates believes the same about himself and Meno concerning virtue; but if the perplexed slave is completely unaided, he will not guide others to the correct answer, no more than an unaided Meno will tell Socrates the correct definition of virtue. By contrast, the person 'believing correctly' about the route to Larisa can simply be asked for guidance or directions. So the attribution in [T5] cannot be the equivalent of saying that the slave 'believes correctly', in the same sense as the person guiding to Larisa.

I conclude that for a *doxa* to 'be in' a person or a soul is not, at least in [T5], the same as for the person to 'believe'. Confirmation, if it is still needed, comes in the apparent discrepancy between these two passages:

[T7] Εἰ οὖν ὅν τ' ἂν ᾖ ᾖ χρόνον καὶ ὃν ἂν μὴ ᾖ ᾖ ἄνθρωπος, ἐνέσονται αὐτῷ ἀληθεῖς δόξαι, αἳ ἐρωτήσει ἐπεγερθεῖσαι ἐπιστῆμαι γίγνονται, ἆρ' οὖν τὸν ἀεὶ χρόνον μεμαθηκυῖα ἔσται ἡ ψυχὴ αὐτοῦ; (86 A 6–9)

such-and-such, but that does not mean that he believed that so-and-so or such-and-such' (*Forms*, 231). Dancy, *Forms*, 231–2 then applies the same distinction to knowledge. Usually in the scholarship on recollection (the exceptions are Gentzler, 'Recollection' and Dancy, *Forms*), the questions of innate, implicit, or latent knowledge get more attention than the corresponding questions about belief.

[44] 'Having' true *doxa* is used also in the discussion of recollection (ἔχει δὲ ταύτας τὰς δόξας, 85 E 7). This expression can be used, I suggest, of *both* the conditions between which I distinguish: it can mean either that true *doxa* 'is in' the person, as in [T5] and the surrounding passages, or that the person 'believes correctly'—that is, that he or she has the relevant cognitive state, like the reliable guide to Larisa in 97 A.

If, then, there are going to be true *doxai* in him [the slave] both for the time when he is a human being and for the time when he isn't, *doxai* which become knowledge when awoken by questioning, then for time everlasting won't his soul be in a state of having learned?

[T8] καὶ γὰρ αἱ δόξαι αἱ ἀληθεῖς, ὅσον μὲν ἂν χρόνον παραμένωσιν, καλὸν τὸ χρῆμα καὶ πάντ᾽ ἀγαθὰ ἐργάζονται· πολὺν δὲ χρόνον οὐκ ἐθέλουσι παραμένειν, ἀλλὰ δραπετεύουσιν ἐκ τῆς ψυχῆς τοῦ ἀνθρώπου... (97 E 6–98 A 2)

For true *doxai* are also a thing of beauty, as long as they stay with one, and all their consequences are good. But they are not prepared to stay with one for long. Instead they run away from the person's soul.

The passages seem to contradict one another on the duration of true *doxai*: are they present for all time ([T7]) or only briefly ([T8])? Evidently there must be a distinction between *doxai* 'being in' a person, as in [T5] and [T7], and the person believing (such as the reliable guide to Larisa and, given its context, in [T8]).

What Socrates means by the former, *doxai* 'being in' the slave or Meno, is best measured by the discussion with the slave. The first hint that *doxai* will become relevant comes when Socrates talks about the slave's attitude to his own answers: 'reply by saying what you believe' (τὸ γάρ σοι δοκοῦν τοῦτο ἀποκρίνου, 83 D 2). Later, as we saw above, he asks Meno whether the slave gave 'his own *doxai*' in his answers (85 B 8–9; compare 84 D 1–2). The slave is giving as his answers not only what has (as we might put it) crossed his mind, but what he believes, at the time when he gives the answers. So the prior condition, when the slave is still perplexed but, according to [T5], containing true *doxai*, is one in which the appropriate sequence of questions will not only elicit from him the right answer but prompt in him a certain attitude to it: he will not only think of the answer to Socrates but also think it true. But, to repeat, this is not equivalent to already *believing* that answer before the question has been put to him.[45]

---

[45] As I finalized this paper, I was fortunate to read D. Bronstein and W. Schwab, 'Is Plato an Innatist in the *Meno*?', *Phronesis*, 64 (2019) 392–430. Bronstein and Schwab argue that the *doxai* already inside the slave are the contents or truths that he comes to believe, not the cognitive state of believing itself. In this paper, I confine myself to the negative point that the *doxa* is not such a cognitive state, but, as long as one can explain what it means to possess an uncognized truth (a challenge they address in the last section of their paper), their interpretation is an attractive account of [T5]. My thanks to David Bronstein for sending me before publication a copy of their paper.

If we choose to express the point in terms of dispositions, we must not say that Plato presents 'believing that p' as 'having the disposition to give p as an answer', or something similar.[46] That behavioural disposition is closer to what Socrates calls 'containing the *doxa*' or, more literally, the *doxa* 'being in' the person. Closer, but not quite identical: a *doxa* is inside a person if he or she has the disposition not only to give certain answers but, at the time of answering particular questions, to take a certain attitude to their answers, such that Socrates' 'say what you believe' requirement is met. In other words, the relevant disposition is to give, in the appropriate context, the answer sincerely.[47] (In a different context, such as when the slave is first asked to solve the problem, he may give a different and incorrect answer.) As we have seen, the presence of a *doxa* in someone, as in [T5], is not the same as believing. Indeed, it is not even described as a kind or way of believing, as some of our adverbial expressions, such as believing latently or implicitly, might be taken to suggest. So I am not interpreting Plato as, in Fine's phrase, a 'dispositional innatist', at least about *believing*.[48]

To conclude: in the *Meno* to say that a *doxa* 'is inside' a person does not imply that the person 'believes' or 'judges'. The former describes the relationship between the slave and the solution to the geometrical problem at the time when the slave was confused and unable to give Socrates an answer: the *doxa* about the solution was inside him even then, despite his not having affirmed the solution

---

[46] Compare the following (E. Schwitzgebel, 'A Phenomenal, Dispositional Account of Belief', *Noûs*, 36 (2002), 249–75 at 250): 'I call it a dispositional account because it treats believing as nothing more or less than being disposed to do and experience certain kinds of things.' Schwitzgebel then immediately contrasts his own account with other dispositional accounts that say less than his about conscious experience.

[47] Contrast Dancy, who admittedly speaks of an ability rather than a disposition: 'the boy has in him the belief that the side of the double square is the diagonal in the sense that, once he is asked questions in the right order, he will be able to say, on his own, that it is' (*Forms*, 232). On my account, the slave must also have a certain attitude to the answer at the time when he gives it. Dancy's earlier formulation ('he [the slave] can see, by himself, the truth of the matter', *Forms*, 231) is in this respect better. See also Gentzler, 'Recollection', 281 n. 49: the true beliefs in the soul 'are mere propensities to give mental assent to true propositions'. (This is one of two interpretations Gentzler considers possible, the other of which is that the true belief is 'explicit, but unconscious belief'.)

[48] Fine, *Inquiry*, 147. Compare the contrast in Audi, 'Dispositions' between a dispositional belief and a disposition to believe.

internally, or assented to it, during his current life. The latter, believing, describes the guide to Larisa, reliable whenever he believes truly; and Socrates does not say whether or not an internal assertion about the way to Larisa has occurred within the guide, as is required by his discussion of *doxa* in the *Theaetetus*. 'Having' a *doxa* can be used of both conditions, and so this wording alone cannot be relied upon to show into which of the two categories a person falls.[49] In my view, these distinctions can be used to clarify what Socrates says about knowledge as well as *doxa*,[50] but that is not a task for this paper. Our task is to see whether assent and internal assertion are needed for *doxa* in the *Theaetetus* and other texts. The *Meno* is silent about whether they are necessary for *believing*, although it suggests that a *doxa* can *be in* a person without either of them having occurred in his or her current life.

Conclusion

In the *Gorgias*, Socrates gainsays his interlocutors about their own positions when they are unaware of, or distance themselves from, the consequences of what they accept or have said. To that extent Socrates represents himself as knowing other people better than they know themselves. But there is no consistent preference for speaking of their *beliefs* in such passages; sometimes he speaks of what they are claiming or putting forward in the debate. In the one passage where he attributes a belief to an astounded Polus, he is addressing Polus' tendency to defer to what other people believe and say; it is essential to recognize that the attribution comes in this context and involves an attribution not only to Polus but to other people as well. So when in the *Theaetetus* Socrates stipulates that every *doxa* involves an internal assertion, he is not contradicting a conception of belief that he holds throughout the *Gorgias*. Rather, in the *Theaetetus* Socrates is making unavailable to himself an *ad hominem* move made against Polus—and, by his own account, made against him by Diotima.

---

[49] See n. 44.

[50] See Dancy, *Forms*, 232, although Dancy uses 'have a belief' as equivalent to 'the belief is in'. I agree that this is one use of the phrase, but 'having the belief' and 'having knowledge' can also be used as equivalents of 'believing' and 'knowing'.

In the *Meno*, he says that there are *doxai* 'in' people which they have not yet, at least in this life, assented to or asserted internally, but this attribution must be distinguished from saying that these people believe, when they are in that condition. The *Meno* is silent about whether believing requires assent or internal assertion—not unreasonably, as in that dialogue Socrates does not need to confront the problem of falsehood whose solution requires *doxa* to have the same structure as what we say to others. In my discussion of the *Meno*, as elsewhere in the paper, I have prioritized the question of *doxa*-attribution, not the question of what Socrates means by *doxa*. But shifting to the first question allows us to see that Socrates is not, despite appearances, saying that the slave enters the conversation already believing the solution to the problem, and that is an important first step for a proper understanding of what *doxa* means in the passage on recollection. Whereas my discussion of the *Gorgias* does not require us to distinguish Polus' 'belief' from the cognitive state called a *doxa* in [T1], I do distinguish that state from what is attributed to the slave in [T5].

As my account depends on contextualization to a greater extent at some points than at others, I will close with a brief and (I expect) provocative comment on literary context and what remains 'perhaps the most burning question in Platonic scholarship today', the relation and interplay between literary and philosophical accounts of the dialogues.[51] The contrast between my accounts of [T1] and [T2], from the *Theaetetus* and *Gorgias*, respectively, and my extended discussion of the dialogues to which they belong, illustrate that a reasoned case can be made for giving the literary and dramatic context of one passage a kind of significance that is not given to another. Considering whether or not to interpret a certain argument or conception as *ad hominem* need not come down to intellectual temperament or the a priori adoption of a single

---

[51] C. H. Kahn, 'From *Republic* to *Laws*: A Discussion of Christopher Bobonich, *Plato's Utopia Recast*', *Oxford Studies in Ancient Philosophy*, 26 (2004), 337–62 at 343, which remains (especially at 343–53) a powerful commentary on contemporary approaches to the dialogues. Kahn asks (343): 'how far can the historical and dramatic setting, the character of the interlocutors, the artistic diversity of the dialogues, or the absence of Plato's own voice be an essential factor for the understanding of Plato's philosophy?' The present paper suggests, at least concerning dramatic setting and character, that we should refrain from a once-and-for-all account of their bearing on what Socrates says.

88 *Alex Long*

approach to every part of every dialogue. The dialogues themselves can furnish us with grounds for sensitive discrimination.[52]

University of St Andrews

BIBLIOGRAPHY

Audi, R., *The Possibility of Inquiry: Meno's Paradox from Socrates to Sextus* [*Inquiry*] (Oxford, 2014).

Audi, R., 'Dispositional Beliefs and Dispositions to Believe' ['Dispositions'], *Noûs*, 28 (1994), 419–34.

Benitez, R., 'Boy! What Boy? (A Plea for Meno's Slave)', *Ancient Philosophy*, 36 (2016), 107–14.

Bluck, R. S., *Plato's* Meno (Cambridge, 1961).

Bobonich, C., *Plato's Utopia Recast: His Later Ethics and Politics* (Oxford, 2002).

Broadie, S., 'The Knowledge Unacknowledged in the *Theaetetus*', *Oxford Studies in Ancient Philosophy*, 51 (2016), 87–117.

Bronstein, D. and Schwab, W. 'Is Plato an Innatist in the *Meno*?', *Phronesis*, 64 (2019) 392–430.

Brown, L., 'Connaissance et réminiscence dans le "Ménon"', *Revue philosophique de la France et de l'étranger*, 181. 4 (1991), 603–19.

Burnyeat, M., 'Idealism and Greek Philosophy: What Descartes Saw and Berkeley Missed', *Philosophical Review*, 90 (1982), 3–40.

Burnyeat, M., *The* Theaetetus *of Plato* [*Theaetetus*], with a translation by M. J. Levett (Indianapolis and Cambridge, 1990).

Burnyeat, M. and Frede, M., *The Pseudo-Platonic Seventh Letter*, ed. by D. Scott (Oxford, 2015).

Cohen, L. J., 'Belief and Acceptance', *Mind*, 98 (1989), 367–89.

Dancy, R. M., *Plato's Introduction of Forms* [*Forms*] (Cambridge, 2004).

Dickey, E., *Greek Forms of Address: From Herodotus to Lucian* (Oxford, 1996).

Dodds, E. R., *Plato: Gorgias* (Oxford, 1959).

Doyle, J., 'The Fundamental Conflict in Plato's *Gorgias*', *Oxford Studies in Ancient Philosophy*, 30 (2006), 87–100.

Duncombe, M., 'Thought as Internal Speech in Plato and Aristotle' ['Thought'], *Logical Analysis and History of Philosophy*, 19 (2016), 105–25.

[52] My thanks to the editor, the two anonymous readers for the journal, Ursula Coope, Luca Castagnoli, and those who commented on parts of the paper when they were presented at St Andrews and the Southern Association for Ancient Philosophy in Cambridge.

Fine, G., *Plato on Knowledge and Forms: Selected Essays* [*Knowledge*] (Oxford, 2003).

Gentzler, J., 'Recollection and "The Problem of the Socratic Elenchus"' ['Recollection'], *Proceedings of the Boston Area Colloquium in Ancient Philosophy*, 10 (1994), 257–95.

Griffith, T. and Schofield, M., *Plato:* Gorgias, Menexenus, Protagoras [*Gorgias*] (Cambridge, 2010).

Howatson, M. C. and Sheffield, F. C. C., *Plato: The* Symposium (Cambridge, 2008).

Irwin, T., *Plato:* Gorgias (Oxford, 1979).

Kahn, C. H., 'From *Republic* to *Laws*: A Discussion of Christopher Bobonich, *Plato's Utopia Recast*', *Oxford Studies in Ancient Philosophy*, 26 (2004), 337–62.

Kamtekar, R., *Plato's Moral Psychology: Intellectualism, the Divided Soul, and the Desire for Good* [*Psychology*] (Oxford, 2017).

Kerschensteiner, J., *Kosmos: Quellenkritische Untersuchungen zu den Vorsokratikern* (Munich, 1962).

Lee, M.-K., *Epistemology after Protagoras: Responses to Relativism in Plato, Aristotle, and Democritus* (Oxford, 2004).

Long, A. G., *Conversation and Self-Sufficiency in Plato* (Oxford, 2013).

Menn, S., *Plato on God as* Nous (Carbondale, 1995).

Moss, J., 'Plato's Appearance-assent Account of Belief' ['Belief'], *Proceedings of the Aristotelian Society*, 114 (2014), 213–38.

Rowe, C., *Plato:* Theaetetus *and* Sophist (Cambridge, 2015).

Schofield, M., 'Callicles' Return: *Gorgias* 509–22 Reconsidered', *Philosophie Antique*, 17 (2017), 7–30.

Schwab, W., 'Explanation in the Epistemology of the *Meno*', *Oxford Studies in Ancient Philosophy*, 48 (2015), 1–36.

Schwitzgebel, E., 'A Phenomenal, Dispositional Account of Belief', *Noûs*, 36 (2002), 249–75.

Scott, D., *Plato's* Meno [*Meno*] (Cambridge, 2006).

Sedley, D., *The Midwife of Platonism: Text and Subtext in Plato's* Theaetetus [*Midwife*] (Oxford, 2004).

Sedley, D. N. and Long, A. G., *Plato:* Meno *and* Phaedo (Cambridge, 2010).

Sharples, R. W., *Plato:* Meno (Warminster, 1991).

Smyth, H. W., *Greek Grammar*, rev. Messing (Cambridge, MA, 1956).

Versnel, H. S., *Coping with the Gods: Wayward Readings in Greek Theology* (Leiden, 2011).

Woolf, R., 'Socratic Authority' ['Authority'], *Archiv für Geschichte der Philosophie*, 90 (2008), 1–38.

DEMONSTRATION BY *REDUCTIO AD IMPOSSIBILE* IN *POSTERIOR ANALYTICS* 1. 26

MARKO MALINK

1. Aristotle's thesis in *Posterior Analytics* 1. 26

AT the beginning of the *Analytics*, Aristotle states that the subject of the treatise is demonstration (ἀπόδειξις). A demonstration, for Aristotle, is a kind of deductive argument. It is a deduction through which, when we possess it, we have scientific knowledge (ἐπιστήμη). While the *Prior Analytics* deals with deduction in general, the nature of demonstration is studied in the *Posterior Analytics*.

In *Posterior Analytics* 1. 24–6, Aristotle sets out to compare different kinds of demonstration. He begins by explaining why, in his view, universal demonstrations are better than particular ones, and positive demonstrations are better than negative ones (1. 24–5). He goes on, in chapter 1. 26, to argue that direct demonstrations are better than those that proceed by *reductio ad impossibile*. In the opening sentence of the chapter, Aristotle writes:

ἐπεὶ δ' ἡ κατηγορικὴ τῆς στερητικῆς βελτίων, δῆλον ὅτι καὶ τῆς εἰς τὸ ἀδύνατον ἀγούσης.[1] (*Post. An.* 1. 26, 87ᵃ1–2)

Since positive demonstration is better than privative demonstration, clearly it is also better than that which leads to the impossible.

Aristotle is here referring to the main result of the preceding chapter, that direct positive demonstrations are better than direct negative (or privative) ones. Based on this, he seeks to establish in 1. 26 that direct positive demonstrations are better than those by *reductio ad impossibile*. He does so by arguing that direct negative demonstrations are better than those by *reductio*.[2]

---

[1] For the Greek text of Aristotle's *Analytics*, I follow the edition of T. Waitz, *Aristotelis Organon Graece* [*Organon*], 2 vols. (Leipzig, 1844–6). All translations are my own unless otherwise noted.

[2] See Philop. *In An. Post.* 290. 32–291. 5 Wallies; J. Zabarella, *Opera logica* [*Opera logica*] (Frankfurt a.M., 1608), 972 E–F.

Marko Malink, *Demonstration by* reductio ad impossibile *in* Posterior Analytics *1. 26*. In: Oxford Studies in Ancient Philosophy Volume LVIII. Edited by: Victor Caston, Oxford University Press (2020). © Marko Malink.
DOI: 10.1093/oso/9780198858997.003.0004

To show that direct negative demonstrations are better than those by *reductio*, Aristotle argues that the former are superior in explanatory power to the latter in that they proceed from premisses which are prior to the conclusion. In the final section of the chapter, he states this thesis as follows:

εἰ οὖν ἡ ἐκ γνωριμωτέρων καὶ προτέρων κρείττων, εἰσὶ δ' ἀμφότεραι ἐκ τοῦ μὴ εἶναί τι πισταί, ἀλλ' ἡ μὲν ἐκ προτέρου ἡ δ' ἐξ ὑστέρου, βελτίων ἁπλῶς ἂν εἴη τῆς εἰς τὸ ἀδύνατον ἡ στερητικὴ ἀπόδειξις, ὥστε καὶ ἡ ταύτης βελτίων ἡ κατηγορικὴ δῆλον ὅτι καὶ τῆς εἰς τὸ ἀδύνατόν ἐστι βελτίων. (*Post. An.* 1. 26, 87ᵃ25–30)

Thus, if a demonstration which proceeds from what is more known and prior is superior, and if in both kinds of demonstration conviction proceeds from something's not holding, but in the one from something prior and in the other from something posterior, then privative demonstration will be better without qualification than demonstration leading to the impossible. Consequently, it is also clear that positive demonstration, which is better than privative demonstration, is also better than that which leads to the impossible.

In this passage, Aristotle compares direct negative demonstrations and those by *reductio*. Both kinds of demonstration make use of negative propositions, that is, propositions asserting that 'something does not hold'.[3] They differ from each other with respect to the priority relations that obtain between the premisses and the conclusion. While direct negative demonstrations proceed from premisses that are more known than and prior to the conclusion, demonstrations by *reductio* proceed from premisses that are posterior to the conclusion.

In *Posterior Analytics* 1. 2, Aristotle distinguishes between priority 'in nature' and priority 'to us'. Likewise, he distinguishes between being more known 'in nature' and being more known 'to us'. He regards the latter distinction as equivalent to the former, using the phrases 'prior' and 'more known' interchangeably in this context.[4] In chapter 1. 26, Aristotle makes it clear that the sense in which the premisses of a direct negative demonstration are prior to

---

[3] Philop. *In An. Post.* 298. 28–299. 4; M. Mignucci, *L'argomentazione dimostrativa in Aristotele: commento agli* Analitici secondi *I* [*L'argomentazione dimostrativa*] (Padua, 1975), 566. The phrase τὸ μὴ εἶναί τι at 87ᵃ26 is used by Aristotle to designate negative as opposed to affirmative propositions (similarly, *Post. An.* 1. 2, 72ᵃ20; 1. 23, 84ᵇ30–1; 1. 25, 86ᵇ8–9).

[4] *Post. An.* 1. 2, 71ᵇ33–72ᵃ5; see R. D. McKirahan, *Principles and Proofs: Aristotle's Theory of Demonstrative Science* [*Principles*] (Princeton, 1992), 30–1;

the conclusion is priority in nature (φύσει, 87ᵃ17). Accordingly, when he refers to these premisses as 'more known', he does not mean that they are necessarily more known to us, but that they are more known in nature.[5]

By contrast, the premisses of a demonstration by *reductio* are not prior but posterior in nature to the conclusion. Aristotle does not specify whether this claim holds for all demonstrations by *reductio* or whether it is a claim that admits of exceptions. The answer to this question will emerge from his argument in chapter 1. 26. For now, what is important is that Aristotle draws a clear contrast between direct negative demonstrations and those by *reductio*: the former proceed from premisses that are prior in nature to the conclusion, the latter from premisses that are posterior in nature to the conclusion.[6]

In Aristotle's view, premisses that are not prior in nature to the conclusion fail to reveal the cause (αἰτία) of the *demonstrandum*, and hence are not explanatory of the conclusion (αἴτια τοῦ συμπεράσματος, 1. 2, 71ᵇ22).[7] Thus, the premisses of demonstrations by *reductio* are not explanatory of the conclusion. At the same time, Aristotle holds that, in order to have scientific knowledge of a thing, one needs to grasp the cause, or explanation, of that thing (71ᵇ9–12). Hence, demonstrations by *reductio* in which the premisses are posterior in nature to the conclusion are not capable of producing scientific knowledge of the conclusion. This does not mean that Aristotle takes these demonstrations to be invalid. There is no doubt that he regards them as valid deductive arguments in which the conclusion follows necessarily from the premisses.[8] Accordingly, he takes them to be capable of producing conviction (πίστις) of the

J. Barnes, *Aristotle's* Posterior Analytics, 2nd edn. [*Posterior Analytics 2nd edn.*] (Oxford, 1993), 95–7.

[5] J. H. von Kirchmann, *Erläuterungen zu den zweiten Analytiken des Aristoteles* [*Erläuterungen*] (Leipzig, 1878), 116.

[6] See R. Grosseteste, *Commentarius in Posteriorum Analyticorum libros* [*Commentarius*], ed. P. Rossi (Florence, 1981), 253–4.

[7] Aristotle maintains that, in order for the premisses of a demonstration to be explanatory (αἴτια) of the conclusion, they must be prior in nature to the conclusion (1. 2, 71ᵇ31; 2. 15, 98ᵇ17); see Zabarella, *Opera logica*, 660 c–d; D. Bronstein, *Aristotle on Knowledge and Learning: The* Posterior Analytics [*Knowledge and Learning*] (Oxford, 2016), 128. For the premisses to be explanatory of the conclusion is for them to reveal the cause (αἰτία) of the *demonstrandum* (1. 2, 71ᵇ30–1 and 71ᵇ9–12); cf. Bronstein, *Knowledge and Learning*, 35–8.

[8] See *Pr. An.* 2. 11, 62ᵃ11–17.

conclusion.[9] He denies, however, that they can produce scientific knowledge (ἐπιστήμη).

In *Posterior Analytics* I. 2, Aristotle defines a demonstration as a deduction that is capable of producing scientific knowledge (71ᵇ18–19). In order to have this capacity, he argues, the premisses of a demonstration must be more known in nature than the conclusion, prior in nature to the conclusion, and explanatory of the conclusion (71ᵇ19–25).[10] Insofar as demonstrations by *reductio* fail to meet these conditions, they are not genuine demonstrations as defined in chapter I. 2. Instead, they are demonstrations in a broader sense. Aristotle countenances such a broader sense, for example, in *Posterior Analytics* I. 13, when he distinguishes between deductions 'of the why' (τοῦ διότι) and those 'of the fact' (τοῦ ὅτι). Although deductions 'of the fact' are not explanatory and do not reveal the cause of the *demonstrandum*, Aristotle is willing to refer to them as 'demonstrations' (78ᵃ30, 78ᵇ14). Similarly, when he speaks of 'demonstration' by *reductio ad impossibile* in I. 26, it may be a demonstration 'of the fact' but not a genuine demonstration.[11] By contrast, direct negative demonstrations proceed from premisses that are prior in nature to the conclusion. Thus, provided that they satisfy the other conditions laid down in Aristotle's characterization of demonstration in chapter I. 2, they are genuine demonstrations in which the premisses are explanatory of the conclusion. As such, they are capable of producing scientific knowledge.

Aristotle's view that demonstrations by *reductio* are not explanatory proved influential. For example, the view is endorsed by Proclus in his commentary on the first book of Euclid's *Elements*:

ὅταν μὲν οὖν ὁ συλλογισμὸς ᾖ δι' ἀδυνάτου τοῖς γεωμέτραις, ἀγαπῶσι τὸ σύμπτωμα μόνον εὑρεῖν, ὅταν δὲ διὰ προηγουμένης ἀποδείξεως, τότε πάλιν, εἰ μὲν ἐπὶ μέρους αἱ ἀποδείξεις γίγνοιντο, οὔπω δῆλον τὸ αἴτιον, εἰ δὲ καθ' ὅλον καὶ ἐπὶ πάντων τῶν ὁμοίων, εὐθὺς καὶ τὸ διὰ τί γίγνεται καταφανές. (Proclus *In Eucl.* I 202. 19–25 Friedlein)

---

[9] This is clear from the fact that Aristotle regards demonstrations by *reductio*, just like direct negative ones, as 'convincing' (πισταί, 87ᵃ26); see Philop. *In An. Post.* 298. 28–299. 2.

[10] See Philop. *In An. Post.* 29. 1–14; Zabarella, *Opera logica*, 653 F–654 B; McKirahan, *Principles*, 31; Bronstein, *Knowledge and Learning*, 127–8.

[11] Avicenna *al-Shifā': al-Burhān* 1. 8, 90. 15 Afifi. Thanks to Riccardo Strobino for sharing parts of his translation of Avicenna's *al-Burhān*.

When geometers reason through the impossible, they are content merely to discover the property [of a given subject]. But when their reasoning proceeds through a principal demonstration, then, if the demonstrations are partial, the cause is not yet clear, whereas if it is universal and applies to all like things, the 'why' at once becomes evident.[12]

According to Proclus, demonstrations by *reductio ad impossibile* serve to establish the fact that a given subject has a certain property. They do not, however, reveal the cause, or the 'why', of that fact. Instead, the cause can be revealed by means of a 'principal' demonstration, that is, a direct one.[13] Provided that the direct demonstration exhibits the appropriate level of generality, it succeeds in revealing the cause of the *demonstrandum*. Thus, like Aristotle, Proclus holds that direct demonstrations possess an explanatory power that those by *reductio* lack. Now, Proclus was thoroughly familiar with Aristotle's logical works and wrote a commentary on the *Posterior Analytics*.[14] His commentary on the *Elements* contains numerous references to the *Posterior Analytics*, including an exposition of Aristotle's account of exactness in chapter 1. 27.[15] Thus, it seems clear that, in his remarks on demonstration by *reductio*, Proclus is following Aristotle's treatment in chapter 1. 26.

The same view of demonstration by *reductio* was held by a number of thinkers in the early modern period.[16] For example, in his 1615 essay *De mathematicarum natura dissertatio*, Giuseppe Biancani

---

[12] The translation follows the one given by T. L. Heath, *The Thirteen Books of Euclid's* Elements, vol. i: Introduction and Books I, II [*Elements*] (Cambridge, 1908), 150 n. 1, with some modifications.

[13] As Heath (*Elements*, 150 n. 1) notes, the phrase 'principal demonstration' (προηγουμένη ἀπόδειξις) at 202. 21–2 is used by Proclus to refer to direct demonstrations. *Pace* G. R. Morrow, *Proclus: A Commentary on the First Book of Euclid's* Elements, 2nd edn. [*Proclus*] (Princeton, 1992), 158–9.

[14] As a student, Proclus learned Aristotle's logical works by heart (Marinus *Vita Procli* 9. 33–6 Saffrey and Segonds). For Proclus' (lost) commentary on the *Posterior Analytics*, see C. Helmig, 'Proclus' Criticism of Aristotle's Theory of Abstraction and Concept Formation in *Analytica Posteriora* II 19', in F. A. J. de Haas, M. Leunissen, and M. Martijn (eds.), *Interpreting Aristotle's* Posterior Analytics *in Late Antiquity and Beyond* (Leiden, 2010), 27–54 at 27–9.

[15] For Proclus' exposition of *Post. An.* 1. 27, see *In Eucl. I* 59. 10–60. 1; cf. Morrow, *Proclus*, 47.

[16] See P. Mancosu, 'On the Status of Proofs by Contradiction in the Seventeenth Century', *Synthese*, 88 (1991), 15–41 at 15–36; id., *Philosophy of Mathematics and Mathematical Practice in the Seventeenth Century* [*Mathematics*] (Oxford, 1996), 24–8, 58–64, 83–4, and 100–15; id., 'On Mathematical Explanation', in E. Grosholz and H. Berger (eds.), *The Growth of Mathematical Knowledge* (Dordrecht, 2000), 103–19 at 108–16.

denied that demonstrations by *reductio* proceed 'from a cause', citing the passage from Proclus' commentary just quoted.[17] In his *Lectiones mathematicae* from the 1660s, Isaac Barrow asserts that, as for reasoning by *reductio ad impossibile*, 'Aristotle teaches, and everyone grants, that reasoning of this sort does not at all furnish knowledge that is very perspicuous and pleasing to the mind'.[18] The point is made more explicit by Arnauld and Nicole in the *Port-Royal Logic*:

> Those demonstrations which show that a thing is such, not by its principles, but by some absurdity which would follow if it were not so, are very common in Euclid. It is clear, however, that while they may convince the mind, they do not enlighten it, which ought to be the main result of science. For our mind is not satisfied unless it knows not only that a thing is, but why it is, which cannot be learned from a demonstration by reduction to the impossible.[19]

Arnauld and Nicole criticize Euclid and other geometers for giving demonstrations by *reductio* in cases when a direct demonstration is available. These geometers, they argue, 'have not sufficiently observed that, in order to have perfect knowledge of a truth, it is not enough to be convinced that it is true, if beyond this we do not penetrate into the reasons, derived from the nature of the thing itself, why it is true'.[20]

---

[17] G. Biancani, *De mathematicarum natura dissertatio* (Bologna, 1615), 10, 12, and 20.

[18] 'Certe docet philosophus, et omnes fatentur, ejusmodi ratiociniis haud ita perspicuam animoque blandientem comparari scientiam', I. Barrow, *The Mathematical Works of Isaac Barrow*, ed. W. Whewell (Cambridge, 1860), 377. Accordingly, Barrow maintains that 'this mode of demonstration, as all acknowledge, is rather obscure and ignoble' ('qui demonstrandi modus, ut omnes agnoscunt, obscurior est et ignobilior', 357).

[19] 'Ces sortes de démonstrations qui montrent qu'une chose est telle, non par ses principes, mais par quelque absurdité qui s'ensuivrait si elle était autrement, sont très ordinaires dans Euclide. Cependant il est visible qu'elles peuvent convaincre l'esprit, mais qu'elles ne l'éclairent point, ce qui doit être le principal fruit de la science. Car notre esprit n'est point satisfait, s'il ne sait non seulement que la chose est, mais pourquoi elle est; ce qui ne s'apprend point par une démonstration qui réduit à l'impossible.' A. Arnauld and P. Nicole, *La Logique ou l'art de penser* [*Logique*], ed. P. Clair and F. Girbal, 2nd edn. (Paris, 1993), 4. 9. 3, 328.

[20] '. . . il semble qu'ils n'ont pas assez pris garde qu'il ne suffit pas pour avoir une parfaite science de quelque vérité, d'être convaincu que cela est vrai, si de plus on ne pénètre par des raisons prises de la nature de la chose même pourquoi cela est vrai.' Arnauld and Nicole, *Logique*, 4. 9. 1, 326.

A similar view is expressed by Kant in the *Critique of Pure Reason*. In the course of specifying the methods of proof admissible in the discipline of pure reason, Kant excludes proof by *reductio ad impossibile*, or 'apagogic' proof, on the following grounds:

The third special rule of pure reason, if it is subjected to a discipline in regard to transcendental proofs, is that its proofs must never be apagogic but always ostensive. Direct or ostensive proof, in all kinds of cognition, is that which combines with the conviction of truth insight into the sources of the truth; apagogic proof, by contrast, can produce certainty, but cannot enable us to comprehend the truth in its connection with the grounds of its possibility. Hence the latter is more of an emergency aid than a procedure which satisfies all the aims of reason.[21]

This view of 'apagogic' proof was common among theorists working in the Kantian tradition in the nineteenth century.[22] In his *Theory of Science*, Bolzano argues that proofs by *reductio*, while they can produce conviction, cannot exhibit 'the objective ground' of the *demonstrandum*.[23] Similarly, Trendelenburg states in his *Logical Investigations* that 'indirect proof, as Aristotle has already shown, possesses less scientific value than direct proof.... Indirect proof does not provide any insight into the inner grounds of the thing.'[24] Among more recent authors, Lipton suggests that proofs

---

[21] 'Die dritte eigenthümliche Regel der reinen Vernunft, wenn sie in Ansehung transscendentaler Beweise einer Disciplin unterworfen wird, ist: daß ihre Beweise niemals apagogisch, sondern jederzeit ostensiv sein müssen. Der directe oder ostensive Beweis ist in aller Art der Erkenntniß derjenige, welcher mit der Überzeugung von der Wahrheit zugleich Einsicht in die Quellen derselben verbindet; der apagogische dagegen kann zwar Gewißheit, aber nicht Begreiflichkeit der Wahrheit in Ansehung des Zusammenhanges mit den Gründen ihrer Möglichkeit hervorbringen. Daher sind die letzteren mehr eine Nothhülfe, als ein Verfahren, welches allen Absichten der Vernunft ein Genüge thut.' I. Kant, *Kritik der reinen Vernunft*, in *Kant's gesammelte Schriften I*, Königlich Preußische Akademie der Wissenschaften (Berlin, 1911), vol. iii, A 789/B 817.

[22] For example, L. H. Jakob, *Grundriß der allgemeinen Logik und kritische Anfangsgründe der allgemeinen Metaphysik*, 4th edn. (Halle/Saale, 1800), 130; W. T. Krug, *System der theoretischen Philosophie*, 1. Theil: Denklehre oder Logik (Königsberg, 1806), 595–7; J. G. C. C. Kiesewetter, *Grundriß einer allgemeinen Logik nach Kantischen Grundsätzen*, 1. Theil: Reine allgemeine Logik, 4th edn. (Leipzig, 1824), i. 149 and ii. 493; E. Reinhold, *Die Logik oder die allgemeine Denkformenlehre* (Jena, 1827), 409–10.

[23] B. Bolzano, *Wissenschaftslehre: Versuch einer ausführlichen und größtentheils neuen Darstellung der Logik mit steter Rücksicht auf deren bisherige Bearbeiter [Wissenschaftslehre]*, 4 vols. (Sulzbach, 1837), iv. 270–1 and 278 n. 2 (§530).

[24] 'Der indirekte Beweis hat, wie schon Aristoteles zeigt, geringeren wissenschaftlichen Werth, als der direkte.... Der indirekte Beweis öffnet daher keine

by *reductio* 'work by showing necessity but without providing an explanation', and that they fail to be explanatory 'because they do not show what "makes" the theorem true'.[25] Similarly, Poston holds that '*reductio* proofs provide conclusive grounds *that* a claim is true without removing the mystery as to *why* the claim is true'.[26] Of course, this is not to say that all these theorists agree with Aristotle, or with each other, on why it is that proofs by *reductio* fail to be explanatory. Far from it. Nonetheless, they share a commitment to the same general thesis, which derives from Aristotle's discussion in *Posterior Analytics* I. 26.

While Aristotle's thesis in *Posterior Analytics* I. 26 exerted a long-lasting influence, its precise import has remained somewhat obscure. There is no consensus in the literature on why exactly demonstrations by *reductio* fail to be explanatory in Aristotle's view. This is mainly because the argument Aristotle gives in support of his thesis is compressed and raises a number of interpretive questions. In fact, Aristotle's argument in chapter I. 26 has been regarded as problematic since antiquity. Philoponus reports that 'all commentators together have attacked Aristotle on the exposition of these things, saying that he gives an incorrect account of deduction through the impossible'.[27] Accordingly, Zabarella notes that 'I have considered this passage for a very long time and have not found anything in other commentators in which I could quite

---

Einsicht in die inneren Gründe der Sache', F. A. Trendelenburg, *Logische Untersuchungen*, 2. Band, 3rd edn. (Leipzig, 1870), 440. For Trendelenburg's discussion of *Post. An.* I. 26, see id., *Elementa logices Aristoteleae*, 5th edn. (Berlin, 1862), 127–9. By contrast, Lotze argues that some indirect proofs are explanatory in that they derive the conclusion from its grounds; H. Lotze, *System der Philosophie*, I. Theil: Drei Bücher der Logik [*Logik*] (Leipzig, 1874), 263–76.

[25] P. Lipton, 'Understanding without Explanation', in H. W. de Regt, S. Leonelli, and K. Eigner (eds.), *Scientific Understanding: Philosophical Perspectives* (Pittsburgh, 2009), 43–63 at 48; id., 'Mathematical Understanding', in J. Polkinghorne (ed.), *Meaning in Mathematics* (Oxford, 2011), 49–54 at 50.

[26] T. Poston, *Reason and Explanation: A Defense of Explanatory Coherentism* (New York, 2014), 79. Against this, others argue that some proofs by *reductio* are explanatory, e.g. M. Colyvan, *An Introduction to the Philosophy of Mathematics* (Cambridge, 2012), 80; M. Lange, *Because Without Cause: Non-Causal Explanations in Science and Mathematics* (Oxford, 2017), 234 and 445 n. 9; G. Hanna, 'Reflections on Proof as Explanation', in A. J. Stylianides and G. Harel (eds.), *Advances in Mathematics Education Research on Proof and Proving* (Cham, 2018), 3–18 at 13–14.

[27] Philop. *In An. Post.* 291. 10–12: ἐν αὐτῇ τῇ ἐκθέσει τούτων ἁπαξάπαντες οἱ ἐξηγηταὶ ἐπελάβοντο τοῦ Ἀριστοτέλους ὡς κακῶς τὸν διὰ τοῦ ἀδυνάτου ἐκτιθεμένου συλλογισμόν.

acquiesce'.[28] Modern readers are in no better a position than Zabarella. Thus, Mignucci concludes that 'it is difficult to make sense of the confused argument that Aristotle advances' in *Posterior Analytics* 1. 26.[29] Smith holds that the argument is 'very unsatisfactory' and that 'we cannot actually make c. 26 into a coherent account of *per impossibile* proof'.[30] Likewise, Detel regards the argument as 'muddled' and, 'as a matter of fact, unsuccessful'.[31]

The plan of this paper is as follows. I begin by considering the preliminary part of Aristotle's argument in chapter 1. 26, in which he explains the difference between direct negative demonstrations and those by *reductio* (Section 2). Next, I turn to the core part of the argument, which appeals to the relation of priority in nature between scientific propositions (Section 3). I argue that this priority relation is determined by the order of terms in acyclic chains of immediate universal affirmations (Sections 4 and 5). Given this characterization of priority in nature, Aristotle's argument in *Posterior Analytics* 1. 26 turns out to be coherent and successful (Section 6). Finally, I discuss how Aristotle answers an objection to his argument by emphasizing the mereological structure of direct demonstrations (Section 7).

2. Direct negative demonstration versus demonstration by *reductio*

In the *Analytics*, demonstrations take the form of deductions governed by the three syllogistic figures. Aristotle focuses on deductions that consist of four kinds of categorical proposition:

AaB	A belongs to all B	(universal affirmative)
AeB	A belongs to no B	(universal negative)
AiB	A belongs to some B	(particular affirmative)
AoB	A does not belong to some B	(particular negative)

---

[28] 'locum hunc diutissime consideravi & apud alios nihil inveni, in quo plane possem acquiescere', Zabarella, *Opera logica*, 976 A.

[29] 'È difficile dare un senso alla confusa argomentazione che Aristotele avanza . . .', Mignucci, *L'argomentazione dimostrativa*, 559; similarly, id., *Aristotele*: Analitici secondi (Rome, 2007), 233.

[30] R. Smith, 'The Syllogism in *Posterior Analytics* I' ['Syllogism'], *Archiv für Geschichte der Philosophie*, 64 (1982), 113–35 at 133–4.

[31] 'verkorkst' and 'faktisch erfolglos', W. Detel, *Aristoteles:* Analytica posteriora, 2 vols. [*Analytica posteriora*] (Berlin, 1993), ii. 450.

A demonstration is positive if its conclusion is an a- or i-proposition; it is negative (or privative) if its conclusion is an e- or o-proposition.

In *Posterior Analytics* 1. 25, Aristotle has argued that direct positive demonstrations are better than direct negative ones. His aim in chapter 1. 26 is to show that direct negative demonstrations are better than those by *reductio*. He begins by explaining the difference between these two kinds of demonstration, as follows:

δεῖ δ' εἰδέναι τίς ἡ διαφορὰ αὐτῶν. ἔστω δὴ τὸ Α μηδενὶ ὑπάρχον τῷ Β, τῷ δὲ Γ τὸ Β παντί· ἀνάγκη δὴ τῷ Γ μηδενὶ ὑπάρχειν τὸ Α. οὕτω μὲν οὖν ληφθέντων δεικτικὴ ἡ στερητικὴ ἂν εἴη ἀπόδειξις ὅτι τὸ Α τῷ Γ οὐχ ὑπάρχει. ἡ δ' εἰς τὸ ἀδύνατον ὧδ' ἔχει. εἰ δέοι δεῖξαι ὅτι τὸ Α τῷ Β οὐχ ὑπάρχει, ληπτέον ὑπάρχειν, καὶ τὸ Β τῷ Γ, ὥστε συμβαίνει τὸ Α τῷ Γ ὑπάρχειν. τοῦτο δ' ἔστω γνώριμον καὶ ὁμολογούμενον ὅτι ἀδύνατον. οὐκ ἄρα οἷόν τε τὸ Α τῷ Β ὑπάρχειν. εἰ οὖν τὸ Β τῷ Γ ὁμολογεῖται ὑπάρχειν, τὸ Α τῷ Β ἀδύνατον ὑπάρχειν. (*Post. An.* 1. 26, 87^{a}2–12)

We must understand what the difference between them is [i.e. between direct negative demonstration and demonstration by *reductio ad impossibile*]. Let A belong to no B and B to all C; it follows necessarily that A belongs to no C. If these premisses are assumed, the privative demonstration that A does not belong to C will be ostensive. Demonstration leading to the impossible, on the other hand, proceeds as follows. If it is required to prove that A does not belong to B, we must assume that it does belong, and that B belongs to C; hence it follows that A belongs to C. But let it be known and agreed that this is impossible. Therefore, A cannot belong to B. If, then, it is agreed that B belongs to C, it is impossible for A to belong to B.

In the first part of this passage, Aristotle considers a negative demonstration that is direct (or 'ostensive').[32] This demonstration takes the form of the syllogistic mood Celarent in the first figure:

---

[32] In the *Prior Analytics*, the term 'ostensive' (δεικτικός) is used to designate direct deductions as opposed to deductions by *reductio ad impossibile* and other deductions 'from a hypothesis' (ἐξ ὑποθέσεως); see *Pr. An.* 1. 7, 29^{a}31–3; 1. 23, 40^{b}25–9, 41^{a}21–37; 1. 29, 45^{a}23–^{b}15; 2. 14 *passim*. In the *Posterior Analytics*, δεικτικός is sometimes used to designate positive as opposed to negative demonstrations (1. 23, 85^{a}2; 1. 25, 86^{a}32, 86^{b}30–9); see M. Frede, 'Stoic vs. Aristotelian Syllogistic', *Archiv für Geschichte der Philosophie*, 56 (1974), 1–32 at 29. At 1. 26, 87^{a}5, however, the term designates direct deductions; see Philop. *In An. Post.* 296. 3; G. R. G. Mure, *Aristotle's* Analytica posteriora [*Posteriora*], in *The Works of Aristotle Translated into English*, ed. W. D. Ross and J. A. Smith, vol. i (Oxford, 1928), ad loc.; P. Pellegrin, *Aristote:* Seconds Analytiques [*Seconds Analytiques*] (Paris, 2005), 388 n. 3; J. Tricot, *Aristote:* Seconds Analytiques [*Seconds Analytiques*] (Paris, 2012), 145; *pace* Mignucci, *L'argomentazione dimostrativa*, 560.

AeB, BaC, therefore AeC

In the second part of the passage, Aristotle goes on to consider a demonstration by *reductio*. One might have expected this demonstration to derive the same conclusion as the preceding direct demonstration, AeC.[33] Aristotle would then be able to compare the two demonstrations with respect to their explanatory value regarding this conclusion. As reasonable as this strategy may seem, it is not the one adopted by Aristotle. Instead, he chooses to consider a demonstration by *reductio* that derives the conclusion 'A does not belong to B'. Accordingly, the assumption for *reductio* is the proposition 'A belongs to B'. Since Aristotle's formulation of these propositions does not contain any quantifying expressions such as 'no' or 'all', there is some ambiguity as to their quantity. The conclusion derived in the demonstration by *reductio* may be either an e- or an o-proposition, while the assumption for *reductio* may be either an a- or an i-proposition. Now, Aristotle takes the assumption for *reductio* to be the major premiss of a deduction in the first figure, the minor premiss being BaC. Since there are no (valid) first-figure deductions with a major i-premiss, it is clear that the assumption for *reductio* is not an i- but an a-proposition.[34] Thus, the subordinate deduction initiated by the assumption for *reductio* takes the form of the first-figure mood Barbara:

AaB, BaC, therefore AaC

Aristotle takes it that, in the demonstration by *reductio*, the proposition AaC is known and agreed to be 'impossible'. This allows him

---

The label 'direct' is not used by Aristotle, but derives from later authors who referred to direct deductions by the phrases ἐξ εὐθείας or ἐπ' εὐθείας. For ἐξ εὐθείας, see Galen *De sophismatis* 593. 17 Kühn; cf. R. B. Edlow, *Galen on Language and Ambiguity* (Leiden, 1977), 79 and 104. For ἐπ' εὐθείας, see Philop. *In An. Pr.* 248. 3, 300. 27 Wallies, *In An. Post.* 273. 27–8, 290. 32–291. 22, 296. 3 Wallies; ps.-Themist. *In An. Pr.* 107. 32, 108. 6 Wallies; ps.-Ammon. *In An. Pr.* 66. 33–6 Wallies.

[33] According to Philoponus, some ancient commentators criticized Aristotle for not considering a demonstration by *reductio* that derives the same conclusion as the direct demonstration (Philop. *In An. Post.* 294. 12–14). A similar criticism is expressed by Detel, *Analytica posteriora*, ii. 456–7.

[34] J. Pacius, *Aristotelis Stagiritae Peripateticorum principis Organum*, 2nd edn. [*Organum*] (Frankfurt a.M., 1597), 488. In the *Prior Analytics*, Aristotle considers 'indeterminate' propositions, which lack any quantifying expressions (*Pr. An.* 1. 1, 24ᵃ16–22; see Ammon. *In An. Pr.* 18. 15–38 Wallies). However, since there are no (valid) first-figure deductions with an indeterminate major premiss (*Pr. An.* 1. 4, 26ᵃ30–9 and 26ᵇ21–5), the assumption for *reductio* cannot be indeterminate.

to conclude the *reductio* by inferring the conclusion of the demonstration. The conclusion thereby obtained is the contradictory opposite of the assumption for *reductio*. Given that this assumption is the universal affirmative AaB, the conclusion inferred in the demonstration by *reductio* is the particular negative AoB.

Against this, it is often thought that the conclusion of the demonstration by *reductio* is not AoB but the universal negative AeB.[35] In adopting this view, commentators are presumably guided by the idea that the demonstration by *reductio* is intended to derive the major premiss of the direct demonstration.[36] At the same time, they acknowledge that the assumption for *reductio* is the a-proposition AaB. Thus Aristotle would seem to commit the fallacy of concluding the *reductio* by inferring not the contradictory but the contrary opposite of the assumption for *reductio*. Yet, as Philoponus points out, 'it is not likely that Aristotle, the first and only one to have provided the logical methods, would commit such a grave error'.[37] In *Prior Analytics* 2. 11, Aristotle emphasizes that the conclusion of a deduction by *reductio* must be the contradictory opposite, not the contrary opposite, of the assumption for *reductio*.[38] He regards this as a constraint on *reductio* which is generally accepted (ἔνδοξον).[39]

---

[35] Philop. *In An. Post.* 294. 2–4 Wallies; Grosseteste, *Commentarius*, 253; R. Kilwardby, *Notule libri Posteriorum* [*Notule*], ed. D. Cannone (Cassino, 2003–4), 281; Albertus Magnus, *Opera omnia*, vol. ii, ed. A. Borgnet (Paris, 1890), 136; D. Soto, *In libros Posteriorum Aristotelis sive de demonstratione absolutissima commentaria* (Venice, 1574), 367–8; Zabarella, *Opera logica*, 973 A–B; Mignucci, *L'argomentazione dimostrativa*, 560–2; G. Striker, 'Review of J. Barnes, *Aristotle's Posterior Analytics*' ['Review of Barnes'], *Zeitschrift für philosophische Forschung*, 31 (1977), 316–20 at 317 n. 1; Smith, 'Syllogism', 132; H. Seidl, *Aristoteles:* Zweite Analytiken, 2nd edn. [*Zweite Analytiken*] (Würzburg, 1987), 265–6; Barnes, *Posterior Analytics 2nd edn.*, 188; Detel, *Analytica posteriora*, ii. 451; Tricot, *Seconds Analytiques*, 145–6 nn. 2–3.

[36] Thus, Crivelli takes there to be an 'intuition that the conclusion of the demonstration through the impossible is the same as one of the premisses of the negative ostensive demonstration', P. Crivelli, 'Aristotle on Syllogisms from a Hypothesis' ['Hypothesis'], in A. Longo, *Argument from Hypothesis in Ancient Philosophy* (Naples, 2011), 95–184 at 165.

[37] Philop. *In An. Post.* 295. 21–3: οὐ γὰρ ἦν εἰκὸς τὸν Ἀριστοτέλη πρῶτον καὶ μόνον τὰς μεθόδους τὰς λογικὰς παραδεδωκότα τηλικοῦτον ἁμαρτεῖν ἁμάρτημα. Transl. by O. Goldin and M. Martijn, *Philoponus:* On Aristotle, *Posterior Analytics* 1. 19–34 (London, 2012), 98. A similar point is made by Smith, 'Syllogism', 121.

[38] *Pr. An.* 2. 11, 62ᵃ11–19; see also 2. 12, 62ᵃ28–32.

[39] *Pr. An.* 2. 11, 62ᵃ12–13 and 62ᵃ15–19; see R. Smith, *Aristotle:* Prior Analytics [*Prior Analytics*] (Indianapolis, 1989), 200.

Some commentators try to alleviate this problem by arguing that in the *Posterior Analytics* Aristotle adopts a framework in which a- and e-propositions are treated as exhaustive alternatives, so that the falsehood of an a-proposition entails the truth of the correspond-ing e-proposition.[40] This proposal, however, is problematic. Not only does Aristotle not give any indication of adopting such a framework in the *Posterior Analytics*; doing so would commit him to the implausible view that the e-proposition *No animal is human* is true, given that the a-proposition *Every animal is human* is false.[41] Zabarella suggests that in *Posterior Analytics* 1. 26 Aristotle treats a- and e-propositions as exhaustive alternatives because he ignores particular propositions and deals exclusively with universal prop-ositions.[42] Again, this is dubious. While it is true that Aristotle tends to focus on universal propositions in the *Posterior Analytics*, he countenances particular propositions as well. For example, he considers third-figure deductions in *Posterior Analytics* 1. 14, not-ing that they do not derive a universal but a particular conclusion (79^a27–8). Moreover, he discusses demonstrations of the form Bocardo and Baroco in chapters 1. 21 and 1. 23.[43] Given this, why

[40] Zabarella, *Opera logica*, 973 A–B; Smith, 'Syllogism', 118–21 and 131–3; Barnes, *Posterior Analytics 2nd edn.*, 146 and 188.

[41] Barnes claims that, in addition to chapter 1. 26, there are three more passages in the *Posterior Analytics* in which Aristotle takes the falsehood of an a-proposition to entail the truth of the corresponding e-proposition: 1. 11, 77^a10–15; 1. 13, 78^b13–28; 1. 15, 79^a36–$^b4$ (Barnes, *Posterior Analytics 2nd edn.*, 146, 158, and 163). These pas-sages, however, are far from conclusive since all of them can be interpreted without attributing to Aristotle this problematic assumption.

[42] Zabarella, *Opera logica*, 973 A–B. More generally, Solmsen suggests that par-ticular propositions are absent from Aristotle's theory of demonstration in the *Posterior Analytics*; F. Solmsen, *Die Entwicklung der Aristotelischen Logik und Rhetorik* [*Entwicklung*] (Berlin, 1929), 143. Similarly, R. Smith, 'The Relationship of Aristotle's Two *Analytics*' ['Relationship'], *Classical Quarterly*, NS, 32 (1982), 327–35 at 327; Barnes, *Posterior Analytics 2nd edn.*, 114, 158, and 188.

[43] *Post. An.* 1. 21, 82^b21–8; 1. 23, 85^a7–12. Some commentators excise the refer-ence to Baroco in 1. 23 by deleting the phrase ἢ μὴ παντί at 85^a9; e.g. W. D. Ross, *Aristotle's* Prior *and* Posterior Analytics: *A Revised Text with Introduction and Commentary* [*Analytics*] (Oxford, 1949), 587; H. Tredennick, *Aristotle:* Posterior Analytics [*Posterior Analytics*] (Cambridge, MA, 1960), 134; Barnes, *Posterior Analytics 2nd edn.*, 183; Detel, *Analytica posteriora*, ii. 411. In addition, Barnes (*Posterior Analytics 2nd edn.*, 173) excises the reference to Bocardo at 1. 21, 82^b21–8. These excisions, however, are not convincing and it is preferable to retain the text of the manuscripts in both passages; see A. D. Crager, *Meta-Logic in Aristotle's Epi-stemology* (diss. Princeton, 2015), 104–20; M. Malink, 'Aristotle on Principles as Elements' ['Elements'], *Oxford Studies in Ancient Philosophy*, 53 (2017), 163–213 at 184–5 nn. 63–4.

should particular propositions be excluded from consideration in 1. 26? In any case, even if particular propositions are less prominent in the *Posterior Analytics* than universal ones, this does not justify inferring the truth of an e-proposition from the falsehood of the corresponding a-proposition.

It is preferable, then, to take the conclusion of the demonstration by *reductio* to be the particular negative AoB rather than the universal negative AeB. After all, Aristotle never asserts that the demonstration by *reductio* is intended to derive the universal negative premiss of the direct demonstration. It may at first glance seem natural to suppose that it is intended to derive this premiss; but, as we have already seen, we cannot presume that Aristotle's argument in 1. 26 conforms to our antecedent expectations.

Having specified the two demonstrations, Aristotle points out a difference that obtains between them concerning the epistemic status of their negative premiss:

οἱ μὲν οὖν ὅροι ὁμοίως τάττονται, διαφέρει δὲ τὸ ὁποτέρα ἂν ᾖ γνωριμωτέρα ἡ πρότασις ἡ στερητική, πότερον ὅτι τὸ *A* τῷ *B* οὐχ ὑπάρχει ἢ ὅτι τὸ *A* τῷ *Γ*. ὅταν μὲν οὖν ᾖ τὸ συμπέρασμα γνωριμώτερον ὅτι οὐκ ἔστιν, ἡ εἰς τὸ ἀδύνατον γίνεται ἀπόδειξις, ὅταν δ' ἡ ἐν τῷ συλλογισμῷ, ἡ ἀποδεικτική. (*Post. An.* 1. 26, 87ᵃ12–17)

Thus the terms are similarly arranged [in both demonstrations], but there is a difference as to which of the two privative propositions is more known, the one that A does not belong to B or the one that A does not belong to C. When the conclusion that it does not hold is more known, the demonstration leading to the impossible comes about; and when the proposition in the deduction is more known, the demonstrative proof comes about.

Aristotle first notes that the two demonstrations employ terms that are 'similarly arranged'. Thus, he takes the two demonstrations to be related in that they are based on the same underlying structure of terms. In particular, they are based on a structure in which BaC is true and in which negative propositions concerning AB and AC are true.[44] There is, however, a difference as to 'which of the two' (ὁποτέρα) negative propositions is more known. One of the two

---

[44] Kirchmann, *Erläuterungen*, 114–15; Ross, *Analytics*, 595; Pellegrin, *Seconds Analytiques*, 388 n. 5. By contrast, Zabarella (*Opera logica*, 976 A–977 B) denies that the two demonstrations discussed at 87ᵃ3–17 are based on the same underlying structure of terms, arguing instead that they are unrelated and that the schematic letters 'A', 'B', and 'C' are meant to denote different terms in them. This interpretation, however, is not plausible since it conflicts with Aristotle's statement that 'the terms are similarly arranged' in the two demonstrations.

negative propositions in question is identified by Aristotle as 'the conclusion that it does not hold'.[45] This is the conclusion of the direct demonstration, AeC. The other negative proposition is identified as the one 'in the deduction'. This is the major premiss of the direct demonstration, AeB.

Aristotle maintains that in some cases AeB is more known than AeC, while in other cases the latter proposition is more known than the former. Since the relation of being more known in nature is not variable in this way, he presumably has in mind the varying degree to which each of these propositions may be known to the demonstrator.[46] Thus, given the truth of AeB, BaC, and AeC, Aristotle is describing the conditions under which a demonstrator will choose to employ either the direct demonstration or the one by *reductio*. If AeB is more known to the demonstrator than AeC, they will choose the direct demonstration, establishing the latter proposition on the basis of the former. If, on the other hand, AeC is more known to the demonstrator than AeB, they will choose the demonstration by *reductio*. In this case, the demonstrator cannot derive the universal proposition AeB, but at least is able to establish its particular counterpart, AoB.

---

[45] 87ᵃ15: τὸ συμπέρασμα . . . ὅτι οὐκ ἔστιν. In this phrase, τὸ συμπέρασμα refers to the conclusion of the direct demonstration, AeC, while the qualification ὅτι οὐκ ἔστιν indicates that this conclusion is a negative proposition; see Philop. *In An. Post.* 297. 1–13; Tredennick, *Posterior Analytics*, 151; Mignucci, *L'argomentazione dimostrativa*, 563; Barnes, *Posterior Analytics 2nd edn.*, 41; Detel, *Analytica posteriora*, i. 53; Pellegrin, *Seconds Analytiques*, 209 and 388 n. 6; Tricot, *Seconds Analytiques*, 146. By contrast, some commentators take τὸ συμπέρασμα at 87ᵃ15 to refer to the conclusion AaC of the subordinate deduction, rendering 87ᵃ14–15 as follows: 'when it is more known that the conclusion AaC is not (i.e. is false)'; Pacius, *Organum*, 489; Zabarella, *Opera logica*, 978 D; H. Maier, *Die Syllogistik des Aristoteles*, ii/1: Formenlehre und Technik des Syllogismus (Tübingen, 1900), 232–3 n. 1; Mure, *Posteriora*, ad loc.; Ross, *Analytics*, 594; Crivelli, 'Hypothesis', 165. However, this reading fits less well with the context than the former reading. All three occurrences of συμπέρασμα at 87ᵃ18–20 refer to the conclusion of the direct demonstration, AeC. Moreover, since συλλογισμός at 87ᵃ16 refers to the direct demonstration, it is natural to take συμπέρασμα at 87ᵃ15 to refer to the conclusion of this demonstration rather than to the conclusion of some other deduction. Finally, the two readings differ in the interpretation of οὐκ ἔστιν at 87ᵃ15. On the former reading, this phrase serves to demarcate negative from affirmative propositions. On the latter reading, the phrase is used to indicate that a proposition does not hold (or is false), whether this proposition is affirmative or negative (see e.g. *Pr. An.* 2. 2, 53ᵇ12–13; 2. 4, 57ᵇ1–2). While the former use of οὐκ ἔστιν appears at *Post. An.* 1. 26, 87ᵃ26 (see n. 3 above), the latter use does not appear elsewhere in chapter 1. 26.

[46] Kilwardby, *Notule*, 282; Kirchmann, *Erläuterungen*, 114–16; Ross, *Analytics*, 595; Crivelli, 'Hypothesis', 165–7.

In the demonstration by *reductio*, the proposition AaC is 'known and agreed' to be impossible ($87^a9–10$). This is because its contrary opposite, AeC, is known and accepted by the demonstrator and their interlocutors.[47] Thus, the demonstrator accepts both AeC and BaC, and uses these two propositions to establish AoB by *reductio*, as follows:

1.	AeC	(premiss)
2.	BaC	(premiss)
3.	AaB	(assumption for *reductio*)
4.	BaC	(iterated from 2)
5.	AaC	(from 3, 4, by Barbara)
6.	AoB	(*reductio*: 1, 3–5)

In this derivation, the first two lines contain the premisses accepted by the demonstrator, and line 6 contains the conclusion of the demonstration, AoB.[48] The inference from the two premisses to the conclusion takes the form of the third-figure mood Felapton:

AeC, BaC, therefore AoB

A similar proof by *reductio* in which the premisses and the conclusion constitute an instance of Felapton is given by Aristotle in *Posterior Analytics* 1. 16. Having posited the minor premiss BaC ($80^a28–9$), Aristotle reasons as follows:

πάλιν ὃ τῷ Γ μηδενὶ ὑπάρχει, οὐδὲ τῷ B παντὶ ὑπάρξει· εἰ γὰρ τῷ B, καὶ τῷ Γ· ἀλλ' οὐχ ὑπῆρχεν.[49] (*Post. An.* 1. 16, $80^b2–4$)

That which belongs to no C will not belong to all B either; for if it belongs to B, it also belongs to C, but it was assumed that it does not belong.

In this passage, Aristotle makes it clear that the conclusion of the proof by *reductio* is the o-proposition that A does not belong to all B (οὐδὲ τῷ B παντὶ ὑπάρξει). If I am correct, he presents a proof of

---

[47] Seidl, *Zweite Analytiken*, 265–6.

[48] The application of *reductio* in the last line relies on the fact that the conclusion of the subordinate deduction, AaC, is the contrary opposite of an accepted premiss, AeC. For similar proofs by *reductio* in which the conclusion of the subordinate deduction is the contrary rather than the contradictory opposite of an accepted premiss, see *Pr. An.* 1. 2, $25^a17–19$; 1. 7, $29^a36–9$; cf. P. Thom, *The Syllogism* [*Syllogism*] (Munich, 1981), 39–41; Crivelli, 'Hypothesis', 156–8.

[49] For continuity, I use the schematic letters 'A', 'B', 'Γ' in place of Aristotle's 'Γ', 'A', 'B' at $80^a28–^b4$.

the same form, giving rise to an instance of Felapton, in his discussion of demonstration by *reductio* in chapter 1. 26.

3. Aristotle's argument from priority in nature

So far, Aristotle has compared the two demonstrations with respect to what is more known to the demonstrator. He now goes on, in what is the core argument of the chapter, to compare them with respect to what is prior in nature:

φύσει δὲ προτέρα ἢ ὅτι τὸ Α τῷ Β ἢ ὅτι τὸ Α τῷ Γ. πρότερα γάρ ἐστι τοῦ συμπεράσματος ἐξ ὧν τὸ συμπέρασμα. ἔστι δὲ τὸ μὲν Α τῷ Γ μὴ ὑπάρχειν συμπέρασμα, τὸ δὲ Α τῷ Β ἐξ οὗ τὸ συμπέρασμα. (*Post. An.* 1. 26, 87ᵃ17–20)

By nature, however, the proposition that A does not belong to B is prior to the proposition that A does not belong to C. For the things from which a conclusion derives are prior to the conclusion; and that A does not belong to C is a conclusion, whereas that A does not belong to B is that from which the conclusion derives.

Aristotle claims that the proposition AeB is prior in nature to AeC. He takes this claim to help establish the main thesis of the chapter, that direct negative demonstration is better than that by *reductio* because it proceeds from premisses that are prior in nature to the conclusion (87ᵃ25–8).[50] In the direct negative demonstration discussed by Aristotle, the premiss AeB is prior in nature to the conclusion, AeC. In the demonstration by *reductio*, by contrast, the premiss AeC is not prior in nature to the conclusion, AoB. Instead, Aristotle seems to regard AeC as posterior in nature to AoB. At least, this is suggested by his remark that demonstration by *reductio* proceeds from premisses that are posterior in nature (87ᵃ27). Thus, there is a clear sense in which the direct negative demonstration considered by Aristotle in 1. 26 is better than the demonstration by *reductio*.

This argument from priority in nature raises a number of questions. One of them, pointed out by Zabarella, concerns Aristotle's discussion of *reductio ad impossibile* in *Prior Analytics* 2. 14.[51] In this chapter, Aristotle argues that 'whatever is proved through the

---

[50] See Philop. *In An. Post.* 297. 14–22 Wallies.
[51] Zabarella, *Opera logica*, 975 F–976 A.

impossible can also be concluded ostensively'.[52] He shows that every conclusion deducible from given premisses by *reductio ad impossibile* can also be deduced from these premisses without *reductio* by means of a direct deduction.[53] For example, consider the following derivation by *reductio* (63^a14-16):

1.	CaA	(premiss)
2.	CoB	(premiss)
3.	AaB	(assumption for *reductio*)
4.	CaA	(iterated from 1)
5.	CaB	(from 3, 4, by Barbara)
6.	AoB	(*reductio*: 2, 3–5)

Aristotle points out that, in this derivation, the conclusion in line 6 can be deduced directly from the premisses in lines 1 and 2 without the use of *reductio* by applying the second-figure mood Baroco ($2.\ 14,\ 63^a7-16$).[54] Thus, the derivation can be turned into a direct deduction simply by omitting the steps in lines 3–5. In the same way, the conclusion of the demonstration by *reductio* discussed by Aristotle in *Posterior Analytics* 1. 26 can be deduced from the two premisses directly without *reductio* by applying the third-figure mood Felapton. In the resulting direct negative demonstration, the premiss AeC fails to be prior in nature to the conclusion, AoB. Hence, there is a direct negative demonstration in which the premisses are not prior in nature to the conclusion.

Conversely, Aristotle asserts in *Prior Analytics* 2. 14 that whenever a conclusion is deducible from given premisses by means of a direct deduction, it can also be deduced from them by *reductio ad impossibile* (63^b14-18).[55] In particular, the conclusion of Aristotle's direct demonstration in Celarent can be deduced from the same premisses by *reductio*.[56] The result is a demonstration by *reductio* in which the premisses, AeB and BaC, are prior in nature to the conclusion, AeC. Thus, given the interchangeability of direct deduction and *reductio ad impossibile* stated by Aristotle in *Prior Analytics* 2. 14, it is not clear how he can maintain that direct negative

---

[52] *Pr. An.* 2. 14, 62^b38-40: ἅπαν δὲ τὸ δεικτικῶς περαινόμενον καὶ διὰ τοῦ ἀδυνάτου δειχθήσεται, καὶ τὸ διὰ τοῦ ἀδυνάτου δεικτικῶς.
[53] *Pr. An.* 2. 14, 62^b38-63^b13; see also 1. 29, 45^a23-^b8.
[54] See Ross, *Analytics*, 455.
[55] See also *Pr. An.* 1. 29, 45^a26-7.
[56] See *Pr. An.* 2. 14, 63^a32-5; cf. Ross, *Analytics*, 456.

demonstrations differ from those by *reductio* in that they proceed
from premisses that are prior in nature to the conclusion.
In view of this problem, Gisela Striker argues that Aristotle's
argument in *Posterior Analytics* 1. 26 does not turn on the priority
relations that obtain, or fail to obtain, between the premisses and
the conclusion in the two kinds of demonstration. Instead, she
suggests, the argument turns on the way the conclusion is inferred
from the premisses in each case:

As Aristotle himself shows in *An. Pr.* B 14, one can form a 'genuine' premiss pair for the *demonstrandum* from the true premiss of the syllogism [i.e.
the true premiss of the direct deduction initiated by the assumption for
reductio] and the negation of the impossible conclusion. However, this further syllogism is not regarded by Aristotle as a part of the *reductio*, but as a
different proof of the same *demonstrandum*—in the *reductio* the proposition
to be proved is inferred 'from a hypothesis'.... Aristotle's argument for the
superiority of 'categorical' proofs presumably relies on the fact that *reductio*
proofs are not purely syllogistic.[57] (Striker, 'Review of Barnes', 318)

Striker is drawing attention to the fact that Aristotle regards arguments by *reductio ad impossibile* as deductions 'from a hypothesis'
(ἐξ ὑποθέσεως, *Pr. An.* 1. 23, 40ᵇ23–9). According to Aristotle, every
argument by *reductio* contains a part that can be analysed as a direct
deduction in the three syllogistic figures. This part of the argument appears within the subordinate deduction initiated by the
assumption for *reductio*.[58] In Aristotle's view, no such syllogistic
analysis is available for the final step of the argument, in which the
assumption for *reductio* is discharged and the desired conclusion
inferred. Aristotle describes this latter inference as being 'from a
hypothesis' and acknowledges that it cannot be justified within his

---

[57] 'Man kann ja, wie Aristoteles selbst in *An. Pr.* B 14 zeigt, aus der wahren
Prämisse des Syllogismus und der Negation der unmöglichen Conclusio ein "ech-
tes" Prämissenpaar für das Demonstrandum bilden. Dieser zweite Syllogismus
wird aber von Aristoteles nicht als ein Teil der *reductio* angesehen, sondern als ein
anderer Beweis für dasselbe Demonstrandum—in der *reductio* erschließt man den
zu beweisenden Satz "aus der Hypothese".... Aristoteles' Argument für die
Überlegenheit der "kategorischen" Beweise stützt sich vermutlich darauf, daß die
reductio-Beweise nicht rein syllogistisch sind.'

[58] See *Pr. An.* 1. 23, 41ᵃ32–4; 1. 44, 50ᵃ29–32; cf. Alex. Aphr. *In An. Pr.* 259. 9–11,
261. 24–8, 262. 3–4 Wallies; ps.-Ammon. *In An. Pr.* 66. 39–67. 4 Wallies; J. Lear,
Aristotle and Logical Theory [*Logical Theory*] (Cambridge, 1980), 34; Crivelli,
'Hypothesis', 125.

theory of syllogistic moods.[59] According to Striker, this is what underlies Aristotle's argument in *Posterior Analytics* 1. 26.[60]

It may well be that Aristotle accepted the considerations put forward by Striker, taking them to show that direct demonstrations are superior to those by *reductio*. Nonetheless, there is little evidence to suggest that Aristotle in fact appeals to these considerations in *Posterior Analytics* 1. 26. In the core argument of the chapter (87^a17–20 and 25–8), Aristotle does not address the way in which the conclusion is derived from the premisses in a demonstration by *reductio*, nor does he allude to the fact that this derivation is 'from a hypothesis'. Instead, he focuses on the relations of priority in nature that obtain between the premisses and the conclusion of the respective demonstrations. This is in tension with the interpretation proposed by Striker. For relations of priority in nature obtain, or fail to obtain, between the premisses and the conclusion of a demonstration regardless of how the latter is derived from the former. If the same conclusion can be derived from the same premisses either directly or by *reductio*, the choice of derivation does not affect the priority relations obtaining between them. Consequently, Barnes rejects Striker's interpretation of 1. 26, noting that 'Aristotle's argument does not turn on the nature of *reductio* as such'.[61]

Moreover, Striker's interpretation does not sit well with the elaborate exposition of the two kinds of demonstration given by Aristotle in the first half of the chapter (87^a2–17). For, if Aristotle had in mind the point attributed to him by Striker, he could have provided simpler examples of the two kinds of demonstration than he does. He could have chosen examples in which the same conclusion is derived from the same premisses—or he could have omitted the examples altogether, since Striker's point can easily be stated in a general manner without appealing to any particular examples.

Finally, Striker's interpretation makes it difficult to see why the argument in 1. 26 appeals to priority in nature at all. For, on this interpretation, the argument turns on general features of *reductio* described by Aristotle in the *Prior Analytics*, and it is not clear how

---

[59] *Pr. An.* 1. 23, 41^a34; 1. 44, 50^a29–32.

[60] Similar suggestions have been made by Themist. *In An. Post.* 37. 3–7 Wallies; Avicenna *al-Shifā': al-Burhān* 1. 8, 90. 15–17; 3. 7, 244. 14–245. 14 Afifi; Zabarella, *Opera logica*, 976 E–977 D; and Crivelli, 'Hypothesis', 170 n. 157.

[61] Barnes, *Posterior Analytics 2nd edn.*, 188.

these features bear on considerations concerning priority in nature.[62] No doubt Aristotle's discussion in the *Prior Analytics* implies that demonstrations by *reductio* are inferior to direct ones in a number of respects. For example, it implies that demonstrations by *reductio*, unlike direct ones, involve false propositions.[63] Moreover, when Aristotle argues in *Prior Analytics* 2. 14 that every deduction by *reductio* corresponds to a direct deduction deriving the same conclusion from the same premisses, the direct deduction is significantly shorter than the one by *reductio*. Thus, direct demonstration is better than that by *reductio* for reasons of economy, since, as Aristotle notes in *Posterior Analytics* 1. 25, 'other things being equal, a demonstration through fewer items is better'.[64] Crucially, however, Aristotle does not put forward such straightforward arguments in 1. 26. Instead, he appeals to considerations of priority in nature, which do not follow from his general characterization of *reductio* in the *Prior Analytics*.

Thus, we are left with Zabarella's problem of how to reconcile Aristotle's argument in 1. 26 with his treatment of *reductio* in *Prior Analytics* 2. 14. To address this problem, it is helpful to take a closer look at the deductive frameworks employed in these two chapters. In *Prior Analytics* 2. 14, Aristotle takes for granted the fourteen syllogistic moods in the three figures established in *Prior Analytics* 1. 4–6:

First figure: Barbara, Celarent, Darii, Ferio
Second figure: Cesare, Camestres, Festino, Baroco
Third figure: Darapti, Disamis, Datisi, Felapton, Ferison, Bocardo

In *Prior Analytics* 2. 14, Aristotle takes each of these moods to license a direct deduction from the two premisses to the conclusion. With respect to this system, he argues in 2. 14 that any conclusion deducible from given premisses by *reductio ad impossibile*

---

[62] Thus, when Crivelli ('Hypothesis', 159–73) interprets 1. 26 along the lines suggested by Striker, he neglects to explain Aristotle's appeal to priority in nature in the chapter.

[63] The fact that proofs by *reductio* involve false propositions has been taken to show that they are inferior to direct ones, e.g. by G. Galilei, *Tractatus de praecognitionibus et praecognitis and Tractatio de demonstratione*, ed. W. F. Edwards (Padua, 1988), 97; and L. Löwenheim, 'On Making Indirect Proofs Direct', *Scripta Mathematica*, 12 (1946), 125–39 at 126.

[64] *Post. An.* 1. 25, 86^{b}5–7: καὶ ἡ διὰ τῶν ἐλαττόνων ἄρα ἀπόδειξις βελτίων τῶν ἄλλων τῶν αὐτῶν ὑπαρχόντων.

can also be deduced from these premisses by means of a direct deduction using the fourteen moods.[65] Thus, the rule of *reductio ad impossibile* is redundant in Aristotle's full syllogistic system in which all fourteen moods are taken to license direct deductions.

This does not mean, however, that the rule of *reductio* is redundant in Aristotle's theory of the assertoric syllogism as a whole. In *Prior Analytics* 1. 1–7, Aristotle presents two deductive systems in which the rule of *reductio* plays an indispensable role. The first of these systems, expounded in *Prior Analytics* 1. 2 and 1. 4–6, includes among its principles the four first-figure moods which Aristotle regards as 'perfect' (*Pr. An.* 1. 4). In addition, the system includes three conversion rules (*Pr. An.* 1. 2), and a rule of *reductio ad impossibile*:[66]

1. Perfect moods:	AaB, BaC, therefore AaC	(Barbara)
	AeB, BaC, therefore AeC	(Celarent)
	AaB, BiC, therefore AiC	(Darii)
	AeB, BiC, therefore AoC	(Ferio)
2. Conversion:	AeB, therefore BeA	(e-conversion)
	AiB, therefore BiA	(i-conversion)
	AaB, therefore BiA	(a-conversion)
3. Rule of *reductio ad impossibile*		

In *Prior Analytics* 1. 5–6, Aristotle employs these principles to establish the validity of syllogistic moods in the second and third figures. In most cases, he does so by means of direct deductions employing the perfect first-figure moods and conversion rules. There are, however, two valid moods that cannot be established in this way: Baroco and Bocardo. Aristotle establishes these moods by *reductio ad impossibile*, using the perfect mood Barbara.[67] Thus, the rule of *reductio* is not redundant in this deductive system, since Baroco and Bocardo cannot be established directly but only by *reductio*.[68]

---

[65] See e.g. Ross, *Analytics*, 454–6; N. Strobach, *Aristoteles: Analytica priora, Buch II* (Berlin, 2015), 348.

[66] See e.g. J. Corcoran, 'Completeness of an Ancient Logic', *Journal of Symbolic Logic*, 37 (1972), 696–702 at 697–8; id., 'Aristotle's Natural Deduction System', in id. (ed.), *Ancient Logic and its Modern Interpretations* (Dordrecht, 1974), 85–131 at 109–10; Smith, *Prior Analytics*, xix–xxi.

[67] *Pr. An.* 1. 5, 27^{a}36–27^{b}1; 1. 6, 28^{b}15–20.

[68] See Alex. Aphr. *In An. Pr.* 83. 12–25 Wallies; J. Łukasiewicz, *Aristotle's Syllogistic from the Standpoint of Modern Formal Logic*, 2nd edn. (Oxford, 1957),

In *Prior Analytics* 1. 7, Aristotle goes on to present a second deductive system, in which the rule of *reductio* plays an even more prominent role. In this system, Aristotle no longer includes the particular first-figure moods Darii and Ferio in the list of principles. Instead, he establishes these moods by *reductio ad impossibile*, using the first-figure mood Celarent.[69] In addition, Aristotle derives the rules of i- and a-conversion by *reductio* from e-conversion.[70] Thus, the deductive system presented by Aristotle in *Prior Analytics* 1. 7 can be taken to rest on the following principles:

1. Perfect moods: AaB, BaC, therefore AaC (Barbara)
   AeB, BaC, therefore AeC (Celarent)
2. Conversion: AeB, therefore BeA (e-conversion)
3. Rule of *reductio ad impossibile*

Although this deductive system contains fewer principles than the previous one, it has the same deductive power. In particular, the system is strong enough to derive all fourteen moods of Aristotle's assertoric syllogistic. There are, however, only four moods that can be established by means of a direct deduction in this system, namely, the four universal moods Barbara, Celarent, Cesare, and Camestres. The remaining ten moods, including Felapton, cannot be established directly but only by *reductio*. Thus, in this system, a significant portion of the assertoric syllogistic turns out to depend on the rule of *reductio ad impossibile*. At the same time, Aristotle takes this system to be significant because it allows him to reduce all syllogistic moods to the universal first-figure moods Barbara and Celarent

54. In the case of Bocardo, Aristotle mentions an alternative proof using the method of ecthesis instead of *reductio* (*Pr. An.* 1. 6, 28ᵇ20–1). He does not mention a proof by ecthesis for Baroco and it is not clear whether such a proof is available. For example, the formulation of the rule of ecthesis given by Parsons allows for a proof of Bocardo but not of Baroco; T. Parsons, *Articulating Medieval Logic* (Oxford, 2014), 36–7; similarly, T. Ebert and U. Nortmann, *Aristoteles: Analytica priora, Buch I [Analytica priora]* (Berlin, 2007), 333–7. Without appealing to ecthesis, the only way for Aristotle to establish Baroco and Bocardo in his deductive system is by *reductio*.

[69] *Pr. An.* 1. 7, 29ᵇ1–19. See Alex. Aphr. *In An. Pr.* 113. 5–114. 30 Wallies; H. Weidemann, 'Aristotle on the Reducibility of All Valid Syllogistic Moods to the Two Universal Moods of the First Figure (*APr* A7, 29ᵇ1–25)', *History and Philosophy of Logic*, 25 (2004), 73–8; J. Barnes, *Truth, etc.: Six Lectures on Ancient Logic* (Oxford, 2007), 364–6.

[70] *Pr. An.* 1. 2, 25ᵃ17–22. For Aristotle's proof by *reductio* of a-conversion, see n. 48 above.

(1. 7, 29^{b}1–2 and 29^{b}24–5). Thus, when Aristotle summarizes the results of *Prior Analytics* 1. 1–7 in 1. 23, he makes special mention of the system introduced in 1. 7, emphasizing that he has shown how 'every deduction is completed through the first figure and is reduced to the universal deductions in this figure'.[71]

All told, then, we must distinguish three different syllogistic frameworks employed by Aristotle in the *Prior Analytics*. While of equal deductive power, these frameworks differ from each other in the extent to which they rely on *reductio ad impossibile*. In the full system of the assertoric syllogistic, *reductio* is redundant and is not needed to establish any moods. In the deductive system of chapters 1. 4–6, *reductio* is not redundant but is needed to establish Baroco and Bocardo. Finally, in the streamlined system of chapter 1. 7, *reductio* is needed to establish most syllogistic moods, with the exception only of the four universal moods.

In the *Posterior Analytics*, Aristotle does not specify the syllogistic framework that is meant to underlie his theory of demonstration. It is clear that, in chapters 1. 14–26, he relies on elements of the syllogistic theory developed in the *Prior Analytics*, but he does not describe them in any detail. For the most part, it is not necessary for Aristotle to do so in the *Posterior Analytics*. His account of demonstration is to a large extent compatible with different syllogistic frameworks, and entering into a discussion of these frameworks would be extraneous to his main aims in the *Posterior Analytics*. In chapter 1. 26, however, it is important for Aristotle to demarcate the moods that rely on *reductio ad impossibile* from those that do not. This demarcation depends on exactly which syllogistic framework is adopted.

As we have seen, the full system of the assertoric syllogistic, in which all fourteen moods are taken to license direct deductions, does not fit well with Aristotle's argument in *Posterior Analytics* 1. 26. The same is true for the deductive system presented in *Prior Analytics* 1. 4–6. For, in this system, the mood Felapton does not rely on *reductio*, but can be established by means of a direct deduction (*Pr. An.* 1. 6, 28^{a}26–9). Hence, in this system, Aristotle's

---

[71] *Pr. An.* 1. 23, 41^{b}3–5: ἅπας τε συλλογισμὸς ἐπιτελεῖται διὰ τοῦ πρώτου σχήματος καὶ ἀνάγεται εἰς τοὺς ἐν τούτῳ καθόλου συλλογισμούς. Similarly, 1. 23, 40^{b}17–19. See G. Striker, 'Perfection and Reduction in Aristotle's *Prior Analytics*', in M. Frede and G. Striker (eds.), *Rationality in Greek Thought* (Oxford, 1996), 203–19 at 205 n. 5; ead., *Aristotle's Prior Analytics, Book 1* [*Prior Analytics*] (Oxford, 2009), 108 and 170–1; Ebert and Nortmann, *Analytica priora*, 740 and 747.

demonstration by *reductio* in *Posterior Analytics* 1. 26 can be replaced by a direct deduction deriving the same conclusion from the same premises, thus giving rise to Zabarella's problem. By contrast, this problem does not arise in the streamlined system from *Prior Analytics* 1. 7. For, in this system, Felapton cannot be established by means of a direct deduction but only by *reductio*. Hence, among the three systems, the one from chapter 1. 7 fits best with Aristotle's argument in *Posterior Analytics* 1. 26.

More generally, Aristotle's argument in 1. 26 fits with any variant of the system from *Prior Analytics* 1. 7 that yields the same demarcation between moods that rely on *reductio* and those that do not. For example, Aristotle might be taken to employ a variant of this system in which the second-figure moods Cesare and Camestres are not reduced by e-conversion to Celarent, but are posited as additional principles along with Barbara and Celarent. This would be in accordance with the fact that, in the first book of the *Posterior Analytics*, Aristotle does not mention any conversion rules and does not undertake to reduce second- and third-figure moods to those in the first figure.[72] In any case, all that is important for our purposes is that in *Posterior Analytics* 1. 26, Aristotle employs a deductive system in which the only moods that can be established by means of a direct deduction are the purely universal moods, with all other moods relying on *reductio*.[73]

Given such a deductive system, the only direct negative demonstrations in the three figures are those of the form Celarent, Cesare, and Camestres. Aristotle does not explicitly state in 1. 26 that direct affirmative demonstrations proceed from premises that are prior in nature to the conclusion, but it seems clear that he is committed to this view.[74] In the present deductive system, the only

---

[72] See Smith, 'Syllogism', 115–17 and 121–2; id., 'Relationship', 331–3.

[73] *Pace* Lear (*Logical Theory*, 53), who maintains that in *Posterior Analytics* 1. 26, every demonstration by *reductio* can be replaced by a direct demonstration deriving the same conclusion from the same premises. Lear suggests that, 'when Aristotle comes to criticize proof *per impossibile*, in *Posterior Analytics* A26, all he can say is that the premises which are prior in nature—those from which the conclusion can be proved directly—are not sufficiently familiar to us' (Lear, *Logical Theory*, 53). This, however, is not correct. Aristotle's point at 1. 26, 87ᵃ17–20 and 87ᵃ25–30, is not that the premises of demonstrations by *reductio* fail to be familiar to us, but that they fail to be prior in nature to the conclusion.

[74] Having argued that direct negative demonstrations are better than those by *reductio* in that they proceed from premises which are prior in nature to the conclusion (87ᵃ25–8), Aristotle goes on to infer: 'consequently, it is also clear that positive demonstration, which is better than privative demonstration, is also better than that

direct affirmative demonstrations in the three figures are those of the form Barbara.

Thus, Aristotle's thesis in 1. 26 amounts to the claim that all demonstrations of the form Barbara, Celarent, Cesare, and Camestres proceed from premises that are prior in nature to the conclusion, whereas this is not the case in general for demonstrations that employ the rule of *reductio ad impossibile*. In order to be able to verify this claim, we need an account of what it is for one proposition to be prior in nature to another. In what follows, I provide such an account for both affirmative and negative propositions.

4. Priority in nature for a-propositions

As we have seen, when Aristotle speaks of 'demonstration' by *reductio ad impossibile* in 1. 26, he uses the term 'demonstration' in a broader sense than the one defined in *Posterior Analytics* 1. 2. Otherwise his claim in 1. 26 that demonstrations by *reductio* do not proceed from premises that are prior in nature to the conclusion would be contradictory. Conversely, his claim that direct demonstrations do proceed from such premises would be trivially true, simply in virtue of the definition of demonstration. What, then, is the intended reference of the term 'demonstration' in these claims?

Minimally, a demonstration is a deduction (συλλογισμός). Yet it is unlikely that Aristotle uses 'demonstration' in chapter 1. 26 to refer indiscriminately to all deductions. For he is clear that not every direct deduction has premises that are prior in nature to the conclusion. For example, as he points out in *Posterior Analytics* 1. 6, a true conclusion may be deduced from false premises, which are surely not prior in nature to the true conclusion.[75] Perhaps Aristotle uses 'demonstration' to denote all deductions in which the premisses are true? Again, such a use of the term would seem too broad. For, in Aristotle's view, demonstration is closely tied to scientific knowledge (ἐπιστήμη), and there are many true propositions that

---

which leads to the impossible' (ὥστε καὶ ἡ ταύτης βελτίων ἡ κατηγορικὴ δῆλον ὅτι καὶ τῆς εἰς τὸ ἀδύνατόν ἐστι βελτίων, 87ᵃ28–30). This would be odd if Aristotle did not think that direct affirmative demonstrations are better than those by *reductio* in the same respect as direct negative ones.

[75] *Post. An.* 1. 6, 75ᵃ3–4; see also *Pr. An.* 2. 2–4.

fall outside the purview of scientific knowledge. In particular, as he explains in *Posterior Analytics* 1. 30, truths about contingent chance events do not admit of demonstration and hence cannot be objects of scientific knowledge.[76] One would, therefore, not expect Aristotle in 1. 26 to refer to deductions that involve such truths as 'demonstrations'.

Instead, Aristotle may be taken to use 'demonstration' in 1. 26 to denote those deductions in which the premisses are scientific propositions. Scientific propositions are all indemonstrable premisses of a given science and the theorems derivable from them by means of demonstrations in the strict sense defined in *Posterior Analytics* 1. 2. Whenever the premisses of a deduction are such scientific propositions, the deduction counts as a 'demonstration' in the broader sense of the term employed in 1. 26. Thus, given a class of indemonstrable premisses, the strict demonstrations defined in 1. 2 determine the class of scientific propositions of the science under consideration. A 'demonstration' in the broader sense is then taken to be any deduction in which all premisses are scientific propositions, whether or not it satisfies the definition of demonstration given in 1. 2. Although Aristotle does not explicitly introduce this sense of 'demonstration', it is a natural way for him to use the term. It guarantees that 'demonstrations' are restricted to truths that fall under the purview of demonstrative science, while at the same time being broad enough to allow for a coherent reading of Aristotle's thesis in *Posterior Analytics* 1. 26.

Given this sense of 'demonstration', Aristotle's thesis in 1. 26 amounts to the following claim: in every deduction of the form Barbara, Celarent, Cesare, and Camestres in which the premisses are scientific propositions, the premisses are prior in nature to the conclusion; by contrast, there are deductions by *reductio* in which the premisses are scientific propositions but not prior in nature to the conclusion. While this is a substantive claim, it is not incoherent but stands a chance of being verified. As we will see, the claim can in fact be verified provided there is a suitable characterization of priority in nature.

In *Posterior Analytics* 1. 2–3, Aristotle emphasizes that the premisses of genuine demonstrations are prior in nature to the

---

[76] *Post. An.* 1. 30, 87^{b}19–27. See also *Pr. An.* 1. 13, 32^{b}18–22.

conclusion.[77] He does not, in these chapters, provide an account of what it is for one proposition to be prior in nature to another. Aristotle does, however, offer some guidance on this question in *Posterior Analytics* 1. 15–25. There he considers chains of terms connected by universal affirmations, such as the following:

ἔστω δὴ τὸ Γ τοιοῦτον, ὃ αὐτὸ μὲν μηκέτι ὑπάρχει ἄλλῳ, τούτῳ δὲ τὸ Β πρώτῳ, καὶ οὐκ ἔστιν ἄλλο μεταξύ. καὶ πάλιν τὸ Ε τῷ Ζ ὡσαύτως, καὶ τοῦτο τῷ Β. (*Post. An.* 1. 19, 81ᵇ30–2)

Let C be such that it itself does not further belong to any other thing, and that B belongs to it primitively, with nothing else between them. Again, let E belong to F in the same way, and F to B.

If universal affirmation is indicated by arrows pointing from the predicate to the subject term, the chain of universal affirmations described in this passage can be represented as follows:[78]

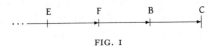

FIG. I

In this diagram, each of the terms B, F, E, … belongs to its successor 'primitively' (πρώτῳ), that is, in such a way that there is no other term between them. Thus, each of these universal affirmations is immediate (ἄμεσος).[79]

Aristotle maintains that if a scientific proposition is immediate, there is no proposition that is prior in nature to it.[80] As such, immediate propositions are indemonstrable principles of a science.[81] For example, given that the a-proposition BaC is immediate, no proposition is prior in nature to it and there is no middle term by means of which it can be demonstrated. The indemonstrable a-propositions

---

[77] *Post. An.* 1. 2, 71ᵇ19–72ᵃ5; 1. 3, 72ᵇ25–32; cf. n. 10 above.

[78] It is clear from the context (81ᵇ10–18) that the verb ὑπάρχειν at 81ᵇ30–2 is meant to indicate universal affirmations.

[79] Aristotle holds that A belongs to B primitively (πρώτῳ or πρώτως) just in case the a-proposition AaB is immediate (ἄμεσος); cf. 1. 16, 79ᵇ25, with 1. 17, 81ᵃ36; see also Philop. *In An. Post.* 194. 6–8, 186. 5–8, 186. 30–187. 6 Wallies. Accordingly, it is widely agreed that the primitive universal affirmations described by Aristotle at 1. 19, 81ᵇ30–2 are immediate; Philop. *In An. Post.* 220. 18–20; Pacius, *Organum*, 464; Zabarella, *Opera logica*, 895 F; O. F. Owen, *The* Organon, *or Logical Treatises, of Aristotle*, vol. i [*Organon*] (London, 1889), 287; Mure, *Posteriora*, ad 81ᵇ30; Mignucci, *L'argomentazione dimostrativa*, 404.

[80] *Post. An.* 1. 2, 72ᵃ7–8; cf. R. Smith, 'Immediate Propositions and Aristotle's Proof Theory' ['Immediate Propositions'], *Ancient Philosophy*, 6 (1986), 47–68 at 48–55.

[81] *Post. An.* 1. 2, 72ᵃ7–8; 1. 3, 72ᵇ18–22.

of a science determine chains of terms connected by immediate universal affirmations. Aristotle refers to these chains as 'series' (συστοιχίαι).[82] In what follows, I refer to them as 'a-paths'. In Aristotle's example, there is an a-path from E to C and an a-path from F to B, the latter being a proper part of the former.

In Aristotle's syllogistic theory, the only way to deduce a universal affirmative conclusion AaB is by means of a-premisses forming a chain of universal affirmations leading from A to B.[83] If these premisses are immediate scientific propositions, they constitute an a-path from A to B. Aristotle holds that any such a-path gives rise to a demonstration of AaB.[84] For example, if there is an a-path from A to B through a single middle term C, there is a demonstration of AaB from the immediate premisses AaC and CaB. Hence each of these premisses is prior in nature to AaB.

More generally, if there is an a-path from A to B, every a-proposition that corresponds to a proper part of this a-path is prior in nature to AaB. Thus, for example, in *Posterior Analytics* I. 25, Aristotle considers a structure of a-paths in which the proposition AaD is prior in nature to AaE:

ἔστω ἡ μὲν διὰ μέσων ἀπόδειξις τῶν Β Γ Δ ὅτι τὸ Α τῷ Ε ὑπάρχει, ἡ δὲ διὰ τῶν Ζ Η ὅτι τὸ Α τῷ Ε. ὁμοίως δὴ ἔχει τὸ ὅτι τὸ Α τῷ Δ ὑπάρχει καὶ τὸ Α τῷ Ε. τὸ δ' ὅτι τὸ Α τῷ Δ πρότερον καὶ γνωριμώτερον ἢ ὅτι τὸ Α τῷ Ε· διὰ γὰρ τούτου ἐκεῖνο ἀποδείκνυται. (*Post. An.* I. 25, 86ᵃ39–86ᵇ5)

Let one demonstration show that A belongs to E through the middle terms B, C, and D, and let the other show that A belongs to E through F and G. Thus the proposition that A belongs to D and the one that A belongs to

---

[82] *Post. An.* I. 15, 79ᵇ7–11; I. 17, 80ᵇ27, 81ᵃ21; I. 29, 87ᵇ5–14; see Smith, 'Syllogism', 122–6. See also Philop. *In An. Post.* 189. 11–13; Zabarella, *Opera logica*, 862 D; Mignucci, *L'argomentazione dimostrativa*, 341; Barnes, *Posterior Analytics* 2nd edn., 163.

[83] *Pr. An.* I. 26, 42ᵇ32–3; see T. J. Smiley, 'What is a Syllogism?', *Journal of Philosophical Logic*, 2 (1973), 136–54 at 139–45; id., 'Aristotle's Completeness Proof', *Ancient Philosophy*, 14 (1994), 25–38 at 27; Thom, *Syllogism*, 181–3.

[84] See Smith, 'Syllogism', 126; McKirahan, *Principles*, 210–12 and 217. With respect to a-paths of immediate universal affirmations, Aristotle holds that 'when A belongs to B, then, if there is some middle term, it is possible to prove [i.e. demonstrate] that A belongs to B' (ὅταν τὸ Α τῷ Β ὑπάρχῃ, εἰ μὲν ἔστι τι μέσον, ἔστι δεῖξαι ὅτι τὸ Α τῷ Β ὑπάρχει, *Post. An.* I. 23, 84ᵇ19–20). Similarly, he writes: '…terms so related to a subject that there are other terms prior to them predicated of the subject are demonstrable [of the subject]' (…ὧν πρότερα ἄττα κατηγορεῖται, ἔστι τούτων ἀπόδειξις, I. 22, 83ᵇ33–4; transl. Mure, *Posteriora*, modified).

E are on a par. But that A belongs to D is prior to and more known than that A belongs to E; for the latter is demonstrated through the former.

In this passage, the terms A and E are connected by two distinct a-paths of immediate universal affirmations:[85]

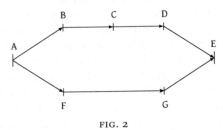

FIG. 2

The propositions AaD and AaE are 'on a par' in that both of them are demonstrable through the same number of middle terms (the former through B and C, and the latter through F and G).[86] At the same time, Aristotle asserts that AaD is prior in nature to, and more known in nature than, AaE.[87] Specifically, AaD is prior in nature to AaE in virtue of the fact that the a-path from A to D is a proper part of the a-path from A to E. If there are multiple a-paths from A to D, each of them is a proper part of some a-path from A to E. For the same reason, the proposition CaE is prior in nature to AaE, given that any a-path from C to E is a proper part of some a-path from A to E.[88]

In this way, a-paths provide a characterization of priority in nature between scientific a-propositions: for any arbitrary A, B, C, and D, the a-proposition AaB is prior in nature to CaD just in case

---

[85] See Zabarella, *Opera logica*, 964 E–F.

[86] Philop. *In An. Post.* 287. 22–5 Wallies; Mignucci, *L'argomentazione dimostrativa*, 548; Barnes, *Posterior Analytics 2nd edn.*, 187.

[87] When Aristotle writes πρότερον καὶ γνωριμώτερον at 86ᵇ3–4, he does not mean priority and being more known 'to us' but 'in nature'; see M. F. Burnyeat, 'Aristotle on Understanding Knowledge' ['Understanding Knowledge'], in E. Berti (ed.), *Aristotle on Science: The* Posterior Analytics, *Proceedings of the Eighth Symposium Aristotelicum* (Padua, 1981), 97–139 at 127–8.

[88] However, this does not mean that the proposition CaE appears in a demonstration of AaE. In *Posterior Analytics* 2. 18, Aristotle argues that when AaE is demonstrated through B, C, and D, the final step of the demonstration should employ the least universal middle term, D, inferring AaE from AaD and DaE (99ᵇ9–14; see Detel, *Analytica posteriora*, ii. 823 and 827; Tricot, *Seconds Analytiques*, 237 n. 4). Likewise, AaD should be inferred from AaC and CaD. On this account, the proposition CaE, though prior in nature to AaE, does not appear in the demonstration of AaE.

(i) there is an a-path from A to B, and (ii) any a-path from A to B is a proper part of some a-path from C to D.

Now, as Aristotle points out in *Posterior Analytics* 1. 3, priority is an asymmetric relation: if one proposition is prior in nature to another, the latter is not prior in nature to the former.[89] Does the proposed characterization of priority in nature satisfy this requirement of asymmetry? As it turns out, it fails to do so if there are cycles of immediate universal affirmations such as:

AaB, BaC, CaA

If each of these propositions is immediate, AaB is prior in nature to AaC since every a-path from A to B is a proper part of some a-path from A to C. At the same time, AaC is prior in nature to AaB, since every a-path from A to C can be extended to B. For example, the shortest a-path from A to C is a proper part of the following a-path from A to B:

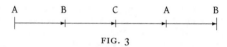

FIG. 3

Thus, the proposed characterization of priority in nature would fail to be asymmetric if there were cyclic a-paths. There is, however, evidence that Aristotle intends to exclude cyclic a-paths in the first book of the *Posterior Analytics*. In particular, he seems to exclude them in his discussion of reciprocal predication, or 'counterpredication', in chapter 1. 22. Based on the theory of predication developed in 1. 22, Aristotle argues against the possibility of counterpredication as follows:

ἔτι εἰ μή ἐστι τοῦτο τουδὶ ποιότης κἀκεῖνο τούτου, μηδὲ ποιότητος ποιότης, ἀδύνατον ἀντικατηγορεῖσθαι ἀλλήλων οὕτως, ἀλλ' ἀληθὲς μὲν ἐνδέχεται εἰπεῖν, ἀντικατηγορῆσαι δ' ἀληθῶς οὐκ ἐνδέχεται. ἢ γάρ τοι ὡς οὐσία κατηγορηθήσεται, οἷον ἢ γένος ὂν ἢ διαφορὰ τοῦ κατηγορουμένου.... ὡς μὲν δὴ γένη ἀλλήλων οὐκ ἀντικατηγορηθήσεται· ἔσται γὰρ αὐτὸ ὅπερ αὐτό τι. οὐδὲ μὴν τοῦ ποιοῦ ἢ τῶν ἄλλων οὐδέν, ἂν μὴ κατὰ συμβεβηκὸς κατηγορηθῇ· πάντα γὰρ ταῦτα συμβέβηκε καὶ κατὰ τῶν οὐσιῶν κατηγορεῖται. (*Post. An.* 1. 22, 83ᵃ36–ᵇ12)

If this is not a quality of that and that of this (a quality of a quality), it is impossible for one thing to be counterpredicated of another in this way. It is possible to make a true statement, but it is not possible to counterpredicate

[89] *Post. An.* 1. 3, 72ᵇ27–8; see also 2. 15, 98ᵇ16–21.

truly. For one alternative is that it is predicated as substance, i.e. being either
the genus or the differentia of what is predicated.... Surely they will not be
counterpredicated of one another as genera, for then something would be
just what is some of itself. Nor will anything be counterpredicated⁹⁰ of a
quality or of the other kinds of thing—unless it is predicated accidentally;
for all these things are accidents, and they are predicated of substances.

While this passage presents many difficulties, it seems clear that its
main focus is on counterpredication (ἀντικατηγορεῖσθαι).⁹¹ By counterpredication, Aristotle means reciprocal predication—that is,
cases in which A is predicated of B and B is predicated of A.⁹² He
considers various putative cases of counterpredication and argues
that they are not admissible in the theory of predication developed
in chapter 1. 22. He begins by noting that A and B cannot be counterpredicated of one another in such a way that one is a quality of
the other and vice versa. Thus, for example, if *pale* and *musical* are

⁹⁰ It is natural to supply ἀντικατηγορηθήσεται from 83ᵇ9 as the main verb of this
sentence; Waitz, *Organon*, ii. 357; Mure, *Posteriora*, ad loc.; Tredennick, *Posterior
Analytics*, 123; J. Barnes, *Aristotle's* Posterior Analytics, 1st edn. [*Posterior Analytics
1st edn.*] (Oxford, 1975), 35; id. (ed.), *The Complete Works of Aristotle: The Revised
Oxford Translation* [*Complete Works*], 2 vols. (Princeton, 1984), i 136; Seidl, *Zweite
Analytiken*, 107; Tricot, *Seconds Analytiques*, 120. On the other hand, some authors
take κατηγορηθήσεται to be the main verb of the sentence; Mignucci, *L'argomentazione
dimostrativa*, 468–9; Barnes, *Posterior Analytics 2nd edn.*, 32; Pellegrin, *Seconds
Analytiques*, 177 and 381 n. 14. Moreover, I take τοῦ ποιοῦ ἢ τῶν ἄλλων to be the genitive object of the verb of the sentence; Tredennick, *Posterior Analytics*, 123; Seidl,
Zweite Analytiken, 107; Barnes, *Posterior Analytics 2nd edn.*, 32; Pellegrin, *Seconds
Analytiques*, 177 (*pace* Barnes, *Posterior Analytics 1st edn.*, 35; id., *Complete Works*,
i 136).
⁹¹ Waitz, *Organon*, ii. 356–7; Mure, *Posteriora*, ad loc.; Ross, *Analytics*, 578–9;
D. W. Hamlyn, 'Aristotle on Predication' ['Predication'], *Phronesis*, 6 (1961),
110–26 at 119–20; Barnes, *Posterior Analytics 1st edn.*, 169–70; J. Lear, 'Aristotle's
Compactness Proof' ['Compactness'], *Journal of Philosophy*, 76 (1979), 198–215 at
214; id., *Logical Theory*, 31; Tricot, *Seconds Analytiques*, 118–20. Pace Mignucci,
L'argomentazione dimostrativa, 460–9; Barnes, *Posterior Analytics 2nd edn.*, 177–8.
⁹² Ross, *Analytics*, 578; Hamlyn, 'Predication', 119–20; Lear, 'Compactness',
214; id., *Logical Theory*, 31; Barnes, *Posterior Analytics 2nd edn.*, 178. This notion
of counterpredication differs from the one employed by Aristotle in *Topics* 1. 5,
according to which A is counterpredicated of B just in case A is true of every individual of which B is true and vice versa (*Top.* 1. 5, 102ᵃ18–30); see J. Brunschwig,
Aristote, Topiques, Livres I–IV (Paris, 1967), 122. Thus, in the *Topics*, two terms
are counterpredicated of one another if they are coextensive in the sense that they
are true of the same class of individuals; see J. Barnes, 'Property in Aristotle's
Topics', *Archiv für Geschichte der Philosophie*, 52 (1970), 136–55 at 137; O. Primavesi,
*Die Aristotelische Topik: Ein Interpretationsmodell und seine Erprobung am Beispiel
von Topik B* (München, 1996), 92. If A and B are coextensive, it does not follow
that A is predicated of B or vice versa (see n. 103 below).

accidents in the category of quality, they are not counterpredicated of one another. Aristotle admits that if Callias is both pale and musical, there is a sense in which it is true to say that the pale thing is musical and the musical thing is pale (1. 22, 83ᵃ7–12). He insists, however, that this is not an instance of true counterpredication.

In the last sentence of the passage, Aristotle strengthens this claim, asserting that nothing is counterpredicated of an accident that is in the category of quality or in any other non-substance category. Thus, if such an accident is predicated of a subject, the subject is not predicated of it. For example, if *large* is predicated of *log*, the latter is not predicated of the former. Again, Aristotle admits that there is a sense in which it is true to say that the large thing is a log (1. 22, 83ᵃ1–3). In his view, however, such predications are merely accidental.[93] They are not proper predications and are not admissible in demonstrations (83ᵃ14–21). For the same reason, the accident *musical* is not predicated of the accident *pale*. While it may be true to say that the pale thing is musical, Aristotle is clear that this is not a genuine predication and is not admissible in demonstrations (83ᵃ10–21). More generally, he holds that no accident is the subject of a genuine predication (83ᵇ21–2). Hence, if either A or B is an accident, they are not predicated of one another.

In the middle part of the passage, Aristotle discusses the possibility of counterpredication between items that are not accidents but are predicated 'as substance'. He states that two items cannot be counterpredicated of one another in such a way that one is a genus of the other and vice versa. It is not entirely clear whether he intends to exclude counterpredications between a definiendum and its definiens, such as *man* and *biped animal*. Philoponus argues that Aristotle intends to exclude them on the grounds that, in these cases, the counterpredicated items are the same whereas the predicate and the subject of genuine predications must be distinct.[94] If this is correct, Aristotle can be taken to exclude any counterpredications between items that are not accidents.

Accordingly, it is widely agreed that, in the passage just quoted, Aristotle excludes the possibility of any counterpredication.[95] This

[93] *Post. An.* 1. 22, 83ᵃ1–18; see also 1. 19, 81ᵇ23–9; *Pr. An.* 1. 27, 43ᵃ33–6.
[94] Philop. *In An. Post.* 246. 14–24 Wallies.
[95] Waitz, *Organon*, ii. 356; Mure, *Posteriora*, ad loc.; Ross, *Analytics*, 578–9; Hamlyn, 'Predication', 120; Barnes, *Posterior Analytics 1st edn.*, 169–70; Lear, 'Compactness', 214; id., *Logical Theory*, 31; Tricot, *Seconds Analytiques*, 119–20.

is confirmed by his statement in chapter 1. 22 that all demonstrations in Barbara are based on chains of immediate, or primitive, predications. In all demonstrations by Barbara, Aristotle writes, 'it is necessary for there to be an item of which something is predicated primitively, and something else of this; and this must come to a stop, and there must be an item which is no longer predicated of anything prior and of which nothing else prior is predicated'.[96] At the same time, he denies that there are any such chains of primitive predications among counterpredicated items:

οὐ γὰρ ἔστιν ἐν τοῖς ἀντικατηγορουμένοις οὗ πρῶτου κατηγορεῖται ἢ τελευταίου· πάντα γὰρ πρὸς πάντα ταύτῃ γε ὁμοίως ἔχει. (*Post. An.* 1. 19, 82ᵃ15–17)

Among counterpredicated items, there is none of which any is predicated primitively or of which it is predicated last; for in this respect at least every such item is related to every other in the same way.

In a class of counterpredicated items, every item is predicated of every other item. Thus, as far as predication is concerned, 'every such item is related to every other in the same way'. Aristotle infers from this that there is no basis for distinguishing immediate (or primitive) from mediate predications, and hence that there are no immediate predications among such items.[97] By the same reasoning, if an item is counterpredicated of something, it is not predicated immediately of anything and nothing is predicated immediately of it. Thus, in maintaining that all demonstrations in Barbara are based on chains of immediate predications, Aristotle in effect excludes counterpredication from the domain of demonstration.[98]

In *Posterior Analytics* 1. 19–22, Aristotle uses his account of predication to characterize the relation of universal affirmation in scientific propositions. In doing so, he assumes that if AaB is a scientific proposition, then A is predicated of B.[99] Hence, by excluding

---

[96] *Post. An.* 1. 22, 83ᵇ28–31: ἀνάγκη ἄρα εἶναί τι οὗ πρῶτόν τι κατηγορεῖται καὶ τούτου ἄλλο, καὶ τοῦτο ἵστασθαι καὶ εἶναί τι ὃ οὐκέτι οὔτε κατ᾽ ἄλλου προτέρου οὔτε κατ᾽ ἐκείνου ἄλλο πρότερον κατηγορεῖται. For πρῶτον at 83ᵇ29 indicating immediate predication, see Pacius, *Organum*, 474; Owen, *Organon*, 294; Barnes, *Posterior Analytics* 2nd edn., 179.

[97] Waitz, *Organon*, ii. 350.

[98] Accordingly, Smith takes 82ᵃ15–17 to show that 'propositions involving convertible [i.e. counterpredicated] terms are somehow disqualified because of the lack of any priority' (Smith, 'Immediate Propositions', 62).

[99] *Post. An.* 1. 22, 83ᵃ18–21; see Zabarella, *Opera logica*, 909 F–910 A; Mignucci, *L'argomentazione dimostrativa*, 454–5. See also Lear, 'Compactness', 201–14; id.,

counterpredication, Aristotle excludes a-paths of the form AaB, BaA. More generally, he excludes any cyclic a-paths of the form A_1aA_2, A_2aA_3, ..., A_naA_1.[100] For, if there were such a-paths, both A_1aA_2 and A_2aA_1 would be scientific propositions, and hence A_1 and A_2 would be counterpredicated of one another.

Of course, Aristotle recognizes that sciences deal with terms that are coextensive in the sense that they are true of the same class of individuals.[101] For example, in the science of geometry, *triangle* is coextensive with *2R* (i.e. *having interior angles equal to two right angles*). Nevertheless, Aristotle denies in *Posterior Analytics* 1. 22 that coextensive terms such as *triangle* and *2R* are predicated of one another. As Philoponus notes in his commentary on 1. 22, Aristotle accepts that *2R* is predicated of *triangle* but denies that the latter is predicated of the former.[102] Consequently, while there is a demonstrable scientific a-proposition in which *2R* is the predicate and *triangle* the subject term, the converse a-proposition is not a scientific proposition. Thus, in Aristotle's theory of demonstration, the fact that A and B are coextensive does not imply that the proposition AaB is a demonstrable theorem or an indemonstrable principle of the science under consideration. This allows Aristotle to countenance coextensive terms while maintaining that there are no cyclic a-paths in a demonstrative science.[103]

Logical Theory, 18–31; R. Smith, 'Predication and Deduction in Aristotle: Aspirations to Completeness', *Topoi*, 10 (1991), 43–52 at 48–51.

[100] See Ross, *Analytics*, 578–9; Lear, 'Compactness', 214; id., *Logical Theory*, 31; Tricot, *Seconds Analytiques*, 118–19 n. 3. Smith argues that Aristotle's rejection of cyclic a-paths plays an important role in his argument for the finitude of demonstration in *Posterior Analytics* 1. 22; R. Smith, 'Aristotle as Proof Theorist', *Philosophia Naturalis*, 27 (1984), 590–97 at 593–4. See also Smith, 'Immediate Propositions', 62; id., 'Aristotle's Regress Argument' ['Regress'], in I. Angelelli and M. Cerezo (eds.), *Studies on the History of Logic: Proceedings of the III. Symposium on the History of Logic* (Berlin, 1996), 21–32 at 27.

[101] He refers to them as terms that 'follow one another' (ἀλλήλοις ἕπεσθαι, *Post. An.* 1. 3, 73ᵃ7) or terms that 'convert' (ἀντιστρέφειν, 1. 13, 78ᵃ27; 1. 19, 82ᵃ15; 2. 4, 91ᵃ16; 2. 16, 98ᵇ36).

[102] Philop. *In An. Post.* 246. 24–30 Wallies.

[103] In *Posterior Analytics* 1. 13, Aristotle states that the terms *near* and *non-twinkling* are counterpredicated of one another (ἀντικατηγορεῖσθαι, 78ᵃ28). Smith ('Immediate Propositions', 62) argues that this conflicts with Aristotle's rejection of counterpredication in *Posterior Analytics* 1. 19–22. However, the apparent conflict can be resolved. In chapter 1. 13, the term ἀντικατηγορεῖσθαι presumably does not express that two terms are predicated of one another in the sense of predication described in chapters 1. 19–22, for this sense of predication has not yet been introduced in 1. 13, but is only defined at 1. 19, 81ᵇ23–9 and 1. 22, 83ᵃ1–21. Instead,

Given that a-paths are acyclic, the proposed characterization of priority in nature satisfies Aristotle's requirement of asymmetry. To see this, recall that an a-proposition AaB is prior in nature to CaD just in case (i) there is an a-path from A to B, and (ii) any a-path from A to B is a proper part of some a-path from C to D. Hence, if AaB were prior in nature to CaD and vice versa, some a-path from A to B would be a proper part of some a-path from A to B, violating the condition of acyclicity. Thus, we have a well-defined, asymmetric relation of priority in nature between scientific a-propositions.

A-paths can naturally be represented by acyclic directed graphs such as the following:

FIG. 4

In this diagram, the demonstrable theorem AaB corresponds to an a-path containing the middle terms $C_1, \ldots, C_4$. Aristotle employs such diagrammatic representations in *Posterior Analytics* 1. 23, when he refers to immediate a-propositions as indivisible constituents of the theorems demonstrated from them ($84^b19–31$).[104] He states that every demonstrable a-proposition corresponds to an a-path containing one or more middle terms ($84^b31–85^a4$). Indemonstrable a-premisses, on the other hand, correspond to immediate a-paths. Thus, any scientific proposition AaB, demonstrable or otherwise, is underwritten by an a-path from A to B.

This allows us to verify part of Aristotle's claim in *Posterior Analytics* 1. 26 that the premises of direct demonstrations are prior in nature to the conclusion. In particular, the claim can be verified for direct demonstrations of the form Barbara: whenever the premises of a deduction in Barbara are scientific propositions, they are prior in nature to the conclusion. To see this, consider an instance of Barbara inferring AaC from AaB and BaC. Given that both premises are scientific propositions, there is an a-path from A to B and an a-path

---

ἀντικατηγορεῖσθαι in 1. 13 can be understood in the weaker sense introduced in the *Topics*, in which it does not express that two terms are predicated of one another but only that they are coextensive (see n. 92). On this reading, Aristotle's acceptance of 'counterpredicated' terms in 1. 13 is consistent with his rejection of counterpredication in 1. 19–22.

[104] See Malink, 'Elements', 174–86.

from B to C. These two a-paths can be combined to form an a-path from A to C of which they are proper parts. More generally, any two a-paths from A to B and from B to C compose an a-path from A to C of which they are proper parts. Hence, both AaB and BaC are prior in nature to AaC.

Thus, Aristotle's claim holds for direct demonstrations of the form Barbara. To establish the claim for all direct demonstrations, it remains to verify it for those of the form Celarent, Cesare, and Camestres. This can be done in an analogous manner, by extending the present account to include not only a-paths but also e-paths.

5. Priority in nature for e-, i-, and o-propositions

In addition to immediate a-propositions, Aristotle countenances immediate e-propositions in the *Posterior Analytics*.[105] If an e-proposition is immediate, it is an indemonstrable principle of a science. It is atomic in the sense that there is no middle term through which it can be demonstrated:

ὥσπερ δὲ ὑπάρχειν τὸ A τῷ B ἐνεδέχετο ἀτόμως, οὕτω καὶ μὴ ὑπάρχειν ἐγχωρεῖ. λέγω δὲ τὸ ἀτόμως ὑπάρχειν ἢ μὴ ὑπάρχειν τὸ μὴ εἶναι αὐτῶν μέσον· οὕτω γὰρ οὐκέτι ἔσται κατ' ἄλλο τὸ ὑπάρχειν ἢ μὴ ὑπάρχειν. (*Post. An.* 1. 15, 79ᵃ33–6)

Just as it is possible for A to belong to B atomically, so it is also possible for it atomically not to belong. By atomically belonging or not belonging I mean that there is no middle term between them; for, in this case, they no longer belong or do not belong by virtue of something else.

If AeB is immediate, B is 'first' (πρῶτον) among the terms to which A does not belong (1. 19, 82ᵃ10–11). Accordingly, if both AeC and CaB are immediate, C is prior (πρότερον) to B among the terms to which A does not belong.[106] This is illustrated by the following diagram, in which the immediate e-proposition AeC is indicated by a zigzag line:

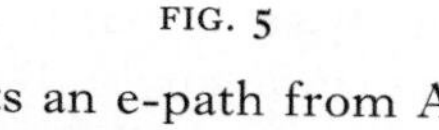

FIG. 5

This diagram represents an e-path from A to B, composed of an atomic e-path from A to C and an atomic a-path from C to B.

---

[105] *Post. An.* 1. 15, 79ᵃ33–ᵇ22; 1. 23, 84ᵇ24–31.
[106] *Post. An.* 1. 19, 82ᵃ9–13; 1. 21, 82ᵇ5–11.

Similarly, if AeB is demonstrated by Camestres from immediate premisses CaA and CeB, the e-path from A to B is composed of an atomic a-path from C to A and an atomic e-path from C to B:

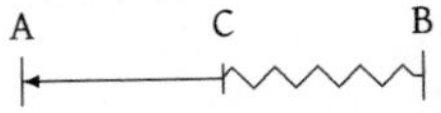

A   C   B

FIG. 6

In the *Posterior Analytics*, Aristotle considers complex negative demonstrations in which an e-conclusion is demonstrated by successive applications of Celarent, Cesare, Camestres, and Barbara.[107] In these demonstrations, the conclusion corresponds to compound e-paths such as the following:[108]

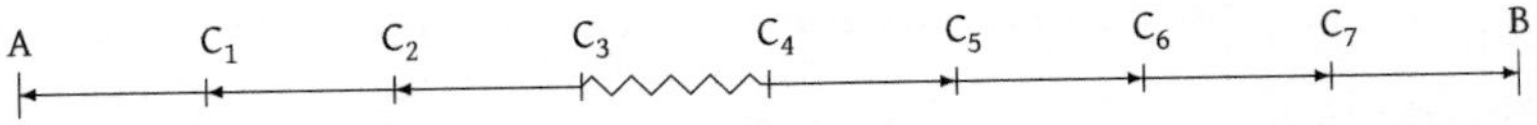

A C_1 C_2 C_3 C_4 C_5 C_6 C_7 B

FIG. 7

In this diagram, the e-path from A to B is composed of an atomic e-path from C_3 to C_4 and two compound a-paths (one from C_3 to A and the other from C_4 to B).

Thus, for Aristotle, any given science determines a demonstrative structure which consists of a set of terms, T, equipped with the two relations of immediate universal affirmation and negation. In what follows, I will indicate these relations by '$\rightarrow$' and '$\sim$', respectively. Thus, '$A \rightarrow B$' means that AaB is an immediate premiss of the science under consideration, and '$A \sim B$' means that AeB is such a premiss. Both $\rightarrow$ and $\sim$ are binary relations on T. As such, they can be represented as subsets of the Cartesian product $T \times T$. Moreover, we write '$\rightarrow^+$' to denote the transitive closure of $\rightarrow$ (i.e. the smallest transitive relation containing $\rightarrow$). Thus, $A \rightarrow^+ B$ just in case there is an a-path from A to B (i.e. just in case there are $C_1, C_2, \ldots, C_n \in T$, $n \geq 1$, such that $A \rightarrow C_1$, $B = C_n$, and $C_i \rightarrow C_{i+1}$ for all $1 \leq i < n$).

Using this notation, the demonstrative structures employed by Aristotle in the *Posterior Analytics* can be characterized as follows:

DEFINITION 1: A *demonstrative structure* is a triple $\langle T, \rightarrow, \sim \rangle$, in which T is a non-empty set of terms, and $\rightarrow$ and $\sim$ are binary relations on T, such that for any A, B $\in T$:

    i. If $A \rightarrow B$, there is no C $\in T$ such that $A \rightarrow^+ C$ and $C \rightarrow^+ B$.

---

[107] *Post. An.* 1. 21, 82^{b}4–21; 1. 23, 85^{a}3–7; 1. 25, 86^{b}10–27.
[108] Smith, 'Regress', 29; id., 'Aristotle's Theory of Demonstration', in G. Anagnostopoulos (ed.), *A Companion to Aristotle* (Oxford, 2009), 51–65 at 57–8.

ii. If A~B, then A≠B and B~A.

iii. If A~B, there is no C ∈ T such that A→$^+$C and either B→$^+$C or B=C.

iv. If A~B, there are no C, D ∈ T such that C~D and C→$^+$A and either D→$^+$B or D=B.

Condition (i) ensures that → is the relation of immediate as opposed to mediate universal affirmation. Moreover, it implies that → is acyclic (i.e. that there is no A ∈ T such that A→$^+$A). Condition (ii) states that the relation of immediate universal negation, ~, is irre-flexive and symmetric. Condition (iii) states that if A~B, then A and B are disjoint in the sense that there is no a-path from A to B or to a third term reachable from B. Finally, (iv) ensures that ~ is immediate as opposed to mediate universal negation.[109]

In a demonstrative structure, an a-path from A to B corresponds to a set of pairs ⟨A, C_1⟩, ⟨C_1, C_2⟩,…, ⟨C_n, B⟩ such that A→C_1, C_i→C_{i+1}, and C_n→B. Thus, a-paths can be defined as subsets of the relation →, as follows:

DEFINITION 2: Let ⟨T, →, ~⟩ be a demonstrative structure. For any A, B ∈ T, an *a-path from A to B* is a set {⟨A, C_1⟩, ⟨C_1, C_2⟩,…, ⟨C_{n-1}, C_n⟩} ⊆ → ($n ≥ 1$) such that C_n=B.

As we have seen, an e-path from A to B consists of an atomic e-path from C to D together with an a-path from C to A (unless C=A) and an a-path from D to B (unless D=B). Thus, if the atomic e-path is represented by the singleton {⟨C, D⟩} and the two pos-sible a-paths by sets P and Q, e-paths can be defined as the union of these three sets:

DEFINITION 3: Let ⟨T, →, ~⟩ be a demonstrative structure. For any A, B ∈ T, an *e-path from A to B* is a set {⟨C, D⟩}∪P∪Q such that:

i. C~D,

ii. either C=A and P=∅ or P is an a-path from C to A, and

iii. either D=B and Q=∅ or Q is an a-path from D to B.

---

[109] In addition to conditions (i)–(iv), the demonstrative structures considered by Aristotle in the *Posterior Analytics* satisfy a number of further conditions. For example, Aristotle holds that they do not contain any infinite chains of the form A_1→A_2, A_2→A_3,… (1. 22, 84^{a}7–11 and 84^{a}29–^{b}2). For our present purposes, it is not necessary to make these additional conditions explicit.

Just like a-paths, e-paths are subsets of $T \times T$. Accordingly, parthood between these paths is given by the subset relation: an a- or e-path is a proper part of another a- or e-path just in case the former is a proper subset of the latter.[110]

Given this account of e-paths, the above characterization of priority in nature can be extended to cover e-propositions: AeB is prior in nature to CeD just in case (i) there is an e-path from A to B, and (ii) any e-path from A to B is a proper subset of some e-path from C to D. Likewise, AaB is prior in nature to CeD just in case there is an a-path from A to B and any such a-path is a proper subset of some e-path from C to D.

This allows us to verify Aristotle's claim in *Posterior Analytics* 1. 26 that the premises of every direct negative demonstration are prior in nature to the conclusion. For any deduction of the form Celarent, Cesare, and Camestres, if the premises are scientific propositions, they are prior in nature to the conclusion. To see this, consider an instance of Celarent in which AeC is deduced from AeB and BaC. Given that both premises are scientific propositions, there is an e-path from A to B and an a-path from B to C. The union of these two paths is an e-path from A to C of which the first two paths are proper subsets. Likewise, any e-path from A to B and any a-path from B to C can be composed to form an e-path from A to C of which they are proper subsets. Hence, both AeB and BaC are prior in nature to AeC.

Similarly, consider an instance of Camestres in which the premisses, BaA and BeC, are scientific propositions. There is an a-path from B to A and an e-path from B to C. Their union is an e-path from A to C of which they are proper subsets. The same is the case for any a-path from B to A and any e-path from B to C. Hence, BaA and BeC are prior in nature to AeC. The same argument applies in the case of Cesare. Hence, given that the only direct deductions in the three syllogistic figures are those of the form Barbara, Celarent, Cesare, and Camestres, it follows that the premises of every direct demonstration are prior in nature to the conclusion.

While a- and e-paths determine an order of priority in nature among scientific a- and e-propositions, they do not determine such an order for scientific i- and o-propositions. To this end, we need

---

[110] I am grateful to Kit Fine for suggesting to me this way of modelling parthood between paths.

to introduce i- and o-paths. Aristotle does not mention immediate
i- or o-propositions in the *Posterior Analytics*, nor does he explain
when an i- or o-proposition is prior in nature to another. His
account of demonstration is therefore compatible with different
ways of characterizing i- and o-paths. In what follows, I will adopt
a simple characterization of these paths in terms of a- and e-paths.
An i-path will be taken to consist of two a-paths with a common
endpoint. For example, the following i-path from A to B consists
of two a-paths from A and B to C_4:

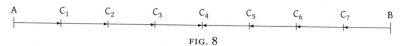

FIG. 8

Thus, i-paths can be defined as follows:

> DEFINITION 4: Let $\langle T, \rightarrow, \sim \rangle$ be a demonstrative structure. For
> any A, B $\in$ T, an *i-path from A to B* is a set P$\cup$Q such that for
> some C $\in$ T:
>
> i.   P is an a-path from A to C,
> ii. Q is an a-path from B to C, and
> iii. the sets P and Q are disjoint.

For example, if there are atomic a-paths from both *biped* and *animal*
to *human*, they compose an i-path from *biped* to *animal*. It follows
that the a-propositions *All humans are biped* and *All humans are animals* are prior in nature to the i-proposition *Some animals are biped*.

Condition (iii) in the definition excludes prolix i-paths that contain superfluous parts not needed to establish an i-proposition. For
example, suppose that there is a unique a-path from *human* to
Greek. Hence there are a-paths from both *biped* and *animal* to
Greek, but these two a-paths are not disjoint since they both contain the a-path from *human* to *Greek*. Thus, condition (iii) ensures
that they do not compose an i-path from *biped* to *animal*. This
accounts for the intuition that *All Greeks are human* is not prior in
nature to *Some animals are biped*.[111]

Similarly, an o-path can be taken to consist of an e-path and an
a-path that have a common endpoint. For example, the following

---

[111] Condition (iii) may be strengthened, e.g. by requiring that no term other than
C appear on both P and Q. For present purposes, however, it is not necessary to add
this stronger condition.

o-path from A to B consists of an e-path from A to C_5 and an a-path from B to C_5:

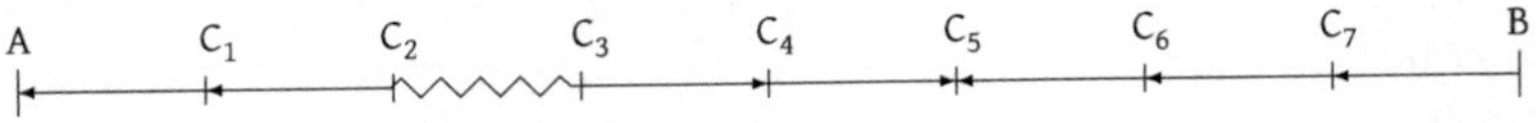

FIG. 9

Thus, o-paths can be defined as follows:

> DEFINITION 5: Let $\langle T, \to, \sim \rangle$ be a demonstrative structure. For any A, B $\in$ T, an *o-path from A to B* is a set P$\cup$Q such that for some C $\in$ T:
>
> i. P is an e-path from A to C,
> ii. Q is an a-path from B to C, and
> iii. the sets P and Q are disjoint.

For example, if there is an atomic e-path from *four-footed* to *human* and an a-path from *animal* to *human*, they compose an o-path from *four-footed* to *animal*. It follows that the propositions *No humans are four-footed* and *All humans are animals* are prior in nature to the o-proposition *Some animals are not four-footed*.

As before, condition (iii) excludes prolix o-paths that contain superfluous parts not needed to establish an o-proposition. Suppose, for example, that there is a unique e-path from *four-footed* to *Greek* and a unique a-path from *animal* to *Greek*. Since both of these paths contain the a-path from *human* to *Greek*, they are not disjoint and hence fail to compose an o-path from *four-footed* to *animal*. In this way, condition (iii) accounts for the intuition that *All Greeks are human* is not prior in nature to the o-proposition *Some animals are not four-footed*.

In a demonstrative structure, an i-proposition may be underwritten either by an i-path or by an a-path. Likewise, an o-proposition may be underwritten by an o- or e-path. If a path underwrites a proposition, the former is called a 'path for' the latter:

> DEFINITION 6: Let $\langle T, \to, \sim \rangle$ be a demonstrative structure. For any A, B $\in$ T:
>
> an a-path from A to B is a *path for* the propositions AaB, AiB, and BiA,
> an e-path from A to B is a *path for* the propositions AeB and AoB,
> an i-path from A to B is a *path for* the proposition AiB, and
> an o-path from A to B is a *path for* the proposition AoB.

A proposition is satisfied in a demonstrative structure if there is a path for it in this structure:

DEFINITION 7: Let $\langle T, \rightarrow, \sim \rangle$ be a demonstrative structure with A, B $\in$ T. For any proposition AxB (where 'x' stands for 'a', 'e', 'i', or 'o'): AxB is *satisfied in* $\langle T, \rightarrow, \sim \rangle$ just in case there is a path for AxB in $\langle T, \rightarrow, \sim \rangle$.

Given this definition of satisfaction, all fourteen moods and conversion rules of Aristotle's assertoric syllogistic are sound with respect to the class of demonstrative structures. Whenever the premisses of any of these moods and conversion rules are satisfied in a demonstrative structure, the conclusion is satisfied in this structure.[112] Hence, assuming that all immediate premisses of a given science are satisfied in the underlying demonstrative structure, all theorems derivable from them by means of the deductive resources of Aristotle's assertoric syllogistic are satisfied in this structure. Thus, all scientific propositions—immediate premisses and demonstrable theorems alike—are satisfied in the demonstrative structure determined by the science under consideration.

It should be noted that there are cases in which neither AeB nor AiB is satisfied in a demonstrative structure.[113] Since Aristotle requires that one of these propositions be true, satisfaction in a demonstrative structure does not capture the truth-conditions of categorical propositions. Instead, it captures their status as scientific propositions: a proposition is satisfied in a demonstrative structure just in case it is either an immediate premiss or a demonstrable theorem of the science under consideration. Thus, if neither AeB nor AiB is satisfied in a demonstrative structure, one of them is true but neither is a scientific proposition of the science.

We are now in a position to provide a general characterization of priority in nature between scientific a-, e-, i-, and o-propositions:

DEFINITION 8: Let $\langle T, \rightarrow, \sim \rangle$ be a demonstrative structure with A, B, C, D $\in$ T. For any propositions AxB and CyD (where 'x'

---

[112] This can be verified by checking each mood and conversion rule. Consider, for example, the case of Baroco: BaA, BoC, therefore AoC. Given that both premisses are satisfied in a demonstrative structure, there is an a-path or from B to A and either an e- or o-path from B to C. It can be shown that the union of these two paths is an e-path or o-path from A to C, respectively. The other cases are similar.

[113] Similarly, there are cases in which neither AaB nor AoB is satisfied in a demonstrative structure.

and 'y' stand for 'a', 'e', 'i', or 'o'), AxB is *prior in nature to* CyD
in $\langle T, \rightarrow, \sim \rangle$ just in case:

    i. AxB is satisfied in $\langle T, \rightarrow, \sim \rangle$, and

    ii. every path for AxB is a proper subset of some path for CyD.

Clearly, this relation of priority in nature is transitive. Moreover, given the acyclicity of $\rightarrow$, it is irreflexive, and hence asymmetric.[114] As such, it constitutes a well-defined relation of priority in nature between scientific propositions.

Of course, the present characterization of priority in nature is not stated by Aristotle in the *Posterior Analytics*. Nonetheless, it captures the way in which he took the relation of priority in nature between scientific propositions to be determined by a- and e-paths. Moreover, as we will see, this characterization allows us to verify Aristotle's thesis in *Posterior Analytics* 1. 26.

6. Accounting for Aristotle's thesis in *Posterior Analytics* 1. 26

The thesis of 1. 26 states that direct demonstrations proceed from premisses that are prior in nature to the conclusion, whereas demonstrations by *reductio* proceed from premisses that are posterior in nature to the conclusion. The first part of this thesis, regarding direct demonstrations, is captured by the following theorem:

> THEOREM 1: Let $\langle T, \rightarrow, \sim \rangle$ be a demonstrative structure. For any deduction of the form Barbara, Celarent, Cesare, and Camestres, if both premisses are satisfied in $\langle T, \rightarrow, \sim \rangle$, then each premiss is prior in nature to the conclusion in $\langle T, \rightarrow, \sim \rangle$.

The theorem holds because, as we have seen, reasoning by Barbara from premisses satisfied in a demonstrative structure amounts to extending a-paths in this structure, and reasoning by Celarent, Cesare, and Camestres from such premisses amounts to extending e-paths.

Since all scientific propositions are satisfied in a demonstrative structure, every deduction of the form Barbara, Celarent, Cesare, and Camestres in which both premisses are scientific propositions

---

[114] If a proposition AxB were prior in nature to itself, every path for AxB would be a proper subset of some path for AxB. But, given that $\rightarrow$ is acyclic, no a- or e-path for AxB is a proper subset of another a- or e-path for AxB, and no i- or o-path for AxB is a proper subset of any path for AxB.

proceeds from premisses that are prior in nature to the conclusion. Given that a 'demonstration' is any deduction in which the premisses are scientific propositions, this claim covers all demonstrations instantiating the four universal moods. Hence, in a deductive system in which these are the only direct demonstrations in the three figures, every direct demonstration proceeds from premisses that are prior in nature to the conclusion.

By contrast, this is not the case for demonstrations that employ the rule of *reductio ad impossibile*. Consider, for example, Aristotle's demonstration by *reductio* in which the premisses and the conclusion constitute an instance of Felapton, deriving AoB from AeC and BaC. There are demonstrative structures in which both premisses of this demonstration are satisfied while neither premiss is prior in nature to the conclusion, but instead the conclusion is prior in nature to one of the premisses. Such a demonstrative structure can be specified using exactly the same arrangement of terms given by Aristotle in *Posterior Analytics* 1. 26 (87^{a}3–12):

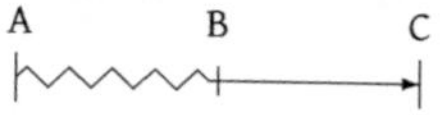

A   B   C

FIG. 10

The two premisses AeC and BaC are satisfied in this structure, since there is an e-path from A to C and an a-path from B to C. These two paths, however, are not disjoint and therefore cannot be combined to form an o-path from A to B.[115] Nor can they be combined to form any other path for AoB, since the only path for this proposition in the structure is the e-path from A to B. Thus, the two paths for AeC and BaC are not proper parts of any path for AoB. As a result, the premisses AeC and BaC are not prior in nature to the conclusion AoB. On the contrary, since the e-path from A to B is a proper part of the e-path from A to C, the conclusion AoB is prior in nature to the premiss AeC.

As we have seen, Aristotle takes AeC to be posterior in nature to AoB (1. 26, 87^{a}25–8). Conversely, he takes AoB to be prior in nature to AeC. Of course, this does not mean that AoB can serve as a premiss in a demonstration of AeC, for no particular proposition

---

[115] The e-path from A to C and the a-path from B to C fail to constitute an o-path from A to B because condition (iii) in Definition 5 is violated (since the two paths overlap in the pair ⟨B, C⟩).

can serve as a premiss in deriving a universal conclusion.[116] Instead, Aristotle seems to regard AoB as prior in nature to AeC in virtue of the fact that the former asserts part of the content that is needed to demonstrate the latter. In the above demonstrative structure, this corresponds to the fact that every path for AoB is a path for AeB and part of a path for AeC. In other words, every path underwriting AoB is in fact a path underwriting AeB and is partly constitutive of a path underwriting AeC. This may help to explain why Aristotle does not use any quantifying expressions such as 'all', 'no', or 'some' in describing the demonstration by *reductio* in *Posterior Analytics* 1. 26 (87ᵃ6–12). For the relevant priority relation between AoB and AeC does not depend on the quantity of these two propositions, but only on the nature of the paths that underwrite them in the underlying demonstrative structure.

There are, then, instances of Felapton in which both premisses are satisfied in a demonstrative structure, but the conclusion is prior in nature to one of the premisses. In fact, there are such instances not only of Felapton but of most particular moods in the three figures:

> THEOREM 2: There are deductions of the form Darii, Ferio, Festino, Darapti, Disamis, Datisi, Felapton, Ferison, and Bocardo such that:
>
> i. both premisses are satisfied in a demonstrative structure $\langle T, \rightarrow, \sim \rangle$, and
> ii. the conclusion is prior in nature to one of the premisses in $\langle T, \rightarrow, \sim \rangle$.

For the negative moods listed in this theorem, the claim can be established by means of the same demonstrative structure just described for the case of Felapton. For the affirmative moods listed in the theorem, it can be established by means of a similar demonstrative structure in which A is connected to B by an a-path instead of an e-path.[117] Thus, the demonstrative structure described by Aristotle in *Posterior Analytics* 1. 26 is not limited to the case of

---

[116] See *Pr. An.* 1. 24, 41ᵇ22–7.

[117] Specifically, consider a demonstrative structure in which A→B and B→C. The propositions AaC, BaC, AiC, CiB, and BiC are satisfied in this structure, but AiB is prior in nature to both AaC and AiC (since the only path for AiB, the a-path from A to B, is a proper part of the a-path from A to C).

Felapton (87ª3–12). Instead, Aristotle's discussion of this structure can be viewed as indicating a more general argument to establish Theorem 2 for negative particular moods and, with a simple modification, also for affirmative ones.

Theorem 2 covers all particular moods in Aristotle's three figures except the second-figure mood Baroco. The latter mood is not included because the theorem does not hold for it: whenever the premisses of an instance of Baroco are satisfied in a demonstrative structure, they are prior in nature to the conclusion. For all other particular moods in the three figures, there are instances in which the premisses are satisfied in a demonstrative structure while the conclusion is prior in nature to one of them. At the same time, there are also instances of these moods in which both premisses are prior in nature to the conclusion.[118] Thus, among demonstrations by *reductio*, there are some in which the premisses are prior in nature to the conclusion, as well as some in which the conclusion is prior in nature to one of the premisses.

These results suffice to justify Aristotle's thesis in *Posterior Analytics* 1. 26 that direct demonstration is better than demonstration by *reductio* on the grounds that the former proceeds from premisses that are prior in nature to the conclusion whereas the latter allows for the conclusion to be prior in nature to one of the premisses (87ª25–30). On the present account, this thesis should not be taken to mean that all direct demonstrations are better in this respect than all demonstrations by *reductio*. Rather, Aristotle's claim is that the method of direct demonstration is superior to the method of demonstration by *reductio* because the former guarantees that all premisses are prior in nature to the conclusion, whereas the latter does not come with such a guarantee but allows for cases in which the conclusion is prior in nature to one of the premisses. This differs from the interpretation of 1. 26 given by Gisela Striker and others, who take Aristotle in this chapter to state that all demonstrations by *reductio* are inferior to all direct ones.[119] If I am correct, such a universal thesis is neither intended by Aristotle nor supported by his argument in the chapter. Nonetheless, his argument

---

[118] Consider, for example, an instance of Darii, inferring AiC from AaB and BiC, when both AaB and BaC are satisfied in the underlying demonstrative structure.

[119] See n. 60 above.

succeeds in establishing a clear difference between the two methods of demonstration.

The function of a demonstration, for Aristotle, is to produce scientific knowledge:

... καθ' ἣν μᾶλλον ἐπιστάμεθα ἀπόδειξιν βελτίων ἀπόδειξις· αὕτη γὰρ ἀρετὴ ἀποδείξεως... (*Post. An.* 1. 24, 85ᵃ21–2)

... the demonstration by which we have more scientific knowledge is the better demonstration; for this is the excellence of a demonstration...

In order to have scientific knowledge of a demonstrable theorem, one needs to derive it from premisses that are prior to it in nature. Hence, the method of direct demonstration is better than that of demonstration by *reductio* since it is more reliable at achieving 'the excellence of a demonstration'.[120] As Myles Burnyeat has pointed out, 'given Aristotle's belief that there is real priority and posteriority in nature', a demonstration should be 'not just a preferred ordering of humanly constructed knowledge, but a mapping of the structure of the real'.[121] Direct demonstration is better suited to this task than that by *reductio* because the former, but not the latter, always succeeds in mapping the relation of priority in nature encoded in structures of acyclic a-paths (συστοιχίαι).

Aristotle does not indicate whether those demonstrations by *reductio* in which the premisses are in fact prior in nature to the conclusion can have the status of genuine demonstrations producing scientific knowledge. His argument in *Posterior Analytics* 1. 26 does not preclude that some of them may have this status. On the present account, the only way to derive a scientific i- or o-proposition is by means of *reductio*. Thus, it would seem natural to accept that, for each of these propositions, there is a derivation by *reductio* which has the status of a genuine demonstration producing scientific knowledge of it. Aristotle may have independent reasons for regarding

---

[120] The former method is, so to speak, more demonstrative than the latter. Accordingly, when Aristotle distinguishes direct demonstration from demonstration by *reductio* in 1. 26, he refers to the former as 'demonstrative' (ἀποδεικτική, 87ᵃ17; see Philop. *In An. Post.* 297. 9–12 Wallies). Similarly, he refers to it in 1. 24 as 'that which is said to demonstrate' (ἡ ἀποδεικνύναι λεγομένη, 85ᵃ15–16; see Philop. *In An. Post.* 273. 26–9). The latter phrase suggests that direct demonstration was taken to be superior to demonstration by *reductio* not only by Aristotle but also by other thinkers at his time.

[121] Burnyeat, 'Understanding Knowledge', 126.

such demonstrations by *reductio* as inferior to direct ones—but if so, he does not explain them in *Posterior Analytics* 1. 26.

By contrast, many later theorists have endorsed the universal thesis that all proofs by *reductio* fail to be explanatory. Such a universal thesis is clearly evinced, for example, in the passages from the *Port-Royal Logic* and the *Critique of Pure Reason* quoted above. It is also maintained by Bernard Bolzano, who argues in his *Theory of Science* that no proof by *reductio* can exhibit the 'objective ground' of the *demonstrandum*. Following Aristotle's lead in *Prior Analytics* 2. 14, Bolzano holds that every proof by *reductio* can be transformed into a direct proof.[122] In his view, proofs by *reductio* cannot exhibit the objective ground of the *demonstrandum* because they involve superfluous steps and redundant assumptions that are absent from the corresponding direct proofs.[123] Whatever the merits of Bolzano's account, it differs significantly from Aristotle's argument in *Posterior Analytics* 1. 26. For, as we have seen, this argument relies on a deductive system in which not every proof by *reductio* can be transformed into a direct one, and it does not turn on the fact that proofs by *reductio* involve an assumption for *reductio* and other steps that are absent from direct proofs. Unlike Bolzano's account, Aristotle's argument does not imply that all demonstrations by *reductio* are inferior to direct ones.

In his *Theory of Science*, Bolzano takes a keen interest in the relation of priority in nature introduced by Aristotle in *Posterior Analytics* 1. 2–3. Bolzano argues that this relation can be viewed as a relation of 'grounding' whereby one truth is grounded in one or more other truths.[124] In accordance with this suggestion, the results concerning priority in nature stated in Theorems 1 and 2 have close analogues in modern theories of grounding. These theories explore, among other things, how the relation of grounding interacts with the rules of inference governing logical connectives in deductive systems. Consider, for example, a deductive system for the language of propositional logic using the connectives of negation (¬)

---

[122] Bolzano, *Wissenschaftslehre*, iv. 271–8 (§530. 2–4 and n. 2); see Mancosu, *Mathematics*, 110–15.

[123] Bolzano, *Wissenschaftslehre*, iv. 270–1 (§530. 1). See S. Centrone, 'Das Problem der apagogischen Beweise in Bolzanos *Beyträgen* und seiner *Wissenschaftslehre*', *History and Philosophy of Logic*, 33 (2012), 127–57 at 142–3; S. Roski, *Bolzano's Conception of Grounding* (Frankfurt a.M., 2017), 159–60.

[124] Bolzano, *Wissenschaftslehre*, ii. 364 (§209 n. 1); see also ii. 341 (§198 n. 1).

and conjunction (∧). The system contains four direct rules of inference, where ϕ and ψ are any propositions:

> ϕ, ψ, therefore $\phi \wedge \psi$
> ϕ, therefore $\neg\neg\phi$
> $\neg\phi$, therefore $\neg(\phi \wedge \psi)$
> $\neg\psi$, therefore $\neg(\phi \wedge \psi)$

In addition, the system contains the following rule of *reductio ad impossibile*, where ϕ and ψ are any propositions and Γ any set of propositions:

$$\frac{\Gamma,\ \neg\phi,\ \text{therefore}\ \psi \wedge \neg\psi}{\Gamma,\ \text{therefore}\ \phi}$$

Taken together, these rules suffice to derive all the laws of classical propositional logic. The four direct rules are special in that, when applied to true propositions, the conclusion not only is a logical consequence of the premisses but also is grounded in these premisses. For example, if ϕ and ψ are true, then $\phi \wedge \psi$ is grounded in these two propositions (or the fact that $\phi \wedge \psi$ obtains in virtue of the fact that ϕ and the fact that ψ). More generally, the relation of grounding is usually taken to obey the following laws corresponding to the four direct rules of inference:[125]

> If ϕ and ψ, then ϕ, ψ ground $\phi \wedge \psi$
> If ϕ, then ϕ grounds $\neg\neg\phi$
> If $\neg\phi$, then $\neg\phi$ grounds $\neg(\phi \wedge \psi)$
> If $\neg\psi$, then $\neg\psi$ grounds $\neg(\phi \wedge \psi)$

By contrast, there is no such agreement between the laws of grounding and the derived rules of inference that rely on *reductio ad impossibile* in the deductive system. Consider, for example, the following derived rules which are licensed by the above rule of *reductio*:

---

[125] K. Fine, 'Guide to Ground', in F. Correia and B. Schnieder (eds.), *Metaphysical Grounding: Understanding the Structure of Reality* (Cambridge, 2012), 37–80 at 58 and 62–3; F. Correia, 'Logical Grounds' ['Grounds'], *Review of Symbolic Logic*, 7 (2014), 31–59 at 33–6; id., 'An Impure Logic of Representational Grounding', *Journal of Philosophical Logic*, 46 (2017), 507–38 at 530; similarly, B. Schnieder, 'A Logic for "Because"', *Review of Symbolic Logic*, 4 (2011), 445–65 at 449; J. Korbmacher, 'Axiomatic Theories of Partial Ground I: The Base Theory', *Journal of Philosophical Logic*, 47 (2018), 161–91 at 170.

$\phi \wedge \psi$, therefore ϕ

$\phi \wedge \psi$, therefore ψ

$\neg \neg \phi$, therefore ϕ

When these rules are applied to a true proposition, this proposition does not ground the conclusion. For example, a true conjunction $\phi \wedge \psi$ does not ground either conjunct (the fact that ϕ does not obtain in virtue of the fact that $\phi \wedge \psi$). Thus, while sound deductions instantiating the four direct rules proceed from what grounds to what is grounded, sound deductions using the rule of *reductio* do not.

The four direct rules of inference are analogous to the four universal syllogistic moods in Aristotle's system. When the former are applied to true propositions, the premisses ground the conclusion; when the latter are applied to scientific propositions, the premisses are prior in nature to the conclusion. In both cases, direct deductions proceed in the direction of increasing complexity.[126] In the first case, the conclusion is syntactically more complex than the premisses.[127] In the second case, the conclusion is path-theoretically more complex than the premisses, in the sense that every path for a premiss is a proper part of a path for the conclusion.

In both systems, the direct rules of inference are especially useful in contexts in which preference is given to deductions that proceed from what grounds to what is grounded, or from what is prior in nature to what is posterior in nature. However, these rules and moods do not suffice to generate all deductive consequences of a given set of premisses. To this end, one needs to employ the rule of *reductio ad impossibile* in the two systems. Once this rule is admitted, deductions from true propositions no longer follow the order of grounding, and deductions from scientific propositions no longer follow the order of priority in nature. Instead, the rule of *reductio* licenses deductions in which this order is inverted, inferring the ground from the grounded, or what is prior in nature from what is posterior in nature.

---

[126] This is in accordance with Fine's suggestion that relations of grounding proceed in the direction of increasing complexity for some suitable complexity measure on propositions; K. Fine, 'Some Remarks on Bolzano on Ground', in S. Roski and B. Schnieder (eds.), *Priority Among Truths: Bernard Bolzano's Philosophy of Grounding* (Oxford, *forthcoming*), §5.

[127] See Correia, 'Grounds', 35–7.

Thus, Bolzano's suggestion that the relation of priority in nature employed by Aristotle in the *Posterior Analytics* can be viewed as a relation of grounding is borne out by the parallels between Aristotle's argument in 1. 26 and modern developments in the logic of ground. More specifically, Aristotle's relation of priority in nature corresponds to what is known as strict partial ground. Kit Fine characterizes the latter relation in terms of the idea of a fact verifying a proposition. Facts can be fused to form more complex facts of which they are parts. On Fine's account, if a true proposition is a strict partial ground of another true proposition, every fact verifying the former is part of a fact verifying the latter.[128] Similarly, the present account of priority in nature is based on the idea that paths underwrite scientific propositions. Paths can be combined to form more complex paths of which they are proper parts. If a scientific proposition is prior in nature to another scientific proposition, every path for the former is a proper part of a path for the latter.[129]

7. Parts and wholes

Aristotle's argument in *Posterior Analytics* 1. 26 rests on the claim that the major premiss of the direct negative demonstration, AeB, is prior in nature to the conclusion AeC (87ª17–18). In support of this claim, Aristotle states that the latter proposition is a conclusion while the former is among the propositions 'from which the conclusion derives' (ἐξ ὧν τὸ συμπέρασμα):

πρότερα γάρ ἐστι τοῦ συμπεράσματος ἐξ ὧν τὸ συμπέρασμα. ἔστι δὲ τὸ μὲν Α τῷ Γ μὴ ὑπάρχειν συμπέρασμα, τὸ δὲ Α τῷ Β ἐξ οὗ τὸ συμπέρασμα. (*Post. An.* 1. 26, 87ª18–20)

---

[128] Fine, 'Guide to Ground', 71–3; id., 'The Pure Logic of Ground' ['Pure Logic'], *Review of Symbolic Logic*, 5 (2012), 1–25 at 7–9.

[129] Thus, the account of priority of nature given in Definition 8 can be viewed as a special case of Fine's factual semantics for ground, when a 'fact' is taken to be any set of atomic a- and e-paths, and the operation of 'factual fusion' is taken to be set-theoretic union (see Fine, 'Pure Logic', 7–9). However, while Fine's account applies to any true propositions and the facts that make them true, Definition 8 applies only to scientific truths and the paths that underwrite their status as scientific truths in acyclic demonstrative structures.

For the things from which a conclusion derives are prior to the conclusion; and that A does not belong to C is a conclusion, whereas that A does not belong to B is that from which the conclusion derives.

According to this passage, the propositions 'from which a conclusion derives' are prior in nature to the conclusion. Given that AeC is a conclusion that derives from AeB in the direct negative demonstration, the latter proposition is prior in nature to the former. But what about the demonstration by *reductio*, in which the conclusion AoB is derived from the premisses AeC and BaC? If these premisses are propositions 'from which the conclusion derives', it would seem to follow that AeC is prior in nature to AoB, thereby undermining Aristotle's argument in 1. 26. Aristotle responds to this objection as follows:

οὐ γὰρ εἰ συμβαίνει ἀναιρεῖσθαί τι, τοῦτο συμπέρασμά ἐστιν, ἐκεῖνα δὲ ἐξ ὧν. ἀλλὰ τὸ μὲν ἐξ οὗ συλλογισμός ἐστιν ὃ ἂν οὕτως ἔχῃ ὥστε ἢ ὅλον πρὸς μέρος ἢ μέρος πρὸς ὅλον ἔχειν, αἱ δὲ τὸ ΑΓ καὶ ΑΒ προτάσεις οὐκ ἔχουσιν οὕτω πρὸς ἀλλήλας. (*Post. An.* 1. 26, 87ᵃ20–5)

For it is not the case that if something happens to be rejected, this is a conclusion and the other things are that from which the conclusion derives. Rather, that from which a deduction proceeds is what is related to one another either as whole to part or as part to whole.[130] But the propositions AC and AB are not related to one another in this way.

In this passage, demonstrations by *reductio* are described as arguments in which something is rejected. The thing rejected in them is the assumption for *reductio*.[131] Aristotle emphasizes that the

---

[130] Crivelli ('Hypothesis', 168) takes ἔχειν at 87ᵃ23 to be transitive, translating the clause as follows: 'what is in such a condition as to have a whole in relation to a part or a part in relation to a whole'. Elsewhere Aristotle states that the premisses of a deduction are 'so related as to be one a whole and the other a part' (ἔχει οὕτως ὥστ' εἶναι τὸ μὲν ὡς ὅλον τὸ δ' ὡς μέρος, *Pr. An.* 1. 25, 42ᵃ15–16; similarly, 42ᵃ10; 1. 41, 49ᵇ37–8); see H. Maier, *Die Syllogistik des Aristoteles*, ii/2: *Die Entstehung der Aristotelischen Logik* [*Entstehung*] (Tübingen, 1900), 152 n. 1. Since there is no other passage in which Aristotle states that the premisses of a deduction have a whole in relation to a part, it seems preferable to take ἔχειν at 87ᵃ23 to be intransitive; Philop. *In An. Post.* 298. 7–8; Zabarella, *Opera logica*, 978 ᴇ–980 ᴀ; Kirchmann, *Erläuterungen*, 116; Mure, *Posteriora*, ad loc.; Tredennick, *Posterior Analytics*, 153; Mignucci, *L'argomentazione dimostrativa*, 564; Seidl, *Zweite Analytiken*, 127 and 266; Barnes, *Posterior Analytics* 2nd edn., 41; Detel, *Analytica posteriora*, i. 54; Pellegrin, *Seconds Analytiques*, 211; Tricot, *Seconds Analytiques*, 146.

[131] 'A demonstration reducing to the impossible differs from an ostensive demonstration in that it posits what it wishes to reject by reducing it to an agreed falsehood' (διαφέρει δ' ἡ εἰς τὸ ἀδύνατον ἀπόδειξις τῆς δεικτικῆς τῷ τιθέναι ὃ βούλεται ἀναιρεῖν,

proposition expressing this rejection, the contradictory opposite of the assumption for *reductio*, is not always a 'conclusion' (συμπέρασμα).[132] Thus, he denies that in every demonstration by *reductio* the proposition inferred in the final step is a 'conclusion'. Accordingly, he denies that the premisses of every such demonstration are 'that from which' this proposition derives. With respect to Aristotle's demonstration by *reductio*, this means that AoB is not a conclusion, and the premisses AeC and BaC are not that from which AoB derives.

In denying that AoB is a conclusion, Aristotle departs from his terminology in the *Prior Analytics*, where he refers to any proposition inferred in the final step of a deduction by *reductio* as a 'conclusion'.[133] In the passage just quoted, he adopts a stricter use of the term, in which not every proposition deduced by *reductio* counts as a conclusion. Grosseteste argues that Aristotle uses 'conclusion' here specifically for those propositions that are posterior in nature to the premisses from which they are deduced.[134] If this is correct, the proposition inferred in any direct demonstration is a conclusion and the premisses are 'that from which the conclusion derives'. Aristotle suggests that, in such a demonstration, the conclusion 'derives from' the premisses because the premisses are related to one another 'as whole to part or as part to whole'. Thus, while the premisses of the direct negative demonstration, AeB and BaC, are related to one another 'as whole to part or as part to whole', this is not the case for the premisses of the demonstration by *reductio*, AeC and BaC.

In the last sentence of the passage, Aristotle states that 'the propositions AC and AB are not related to one another in this way'. The first of these propositions is the negative premiss of the demonstration by *reductio*, AeC, and the second is the proposition inferred in this demonstration, AoB. Since AeC and AoB do not form a pair of premisses for any deduction, it makes little sense to point out that they are not premisses related to one another 'as whole to part or as part to whole'. In view of this difficulty, Ross

---

ἀπάγουσα εἰς ὁμολογούμενον ψεῦδος, *Pr. An.* 2. 14, 62ᵇ29–31). See also the use of ἀναιρεῖν at *SE* 5, 167ᵇ22–4.

[132] See F. Biese, *Die Philosophie des Aristoteles*, i: Logik und Metaphysik (Berlin, 1835), 270–1; Waitz, *Organon*, ii. 370; Ross, *Analytics*, 594; Crivelli, 'Hypothesis', 168–9.

[133] *Pr. An.* 2. 11, 61ᵃ20, 61ᵇ17; 2. 14 62ᵇ34–5, 62ᵇ38, 63ᵇ16.

[134] Grosseteste, *Commentarius*, 254.

emends the text of the sentence, printing 'AC and BC' instead of 'AC and AB' at 87^{a}24.[135] The sentence then asserts that the premisses of the demonstration by *reductio*, AeC and BaC, do not stand in the requisite part-whole relation. While this is a natural reading, there is no textual evidence for Ross's emendation.[136] Barnes has suggested reading 'BC and AB' instead of 'AC and AB', but there is no textual support for this emendation either.[137] Instead, all manuscripts have 'AC and AB'.

If we wish to follow the manuscripts, the sentence can be taken to assert that AeC and AoB are not related in such a way that the latter can be derived from AeC and another premiss which stands to AeC 'as whole to part or as part to whole'. On this reading, Aristotle's focus shifts from the part-whole relations that obtain between the premisses of a demonstration to the relation that obtains between one of the premisses and the conclusion. This shift may be facilitated by the fact that Aristotle recognizes part-whole relations not only between the premisses of demonstrations but also between their premisses and the conclusion. For example, in a demonstration by Barbara, Aristotle takes the conclusion to be a part of the major premiss, noting that 'the one is a part and the other a whole' (μέρος γάρ, τὸ δ' ὅλον, 2. 3, 91^{a}4–5).[138] Maier has argued that, for Aristotle, this is just another way of expressing the same thought he has in mind when he says that the minor premiss is related to the major premiss 'as part to whole'.[139] Thus, according

---

[135] Ross, *Analytics*, 595; followed by Tredennick, *Posterior Analytics*, 152; Mignucci, *L'argomentazione dimostrativa*, 564–5; Barnes, *Posterior Analytics 2nd edn.*, i. 54 and ii. 458; Pellegrin, *Seconds Analytiques*, 210 and 388–9 n. 7; Crivelli, 'Hypothesis', 167.

[136] In manuscript c, the phrase καὶ AB at 87^{a}24 is accompanied by the marginal note 'γρ ΒΓ' (see Waitz, *Organon*, ii. 43). Here γρ may stand either for γράφεται, indicating a variant reading, or for γράφε, indicating an emendation; see N. G. Wilson, 'More about γράφεται Variants', *Acta Antiqua Academiae Scientiarum Hungaricae*, 48 (2008), 79–81. Since ΒΓ is not attested in any other manuscripts, it seems more likely that the marginal note in c is meant to indicate an emendation. Ross (*Analytics*, ad 87^{a}24) and Williams (*Studies in the Manuscript Tradition of Aristotle's Analytica* (Königstein, 1984), 64) claim that ΒΓ is found in a secondary hand in manuscript C. This claim, however, is not correct (the error may be due to a misprint in Ross's apparatus, writing 'C' in place of 'c'). I am grateful to Michel Crubellier and Pieter Sjoerd Hasper for discussion of the manuscript situation at 87^{a}24.

[137] Barnes, *Posterior Analytics 1st edn.*, 45 and 181; followed by Striker, 'Review of Barnes', 317, but retracted in id. *Posterior Analytics 2nd edn.*, 41 and 189.

[138] See 91^{a}2–5 and the explanations by Maier, *Entstehung*, 152–3 n. 3; Barnes, *Posterior Analytics 2nd edn.*, 208.

[139] Maier, *Entstehung*, 151–5.

to Maier, a premiss of a demonstration is part of another premiss just in case the conclusion is part of the latter premiss. Hence, asserting that BaC is part of AeB is equivalent to asserting that AeC is part of AeB. Likewise, denying that BaC is part of AeC is equivalent to denying that AoB is part of AeC. This may help to explain why Aristotle transitions from the one denial to the other in the passage just quoted. On this reading, the point of the last sentence is equivalent to the one expressed by Ross's emendation. Thus, whether or not we accept the emendation, Aristotle denies that the premisses of the demonstration by *reductio*, AeC and BaC, are related to one another 'as whole to part or as part to whole'.

In the *Analytics*, Aristotle repeatedly claims that the premisses of a deduction are related to one another 'as whole to part'.[140] He does not explain what it is for two premisses to be related in this way, nor is it clear whether he intends the claim to hold for all deductions in the three figures.[141] In *Posterior Analytics* 1. 26, at any rate, the claim seems to apply only to direct demonstrations but not to those by *reductio*. In all direct demonstrations, the premisses are related to one another 'as whole to part or as part to whole', whereas this is not the case in all demonstrations by *reductio*. Given the deductive framework employed by Aristotle in 1. 26, this means that the claim applies to demonstrations instantiating the four universal moods, but not to other demonstrations in the three figures.[142]

To see how the claim applies to demonstrations in the four universal moods, consider the case of Barbara: AaB, BaC, therefore AaC. The major premiss asserts that, as Aristotle puts it, 'A belongs to the whole of B' ($\tau \grave{o}$ A $\emph{ὅλῳ}$ $\tau \hat{\wp}$ B $\emph{ὑπάρχει}$).[143] The minor premiss

---

[140] *Pr. An.* 1. 25, 42ᵃ9–18; 1. 41, 49ᵇ37–50ᵃ1; *Post. An.* 1. 10, 77ᵃ3–4; 2. 6, 92ᵃ12–13. See Maier, *Entstehung*, 152–5; Barnes, *Posterior Analytics* 2nd edn., 189; Striker, *Prior Analytics*, 183–4.

[141] Some commentators take the claim to apply to all deductions in the three figures (Mignucci, *L'argomentazione dimostrativa*, 565; Barnes, *Posterior Analytics* 2nd edn., 189; Crivelli, 'Hypothesis', 169–70). However, it is not easy to see how the claim applies to deductions in the third figure, e.g. to those of the form Darapti. Thus, Alexander takes Aristotle's claim at *Prior Analytics* 1. 25, 42ᵃ9–17 to apply only to deductions in the first figure (Alex. Aphr. *In An. Pr.* 277. 5–23 Wallies). Similarly, Ross (*Analytics*, 379) holds that the claim 'is most clearly true' of deductions in the first figure.

[142] Kirchmann (*Erläuterungen*, 116) takes Aristotle's claim at 87ᵃ22–3 to be restricted to deductions in the first figure. On the present account, by contrast, the claim applies not only to first-figure deductions in Barbara and Celarent, but also to second-figure deductions in Cesare and Camestres.

[143] *Pr. An.* 2. 2, 53ᵇ30, 54ᵇ4–5, 54ᵇ25–6, 54ᵇ28–9, 55ᵃ6, 55ᵃ37; 2. 3, 55ᵇ27–8, 55ᵇ35–6, 56ᵃ26, 56ᵃ29–30, 56ᵃ33–4, 56ᵇ1; 2. 4, 56ᵇ38, 57ᵃ13–14, 57ᵃ19, 57ᵃ21; 2. 21, 67ᵃ33–4;

asserts that 'C is in B as in a whole' (τὸ Γ ἐν ὅλῳ ἐστὶ τῷ B).[144] Thus, the major premiss makes a universal claim about B as a whole while the minor premiss identifies a part of B that is in B as in a whole. In this sense, the major premiss can be viewed as a 'whole' and the minor premiss as a 'part'.[145] Similarly, in the case of Celarent, the major premiss AeB asserts that 'A does not belong to the whole of B' (τὸ A ὅλῳ τῷ B οὐχ ὑπάρχει).[146] Thus, the major premiss makes a universal negative claim about B as a whole. Likewise, in the case of Cesare and Camestres, the e-premiss asserts that the major or minor term does not belong to the middle term as a whole.

In all four universal moods, then, one premiss makes a universal affirmative or negative claim about the middle term B as a whole, while the other premiss states that the minor term is a part of B which is in B as in a whole. This is not the case for any of the other moods in the three figures. It is therefore natural for Aristotle to characterize the four universal moods as those in which the premisses are related to one another 'as whole to part or as part to whole'. In Barbara, Celarent, and Cesare, the major premiss is related to the minor premiss as whole to part, and in Camestres they are related the other way around. Whenever the premisses of a deduction are scientific propositions that stand in this part-whole relation, they are prior in nature to the conclusion.[147] Grosseteste explains this point in his commentary on *Posterior Analytics* 1. 26 for the cases of Barbara and Celarent as follows:

Cum igitur in demonstrationibus sit semper predicatio directa naturaliter ordinata et minor propositio sit pars, maior vero totum, palam quoniam conclusio erit natura posterior et ea ex quibus est sillogismus erunt priora

---

2. 22, 68ᵃ16–17, 68ᵃ22; 2. 23, 68ᵇ21; *Post. An.* 1. 16, 80ᵃ40–ᵇ1, 80ᵇ4, 80ᵇ8–9; 1. 17, 80ᵇ37–8.

[144] *Pr. An.* 1. 1, 24ᵃ13–14, 24ᵇ26–7; 1. 4, 25ᵇ32–4; 2. 1, 53ᵃ21–4; *Post. An.* 1. 15, 79ᵃ36–ᵇ18; 1. 17, 80ᵇ27–8.

[145] Maier, *Entstehung*, 152–5.

[146] *Pr. An.* 2. 3, 55ᵇ33; 2. 4, 56ᵇ38, 57ᵃ3; *Post. An.* 1. 16, 80ᵇ1, 80ᵇ8.

[147] Lotze attributes to Aristotle the view that the best way to prove a conclusion from its explanatory grounds is by means of a first-figure deduction in Barbara, since 'it is only here that we find the subordination of a given idea under a general truth which enables us to understand not only that [the conclusion] holds, but also why it holds' ('nur hier findet die Unterordnung eines gegebenen Inhalts unter eine allgemeine Wahrheit statt, aus welcher nicht blos begriffen wird, daß [das zu Beweisende] gilt, sondern auch warum es gilt', Lotze, *Logik*, 265). On the present account, explanatory proofs of this sort are found not only in Barbara but in all four universal moods. Whenever these moods are applied to scientific propositions, the premisses stand to the conclusion in the explanatory relation described by Lotze.

natura.... Cum autem in hac: omne C est B, sit predicatio directa secundum ordinem naturalem et ita C sit pars B, et hec propositio: omne C est B, sit sicut pars ad hanc: nullum B est A, manifestum quoniam hec: nullum C est A, est posterior natura quam hec: nullum B est A. (Grosseteste, *Commentarius*, 253–4)

Since in demonstrations the predication is always direct and in natural order, and the minor premiss is a part while the major premiss is a whole, it is plain that the conclusion will be posterior in nature and that from which the deduction proceeds will be prior in nature.... When in the proposition *All C is B* the predication is direct and in accordance with natural order and, in this way, C is a part of B and the proposition *All C is B* is related as a part to the proposition *No B is A*, it is evident that the proposition *No C is A* is posterior in nature to the proposition *No B is A*.

Grosseteste's argument does not apply to deductions in which the premisses do not stand in the part-whole relation exhibited by the four universal moods. When such deductions proceed from scientific propositions, the premisses may fail to be prior in nature to conclusion.

Throughout the first book of the *Posterior Analytics*, Aristotle appeals, more or less directly, to the deductive framework of the assertoric syllogistic. In doing so, he usually focuses on the four universal moods Barbara, Celarent, Cesare, and Camestres, but often does not mention any of the other moods in the three figures.[148] Robin Smith takes this to be an indication that the *Posterior Analytics* was largely written before Aristotle developed the full syllogistic theory presented in the *Prior Analytics*. In Smith's view, 'the *Posterior Analytics* as we have it does not presuppose the *Prior Analytics* but something decidedly simpler'.[149] By contrast, the preceding considerations suggest a different explanation of Aristotle's focus in the *Posterior Analytics* on the four universal moods. These moods constitute the core of the deductive framework employed in *Posterior Analytics* 1. 26, and they are the only ones that license direct demonstrations in this framework. Whenever they are applied to scientific propositions, the premisses are prior in nature to the conclusion. All other moods in the three figures rely on the rule of *reductio ad impossibile*, and they do not guarantee that scientific premisses are prior in nature to the conclusion. As we have seen, Aristotle clearly recognizes such moods in the *Posterior Analytics*.[150]

---

[148] See Smith, 'Relationship', 328–35.
[149] Smith, 'Relationship', 327; see also id., 'Syllogism', 114–35.
[150] See n. 43.

But they are less suitable for the purposes of scientific demonstration than the four universal ones, and therefore play a less prominent role in this treatise. Thus, Aristotle is focusing on the four universal moods in the *Posterior Analytics* not because he was not sufficiently aware of the other moods when he wrote the treatise, but because these are the ones that are most important and useful for the purposes of scientific demonstration.

Smith argues that *Posterior Analytics* 1. 26 was written before *Prior Analytics* 2. 11–14 because otherwise one 'must suppose that Aristotle, after having acquired the sort of understanding of *reductio ad impossibile* reflected in *Pr. An.* 2. 11–14, ... somehow produced the very unsatisfactory treatment of this subject in *Post. An.* 1. 26'.[151] In my view, this argument is not convincing. As we have seen, Aristotle's discussion in *Posterior Analytics* 1. 26 is not incompatible with, or inferior to, his treatment of *reductio* in the *Prior Analytics*.[152] Instead, his aims are different in the two parts. In the *Prior Analytics*, Aristotle studies the nature of deductions by *reductio* in general and their relationship to direct deductions in the assertoric syllogistic. This investigation deals with features common to all deductions by *reductio*, and hence does not appeal to any considerations concerning priority in nature, since these pertain only to scientific demonstrations and not to the other kinds of deduction countenanced by Aristotle. In *Posterior Analytics* 1. 26, on the other hand, he deals specifically with demonstrations by *reductio* and the relations of priority in nature that obtain between their constituent propositions. The latter discussion relies on special assumptions of his theory of demonstration that are absent

---

[151] Smith, 'Syllogism', 134.

[152] Smith ('Syllogism', 119) claims that 'none of [*Posterior Analytics* 1. 26] makes any sense unless Aristotle somehow supposes that the conclusion of an indirect proof must be negative'. In the *Prior Analytics*, on the other hand, Aristotle is clear that deductions by *reductio* can establish not only negative but also affirmative conclusions (*Pr. An.* 2. 14, 62^{b}37–8; see also 1. 6, 28^{a}22–3, 28^{b}14; 1. 7, 29^{a}32–^{b}11). It is true that Aristotle's focus in *Posterior Analytics* 1. 26 is on demonstrations by *reductio* that establish a negative conclusion, but this does not mean that he excludes demonstrations by *reductio* which establish an affirmative conclusion. Given his claim in 1. 25 that direct affirmative demonstrations are better than direct negative ones, it is obvious that direct affirmative demonstrations are also better than demonstrations by *reductio* which establish an affirmative conclusion. For the latter not only involve an application of the rule of *reductio*, but also employ a direct negative deduction (unless they involve nested applications of *reductio*). Thus, it makes sense for Aristotle in chapter 1. 26 to focus on the more interesting question of whether direct negative demonstrations are better than those demonstrations by *reductio* that establish a negative conclusion.

from the *Prior Analytics*. In particular, it relies on the assumption, introduced in *Posterior Analytics* I. 19–22, that demonstrations are based on structures of acyclic a-paths. It is therefore not surprising that the discussion in *Posterior Analytics* I. 26 takes a different form from the treatment of *reductio* in the *Prior Analytics*. Of course, Aristotle's argument in I. 26, like in other parts of the *Posterior Analytics*, is highly compressed and stands in need of extensive interpretation.[153] Nonetheless, the argument is coherent and well suited to the aims of the chapter. It succeeds in establishing that all direct demonstrations, but not all demonstrations by *reductio*, proceed from premises that are prior in nature to the conclusion.

Friedrich Solmsen has argued that the account of demonstration presented in the first book of the *Posterior Analytics* is based on what he calls *Eidosketten*, chains of universal terms arranged in order of generality.[154] In the same vein, Smith maintains that Aristotle's 'theory of demonstration is the theory of the structure of a system of terms arranged in ordered "chains" (συστοιχίαι)'.[155] In accordance with this view, I have argued that any Aristotelian science determines a structure of a-paths in which terms are connected by immediate universal affirmations. Given that a-paths are acyclic, they give rise to a well-defined relation of priority in nature among scientific propositions. It is this relation of priority in nature, I submit, that lies at the heart of Aristotle's argument in *Posterior Analytics* I. 26.[156]

New York University

[153] Kirchmann, *Erläuterungen*, 116–17.

[154] Solmsen, *Entwicklung*, 53–7 and 81–122; id., 'The Discovery of the Syllogism', *Philosophical Review*, 50 (1941), 410–21 at 410 and 420.

[155] Smith, 'Syllogism', 122.

[156] Earlier versions of this paper were presented at Fudan University, Humboldt University Berlin, Peking University, Princeton University, Shandong University Jinan, Tufts University, UCLA, UC San Diego, University of Bologna, University of Campinas, University of Utah, University of Vienna, and Williams College. I would like to thank all those in attendance for their stimulating questions and helpful comments, especially Francesco Ademollo, Lucas Angioni, Rob Bolton, David Charles, Adam Crager, Michel Crubellier, Paolo Fait, Mary-Louise Gill, Katerina Ierodiakonou, Monte Johnson, George Karamanolis, Hendrik Lorenz, Henry Mendell, Stephen Menn, Calvin Normore, Christof Rapp, Samuel Rickless, Anne Siebels Peterson, Gisela Striker, Wei Wang, Eric Watkins, and Breno Zuppolini. In preparing the final version of the paper, I have benefited from generous and detailed written comments by Victor Caston, Paolo Crivelli, Riccardo Strobino, and two anonymous referees for *Oxford Studies in Ancient Philosophy*. Finally, I am very grateful to Kit Fine, Ben Morison, and Jacob Rosen for invaluable discussions and suggestions which led to significant improvements in the paper.

BIBLIOGRAPHY

Albertus Magnus, *Opera omnia*, vol. ii, ed. A. Borgnet (Paris, 1890).

Arnauld, A. and Nicole, P., *La Logique ou l'art de penser* [*Logique*], ed. P. Clair and F. Girbal, 2nd edn. (Paris, 1993).

Barnes, J., 'Property in Aristotle's *Topics*', *Archiv für Geschichte der Philosophie*, 52 (1970), 136–55.

Barnes, J., *Aristotle's* Posterior Analytics, 1st edn. [*Posterior Analytics 1st edn.*] (Oxford, 1975).

Barnes, J. (ed.), *The Complete Works of Aristotle: The Revised Oxford Translation* [*Complete Works*], 2 vols. (Princeton, 1984).

Barnes, J., *Aristotle's* Posterior Analytics, 2nd edn. [*Posterior Analytics 2nd edn.*] (Oxford, 1993).

Barnes, J., *Truth, etc.: Six Lectures on Ancient Logic* (Oxford, 2007).

Barrow, I., *The Mathematical Works of Isaac Barrow*, ed. W. Whewell (Cambridge, 1860).

Biancani, G., *De mathematicarum natura dissertatio* (Bologna, 1615).

Biese, F., *Die Philosophie des Aristoteles*, i: Logik und Metaphysik (Berlin, 1835).

Bolzano, B., *Wissenschaftslehre: Versuch einer ausführlichen und größtentheils neuen Darstellung der Logik mit steter Rücksicht auf deren bisherige Bearbeiter* [*Wissenschaftslehre*], 4 vols. (Sulzbach, 1837).

Bronstein, D., *Aristotle on Knowledge and Learning: The* Posterior Analytics [*Knowledge and Learning*] (Oxford, 2016).

Brunschwig, J., *Aristote*, Topiques, *Livres I–IV* (Paris, 1967).

Burnyeat, M. F., 'Aristotle on Understanding Knowledge' ['Understanding Knowledge'], in E. Berti (ed.), *Aristotle on Science: The* Posterior Analytics, *Proceedings of the Eighth Symposium Aristotelicum* (Padua, 1981), 97–139.

Centrone, S., 'Das Problem der apagogischen Beweise in Bolzanos *Beyträgen* und seiner *Wissenschaftslehre*', *History and Philosophy of Logic*, 33 (2012), 127–57.

Colyvan, M., *An Introduction to the Philosophy of Mathematics* (Cambridge, 2012).

Corcoran, J., 'Completeness of an Ancient Logic', *Journal of Symbolic Logic*, 37 (1972), 696–702.

Corcoran, J., 'Aristotle's Natural Deduction System', in id. (ed.), *Ancient Logic and its Modern Interpretations* (Dordrecht, 1974), 85–131.

Correia, F., 'Logical Grounds' ['Grounds'], *Review of Symbolic Logic*, 7 (2014), 31–59.

Correia, F., 'An Impure Logic of Representational Grounding', *Journal of Philosophical Logic*, 46 (2017), 507–38.

Crager, A. D., *Meta-Logic in Aristotle's Epistemology* (diss. Princeton, 2015).

Crivelli, P., 'Aristotle on Syllogisms from a Hypothesis' ['Hypothesis'], in A. Longo (ed.), *Argument from Hypothesis in Ancient Philosophy* (Naples, 2011), 95–184.

Detel, W., *Aristoteles:* Analytica posteriora, 2 vols. [*Analytica posteriora*] (Berlin, 1993).

Ebert, T. and Nortmann, U., *Aristoteles:* Analytica priora, *Buch I* [*Analytica priora*] (Berlin, 2007).

Edlow, R. B., *Galen on Language and Ambiguity* (Leiden, 1977).

Fine, K., 'Guide to Ground', in F. Correia and B. Schnieder (eds.), *Metaphysical Grounding: Understanding the Structure of Reality* (Cambridge, 2012), 37–80.

Fine, K., 'The Pure Logic of Ground' ['Pure Logic'], *Review of Symbolic Logic*, 5 (2012), 1–25.

Fine, K., 'Some Remarks on Bolzano on Ground', in S. Roski and B. Schnieder (eds.), *Priority Among Truths: Bernard Bolzano's Philosophy of Grounding* (Oxford, *forthcoming*).

Frede, M., 'Stoic vs. Aristotelian Syllogistic', *Archiv für Geschichte der Philosophie*, 56 (1974), 1–32.

Galilei, G., *Tractatus de praecognitionibus et praecognitis and Tractatio de demonstratione*, ed. W. F. Edwards (Padua, 1988).

Goldin, O. and Martijn, M., *Philoponus:* On Aristotle, *Posterior Analytics* 1. 19–34 (London, 2012).

Grosseteste, R., *Commentarius in Posteriorum Analyticorum libros* [*Commentarius*], ed. P. Rossi (Florence, 1981).

Hamlyn, D. W., 'Aristotle on Predication' ['Predication'], *Phronesis*, 6 (1961), 110–26.

Hanna, G., 'Reflections on Proof as Explanation', in A. J. Stylianides and G. Harel (eds.), *Advances in Mathematics Education Research on Proof and Proving* (Cham, 2018), 3–18.

Heath, T. L., *The Thirteen Books of Euclid's* Elements, vol. i: Introduction and Books I, II [*Elements*] (Cambridge, 1908).

Helmig, C., 'Proclus' Criticism of Aristotle's Theory of Abstraction and Concept Formation in *Analytica Posteriora* II 19', in F. de Haas, M. Leunissen, and M. Martijn (eds.), *Interpreting Aristotle's* Posterior Analytics *in Late Antiquity and Beyond* (Leiden, 2010), 27–54.

Jakob, L. H., *Grundriß der allgemeinen Logik und kritische Anfangsgründe der allgemeinen Metaphysik*, 4th edn. (Halle/Saale, 1800).

Kant, I., *Kritik der reinen Vernunft*, in *Kant's gesammelte Schriften I*, Königlich Preußische Akademie der Wissenschaften (Berlin, 1911).

Kiesewetter, J. G. C. C., *Grundriß einer allgemeinen Logik nach Kantischen Grundsätzen*, 1. Theil: Reine allgemeine Logik, 4th edn. (Leipzig, 1824).

Kilwardby, R., *Notule libri Posteriorum* [*Notule*], ed. D. Cannone (Cassino, 2003–4).

Kirchmann, J. H. von, *Erläuterungen zu den zweiten Analytiken des Aristoteles* [*Erläuterungen*] (Leipzig, 1878).

Korbmacher, J., 'Axiomatic Theories of Partial Ground I: The Base Theory', *Journal of Philosophical Logic*, 47 (2018), 161–91.

Krug, W. T., *System der theoretischen Philosophie*, 1. Theil: Denklehre oder Logik (Königsberg, 1806).

Lange, M., *Because Without Cause: Non-Causal Explanations in Science and Mathematics* (Oxford, 2017).

Lear, J., 'Aristotle's Compactness Proof' ['Compactness'], *Journal of Philosophy*, 76 (1979), 198–215.

Lear, J., *Aristotle and Logical Theory* [*Logical Theory*] (Cambridge, 1980).

Lipton, P., 'Understanding without Explanation', in H. W. de Regt, S. Leonelli, and K. Eigner (eds.), *Scientific Understanding: Philosophical Perspectives* (Pittsburgh, 2009), 43–63.

Lipton, P., 'Mathematical Understanding', in J. Polkinghorne (ed.), *Meaning in Mathematics* (Oxford, 2011), 49–54.

Lotze, H., *System der Philosophie*, 1. Theil: Drei Bücher der Logik [*Logik*] (Leipzig, 1874).

Löwenheim, L., 'On Making Indirect Proofs Direct', *Scripta Mathematica*, 12 (1946), 125–39.

Łukasiewicz, J., *Aristotle's Syllogistic from the Standpoint of Modern Formal Logic*, 2nd edn. (Oxford, 1957).

Maier, H., *Die Syllogistik des Aristoteles*, ii/1: Formenlehre und Technik des Syllogismus (Tübingen, 1900).

Maier, H., *Die Syllogistik des Aristoteles*, ii/2: Die Entstehung der Aristotelischen Logik [*Entstehung*] (Tübingen, 1900).

Malink, M., 'Aristotle on Principles as Elements' ['Elements'], *Oxford Studies in Ancient Philosophy*, 53 (2017), 163–213.

Mancosu, P., 'On the Status of Proofs by Contradiction in the Seventeenth Century', *Synthese*, 88 (1991), 15–41.

Mancosu, P., *Philosophy of Mathematics and Mathematical Practice in the Seventeenth Century* [*Mathematics*] (New York, 1996).

Mancosu, P., 'On Mathematical Explanation', in E. Grosholz and H. Berger (eds.), *The Growth of Mathematical Knowledge* (Dordrecht, 2000), 103–19.

McKirahan, R. D., *Principles and Proofs: Aristotle's Theory of Demonstrative Science* [*Principles*] (Princeton, 1992).

Mignucci, M., *L'argomentazione dimostrativa in Aristotele: commento agli Analitici secondi I* [*L'argomentazione dimostrativa*] (Padua, 1975).

Mignucci, M., *Aristotele*: Analitici secondi (Rome, 2007).

Morrow, G. R., *Proclus: A Commentary on the First Book of Euclid's Elements*, 2nd edn. [*Proclus*] (Princeton, 1992).

Mure, G. R. G., *Aristotle's* Analytica posteriora [*Posteriora*], in *The Works of Aristotle Translated into English*, ed. W. D. Ross and J. A. Smith, vol. i (Oxford, 1928).

Owen, O. F., *The* Organon, *or Logical Treatises, of Aristotle*, vol. i [*Organon*] (London, 1889).

Pacius, J., *Aristotelis Stagiritae Peripateticorum principis Organum*, 2nd edn. [*Organum*] (Frankfurt a.M., 1597).

Parsons, T., *Articulating Medieval Logic* (Oxford, 2014).

Pellegrin, P., *Aristote:* Seconds Analytiques [*Seconds Analytiques*] (Paris, 2005).

Poston, T., *Reason and Explanation: A Defense of Explanatory Coherentism* (New York, 2014).

Primavesi, O., *Die Aristotelische Topik: Ein Interpretationsmodell und seine Erprobung am Beispiel von* Topik *B* (München 1996).

Reinhold, E., *Die Logik oder die allgemeine Denkformenlehre* (Jena, 1827).

Roski, S., *Bolzano's Conception of Grounding* (Frankfurt a.M., 2017).

Ross, W. D., *Aristotle's* Prior *and* Posterior Analytics*: A Revised Text with Introduction and Commentary* [*Analytics*] (Oxford, 1949).

Schnieder, B., 'A Logic for "Because"', *Review of Symbolic Logic*, 4 (2011), 445–65.

Seidl, H., *Aristoteles:* Zweite Analytiken, 2nd edn. [*Zweite Analytiken*] (Würzburg, 1987).

Smiley, T. J., 'What is a Syllogism?', *Journal of Philosophical Logic*, 2 (1973), 136–54.

Smiley, T. J., 'Aristotle's Completeness Proof', *Ancient Philosophy*, 14 (1994), 25–38.

Smith, R., 'The Relationship of Aristotle's Two *Analytics*' ['Relationship'], *Classical Quarterly*, NS, 32 (1982), 327–35.

Smith, R., 'The Syllogism in *Posterior Analytics* I' ['Syllogism'], *Archiv für Geschichte der Philosophie*, 64 (1982), 113–35.

Smith, R., 'Aristotle as Proof Theorist', *Philosophia Naturalis*, 27 (1984), 590–7.

Smith, R., 'Immediate Propositions and Aristotle's Proof Theory' ['Immediate Propositions'], *Ancient Philosophy*, 6 (1986), 47–68.

Smith, R., *Aristotle:* Prior Analytics [*Prior Analytics*] (Indianapolis, 1989).

Smith, R., 'Predication and Deduction in Aristotle: Aspirations to Completeness', *Topoi*, 10 (1991), 43–52.

Smith, R., 'Aristotle's Regress Argument' ['Regress'], in I. Angelelli and M. Cerezo (eds.), *Studies on the History of Logic: Proceedings of the III. Symposium on the History of Logic* (Berlin, 1996), 21–32.

Smith, R., 'Aristotle's Theory of Demonstration', in G. Anagnostopoulos (ed.), *A Companion to Aristotle* (Oxford, 2009), 51–65.

Solmsen, F., *Die Entwicklung der Aristotelischen Logik und Rhetorik* [*Entwicklung*] (Berlin, 1929).

Solmsen, F., 'The Discovery of the Syllogism', *Philosophical Review*, 50 (1941), 410–21.

Soto, D., *In libros Posteriorum Aristotelis sive de demonstratione absolutissima commentaria* (Venice, 1574).

Striker, G., 'Review of J. Barnes, *Aristotle's* Posterior Analytics' ['Review of Barnes'], *Zeitschrift für philosophische Forschung*, 31 (1977), 316–20.

Striker, G., 'Perfection and Reduction in Aristotle's *Prior Analytics*', in M. Frede and G. Striker (eds.), *Rationality in Greek Thought* (Oxford, 1996), 203–19.

Striker, G., *Aristotle's* Prior Analytics, *Book 1* [*Prior Analytics*] (Oxford, 2009).

Strobach, N., *Aristoteles: Analytica priora, Buch II* (Berlin, 2015).

Thom, P., *The Syllogism* [*Syllogism*] (Munich, 1981).

Tredennick, H., *Aristotle: Posterior Analytics* [*Posterior Analytics*] (Cambridge, MA, 1960).

Trendelenburg, F. A., *Elementa logices Aristoteleae*, 5th edn. (Berlin, 1862).

Trendelenburg, F. A., *Logische Untersuchungen,* 2. Band, 3rd edn. (Leipzig, 1870).

Tricot, J., *Aristote: Seconds Analytiques* [*Seconds Analytiques*] (Paris, 2012).

Waitz, T., *Aristotelis Organon Graece* [*Organon*], 2 vols. (Leipzig, 1844–6).

Weidemann, H., 'Aristotle on the Reducibility of All Valid Syllogistic Moods to the Two Universal Moods of the First Figure (APr A7, $29^{b}1$–25)', *History and Philosophy of Logic*, 25 (2004), 73–8.

Williams, M., *Studies in the Manuscript Tradition of Aristotle's* Analytica (Königstein, 1984).

Wilson, N. G., 'More about γράφεται Variants', *Acta Antiqua Academiae Scientiarum Hungaricae*, 48 (2008), 79–81.

Zabarella, J., *Opera logica* [*Opera logica*] (Frankfurt a.M., 1608).

ARISTOTLE ON SPONTANEOUS
GENERATION, SPONTANEITY,
AND NATURAL PROCESSES

EMILY KRESS

IN the *Generation of Animals* and other biological works, Aristotle contrasts standard animal generation with what he calls 'spontaneous generation' (γένεσις αὐτόματος). He reports that spontaneous generation happens when some material—often mud, but also cheese, wool, wood, snow, dung, vinegar, figs, and cabbage stalks[1]—begins to putrefy. In so doing, this material gives rise to a new organism. These organisms include some insects, as well as certain hard-shelled sea creatures, such as the oysters, barnacles, cockles, and scallops that Aristotle calls 'testacea' (ὀστρακόδερμα).

Roughly, spontaneous generation differs from standard animal generation in that spontaneously generated organisms lack parents of the same kind. After all, they develop from putrefying stuff, not materials provided by parents. This difference between standard and spontaneous generation is the one Aristotle emphasizes in the opening stages of the *Generation of Animals*, before getting into the muddy details of their generative process (*GA* 1. 1, 715^{a}24–5, 715^{b}4–6).[2] This rough-and-ready statement of the difference, however, is not so much an *explanation* of what makes spontaneous generation special as it is an invitation to find it puzzling.

The puzzle has two components. Both are concerned with what to make of—and where to locate—the difference between standard and spontaneous generation. The first is whether this difference—the absence of parent animals—even matters. In a rough initial formulation, we might ask: is the absence of parents just a *quirky fact* about spontaneously generated organisms—albeit one with

---

[1] For these materials, see especially *History of Animals* 5. 15–16, 19, 31–2, and 6. 15, 16. For an overview of the species, see P. Louis, 'La génération spontanée chez Aristote' ['Génération spontanée'], *Revue de Synthèse*, 89 (1968), 293–305.

[2] The Greek text is taken from H. J. Drossaart Lulofs (ed.), *De generatione animalium* (Oxford, 1965). Translations of Aristotle are my own, but are indebted to those of Peck, Lee, Charlton, and the *Revised Oxford Translation*.

Emily Kress, *Aristotle on Spontaneous Generation, Spontaneity, and Natural Processes*. In: Oxford Studies in Ancient Philosophy Volume LVIII. Edited by: Victor Caston, Oxford University Press (2020).
© Emily Kress.
DOI: 10.1093/oso/9780198858997.003.0005

implications for their level of sophistication[3]—or does it make a difference to the *causal structure* of their generative process?

What makes the question pressing is that spontaneous generation has a number of intriguing features that make it hard to categorize. On the one hand, it produces good outcomes. It is responsible for *every* generation of certain kinds of animals, including various oysters, whelks, and so on. Insofar as processes that generate animals are the sorts of things that happen 'for the sake of' (ἕνεκα) something (*GA* 1. 1, 715ᵃ4–8; 2. 4, 739ᵇ28, 2. 6, 742ᵃ20–ᵇ17), it may not be unreasonable to wonder if spontaneous generation counts as happening for the sake of something too. At the same time, it is not obvious how muddy water might 'putrefy' for the sake of producing oyster life. Surely, putrefying is a paradigmatic destructive process that does *not* happen for the sake of something.

We thus have reason to take spontaneous generation to be— roughly—both the same sort of causal process as standard generation and something totally different. This formulation of the puzzle reveals a parallel to a number of debates, including some in the philosophy of mind about whether hallucination and veridical perception are of a common kind,[4] or whether we should be *disjunctivists* about them. Minimally, disjunctivism about perception holds that the genus to which the experiences we have in veridical perception and hallucination belong is irreducibly *disjunctive*. Consequently, it denies that we should give the same account of these experiences, even if they are subjectively indistinguishable. Disjunctivists sometimes propose to explain the disjunctive nature of this genus in terms of the absence of a common 'fundamental kind' to which veridical perception and hallucination both belong—that is, a common 'kind in virtue of which the event has the nature that it does'.[5]

---

[3] Cf. A. Gotthelf, 'Teleology and Spontaneous Generation in Aristotle: A Discussion' ['Teleology'] in id., *Teleology, First Principles, and Scientific Method in Aristotle's Biology* (Oxford, 2012), 142–50 at 149 and S. Stavrianeas, 'Spontaneous Generation in Aristotle's Biology' ['Spontaneous Generation'], *Rhizai*, 2 (2008), 303–38 at 311 ff.

[4] Or have a 'common element', etc. For options, see A. Byrne and H. Logue, 'Either/Or', in A. Haddock and F. Macpherson (eds.), *Disjunctivism: Perception, Action, Knowledge* [*Disjunctivism*] (Oxford, 2008), 57–94.

[5] M. G. F. Martin, 'The Limits of Self-Awareness' ['Limits'], *Philosophical Studies*, 120 (2004), 37–89 at 60. This formulation leaves open the possibility that these states have a common feature, so long as it is not *fundamental*.

My proposal is that a fully satisfying solution to the puzzle about spontaneous generation sketched above might supply an answer to a parallel question: is the genus to which standard and spontaneous generation belong irreducibly disjunctive? If it is, we might propose to explain this fact by denying that standard and spontaneous generation are causal processes of the same 'fundamental kind'. By framing the first puzzle in terms of disjunctivism, we can see that its resolution will not be of interest only to scholars of ancient biology. It may provide clues to parallel issues elsewhere in Aristotle's philosophy: whether he is a disjunctivist about perception and action, and what form that disjunctivism might take.

The second component of the puzzle is likewise concerned with where to locate the deviancy of spontaneous generation. A natural thought is that spontaneous generation differs from standard generation just by being 'spontaneous' in Aristotle's technical sense. In *Physics* 2. 4–6, Aristotle offers an account of things that happen 'spontaneously' (ἀπὸ τοῦ αὐτομάτου, διὰ τὸ αὐτόματον) and 'by chance' (ἀπὸ τύχης). (For ease of reference, I call these 'spontaneous' or 'spontaneously caused proceedings'.[6]) They include the case of a man who goes to the market with the aim of prosecuting someone in court, but who runs into his debtor and so collects on a debt. The man's action has several significant features. First, it is among things that are for the sake of something, in particular, getting back the money.[7] In addition, it contrasts with standard cases of things that happen for the sake of something in that it is 'accidentally' (κατὰ συμβεβηκός) caused and happens 'neither ... always nor for the most part' (οὔτε ... αἰεὶ οὔτε ὡς ἐπὶ τὸ πολύ, 2. 5, 196ᵇ12–13).

The *Physics* account of spontaneous proceedings bears similarities to the biological works' account of spontaneous generation. Most obviously, the same family of terms—forms of *automaton*—is used to refer to both.[8] Moreover, both are introduced by way of

---

[6] Terminology inspired by S. Kelsey, '*Physics* 199ᵃ8–12', *Apeiron*, 44 (2011), 1–12. 'Spontaneous proceeding' proves to be a more convenient expression than 'things that happen spontaneously', as well as capturing the cautious spirit of *Physics* 2. Of course, the proceedings of interest below are *processes*.

[7] *Phys.* 2. 5, 196ᵇ21–2, 196ᵇ34, 197ᵃ16; 2. 6, 197ᵇ18–20; 2. 8, 199ᵇ21–2.

[8] In the *Generation of Animals*: ὥσπερ αὐτοματιζούσης τῆς φύσεως; αὐτόματα; ἐν τοῖς αὐτομάτοις; αὐτομάτως; φυόμενον αὐτόματον; ἀπὸ συστάσεως αὐτομάτου; ἡ γένεσις αὐτόματος. The *Generation of Animals* uses αὐτόματ- words in three contexts. One is spontaneously generated organisms, my focus here. Another is wind-eggs, which are formed 'spontaneously' (αὐτόματα, 3. 1, 749ᵃ34–ᵇ1)—by the female concocting

contrast with standard cases of *teleological* causation (standard
animal generation, standard cases of collecting a debt).⁹ Finally,
Physics 2 refers to spontaneous proceedings that 'could be done'
(ἂν πραχθείη) 'by nature' (ἀπὸ φύσεως, 2. 5, 196ᵇ22), making it not
unreasonable to look for such cases in the natural world. All these
factors suggest that spontaneous generation may be importantly
like spontaneously caused proceedings.

However, the broad tendency of recent philosophical scholarship—with a few exceptions, most notably Lennox's important
work—has been to argue that the *Physics'* spontaneous proceedings
are spontaneous in a completely different way than spontaneous
generation is.¹⁰ One motivation is an apparent tension between
the *Physics'* claim that spontaneous proceedings happen 'neither
always nor for the most part' and the biological works' claims that
testacea and insects are generated out of rotting materials with a good
deal of regularity.¹¹ How can spontaneous generation be thought

---

her residue without the male. These reach a further stage of generation than is normally possible without male intervention (750ᵇ–751ᵇ). Wind-eggs are not spontaneous in the way testacea are: whereas wind-eggs have a female parent, testacea are
parentless. Still, they undergo a change that normally requires a cause they lack—a
fact that suggests parallels to spontaneous generation. A third context is the 'automatic puppets' to which Aristotle compares the organized changes that give rise to
naturally generated organisms (2. 1, 734ᵇ9–17; 2. 5, 741ᵇ7–15). These are not spontaneous in the *Physics* sense. Cf. L. Judson, 'Chance and "Always or For the Most
Part" in Aristotle' ['Chance'], in id., *Aristotle's* Physics: *A Collection of Essays*
(Clarendon, 1991), 73–99 at 74 n. 2.

⁹ *GA* 1. 1, 715ᵃ25, 715ᵇ4–5, 715ᵇ25–8; 1. 16, 721ᵃ7; 1. 23, 731ᵇ12–13; 2. 1, 732ᵇ11–12;
2. 3, 736ᵇ33 ff.; 2. 6, 743ᵃ35–6; 3. 9, 758ᵃ29–31, 758ᵇ7–8, 758ᵇ21–4.

¹⁰ See D. M. Balme, 'Development of Biology in Aristotle and Theophrastus:
Theory of Spontaneous Generation' ['Development'], *Phronesis*, 7 (1962), 91–104;
D. Hull, 'The Conflict Between Spontaneous Generation and Aristotle's
Metaphysics' ['Conflict'], *Proceedings of the Inter-American Congress of Philosophy*,
7 (1967–8), 245–50; endorsed by Gotthelf, 'Teleology', 143 n. 3; and by D. Henry,
'Themistius and Spontaneous Generation in Aristotle's *Metaphysics'* ['Themistius'],
Oxford Studies in Ancient Philosophy, 24 (2003), 183–207 at 184 n. 1. For the view
that spontaneous generation does not satisfy the *Physics'* criterion but that there is
a distinction between the *Physics'* and *Metaphysics'* projects, see A. Bonello,
Aristotle on Spontaneity [*Spontaneity*], PhD diss., University of Toronto, 2015. For
Lennox's alternative, see his 'Teleology, Chance, and Aristotle's Theory of
Spontaneous Generation' ['Teleology'], in id., *Aristotle's Biology: Studies in the
Origins of Life Science* (Cambridge, 2001), 229–49.

¹¹ Lennox has called this 'the central outstanding problem with Aristotle's doctrine of spontaneity in nature' ('Teleology', 243). In addition to the debate about
the *Physics* 2 notion of spontaneity that I focus on here, there is also one about the
relation to *Metaphysics Z*. 7–9's discussion of spontaneity, focusing especially on the
claims that spontaneously generated products come to be both with and without

to happen neither always nor for the most part when it happens all the time?[12]

My first aim is to show that these two puzzles about the deviancy of spontaneous generation—whether it shares a common 'fundamental' kind with standard generation and whether it is spontaneously caused in the sense of *Physics* 2—turn on the same questions about its *causal structure*. This approach builds on Lennox's suggestion that an adequate interpretation should appeal to Aristotle's views about the *efficient causes* of spontaneous generation.[13] It extends the approach by arguing for the importance of the *types* of *processes* these efficient causes initiate—and their relation to *other* process types involved in spontaneous generation. (The spontaneous 'proceedings' here are, I will argue, efficient causal *processes*.) My overarching aim is to show that attending to these types opens up a fruitful strategy for approaching the puzzles of spontaneous generation.

My procedure is as follows. Sections 1 and 2 sketch some initial motivations for concentrating on the process types of spontaneous generation. Section 2 also provides an outline of the main features of spontaneous proceedings, according to *Physics* 2. Section 3 argues that spontaneous generation can be described (in a way still in need of explanation) in terms of *two* types: putrefaction and concoction. Section 4 begins to offer an explanation for these two descriptions by examining Aristotle's accounts of the putrefaction and concoction types, and how they fit into his theory of efficient causation. Section 5 begins to use this approach to resolve the

---

seed and when the matter moves itself (as well as the compatibility of these ideas with *Physics* 2. 4–6). See Bonello, *Spontaneity*, 81–103; Gotthelf, 'Teleology', 149; Henry, 'Themistius', 183–207; Lennox, 'Teleology', 234; K. Zwier, 'Methodology in Aristotle's Theory of Spontaneous Generation' ['Methodology'], *Journal of the History of Biology*, 51 (2018), 355–86 at 374 ff. My focus here is on *Physics* 2. 4–6.

[12] Zwier cautiously suggests that '[t]he inherited term "spontaneous generation" [. . .] was merely a referring term, and there were good reasons to maintain its usage', which leaves 'room for some inconsistency' ('Methodology', 380). My question is about how much inconsistency there is and where to locate it. For a good account of the context for Aristotle's account of spontaneity, see M. R. Johnson, 'The Medical Background of Aristotle's Theory of Nature and Spontaneity' ['Medical Background'], *Proceedings of the Boston Area Colloquium in Ancient Philosophy*, 27 (2012), 105–52. For a brief suggestion that Aristotle inherits how 'the Greeks used the term', see also C. Panayides, 'Aristotle on Chance and Spontaneous Generation: A Discussion Note', *Filozofia*, 68 (2013), 121–2.

[13] Lennox puts the point in terms of 'formal replication'. See below.

puzzles about the deviancy of spontaneous generation. I argue that Aristotle inclines towards a particularly interesting version of *disjunctivism* about animal generation. He thinks that spontaneous generation and standard generation belong to different 'fundamental' types, because these processes unfold in similar (concoction-like) ways but in virtue of different efficient causal capacities. In the standard case, these causal capacities properly cause concoction, but in the spontaneous one, they properly cause putrefaction. A further upshot is an account of why spontaneous generation is rare and accidentally caused: it is rare for processes of the putrefaction type to unfold in the way the processes of the concoction type do.

1. The importance of process types

Process types provide a crucial tool for addressing the puzzling deviancy of spontaneous generation. In this section, I offer one textual and one philosophical consideration that favour this approach. On the textual side, attending to process types reflects Aristotle's own procedure in the *Generation of Animals*. The task of this work is to specify the *efficient causes* of animal generation (1. 1, 715^{a}13–14). Considering this cause, it argues, is 'in a way the same' (τρόπον τινὰ ταὐτόν) as considering 'the generation of each [animal]' (τῆς γενέσεως τῆς ἑκάστου, 715^{a}14–15). It soon emerges that this project is as much about specifying the causal *processes* involved in efficient causation as it is about specifying their efficient causes. The *Generation of Animals* makes especially frequent appeal to the process type concoction (πέψις).[14] Other types matter too, like *drying* (ξηραίνεσθαι, 2. 4 739^{b}27 ξηραινομένης, 29; 2. 6, 743^{a}18, ^{b}6). This is just what we should expect, for the efficient cause is defined in terms of a *process*: it is 'that from which the process comes' (ὅθεν ἡ κίνησις, *Phys.* 2. 3, 195^{a}8) and 'that from which the process first comes' (ὅθεν ἡ

---

[14] For example, 1. 8, 718^{b}21; 1. 18, 725^{b}21; 1. 19, 726^{b}5; 3. 2, 753^{a}19; 4. 1, 765^{b}15–16; 4. 6, 775^{a}17; 4. 8, 776^{a}22, 776^{b}35; 5. 6, 786^{a}17. On this type, see especially I. Düring, *Aristotle's Chemical Treatise:* Meteorologica, *Book IV,* with introduction and commentary [*Chemical Treatise*] (Elanders, 1944), 35–40, 68 ff.; G. E. R. Lloyd, 'The Master Cook', in id., *Aristotelian Explorations* ['Master Cook'] (Cambridge, 1996), 84–103; and G. Freudenthal, *Aristotle's Theory of Material Substance: Heat and Pneuma, Form and Soul* (Clarendon, 1995), 149–71. For applications to spontaneous generation, see Stavrianeas, 'Spontaneous Generation', 328 ff. and below.

κίνησις πρῶτον, 2. 7, 198ᵃ26). My focus on process types is thus in keeping with the *Generation of Animals*' project of investigating the activity of efficient causes.

The close connection between *process types* and *efficient causes* also reveals a philosophical motivation for my approach. Lennox has made progress in understanding spontaneous generation by observing that its efficient causes differ from those of standard generation. His idea is that standard generation involves 'formal replication', but spontaneous generation does not. In standard generation, as in other processes susceptible to teleological explanation, there is 'a *formal identity* between the source of that process's efficient causes and the process's outcome'.[15] In spontaneous generation, however, the efficient cause and the outcome do *not* share a form.

Lennox's notion of formal replication fits well with *Physics* 3. 2's observation that in a process, 'the changer (τὸ κινοῦν) always bears some form, either this or this such or this much, which is a source and cause of the change (τῆς κινήσεως), when it causes change' (κινῇ, 202ᵃ9–11).[16] If an efficient cause is to transfer a form to a product, it must have this form too. This is why the process it initiates is characterized by formal replication.

This observation is a valuable starting point for making sense of spontaneous generation. Still, it leaves open tricky questions.[17] What is involved in 'bearing' a form? *How* do forms get transmitted to products? These questions are especially pertinent to ask of

[15] Lennox, 'Teleology', 233; cf. 231. Cf. Johnson, 'Medical Background', 127 ff. on the sameness of form of product and producer.

[16] εἶδος δὲ ἀεὶ οἴσεταί τι τὸ κινοῦν, ἤτοι τόδε ἢ τοιόνδε ἢ τοσόνδε, ὃ ἔσται ἀρχὴ καὶ αἴτιον τῆς κινήσεως, ὅταν κινῇ. The text is taken from W. D. Ross (ed.), *Aristotelis Physica* (Oxford, 1950). I translate using 'change' rather than 'process', because English lacks an appropriate process-inspired translation for κινῇ.

[17] I thus aim to provide an account of spontaneous generation that builds on, but also goes beyond, Lennox's formal replication, paying particular to attention to what goes on during the unfolding of the *process*. Having a more determinate account of what counts as formal replication or bearing a form proves useful for tricky cases (like those below), where a process brings out an 'underlying shape'. Moreover, I connect these issues more clearly with the details of *Meteorologica* 4 and show how they are relevant to thinking about spontaneous causation. This, in turn, raises new questions, not considered by Lennox, about whether spontaneous and standard generations are concoctions. In addition, I differ with Lennox on how I understand the requirement that spontaneous generation be *rare*, its application to the material mix that determines the shape the testacean takes (nn. 30 and 32), and about whether the heat in the *pneuma* must be species-specific (n. 64).

Aristotle's *kinēseis*. These are *processes:* the sorts of things that continue and unfold through time.[18] It is appropriate to ask of them not just what results they produce, but *how* they do so. In expounding a contemporary notion of a process, Steward thus writes that 'we have to explain not only the occurrence of its front end, as it were, but also its *course*'. The reason is that '[t]o explain its *initiation* is not to explain everything that needs to be explained'.[19]

In the Aristotelian case, the question is whether there is such a characteristic 'course' by which forms are borne to products—whether a process that does so has a particular structure of stages or unfolds in a particular manner.[20] If there is, we need to know whether it is characteristic of certain process *types*. Does spontaneous generation have this course? If so, does this make it belong to the associated types?

The question is made even more pressing by Aristotle's presentation of the biological facts. As we will see, some of his vocabulary for describing spontaneous generation is markedly similar to that for describing the key process type of standard generation. Without further details about what these *types* are like, it is hard to say exactly how they are alike and how they differ—and so to solve our puzzles.

2. Spontaneous generation and spontaneous causation

Further philosophical support for an approach that emphasizes process types can be obtained by reflecting on the puzzle about whether spontaneous generation is *spontaneously caused* (in the *Physics* 2 sense). Understood correctly, this puzzle is closely connected with

---

[18] In taking a *kinēsis* to be a *process*, I follow D. Charles, 'Aristotle's Processes' ['Processes'], in M. Leunissen (ed.), *Aristotle's Physics: A Critical Guide* (Cambridge, 2015), 186–205. My interpretation is compatible with taking *kinēseis* to be events, so long as these have the right structure.

[19] H. Steward, 'Processes, Continuants, and Individuals', *Mind*, 122 (2013), 781–812 at 810. For a '*structure* of stages', see R. Stout, *Things That Happen Because They Should: A Teleological Approach to Action* (Oxford, 1996), 50.

[20] For an argument that such a 'manner' plays a major role in Aristotle's teleology, see E. Kress, 'How Things Happen for the Sake of Something: The Dialectical Strategy of Aristotle, *Physics* 2. 8' ['How Things Happen'], *Phronesis*, 64 (2019), 321–47. In this paper, I connect this idea of a manner with questions about process *types*.

the issue of what *types* it belongs to. *Physics* 2. 4–6 offers several conditions for spontaneous causation. I focus on three. First, spontaneous proceedings happen 'neither ... always nor for the most part' (οὔτε ... ἀεὶ οὔτε ὡς ἐπὶ τὸ πολύ)—which I abbreviate as 'rarely'.[21] Second, they are accidentally caused.[22] These conditions are related, and 2. 4–6 often substitutes one for the other. 2. 5, for instance, locates spontaneous proceedings 'in the class of things outside of what is necessary and for the most part' (ἐν τοῖς παρὰ τὸ ἀναγκαῖον καὶ τὸ ὡς ἐπὶ πολύ) and specifically those that can be 'for the sake of something' (ἕνεκά του, 196ᵇ19–21). It later offers roughly the same definition, substituting accidental causation for happening rarely: 'chance is an accidental cause in the class of things that are in accord with choice, among the things that are for the sake of something' (197ᵃ5–6).[23] It is thus plausible to think spontaneous proceedings happen rarely *because* they are accidentally caused.[24] Moreover— this is the third condition—they are among things that are *for the sake of something* (196ᵇ33).

My argument is that to determine whether spontaneous generation meets these conditions, we need to know which process types are involved in it. I begin with the requirement that spontaneous proceedings happen *rarely* and accidentally. These conditions concern *types*. It makes no sense to say that an individual happens rarely. Rather, what is rare is occurrences of some type. Moreover, different ways of specifying these types yield different determinations about whether something counts as happening rarely and as accidentally caused. Consider Aristotle's example in *Physics* 2. 5: the housebuilding craft is a *proper* cause of a house, but the musical is an *accidental* cause (2. 5, 196ᵇ24–9). The housebuilding craft and the housebuilding process it causes are of a type that is non-accidentally related to the house type, but the musical type is accidentally related to it. *Metaphysics* E. 2 offers an example with a slightly different structure, closer to what we will find in spontaneous generation: a pastry chef who aims at producing sweet pastries and also, accidentally, produces health (1027ᵃ3–5). The chef's pastry-making

---

[21] *Phys.* 2. 5, 196ᵇ12–13, 196ᵇ20, 196ᵇ36, 197ᵃ4, 197ᵃ19, 197ᵃ31–2, 197ᵃ35.

[22] *Phys.* 2. 5, 196ᵇ23–9, 197ᵃ12–14, cf. 196ᵇ35; 2. 6, 197ᵇ18–20.

[23] ἡ τύχη αἰτία κατὰ συμβεβηκὸς ἐν τοῖς κατὰ προαίρεσιν τῶν ἕνεκά του. Cf. *Metaphysics* Δ. 30 and *E*. 2.

[24] Judson argues for the stronger claim that the two conditions are 'the *same*' ('Chance', 81). I rely only on the weaker claim.

craft aims at making sweet pastries and so it is the non-accidental cause of the sweet pastry, insofar as it is a sweet pastry. However, this craft is only *accidentally* the cause of a healthy thing, when it just so happens that this sweet pastry is also healthy. As before, the point is that saying that this is a case of accidental causation—and that cases like it happen rarely—depends on identifying the pastry as belonging to two types: the healthy one and the sweet one. If the types were different, these might not be examples of accidental causation (or things that happen rarely). The upshot is that to say whether spontaneous generation is spontaneous, we likewise need to know with which *types* it is associated.

In addition, we need to know what it is for occurrences of these types to happen *rarely*. Since my focus is on elucidating spontaneous generation, I just sketch one prominent account of what it is to happen rarely and show how it can be used to set up the puzzle. As I understand it, Aristotle has what Judson has called a *conditional* frequency account. This means that events of type E_I are said to happen regularly (or rarely, or never) *relative to* events of type E_2.[25] The advantage of this interpretation is that makes Aristotle's claims come out true: while heat waves are rare on the whole, they are common *in summer* (*Phys.* 2. 8, 198^{b}34–199^{a}3).[26] The man who goes to goes to court and collects his debt 'by chance' or 'spontaneously' (2. 5, 197^{a}1–5) does so rarely, even if he spends 'more than half his whole life' running into his debtor. What matters is that acting in such a way as to run into one's debtor is rare *relative to* going to court.[27]

These observations recommend the following way of thinking about accidental causation and rarity. In the formulations below, I intend talk of being 'of' a type to be neutral about whether that

[25] Judson, 'Chance', 83.

[26] For a contrasting view, on which these are frequencies in *ideal* circumstances, see K. Nielsen, 'The Private Parts of Animals: Aristotle on the Teleology of Sexual Difference', *Phronesis*, 53 (2008), 373–405 at 398. Mignucci defends an absolute (rather than conditional) frequency interpretation but qualifies it: 'the phrase OETP [ὡς ἐπὶ τὸ πολύ] in ordinary language generally denotes a plurality of *cases*' ('l'expression OETP au niveau du langage courant dénote en général une pluralité de *cas*', M. Mignucci, ' "Ὡς ἐπὶ τὸ πολύ" et nécessaire dans la conception aristotél-icienne de la science', in E. Berti (ed.), *Aristotle on Science: The* 'Posterior Analytics', Proceedings of the Eighth Symposium Aristotelicum (Editrice Antenore, 1981), 173–203 at 186).

[27] Judson, 'Chance', 85. In emphasizing 'such a way', I go beyond Judson.

type is 'fundamental'. In addition, I intend '*F*' and '*G*' to range over types. For simplicity, I speak of a token of these types as 'an *F*' and tokens as '*F*s', etc.

ACCIDENTAL CAUSATION: a *G* is accidentally caused if its cause is properly (i.e. non-accidentally) a cause of *F*s and this *G* is only accidentally an *F*.[28]

RARITY: *G*s are rare relative to *F*s if it is rare for an *F* also to be a *G*.

My project below is to extend this basic model, derived from *Physics* 2, to spontaneous generation.

To determine whether spontaneous generation happens rarely and accidentally, we therefore need to know *relative to what* it might do so. While it may happen all the time relative to *some* sort of thing, it may not happen all the time relative to some *other* sort of thing. This has been the main sticking point for interpreters. Balme, for instance, supposed that Aristotle's idea was 'that in any given product spontaneity appears as an unusual exception'. That is, for each product type, spontaneously generated products are exceptions to what that type is normally like. Balme then objected that whole classes of animals—ticks, some flies, oysters—always come to be spontaneously and never non-spontaneously.[29] A related worry arises from *Generation of Animals* 3. 11's suggestion that specific environmental conditions determine what sort of organism results (762[a]8–32).[30] Thus, we find different testacea being generated in different places: oysters in slimy mud, cockles in sandy mud, and so on.[31] The worry is that if these environmental conditions

---

[28] This formulation reflects the fact that the market example and spontaneous generation turn out to be more like the cook than the builder. Cf. J. Allen, 'Aristotle on Chance as an Accidental Cause' ['Chance'], in Leunissen (ed.), *Critical Guide*, 66–87 at 79.

[29] Balme, 'Development', 96–8.

[30] As Lennox puts it, a spontaneously generated organism's 'pattern of development is a function of the amount of *pneuma* relative to earthen and liquid material in the enclosed mix' and that this 'mix, which can change depending on climatic and geographic variables, will determine whether the enclosure comes to be a sea urchin or an oyster' ('Teleology', 233). On the material mix, cf. Hull, 'Conflict', 247; Zwier, 'Methodology', 373, 384. For a similar worry that these facts make it hard to count spontaneous generation as rare, see Bonello, *Spontaneity*, 26–38. I discuss this 'mix' below.

[31] *HA* 5. 15, 547[b]18–23; cf. 5. 15–16, 19, 31–2; 6. 15–16.

are individuated as just the ones that produce an oyster, it will not be rare for them to do so.[32]

These worries plainly depend on a view about the *types* relative to which spontaneous products count as rare: the *F*s. If these are types of products that are individuated by species, then spontaneous generation is not rare. (If the type is *oyster* products, then it is not rare for those products to be spontaneous.) Similarly, if the types are types of environmental conditions that are individuated by species, then spontaneous generation is not rare. (If the types are just oyster-producing combinations of mud and sun, it is not rare for these conditions to generate oysters.) But if they are different types, individuated in another way, spontaneous generation may turn out to happen rarely after all. A great deal therefore depends on the types relative to which spontaneous generation might count as rare.

Which types are these? To answer this question, it will help to know which category of thing we are looking for. While Balme points to *product* types, the types most relevant for determining whether something happens 'spontaneously' are in fact the *process* types associated with *efficient* causes. This much can be gleaned from *Physics* 2. 6, which argues that spontaneous proceedings have *efficient* causes and that 'chance' and 'spontaneity' are their accidental efficient causes ($198^{a}2$–3). Efficient causes, as we have seen,

---

[32] Lennox suggests his account meets the rarity condition in virtue of a certain indefiniteness of cause: 'while many species of organisms are spontaneously generated with great regularity, they do not come to be always or usually due to the same cause' ('Teleology', 242). This unpacking of the condition may risk obscuring how the market example applies the notion of conditional frequency to spontaneous proceedings: what it takes to be rare relative to what. Aristotle claims that what the man did would *not* have been by chance if he went to the market as he did (e.g. by going to court) always or for the most part *for the sake of collecting his debt* (2. 5, $197^{a}1$–5). Aristotle's idea appears to be that if it were *not* rare for such goings to the market to happen for the sake of this, the type of proceeding the man engaged in would *not* be rare and so *not* by chance. The reason, presumably, is that this regularity would be the result of a non-accidental causal connection between, say, *going to court* and *collecting a debt*. Aristotle's point is thus not that collecting a debt is the sort of thing that happens in a variety of ways and so is only rarely caused in one particular way. There might be many ways of collecting a debt, such that it is rare for collecting a debt to be caused by any one of them, even though each of them non-accidentally and regularly causes one to get one's money. This, surely, would not be a chance proceeding, because there would be no accidental causal connection between the cause and its effect. The fact that there are very many ways of collecting a debt is thus only relevant to whether something happens rarely insofar as it is *good evidence* that it is rare for any one of them to produce the desired result.

are causes of *processes* (*kinēseis*). Aristotle's examples suggest that spontaneous proceedings are rare because it is rare for processes of the type non-accidentally initiated by their accidental efficient causes also to be (somehow) of the type whose *end* is achieved by chance.[33] (In this way, Aristotle's third condition for happening spontaneously helps us to apply the first two.) In the market example, it is rare for a case of *going to court* also to be a case of *collecting a debt*. This is because there is an accidental connection between these types and between the efficient cause in virtue of which the process is of the type *going to court* and the type *collecting a debt* (cf. *Phys.* 2. 5, $196^{b}33-197^{a}1$, $197^{a}14-18$).[34] We may therefore say that these spontaneous 'proceedings' are *processes*, and that the types relative to which they happen rarely are *process* types.

Like *Physics* 2's examples, spontaneous generation is a *process* associated with various *types*. As we have seen, Aristotle's account refers to 'putrefaction' (σῆψις, *GA* 3. 11, $762^{a}11$, $762^{a}14$), things 'concocting' (συμπέττουσα, πέττουσα, 3. 11, $762^{b}8$, $762^{b}15$), being and having been 'concocted' (πεττόμενον, πεφθέντος, 3. 11, $762^{a}14$, $762^{a}15$), and things 'putrefied' (σηπόμενον, $762^{a}14$; σαπρόν, $762^{a}15$). Concoction and putrefaction are among the process types *Meteorologica* 4 takes to happen via the joint actualization of an active power of the agent and a passive power of the patient (4. 1, 378^{b} 26–8)—which is also characteristic of causal processes (κινήσεις, *Phys.* 3. 3, $202^{a}14-16$, $202^{b}26-8$). Like the *Physics'* spontaneous proceedings, the *Generation of Animals'* spontaneous generations are thus efficient causal processes. Whether they happen rarely and accidentally should therefore be understood in terms of the conditional frequency of *process types*. (That is, the *F*s and *G*s will be tokens of process types.) Setting up the puzzle in this way once again reveals that an adequate solution requires an account of the process types involved in spontaneous generation.

---

[33] Judson treats E_1 and E_2 as *event* types, but the machinery of *events* is not particularly important to his view. He recognizes the importance of processes in id., 'What Can Happen When You Eat Pungent Food', in N. Avgelis and F. Peonidis (eds.) *Aristotle on Logic, Language and Science* (Sakkoulas, 1998), 185–204. In moving from substances and products towards agents and the processes they cause, the formulation above is closer to that of Allen, 'Chance', 79.

[34] Whether the process is of the type associated with the end achieved in the same way as it would be if the end were achieved non-spontaneously—that is, whether these processes are of the same 'fundamental kind'—is the question I consider below. Here, and in the conditions below, I speak of being 'of a type' in a preliminary way.

3. The process types of spontaneous generation

The next step is to identify more precisely *which* process types are involved in spontaneous generation and how they are *related*. (Are they, that is, related in such a way that spontaneous generation counts as both rare and accidentally caused?) This section addresses the first of these questions, aiming to identify more carefully the types involved. I argue that it is a significant but overlooked feature of Aristotle's account of spontaneous generation that it is a process that can be described, to some extent, in terms of *both* putrefaction and concoction. This interpretation opposes a common view, which denies that putrefaction plays any significant role in spontaneous generation. In the remaining sections of the paper, I turn to the second question, arguing that Aristotle's account of these types in spontaneous generation allows spontaneous generation to count as spontaneously caused.

My main source of evidence will be Aristotle's account of the spontaneous generation of testacea in *Generation of Animals* 3. 11. This chapter presents testacean generation as having two stages or components.[35] In the first, seasonal heat causes a process that ends in worked-up material.[36] In the second, a 'soul principle'[37] in this material causes a process that ends in a fetation ($762^{b}16$–18).[38] That there are two such components is also clear from *Meteorologica* 4 (4. 2, $379^{b}6$–8; 4. 11, $389^{b}5$–6).

My focus here is on the *first* component (the process initiated by seasonal heat), since it is the *only* one that has a claim to being

---

[35] This is a common reading. In Gotthelf's 'two-stage' view, 'the climatic heat first produces something like a female residue, in which the pneumatic heat then "implants movement"' ('Teleology', 147). Stavrianeas suggests the two stages involve different kinds of concoction: 'boiling' and 'ripening' ('Spontaneous Generation', 320, 330–4). For another two-stage view, see Henry, 'Themistius', 200. I am not committed to talk of 'stages', especially since there is some reason to think that those in question may overlap (e.g. 3. 11, $762^{b}16$–18). I prefer talk of 'components', which puts the emphasis on the fundamental causal structure rather than its temporal ordering.

[36] 3. 11, $762^{a}22$–4, $762^{a}12$, $762^{b}12$–16.

[37] I intend this as a literal translation of ἡ ἀρχὴ ἡ ψυχική ($762^{b}17$). This is the heat that will eventually be the 'proper heat' of the resulting organism. See below for details.

[38] I adopt Peck's translation of κύημα as 'fetation'. Unlike 'fetus', this is broad enough to apply to the things Aristotle refers to as a κύημα, e.g. eggs and larvae. See A. L. Peck (ed. and trans.), *Aristotle: Generation of Animals [Generation of Animals]*, revised and reprinted (Loeb, 1963).

spontaneous.[39] The first step is to determine to which *types* this process belongs. The two main types that *Generation of Animals* 3. 11 mentions in connection with it are *concoction* and *putrefaction*. Concoction, we learn in *Generation of Animals* 1 and 2, is the type by which standard generations occur. In *Meteorologica* 4, we learn it has as its end the form it produces (4. 2, 379^{b}18–35). Putrefaction, in contrast, tends towards the destruction of such forms (4. 1, 379^{a}3–26).

Most interpreters have not focused as explicitly on the process types to which spontaneous generation belongs.[40] Where they have considered the question, most have tended to suppose that it is the same sort of process as standard generation. Gotthelf, for instance, has argued that spontaneous generation resembles standard generation in that it involves an 'irreducible potential' for form: a capacity for an organism that is not reducible to the capacities of the materials in the lagoon.[41] If he is right, we may infer that standard and spontaneous generations are alike in being initiated by a common type of capacity and so (perhaps) of a common process type: *concoction*. Since this type aims at producing an organism, it will *not* be rare for it to do so. Henry and Stavrianeas have more explicitly endorsed the idea that spontaneous generation is like standard generation in being *concoction*.[42]

If this interpretation is correct, it will be hard to understand how spontaneous generation might be rare or accidentally caused. It is *not* unusual for concoction to produce an organism or for putrefaction to destroy something. It is not rare for these processes to unfold in these ways—just as it is not rare for going to court to end in arriving at court.[43] This is a serious cost: Aristotle claims

---

[39] Unless noted, this is the component I focus on below.

[40] For an exception, see Stavrianeas, 'Spontaneous Generation', 320 ff. See below.

[41] Gotthelf suggests that while standard and spontaneous generations both result from such capacities, the capacities of the latter may not be 'species-specific' ('Teleology', 145–9).

[42] Stavrianeas, 'Spontaneous Generation', 320 ff.; Henry, 'Themistius', 197–201 A regularizing impulse is also found in Lloyd, 'Master Cook', 117. S. M. Connell, *Aristotle on Female Animals* (Cambridge, 2016), 239–64 emphasizes this tendency but describes how it proves difficult (256).

[43] This strikes me as the best option for making sense of conditional frequency claims where only one type is specified. It fits Judson's emphasis on such claims being relative to the operations of nature ('Chance', 94), as well as the basic thrust of *Physics* 2. 8 (cf. Kress, 'How Things Happen').

that things that happen *spontaneously* happen rarely[44] and are accidentally caused.[45] Thus while the usual interpretation has the merit
of making sense of the fact that certain organisms are regularly and
reliably produced in certain conditions, it fails to explain what
makes spontaneous generation spontaneous.

This cost provides a reason to look for another interpretation.
Happily, there is one available. Indeed, this new interpretation also
provides a more natural reading of the relevant texts. As we have
already started to see, concoction is only one of the process types
that figure in the *Generation of Animals'* account of spontaneous
generation. In addition, Aristotle also repeatedly mentions *putrefaction*, and does so in central and programmatic passages—including those whose main aim is to contrast spontaneous and standard
generation.[46] In taking spontaneous generation to be a fairly straightforward case of concoction, the usual interpretation is forced to
sideline these references to putrefaction. The natural alternative is
to take Aristotle seriously and assign a more important role to
putrefaction than is usually done. This is the task of the remainder
of this paper. The upshot will be an explanation of why spontaneous generation counts as spontaneously caused: roughly, spontaneous generation can be described in terms of both putrefaction and
concoction, and it is rare for putrefaction processes also to be concoction processes.[47]

But first, the evidence for this alternative interpretation. The
first piece of evidence is the importance that Aristotle assigns to
putrefaction in spontaneous generation, across a wide variety of
passages. Aristotle claims in both the *Generation of Animals* and
History of Animals that spontaneously generated organisms 'come
to be from putrefying matter' (ἐκ σηπομένης τῆς ὕλης), 'putrefying
earth' (ἐκ γῆς σηπομένης), 'putrefying liquids' (ἐκ σηπομένων ὑγρῶν),
and so on.[48] In the *History of Animals*, Aristotle even compares the
seed-like fluid from which honey-combing testacea are generated
to a *waste product* in order to justify the claim that their more typically spontaneous kin are generated from *putrefying* matter (5. 15,

---

[44] *Phys.* 2. 5, 196^{b}12–13, 196^{b}20, 196^{b}36, 197^{a}4, 197^{a}19, 197^{a}32, 197^{a}35.
[45] *Phys.* 2. 5, 196^{b}23–9, 197^{a}12–14; cf. 196^{b}35; 2. 6, 197^{b}18–20.
[46] *GA* 1. 1, 715^{a}25, 715^{b}4–5, 715^{b}27–8; 1. 16, 721^{a}7–8.
[47] Again, I intend to leave open questions about the 'fundamental' type.
[48] *GA* 1. 1, 715^{a}25, 715^{b}4–5, 715^{b}27–8; 1. 16, 721^{a}7–8; *HA* 5. 1, 539^{a}23; 5. 15,
546^{b}24; 5. 19, 551^{a}4, 551^{b}30, 552^{a}13; 5. 31, 556^{b}25; 6. 16, 570^{a}23.

546ᵇ24–5). This point is reinforced in *Meteorologica* 4, which says that animals come to be in *putrefying* material (ἐν τοῖς σαπροῖς; 4. 11, 389ᵇ5) and in *putrefying* stuff (ἐν τῇ ἀποκρίσει σηπομένῃ), and *not* in concoction (οὐκ ἐγγίγνεται ἐν τῇ πέψει, 4. 3, 381ᵇ10–11). The use of '*pepsis*' here further underlines the fact that the contrast is between *process* types.

Meteorologica 4. 1 provides details that support these general indications. It makes clear that spontaneous generation begins with putrefaction: 'animals come to be in putrefying things on account of the fact that the natural heat that has been separated off puts together the things that were separated out.'⁴⁹ Aristotle here distinguishes the two components of spontaneous generation. In one, natural heat is 'separated off' and other materials 'separated out'.⁵⁰ In the other, the natural heat 'puts together' those materials. While it is not here labelled as such, the first of these is evidently a case of *putrefaction*. Not long before this passage, Aristotle had noted that putrefaction just is a process that separates off a body's natural heat, leaving behind dry stuff (379ᵃ3–26). Aristotle has this model in mind when he later remarks that 'animals come to be in putrefying stuff; for the heat that has destroyed each body's proper heat is in them'.⁵¹ It is the heat that destroys a body's natural heat (by forcing it out and so separating it off) that is responsible for the first component of spontaneous generation—where this is just the destructive heat responsible for putrefaction. In contrast, the *second* component is a concoction—a process by which something gets shaped and characterized by *natural heat* (379ᵃ3–ᵇ8).

Similar points are made in the *Physics* and *Metaphysics*. In *Physics* 2. 1, it is precisely the 'rot' (σηπεδών) that is said to send up a shoot in the case of a putrefying bed (193ᵃ13–14).⁵² *Metaphysics* H. 5 claims that whenever an animal comes from a corpse or wine

---

⁴⁹ 379ᵇ6–8: καὶ ζῷα ἐγγίγνεται τοῖς σηπομένοις διὰ τὸ τὴν ἀποκεκριμένην θερμότητα φυσικὴν οὖσαν συνιστάναι τὰ ἐκκριθέντα. Henry and Lloyd respond by listing *two* possibilities for the source of the heat that puts together the fetation: environmental heat and the heat that is separated off, perhaps understood as soul-heat in *pneuma* (Henry, 'Themistius', 200; Lloyd, 'Master Cook', 122). The puzzle is to figure out why Aristotle lists them both.

⁵⁰ For more on these materials, see Section 5.

⁵¹ 389ᵇ5–6: ... ἐν τοῖς σαπροῖς ζῷα ἐγγίγνεται· ἔνεστι γὰρ θερμότης ἡ φθείρασα τὴν ἑκάστου οἰκείαν θερμότητα.

⁵² Incidentally, σηπεδών is used in connection with the spontaneous generation of fleas at *History of Animals* 5. 31, 556ᵇ25.

from vinegar, it does so by 'reverting to the matter' (εἰς τὴν ὕλην...
ἐπανελθεῖν) by processes of 'decay' (αἱ φθοραί, 1044ᵇ34–1045ᵃ6).
What this means is that it is against *this* entire putrefaction-
emphasizing background that *Generation of Animals* 3. 11 sets out
to establish that putrefaction plays a role in spontaneous generation:

ὅσα δὲ μήτε παραβλαστάνει μήτε κηριάζει, τούτων δὲ πάντων ἡ γένεσις αὐτόματός
ἐστιν. πάντα δὲ τὰ συνιστάμενα τὸν τρόπον τοῦτον καὶ ἐν γῇ καὶ ἐν ὕδατι φαίνεται
γιγνόμενα μετὰ σήψεως καὶ μιγνυμένου τοῦ ὀμβρίου ὕδατος· ἀποκρινομένου γὰρ
τοῦ γλυκέος εἰς τὴν συνισταμένην ἀρχὴν τὸ περιττεῦον τοιαύτην λαμβάνει μορφήν.
γίγνεται δ' οὐθὲν σηπόμενον ἀλλὰ πεττόμενον· ἡ δὲ σῆψις καὶ τὸ σαπρὸν περίττωμα
τοῦ πεφθέντος ἐστίν· οὐθὲν γὰρ ἐκ παντὸς γίγνεται καθάπερ οὐδ' ἐν τοῖς ὑπὸ τῆς
τέχνης δημιουργουμένοις—οὐθὲν γὰρ ἂν ἔδει ποιεῖν—νῦν δὲ τὸ μὲν ἡ τέχνη τῶν
ἀχρήστων ἀφαιρεῖ, τὸ δ' ἡ φύσις. (762ᵃ8–18)

The generation of all those that do not produce side shoots or honeycomb
is spontaneous. All things that are put together in this way manifestly
come to be in connection with putrefaction[53] both in earth and in water,
especially while rain water is being mixed in; for while the sweet is being
separated off, the remainder takes on a shape of the sort appropriate for
the principle that is being put together.[54] But nothing comes to be by
putrefying but rather by being concocted; the putrefaction, that is, what is
putrefied, is a residue of what has been concocted; for nothing comes to be
from all of it, just as it does not either in the things that are wrought by
craft—for then there would be no need to *make* things—but as it is, in the
one case craft removes what is useless, and in the other nature does.

The announced aim of this passage is to show that spontaneous
generation occurs in a *certain material* mixture 'in connection with'
(μετά) *putrefaction* (762ᵃ11). This passage is thus in keeping with
Aristotle's approach of giving putrefaction an important role in
spontaneous generation.

---

[53] The *Generation of Animals* uses μετά + the genitive to capture a variety of
relationships. For mere accompaniment, see perhaps 2. 4, 739ᵃ20; 2. 6, 743ᵃ14; 2. 7,
748ᵇ25; 4. 6, 775ᵇ23–4; 5. 3, 783ᵃ36. For essential components, see perhaps 2. 6,
742ᵇ3; 3. 1, 750ᵃ9. The line is not clear; even in the former cases, the words joined
by μετά often designate parts of a single process. None of these passages is an exact
parallel to this use of a verbal noun after μετά alongside a participle.

[54] Alternatively, εἰς τὴν συνισταμένην ἀρχὴν may be taken with the participle,
claiming that the sweet either moves towards (Smyth 1686a) or is destined for
(Smyth 1686d) the 'principle', perhaps as its food, as Aristotle emphasizes at
Generation of Animals 3. 11, 762ᵇ32 and 763ᵃ11–12. Either should be compatible
with my interpretation, which requires simply that the leftover material acquires a
shape that somehow *moulds* the principle (details below). On the principle, see
n. 106. I thank Victor Caston for discussion of this difficult sentence.

The question, of course, is how exactly this important role should be understood. What, exactly, does putrefaction do in spontaneous generation? The argument of the passage takes two steps towards an answer. The first is to say what happens to the materials in a way that is neutral on the question of whether the process type by which it happens is putrefaction or concoction: material in the lagoon, having mixed with rainwater, undergoes a *separating off* (762ᵃ12) that yields two stuffs. These are the 'sweet' stuff (τοῦ γλυκέος, 762ᵃ12), on the one hand, and the 'principle' (ἡ ... ἀρχή, 762ᵃ12–13) and 'remainder' (τὸ περιττεῦον, 762ᵃ13) on the other.⁵⁵ When this happens, the remainder acquires a certain 'shape' (τοιαύτην ... μορφήν, 762ᵃ13). This shape is very important, as we will see below.

The passage's second step is to deepen this neutral explanation by describing the products of this initial separation in terms of *both* putrefaction and concoction. Aristotle begins by drawing a distinction between the concoction and putrefaction types: 'nothing comes to be by putrefying but rather by being concocted' (γίγ-νεται δ' οὐθὲν σηπόμενον ἀλλὰ πεττόμενον, 762ᵃ13–14). Then, he applies this distinction to the products of the separation. The *remainder*, it now emerges, is a product of *putrefaction*: it is 'the putrefaction, that is, what is putrefied' (ἡ ... σῆψις καὶ τὸ σαπρὸν, 762ᵃ14–15). In other words, it is produced by a process of 'putre-faction' and thereby counts as 'what is putrefied'. In this way, the passage makes good on its stated aim of showing how spontaneous generation happens 'in connection with putrefaction' (μετὰ σήψεως, 762ᵃ11). This result, of course, is in keeping with Aristotle's repeated claims that spontaneous generation happens through *putrefaction*.⁵⁶ At the same time, this passage also reveals that this remainder is the 'residue of what has been concocted' (περίττωμα τοῦ πεφθέντος, 762ᵃ15).⁵⁷ By a similar line of reasoning, the remain-der should be so because it is also a product of a process of *concoc-tion*. (In saying this, Aristotle need not be claiming that such a residue or remainder is what concoction *aims* at. It need only be a necessary concomitant of processes of that type. Indeed, Aristotle

---

⁵⁵ See n. 54 for an alternative.

⁵⁶ *GA* 1. 1, 715ᵃ25, 715ᵇ4–5, 715ᵇ27–8; 1. 16, 721ᵃ7–8.

⁵⁷ Aristotle then supports this move with a reference to how things work in the case of craft production, where a concoction-like process of production also involves removing some materials (762ᵃ17–18).

thinks that all natural generation (including concoction) leaves behind a residue (*Meteor.* 2. 3, 358ᵃ7–20; cf. *GA* 1. 18–19, 2. 6).)[58]

The result is an account of the products of the initial separation in terms of *both* putrefaction and concoction. This account, of course, raises a puzzle, both for Aristotle and for his interpreters. What justifies characterizing the product in both these ways, especially given that 'nothing comes to be by putrefying but rather by being concocted' (γίγνεται δ' οὐθὲν σηπόμενον ἀλλὰ πεττόμενον, 762ᵃ 13–14)?[59] The first step in solving the puzzle is to read this observation as a generalizing claim about the nature of the putrefaction and concoction *types*. That is, it need not be a claim in the first place about this particular case, but about whether anything *properly* comes to be by putrefaction. Aristotle's answer is that 'nothing' does: all that properly results from putrefaction, insofar as it is putrefaction, is a putrefied remainder. Of course, to say what properly comes to be from putrefaction is not yet to say what can come to be from it accidentally. The next step is to identify what other features this putrefied remainder just so happens to have: a *shape* that it can contribute to a developing testacean. Below, I will argue this observation is the basis for Aristotle's key insight. His idea is that testacean generation is a process of putrefaction which just so happens, in these particular circumstances, to unfold in some respects as concoction standardly does. In particular, it (accidentally) produces just such a shape.[60]

The fact that the putrefying material has a particular sort of *shape* will thus turn out to be essential to Aristotle's strategy. Already, we can see that there is good reason for him to give shape a key role. Shape is very important to the development of testacea, so much so that Aristotle emphasizes that the shape of the shell is one of the most significant ways in which the various sorts of testacea differ from one another. In *Parts of Animals* 4. 5, for instance, he announces that 'there are many kinds and forms of testeacea'

---

[58] All I require—to get slightly ahead of things—is that facts about this residue allow the same process to be characterized in terms of both *putrefaction* (whose characteristic result is a dry residue, the heat and moisture having been separated off) and also *concoction* (whose characteristic result is producing something *else*— usually, something hot, wet, and with a shape—while leaving behind a residue as a necessary concomitant).

[59] For more on this remark, see discussion later in this section.

[60] For more details on these respects, see n. 58 and especially Section 5.

(ἔστι δὲ γένη καὶ εἴδη πολλὰ τῶν ὀστρακοδέρμων), and then goes on to describe how their shells differ: they are spiral-shelled, bivalves, univalves, spiny, and so on (679ᵇ15–32; for μορφή used of shell shape, see *History of Animals* 4. 4, 530ᵃ14). His idea seems to be that there is an important connection between testacean kinds and shell shape. In fact, the very next section of *Generation of Animals* 3. 11 goes on to argue that it is, in effect, a *shape* formed in the muddy lagoon that determines the *kind* of the resulting testacean:

γίγνονται δ' ἐν γῇ καὶ ἐν ὑγρῷ τὰ ζῷα καὶ τὰ φυτὰ διὰ τὸ ἐν γῇ μὲν ὕδωρ ὑπάρχειν ἐν δ' ὕδατι πνεῦμα, ἐν δὲ τούτῳ παντὶ θερμότητα ψυχικήν, ὥστε τρόπον τινὰ πάντα ψυχῆς εἶναι πλήρη· διὸ συνίσταται ταχέως ὁπόταν ἐμπεριληφθῇ. ἐμπεριλαμβάνεται δὲ καὶ γίγνεται θερμαινομένων τῶν σωματικῶν ὑγρῶν οἷον ἀφρώδης πομφόλυξ. αἱ μὲν οὖν διαφοραὶ τοῦ τιμιώτερον εἶναι τὸ γένος καὶ ἀτιμότερον τὸ συνιστάμενον ἐν τῇ περιλήψει τῆς ἀρχῆς τῆς ψυχικῆς ἐστιν. τούτου δὲ καὶ οἱ τόποι αἴτιοι καὶ τὸ σῶμα τὸ περιλαμβανόμενον. (762ᵃ18–27)

And animals and plants come to be in earth and in water on account of the fact that water is in earth and *pneuma* in water, and in all this [i.e. *pneuma*] there is soul-heat,[61] so that in a way all things are full of soul; for this reason, [things] are put together quickly when it [*sc. pneuma*] is enclosed. And it is enclosed and becomes like a frothy bubble as bodily moisture is being heated. So then, the differences in whether what is being put together is more and less valuable in kind depend on the enclosure of the soul principle.[62] And of this, the places and the body being enclosed are causes.

My suggestion is that the *first* passage (762ᵃ8–18) describes the causal process by which this very 'frothy bubble' (ἀφρώδης πομφόλυξ) forms, which is to say that it describes the process responsible for the *shape* that this bubble (and the materials 'enclosed' [περιλαμβανόμενον] in it) lends to the developing testacean. This *second*

---

[61] I offer 'soul-heat' as a literal translation. Since soul is present in the environment only 'in a way', this is not heat belonging to the soul of an actual existing organism, at least initially. Eventually, it will be heat associated with the resulting organism's soul principle: the one that gets enclosed (762ᵇ16–18).

[62] I follow Gotthelf, citing correspondence with Balme, in taking the sentence in this way ('Teleology', 145–6). The singular verb with the plural subject can be explained as a *constructio ad sensum:* the point is that *the fact that* there are such differences depends on the enclosure of the soul principle. I am grateful to Brad Inwood for discussion of this sentence. I depart slightly from Lennox, who translates τὸ συνιστάμενον as 'the organization' (Lennox, 'Teleology', 233). Against this, Gotthelf points out that τὸ συνιστάμενον 'here and elsewhere clearly refers to the outcome of a process and is a passive, not a middle; it means "that which is (or: is being) constituted"' (146). In correspondence, Lennox has indicated that he intended this translation to refer to 'what is organized'. Cf. n. 64.

passage (762ᵃ18–27) fills in the details about how the process does this: this specially shaped enclosure is responsible for the *kind* of testacean that results ('whether what is being put together is more or less valuable in kind', τοῦ τιμιώτερον εἶναι τὸ γένος καὶ ἀτιμότερον τὸ συνιστάμενον).[63] As I noted above, this reading finds support in *Parts of Animals* 4. 5's project of connecting the *kinds* (γένη) to which testacea belong with the *shape* of their *shells* (679ᵇ15 ff.). Earlier in the *Generation of Animals*, Aristotle also makes clear that animal kinds (2. 1, 732ᵃ17) and souls (2. 3, 736ᵇ32) differ in value (τιμιότητι). The basic idea that emerges is that such differences in *kind*, associated with shell shape, are said at 762ᵃ18–27 to result from 'the places and the body that is being enclosed' (οἱ τόποι ... καὶ τὸ σῶμα τὸ περιλαμβανόμενον)—that is, from earth, water, and *pneuma*, in their environmental conditions.[64] Aristotle's idea may be that shell shape is the feature of testacea most easily affected by the environmental conditions, since different shells are fairly obviously associated with different materials. This may be why the *History of Animals* emphasizes that testacea (and their shells) differ as the mud differs: oysters in slimy mud; cockles, clams, razor-fishes, and scallops in sandy mud; barnacles and limpets on the hollows of rocks; and so on (5. 15, 547ᵇ18–23). In the *Generation of Animals*, too, Aristotle emphasizes that the place (ὁ τόπος) is the cause (αἴτιον) of the sea urchin's long and hard spines (5. 3, 783ᵃ 18–29). In *Parts of Animals* 4. 5, Aristotle is explicit that these spines are features of its *shell* (679ᵇ28–30). Finally, the remainder of the *Generation of Animals* 3. 11 passage supports this suggestion that what the places determine is *shell shape*. Its next lines go on to describe how the bubbly process eventually is followed by what

---

[63] Here, Aristotle refers to the kind (γένος). *Parts of Animals* 4. 5 gives an account of both the kinds (γένη) and species (εἴδη, 679ᵇ15).

[64] This should be a separate issue from whether the soul-*heat* in the *pneuma* is 'generic' or 'species-specific'. (For debate, see Balme, 'Development', 99; Gotthelf, 'Teleology', 144–5; Lennox, 'Teleology', 232–3; Stavrianeas, 'Spontaneous Generation', 322–7, for a particularly detailed discussion of the ingredients and the vital heat.) My focus is on the fact that the causal process that goes on in these conditions (whatever they are) determines the sort of testacea that results (at some level of generality) via determining its shell shape (not necessarily the heat). Indeed, Gotthelf, who opposes the view that the heat is species-specific, still recognizes that the differences of value lie 'in the differences in the enclosing material, e.g. in the different sorts of shells of the testacea', where this is determined by the environmental conditions ('Teleology', 147).

looks like *shell* formation, with earthy material solidifying around a body that has life (762ᵃ27–32).[65]

The upshot is that in determining the shape of the enclosure, 762ᵃ18–32's bubbly causal process—the very one first described at 762ᵃ8–18—determines what kind of testacean comes to be.[66] Moreover, what 762ᵃ8–18 suggests is that it may do so by yielding a *putrefied* residue that happens to have a *shape* (762ᵃ13) which moulds the principle (ἀρχήν) of the organism. This observation helps us to flesh out the solution to the puzzle about why Aristotle describes spontaneous generation in terms of both concoction and putrefaction. My proposal is that our first passage (762ᵃ8–18) begins by describing the causal process that produces the shape as a case of *putrefaction*. Because this putrefaction yields a material that happens to have a shape that can determine the organism's *kind* (as at 762ᵃ18–32), it is legitimate to describe it in terms of the type that characteristically has just this sort of shape as its end: *concoction*.[67]

Spontaneous generation can therefore be described in several ways. On an abstract but causally impoverished level, it is the separation of two stuffs. On a causally rich level, it can be described (for reasons I spell out more fully in Section 5) as putrefaction *and* concoction. The result, as I will argue in Sections 4 and 5, is an interpretation that—unlike the standard interpretation—can explain why spontaneous generation really is spontaneously caused.

The more usual interpretation, however, reads the central passages of *Generation of Animals* 3. 11 differently. While most commentators do not focus as explicitly on process types, many of their interpretations assume that spontaneous generation is a fairly ordinary case of *concoction*. As a result, they deny that *Generation of Animals* 762ᵃ8–18 assigns any real role to putrefaction, despite the fact that it claims that spontaneous generation happens in connection with (μετά) *putrefaction* (762ᵃ11). The appeal of the more usual reading derives from the claim that 'nothing comes to be by putrefying

---

[65] Cf. Gotthelf, 'Teleology', 147. Ultimately, I am neutral about whether the residue moulds the stuff inside the testacean (as a cast moulds plaster; cf. Henry, 'Themistius', 198) or whether it eventually becomes a component of the testacean (its shell) and moulds it that way. See Section 5 for more reasons to think it will be the shell. Either way, the *dry, earthy* (putrefied) stuff lends the principle a shape.

[66] For further support, see discussion below of the 'frothy slime'.

[67] See Sections 4 and 5 for the full picture.

but rather by being concocted' (οὐθὲν σηπόμενον ἀλλὰ πεττόμενον, 762ᵃ13–14). While I interpreted this claim as saying what the putrefaction and concoction *types* are characteristically like, some commentators read it differently: as making a more specific point that *this particular process* must be *not* a case of putrefaction but *only* of concoction. They conclude that while spontaneous generation happens in the vicinity of putrefaction that yields a residue, strictly it consists *only* of a process of *concoction* that yields a testacean. Henry writes:

Aristotle is careful to point out in the *Generation of Animals* that it is not so much the putrefaction of the body that is essential for the spontaneous generation of a *kuema* (an embryo); putrefaction and the thing putrefied are only a by-product of this event (*GA* 762ᵃ13–15). Rather, what is important is the interaction between the heat and moisture being released into the atmosphere that happens in connection with putrefaction. It is here, outside the putrefying ooze, that Aristotle thinks the real excitement takes place.[68]

Drawing on *Meteorologica* 4, he continues:

The process that ensues (the thing that happens 'in connection with putrefaction') includes two important events: *evaporation*, whereby the 'sweet' (the useful material) is extracted from the putrefying materials in the form of a moist vapour (762ᵃ12–13); *recombination*, whereby, as the sweet is being thrown off from the putrescent mixture, it is immediately reorganized and concocted into a new substance by the heat being expelled along with it (379ᵇ7–9, 743ᵃ35–6, 762ᵃ12–13, ᵇ14–16) or, alternatively, by the heat from the surrounding air.[69]

Stavrianeas offers a similar interpretation, adding that concoction 'coincides with' putrefaction and has it as a 'concomitant result', which he takes to mean that 'the rest putrefies'.[70] The upshot is that

---

[68] Henry, 'Themistius', 199. Lloyd writes that at 762ᵃ13–14 Aristotle 'corrects himself and says that, more strictly, nothing comes to be by putrefying, but rather by a process of concoction' ('Master Cook', 118). This reading is endorsed by Zwier, 'Methodology', 363. Cf. Louis, 'Génération spontanée', 302; Bonello, *Spontaneity*, 37.

[69] Henry, 'Themistius', 200. Recombination is a kind of concoction (200). It is less clear whether evaporation is putrefaction, concoction, or something else. The important point is that putrefaction is a by-product.

[70] Stavrianeas, 'Spontaneous Generation', 320. As it turns out, the vocabulary of 'coincidence' does a fairly good job of capturing the relation between the two processes, at least once it is spelled out. Still, he writes that what 'makes them

the component of spontaneous generation described in these passages is not really a case of putrefaction. Indeed, putrefaction cannot even really be said to play a crucial role in getting spontaneous generation *started*, but is only something that happens to its *leftovers*. Spontaneous generation itself is strictly only a case of concoction—despite Aristotle's repeated claims throughout the *Generation of Animals* and elsewhere that putrefaction plays a key role in spontaneous generation.

This common reading is helped along by a sympathetic translation of 762ᵃ13 (τὸ περιττεῦον τοιαύτην λαμβάνει μορφήν). I translated this neutrally as 'the remainder takes on a shape of the sort ...' and suggested that it prompts Aristotle to update his initial claim that spontaneous generation happens 'in connection with putrefaction' (μετὰ σήψεως), so as to add that the putrefying stuff can be described in terms of concoction (while still insisting that it is 'putrefied' or σαπρόν). However, translators sometimes render it in terms that suggest that this remainder *putrefies* and so simply takes on a *putrefied* shape—that is, one of the sort that putrefied things, which are normally mere by-products, tend to have—rather than a shape important for testacean development. Peck translates it as 'that which remains over assumes a putrefying aspect' and adds in a note that this means that it 'putrefies'.[71] Lefebvre likewise notes that 'we must understand that the rest (that which is not the principle) takes on the configuration of what is putrefied'.[72]

Once it is assumed that the residue takes on the shape characteristic of a *putrefied* thing, it starts to look as if putrefaction is a *mere by-product*: one that makes no significant contribution to how testacean generation unfolds (lending it a shape, for instance). We don't think of oysters or anything that contributes to their development as having a 'putrefying aspect'. So, we might reason, whatever has a putrefying aspect must be a leftover by-product that makes no contribution to oyster development—and thus that the only causal process that does so contribute is concoction. This

---

defective is not the absence of regular causes, but differences in the quality of vital heat' (307).

[71] Peck, *Generation of Animals*, 355.

[72] 'Il faut comprendre que le reste (ce qui n'est pas le principe) prend la configuration de ce qui est putréfié' (D. Lefebvre, 'La Génération des animaux', in P. Pellegrin (ed.), *Aristote, Œuvres complètes* (Flammarion, 2014), 1675).

interpretation leaves no room for putrefaction to play a causal role in producing a testacean.

I think we should resist this reading. I will argue for this thesis by examining the contributions of the 'residue' (περίττωμα, 762ᵃ15) and 'remainder' (περιττεῦον, 762ᵃ13), and the processes by which they are formed. If this residue makes no contribution to testacean production and is formed by putrefaction, then it may be reasonable to say, as the common view holds, that putrefaction plays no role in testacean generation, though it does go on 'in the neighbourhood'. On this reading, the only processes that make a real causal contribution to testacean production will be of the concoction type. But if the residue formed by putrefaction itself makes an important contribution to testacean production, then spontaneous generation requires processes that are putrefactions as well as those that are concoctions.

Our first clue that the latter view is closer to the truth is the phrase τοιαύτην λαμβάνει μορφήν. This is an odd way of expressing the thought that the residue takes on a *putrefied* shape. In context, τοιαύτην may point to a variety of things, of which one possibility is a shape of the appropriate sort for the developing principle to have or that is appropriate given the materials and environmental conditions in which the process is unfolding. Moreover, the *Generation of Animals* uses the phrase λαμβάνει μορφήν to describe a shape acquired by the female residue when it is acted on by the male principle to produce something with a certain sort of shape (1. 21, 729ᵇ6–8; 2. 1, 733ᵇ18–21). This shape is the one that is 'proper' (τὴν οἰκείαν μορφήν, 733ᵇ20–1) for the developing organism. What takes it on is, as in *Generation of Animals* 3. 11, a *residue* (περίττωμα, 729ᵇ7–8). The *Generation of Animals*' standard use of the phrase therefore suggests that we take seriously the idea that the remainder takes on a *shape* that contributes to the developing organism.

It bears repeating that in saying this, Aristotle is claiming that what takes on the shape is *putrefying* stuff: stuff properly produced as a result of putrefaction. The implication is that it is *putrefaction* that is responsible for producing material with features that account for a crucial aspect of testacean development (perhaps by moulding the developing organism): its *shaping*. This point is corroborated by a neglected passage later in *Generation of Animals* 3. 11, where

Aristotle says that testacea form on boats when the 'frothy slime putrefies' (σηπομένης τῆς ἀφρώδους ἰλύος, 763ᵃ27–8). As we have seen, testacea develop when a 'frothy bubble' (ἀφρώδης πομφόλυξ, 762ᵃ23–4) forms in the earthy, watery, *pneuma*-filled lagoon (cf. *HA* 6. 15, 569ᵃ22–ᵇ28). In saying that it is *frothy slime* that *putrefies*, Aristotle is saying that what putrefies is the *very same muddy stuff* whose features determine testacean development and is a cause of 'whether what is being put together is more or less valuable' (τοῦ τιμιώτερον εἶναι τὸ γένος καὶ ἀτιμότερον τὸ συνιστάμενον). He is *not* saying that what putrefies is something whose features are inessential to testacean development. The upshot is that the putrefaction this frothy bubble undergoes is (in some way) responsible for a key feature of testacean development: determining its shape or kind.

These passages provide an extra line of defence against Henry's and Stavrianeas's remarks. Even if we were to be persuaded that the 'shape' (μορφή) referred to at 762ᵃ13 is not one that moulds the developing organism, Aristotle's observations that what putrefies is froth and that the way this particular froth just so happens to enclose the other materials determines the kind would still suggest that a product of putrefaction (somehow) plays a kind-determining role. Moreover, as we have seen, an interpretation that gives putrefaction an important causal role is a good fit with the tendency of the biological works and especially the two-component model articulated in *Meteorologica* 4, where spontaneous generation is said crucially to involve both heat that has been separated off and also some materials left behind (4. 1, 379ᵇ6–8; 4. 11, 389ᵇ5–6). On any interpretation, these *Meteorologica* passages indicate that putrefaction must, at the least, play an important role in *getting spontaneous generation going*—that is, in causing the early component described at 762ᵃ8–18.[73] Read in conjunction with the *Generation of Animals* 3. 11 evidence, these passages additionally indicate that a process with this structure—that is, putrefaction—also plays a decisive role in producing something that determines the kind of testacean that results. In Sections 4 and 5, I draw on the details of putrefaction and concoction to sketch further reasons for thinking that this role is that of controlling the initial separation and

---

[73] In the component caused by the environmental heat, rather than soul-heat, as occurs later. See n. 35.

organization of materials, resulting (accidentally) in a specially shaped enclosure.

4. Efficient causation, causal processes, and their types

I have argued that putrefaction has a more important role in spontaneous generation than is usually recognized. In spontaneous testacean generation, a process of the putrefaction type produces a putrefied material that has a shape important to testacean development. Interestingly, Aristotle is also willing to describe this process in terms of concoction. What we need to know next is what *exactly* justifies Aristotle in describing testacean generation in terms of both concoction and putrefaction. Of particular importance is the *relation* between the types: whether they are related in a way that allows spontaneous generation to count as spontaneously caused. In Section 5, I will argue that the capacities that cause testacean generation are those that in situations like this properly cause a process of *putrefaction*, which accidentally happens as processes of the *concoction* type usually do. To support this interpretation, we need an account of the putrefaction and concoction types. This is the project of Section 4.

My strategy here will be to sketch one way we might draw on *Physics* 3. 1–3 to make precise the way in which spontaneous generation can be described in terms of both putrefaction and concoction. As we have seen, in describing spontaneous generation as a case of putrefaction or concoction, Aristotle is treating it as an *efficient causal process*. As *Physics* 3. 1 defines it, such a process (κίνησις) is 'the actuality of what is in capacity insofar as it is such' (ἡ τοῦ δυνάμει ὄντος ἐντελέχεια, ᾗ τοιοῦτον, 201ᵃ10–11). That is, it is fundamentally the *actualization* of a certain kind of *capacity*; this, at bottom, is the sort of thing a process is.[74] As it turns out, there are *two* such capacities: of the *patient* and of the *agent* (the efficient cause). A process is thus 'the actuality of this [what is changeable] by what is capable of changing it' (ἐντελέχεια ... τούτου [καὶ] ὑπὸ τοῦ κινητικοῦ) and is 'the actuality of *both*' (ἐντελέχειαν ἀμφοῖν, 3. 3, 202ᵃ14–16). As

---

[74] I speak indiscriminately of *actuality* and *actualization*. I use the latter to emphasize that this particular actuality is a process, without implying anything about Aristotle's procedure for *defining* a process.

examples, Aristotle offers housebuilding, learning, doctoring, rolling, leaping, etc. (3. 1, 201^{a}18–19). Housebuilding is the actuality of what is *buildable*, insofar as it is such (3. 3, 201^{a}16–17), by what is *capable of building* (cf. 2. 3, 195^{b}23–5; 2. 5, 196^{b}26).[75] It is the actuality of two capacities: of the builder and of the materials.[76]

It is housebuilding, not (say) rolling, because *these* capacities are actualized: the one whose actualization is *building* and the one whose actualization is *being built with*. To say the process actualizes these capacities is to say that *these* capacities, and not others, are being actualized throughout the subsequent unfolding. When the builder acts, they do not just kick off the building. They remain in charge throughout, responding to conditions as they arise; the very same building capacities that kicked the process off are also being actualized throughout it. The builder's action is thus 'not cut off' (ὀυκ ἀποτέμνεσθαι, *Phys.* 3. 3, 202^{b}7–8) from what happens to the patient.[77] This picture gains further support from the observation that a *kinēsis* is a *process*—the sort of thing that continues and unfolds through time, which is directed at a goal, and which can be impeded or interrupted on the way to it.[78] A process is just the sort of thing whose cause helps it unfold in just the way needed to achieve its goal.

For such a process to go well is for it to unfold in a characteristic way—to have an actualization that happens in such a way.[79] *De caelo*, for instance, characterizes the capacity for walking with reference to how walking goes when it goes well—walking a hundred stades (1. 11, 281^{a}1–27). Likewise, when building goes well, its

---

[75] I take it that these are capacities for changes (*building*), rather than end states (*houses*), as in R. Heinaman, 'Is Aristotle's Definition of Change Circular?', *Apeiron*, 27 (1994), 25–38 and Charles, 'Processes', 186–96. However, my argument can be rephrased in terms of the alternative view.

[76] *How* it is the actuality of both is vexed. See Charles, 'Processes', 196–205; U. Coope, 'Aristotle on Action', *Proceedings of the Aristotelian Society*, suppl. vol. 81 (2007), 109–38; 'Change and its Relation to Actuality and Potentiality', in G. Anagnostopoulos (ed.), *A Companion to Aristotle* (Wiley-Blackwell, 2009), 277–91; M. L. Gill, 'Aristotle's Theory of Causal Action in *Physics* III 3', *Phronesis*, 25 (1980), 129–47; A. Marmodoro, 'The Union of Cause and Effect in Aristotle: *Physics* III 3', *Oxford Studies in Ancient Philosophy*, 32 (2007), 205–32 and *Aristotle on Perceiving Objects* (Oxford, 2014).

[77] For further defence, see D. Charles, 'Aristotle on Agency', *Oxford Handbooks Online* (2017), Section IV.1.

[78] Cf. D. Charles, 'Processes, Activities, and Actions', in R. Stout (ed.), *Process, Action, and Experience* (Oxford, 2018), 20–40.

[79] I defend this picture more fully in Kress, 'How Things Happen', 337–45.

steps are in the right order for a house to get built (*Physics* 2. 8, 199ᵃ12–15). Natural teleological processes also unfold in a good manner for achieving a given end (199ᵇ8–12), and they do so because they are actualizations of specific efficient causal capacities whose actualizations unfold in that way if they are not impeded (199ᵇ15–17). This is what it means to say that nature 'acts' (ποιεῖν) for the sake of something (198ᵇ16–17).

This overview helps us to explain what justifies Aristotle in describing spontaneous generation in terms of both putrefaction and concoction. When we describe a process as an instance of a type, we might be saying one or both of two things: which characteristic actualizations it possesses, and *in virtue of what* it possesses them. The latter question is a question about what *capacities* are actualized in the process. What I will argue (in Section 5) is that testacean generation unfolds in the characteristic way—has the characteristic actualization—of *both* putrefaction and concoction. However, it does so for different reasons. It has the characteristic actualization of putrefaction as a result of *in fact being the actualization of* the appropriate capacities: the capacities that are in fact actualized in testacean generation are *proper* (non-accidental) causes of an actualization that goes this way.⁸⁰ This is not so for concoction: although it unfolds in the way characteristic of concoction, it does not do so as a result of capacities that properly cause processes of the concoction type. In this way, it resembles other cases of processes that have certain characteristic features, but not as a result of the appropriate type of cause. In *Nicomachean Ethics* 2. 4, for instance, Aristotle recognizes that there are virtuous actions that are not caused by agents who have full-fledged virtues (1105ᵃ22–6); such actions count as just or temperate, though they are not done just*ly* or temperate*ly* (1105ᵃ28–ᵇ9).

Moreover, what this reveals is that there is reason to think that in identifying the concoction-like unfolding of testacean generation (or the just unfolding of the learner's action) we have not really identified its most 'fundamental' type: the one that it has at least in part in virtue of actualizing the capacities that properly cause it

---

⁸⁰ Recall the market example. What the man is really doing is going to court (*Phys.* 2. 5, 197ᵃ17). What he does is of this type because he is non-accidentally causing himself to be doing this. But in this case, he goes to court in a way that is also characteristic of collecting a debt. Perhaps, the action has a series of stages that result in getting the money (cf. 2. 5, 196ᵇ21–2, 34–6).

and in terms of which it (as a process) is defined—as Martin puts it, 'the kind in virtue of which the event has the nature that it does'.[81] A process, after all, just is the actuality of a capacity of a certain sort, where different capacities have actualizations of different sorts. If we take this definition seriously, we may suspect that if a process unfolds in the way characteristic of a given capacity, but not by actualizing such a capacity, it will have this way of unfolding only *accidentally*, for it will not have it in virtue of its *proper* causes.[82] After all, Aristotle thinks that there are accidental causes and effects, as well as proper ones (*Phys.* 2. 3, 195^{b}3–4, 7). In this case, it would be like a process of typing caused by a monkey, but which unfolds in such a way as to result in *Hamlet*. While it happens in the way that Shakespeare's typing *Hamlet* would, it does so only *accidentally*.[83] While we might still *describe* such a process by highlighting this characteristic unfolding—as we sometimes describe hallucinations in terms of the perceptions they resemble—this will not mean that it is of a 'fundamental' kind that is common to a process that *does* have its characteristic unfolding in virtue of its proper causes.

4. 1. *The concoction type*

The first step in testing out this idea is to find out which capacities and actualizations are characteristic of putrefaction and concoction. We can look to *Meteorologica* 4's account of the processes brought about by the active powers (hot and cold) on the passive powers (moist and dry).[84] We find putrefaction and concoction in

---

[81] Martin, 'Limits', 60. See Section 5 for a more careful formulation.

[82] Compare Stout's contemporary suggestion that 'a process resulting essentially in *P* is/was/will be happening at time *t* if there is/was/will be a mechanism operating at *t* that is characterized by its resulting in *P*' (R. Stout, 'Ballistic Action', in id (ed.), *Process*, 210–27 at 216, where extension to *actions* replaces talk of 'mechanism operating' with 'exercising a power' (226).

[83] Cf. J. Ackrill, 'Aristotle on Action', *Mind*, 87 (1978), 595–601: the action type a person does is '*defined* by features he [the agent who *causes* it] is aware of, since it is only as so defined that he can be said to have done it knowingly and hence to have done it at all (strictly speaking)' (597). There is a contrast between 'doing something, properly speaking, and only doing something *per accidens*' (597), where features of the *cause* make the difference.

[84] On the relation between *Meteorologica* 4 and the biological works, see J. Lennox, 'Aristotle on the Emergence of Material Complexity: *Meteorology* IV and Aristotle's Biology', *HOPOS*, 4 (2014), 272–305 at 297–301.

4. 1–3's account of the activities (ἐργασίαι, 4. 1, 378ᵇ26–8) of the *active* powers. This account highlights two features: first, the heat and cold that cause the process (the *efficient causal capacities*), and second, the kind of actuality that this process is (*how* their heating and cooling go). According to 4. 2:

πέψις μὲν οὖν ἐστιν τελείωσις ὑπὸ τοῦ φυσικοῦ καὶ οἰκείου θερμοῦ ἐκ τῶν ἀντικειμένων παθητικῶν· ταῦτα δ᾽ ἐστὶν ἡ οἰκεία ἑκάστῳ ὕλη. ὅταν γὰρ πεφθῇ, τετελείωταί τε καὶ γέγονεν. καὶ ἡ ἀρχὴ τῆς τελειώσεως ὑπὸ θερμότητος τῆς οἰκείας συμβαίνει, κἂν διά τινος τῶν ἐκτὸς βοηθείας συνεπιτελεσθῇ, οἷον ἡ τροφὴ συμπέττεται καὶ διὰ λουτρῶν καὶ δι᾽ ἄλλων τοιούτων· ἀλλ᾽ ἥ γε ἀρχὴ ἡ ἐν αὐτῷ θερμότης ἐστίν. τὸ δὲ τέλος τοῖς μὲν ἡ φύσις ἐστίν, φύσις δὲ ἣν λέγομεν ὡς εἶδος καὶ οὐσίαν· τοῖς δὲ εἰς ὑποκειμένην τινὰ μορφὴν τὸ τέλος ἐστὶ τῆς πέψεως... (379ᵇ18–27)[85]

Concoction is a completion by the agency of the natural and proper heat from the opposite passive qualities; and these are the proper matter of each thing. For when it has been concocted, it has been completed and it has come to be. And the principle of the completion happens by the agency of the proper heat, even if it is helped in its perfecting by some external aid, as the nourishment is concocted also through baths and other such things; but the principle is the heat in it, and in some cases, the end is the nature, where 'nature' is used in the sense of form and being; but in other cases, the end of the concoction leads to a certain underlying shape ...

This passage describes the capacities and actualizations character-istic of concoction.[86] Its characteristic actualization is a *completion* (τελείωσις) with an end, where this end is either a *formal nature* or an *underlying shape*. According to *Physics* 7. 3, a completion makes something 'most in accordance with [its own] nature' (μάλιστα [τὸ] κατὰ φύσιν, 246ᵃ14–15). As Coope puts it, it 'manifests a nature it already has'; that is, 'properties that it *already has* are more fully developed'.[87] In the case of concoction, this end may be a thing's 'nature ... in the sense of form and being' (φύσις ... ὡς εἶδος καὶ οὐσίαν) or 'a certain underlying shape' (ὑποκειμένην τινὰ μορφήν, *Meteor.* 4. 2, 379ᵇ25–9). Concoctions unfold in this shape-producing way

---

[85] The Greek text is from F. H. Fobes (ed.), *Aristotelis* Meteorologicorum *Libri Quattuor* (Harvard, 1919).

[86] There are different kinds of concoction. Because my focus here is on articulat-ing a new model that can function as the basis for further investigation, I do not discuss these here.

[87] U. Coope, 'Commentary on 246ᵃ10–246ᵇ3', in S. Maso, C. Natali, and G. Seel (eds.), *Reading Aristotle:* Physics VII.3 (Parmenides, 2012), 57–72 at 58, 70.

via the activity of a certain efficient causal capacity ('principle' or ἀρχή): that of the heat that is *proper* or *natural* to the matter it acts on (φυσικοῦ καὶ οἰκείου). It is 'proper' in this sense if it is that 'by which it *naturally* comes to be' (ὑφ' ὧν γίγνεσθαι ... πέφυκεν, *Phys.* 7. 3, 246ᵇ10).[88]

4. 2. *The putrefaction type*

The capacities and characteristic unfolding involved in putrefaction are very different. When the 'proper heat' (οἰκεία θερμότης) cannot do its work, monstrosity or disease results (*GA* 5. 4, 784ᵃ35–ᵇ1); in such cases, 'the heat in the environment' (τῆς ἐν τῷ περιέχοντι θερμότητος) 'putrefies' (σήπεσθαι, 784ᵇ5–6) the material. Likewise, wind-eggs get putrefied when heat is not 'proportionate' to the matter (ἁρμόττουσαν; 3. 2, 753ᵃ28–30). The explanation is that:

τῇ δ' ἁπλῇ γενέσει ἐναντίον μάλιστα κοινὸν σῆψις· ... ὑγρὰ πρῶτον, εἶτα ξηρὰ τέλος γίγνεται τὰ σηπόμενα· ἐκ τούτων γὰρ ἐγένετο, καὶ ὡρίσθη τῷ ὑγρῷ τὸ ξηρὸν ἐργαζομένων τῶν ποιητικῶν. γίγνεται δ' ἡ φθορὰ ὅταν κρατῇ τοῦ ὁρίζοντος τὸ ὁριζόμενον διὰ τὸ περιέχον. ... σῆψις δ' ἐστὶν φθορὰ τῆς ἐν ἑκάστῳ ὑγρῷ οἰκείας καὶ κατὰ φύσιν θερμότητος ὑπ' ἀλλοτρίας θερμότητος· αὕτη δ' ἐστὶν ἡ τοῦ περιέχοντος. ὥστε ἐπεὶ κατ' ἔνδειαν πάσχει θερμοῦ, ἐνδεὲς δὲ ὂν τοιαύτης δυνάμεως ψυχρὸν πᾶν, ἄμφω ἂν αἴτια εἴη, καὶ κοινὸν τὸ πάθος ἡ σῆψις, ψυχρότητός τε οἰκείας καὶ θερμότητος ἀλλοτρίας. διὰ τοῦτο γὰρ καὶ ξηρότερα γίγνεται τὰ σηπόμενα πάντα, καὶ τέλος γῆ καὶ κόπρος· ἐξιόντος γὰρ τοῦ οἰκείου θερμοῦ συνεξατμίζεται τὸ κατὰ φύσιν ὑγρόν, καὶ τὸ σπῶν τὴν ὑγρότητα οὐκ ἔστιν· ἐπάγει γὰρ ἕλκουσα ἡ οἰκεία θερμότης. (*Meteor.* 4. 1, 379ᵃ3–26)

Putrefaction is most generally opposite to simple generation. ... Putrefying things first are moist, then in the end come to be dry; for they came to be out of these, and the dry was made determinate by the moist by the operation of the active qualities. And decay comes to be when what is determined masters what determines it, on account of the environment. ... And putrefaction is the decay of the heat that is proper and in accord with

---

[88] This may show that the capacities of which concoction is an actualization are individuated in terms of a process with an end (e.g. naturally coming to be). We may also note that proper heat is peculiar to kinds of organisms and their parts. It is *natural* heat (φυσικοῦ, 379ᵇ18); thus, Bonitz thinks it synonymous with κατὰ φύσιν (H. Bonitz, *Index Aristotelicus*, 2nd ed. (Akademische Druck, 1955), 499). The importance of this passage is stressed by A. Preus, *Science and Philosophy in Aristotle's Biological Works* (Georg Olms, 1975), 5 n. 4. It may be that proper heat is heat that is proportionate to a thing's nature in the sense that it has *summetria* (*GA* 2. 6, 743ᵃ26–36). In the animal case, it is the correct proportion of heat required to generate offspring (4. 2, 767ᵃ17 ff.). Cf. *PA* 2. 2, 648ᵇ36–649ᵃ1 for proper causation.

nature in each moist thing, by an alien heat; and this is that of the environment. So, since it is affected by lack of heat, and everything lacking this kind of power is cold, both would be the causes, and putrefaction is the common affection of proper cold and alien heat. For on account of this all putrefying things also come to be dry, and its end is earth and dung; for when its proper heat leaves, its natural moisture evaporates along with it, and what draws in moisture is not there; for its proper heat, pulling [the moisture], brings it in.

The capacity that causes putrefaction is therefore that of *alien* heat, such as environmental heat. Its characteristic actuality is one in which this alien heat forces out a body's *natural heat* and *moisture*. Such a body is left dry (as earth or dung), its natural moisture having evaporated with its proper heat.

To get a fix on the roles of putrefaction and concoction in spontaneous generation, we need to know what capacities it actualizes and what this actualization is like: how it unfolds. Given the peculiarities of spontaneous generation, we may expect that the answers to these questions will be so too. This expectation is supported by *Meteorologica* 4. 1, whose account of concoction continues (repeating the very end of the passage just above and continuing),

τὸ δὲ τέλος τοῖς μὲν ἡ φύσις ἐστίν, φύσις δὲ ἦν λέγομεν ὡς εἶδος καὶ οὐσίαν· τοῖς δὲ εἰς ὑποκειμένην τινὰ μορφὴν τὸ τέλος ἐστὶ τῆς πέψεως, ὅταν τοιονδὶ γένηται καὶ τοσονδὶ τὸ ὑγρὸν ἢ ὀπτώμενον ἢ ἑψόμενον ἢ σηπόμενον ἢ ἄλλως πως θερμαινόμενον· τότε γὰρ χρήσιμόν ἐστι καὶ πεπέφθαι φαμέν, ὥσπερ τὸ γλεῦκος καὶ τὰ ἐν τοῖς φύμασιν συνιστάμενα, ὅταν γένηται πύον, καὶ τὸ δάκρυον, ὅταν γένηται λήμη ... (379ᵇ25–32)

In some cases, the end is the nature, where 'nature' is used in the sense of form and being; but in other cases, the end of the concoction leads to a certain underlying shape, when the moist comes to be of such-and-such a kind and quantity by being roasted or boiled or *putrefied* or heated in any other way. For then it is useful and we say it has been concocted, as must, and the things that are put together in growths, when pus comes to be, and tears, when rheum comes to be ...

This passage describes a case in which something acquires an 'underlying shape' (ὑποκειμένην τινὰ μορφήν)—that is, a shape in its *matter*, rather than its formal 'nature' (φύσις).[89] Importantly, for our purposes,

---

[89] Alexander writes that '[s]ince nature is dual, [being] on the one hand *as matter*, on the other as form, he adds what sort of nature the end of concoction is ...' (ἐπεὶ δὲ διττὴ ἡ φύσις, ἡ μὲν ὡς ὕλη, ἡ δὲ ὡς εἶδος, προσέθηκε, ποία φύσις τὸ τῆς πέψεως τέλος,

this thing acquires this underlying shape by *putrefying* (σηπόμενον) and thereby taking on a certain quality and quantity (τοιονδί ... τοσονδί, 379ᵇ26–9).⁹⁰ This case should be familiar. As we saw, *Generation of Animals* 3. 11 claims that spontaneous generation occurs when what *putrefies* takes on a *shape* (μορφήν, 762ᵃ13) of a particular *quality* (τοιαύτην,762ᵃ13).⁹¹ Moreover, just as in 762ᵃ8–18, this happens when a case of *putrefaction* somehow also counts as one of *concoction*.

And just as at 762ᵃ8–18, many scholars have not seen how putrefaction could possibly play the role that the passage appears to assign it.⁹² Lee writes that [t]he sense given by Thurot's alternative reading, "ripened," is better'.⁹³ Thurot, for his part, says:

The word (28) σηπόμενον does not fit here at all, where the topic is the opposite of decomposition. Aristotle enumerates the different species of πέψις (cf. 12 above), and we evidently must read πεπαινόμενον, a term that designates one of the three species, πέπανσις, ἕψησις, ὄπτησις, of which he has just mentioned the two others.⁹⁴

In Meteor. 187. 9–10 Hayduck, trans. Lewis, emphasis added). Düring takes the distinction to be between 'physical' and 'chemical' nature, which he associates with matter and form (*Chemical Treatise*, 15, 69).

⁹⁰ Stavrianeas labels these 'non-assimilatory concoction processes' and identifies the first component of testacean generation as such ('Spontaneous Generation', 333). He does not connect it with *putrefied* residue, and still treats this process as a species of *concoction*. To that extent then, I would contend, his account does not have the resources to ground the thought that the cause is 'external heat that coincidentally heats' and thereby 'turn[s] a portion of it into a proto-organism' (333). This is not enough to make it *coincidentally caused*. A concoction just is a 'completion': the sort of process that is caused by natural heat and that standardly achieves an 'end'—often, as in this case but also, importantly, in others, an 'underlying shape' (379ᵇ18–27). To say that such an underlying shape is coincidentally caused, we need a further step. In particular, we need to consider the process that brings it about as something other than concoction, such as putrefaction. The latter interpretation also does a much better job, more importantly, of capturing Aristotle's remarks on the role of external heat and the formation of the 'shape' in *Generation of Animals* 3. 11 and *Meteorology* 4, as I argue above.

⁹¹ See Section 3.

⁹² σηπόμενον is in the main manuscripts, Alexander's citations, and Olympiodorus' citations, lemmata, and paraphrases. Thurot's alternative appears only in a gloss in Olympiodorus.

⁹³ H. D. P. Lee (ed. and trans.), *Aristotle: Meteorologica* (Loeb, 1952), 299.

⁹⁴ 'Le mot (28) σηπόμενον ne convient nullement ici, où il s'agit du contraire de la décomposition. Aristote énumère les différentes espèces de πέψις (cf. plus haut 12), et il faut évidemment lire πεπαινόμενον, terme qui désigne l'une trois espèces, πέπανσις, ἕψησις, ὄπτησις dont il vient de mentionner deux autres' (C. Thurot, 'Observations critiques sur les Meteorologica d'Aristote (suite et fin)', *Revue archéologique*, nouvelle série, 21 (1870), 396–407 at 398.) Cf. E. Lewis (trans.),

Thurot is certainly correct that there are three kinds of concoction: ripening, boiling, and roasting (*Meteor.* 4. 3). However, this observation does not require that the three cases in which 'the end of the concoction leads to a certain underlying shape' must *also* be ripening, boiling, and roasting—as opposed to putrefying. Aristotle has distinguished cases that bring out an 'underlying shape' from those whose 'end is the nature, where "nature" is used in the sense of form and being'.[95] Only the former are under discussion here. It thus may be that ripening differs from the processes listed here— roasting, boiling, and putrefying—in that ripening is not one of the concoctions that bring out an 'underlying shape' (ὑποκειμένην τινὰ μορφήν). Instead, it may be in the other class of concoctions: those whose 'end is the nature, where "nature" is used in the sense of form and being'. Indeed, Aristotle's account of ripening is explicit that it is a 'completion' (τελέωσις; 4. 3, 380ᵃ13) of which the cause is a thing's nature (ἡ φύσις, 380ᵃ26). In the case of fruit, what this nature ripens is the nourishment (τροφῆς) in the fruit (380ᵃ12). When it does this, it is not bringing out an underlying shape in the nourishing matter, but assimilating that matter to *itself* (380ᵃ25–6)—surely, making it like its form. Aristotle would thus have good reason to put ripening in a different class of concoctions from those that bring out an underlying shape.[96]

Moreover, the idea that putrefaction might produce a shape is compatible with *Meteorologica* 4. 11, which allows that some products of putrefaction have heat in them (389ᵇ8).[97] This means that putrefied material may have a shape in virtue of being affected by seasonal heat in a particular way. We find positive evidence that putrefaction must be able to do this in the fact that *Meteor.* 4. 2,

Alexander of Aphrodisias, *On Aristotle: Meteorology 4* (Duckworth, 1996), 77 n. 50 and Düring, *Chemical Treatise*, 69.

[95] *Meteor.* 4. 2, 379ᵇ25–6: τέλος τοῖς μὲν ἡ φύσις ἐστίν, φύσις δὲ ἣν λέγομεν ὡς εἶδος καὶ οὐσίαν.

[96] In his commentary, Alexander likewise lists as a paradigm case of the first kind of concoction (in which the nature is realized) the realization of the natural form in *fruit*: 'In some cases, then, he says the end of concoction is to realise the natural form itself, as in the case of fruits' (τῆς πέψεως οὖν ἐπί τινων τέλος φησὶν εἶναι τὸ εἶδος τὸ κατὰ φύσιν ἀπολαβεῖν αὐτό, ὡς ἐπὶ τῶν καρπῶν, *In Meteor.* 187. 11–13, trans. Lewis). This is Aristotle's own favoured example of *ripening* in *Meteorologica* 4. 3: 'ripening is a sort of concoction; for concoction of the nourishment in fruits is called ripening' (πέπανσις δ᾽ ἐστὶν πέψις τις· ἡ γὰρ τῆς ἐν τοῖς περικαρπίοις τροφῆς πέψις πέπανσις λέγεται; 380ᵃ11–12).

[97] As Düring notes, calling these the 'so-called συντηκτά' (*Chemical Treatise*, 69).

379^{b}25–32 lists 'pus' (πύον) as the result of concoction that brings out an 'underlying shape' (ὑποκειμένην τινὰ μορφήν). The *Generation of Animals* and *History of Animals* are explicit that pus (πύον) is a product of putrefaction (σαπρότης, *GA* 4. 8, 777^{a}11–12; σηπόμενον, *HA* 3. 19, 521^{a}20). In saying that pus, produced by *putrefaction*, is an example of a product of the relevant kind of *concoction*, Aristotle is underlining his point that a case of putrefaction can sometimes be described as a concoction of that kind. The upshot is that Aristotle really *does* likely mean to say that putrefaction can result in a shape and be described as a concoction. This shape, as this passage also insists, is of course only an underlying one—for it is not the formal nature of the lagoon materials whose enclosure is responsible for the testacean shape (*GA* 3. 11, 762^{a}26–7) to have a testacean shape. These materials have the right ingredients for producing a testacean, but it is not part of their nature to do so.

5. Spontaneous generation and disjunctivism

So far, I have argued that both putrefaction and concoction play a role in spontaneous generation (Section 3). Of particular importance is the fact that putrefaction is causally responsible for producing the material that has a shape that it eventually can lend to developing testacean. I have also sketched the characteristic capacities and actualizations of each type, as well as *Meteorologica* 4's hints about how they might be involved in spontaneous generation (Section 4). The next step is to use these results to explain *exactly* what justifies Aristotle in describing spontaneous generation in terms of both putrefaction and concoction: to examine all the muddy details and to show how they are connected with putrefaction and concoction. The upshot, I will argue, is that spontaneous generation turns out to satisfy Aristotle's criteria for being spontaneously caused.

In fact, it satisfies these criteria in part because Aristotle turns out to hold a particularly interesting *disjunctivist* account of animal generation, one which emerges fairly naturally from his account of efficient causal processes (as we began to see in Section 4). As I began to argue there, this disjunctivist account has it that the 'fundamental' type to which spontaneous generation belongs is a different type than that to which standard generation belongs, despite the fact that the two have in common that they can be described as *unfolding* as concoctions do: as 'being concocted' (as at *GA* 3. 11, 762ᵃ13–14).[98] The 'fundamental' type to which spontaneous generation belongs is a type that has the characteristic unfolding of concoction (the shaping one)—but *as a result of actualizing the capacities that cause putrefaction* in situations like this one.[99] It actualizes *these* capacities and *as a result* unfolds in putrefaction's characteristic way (the natural heat-destroying, dry residue-leaving way)—as well as, accidentally, in concoction's characteristic way. It is thus unlike standard generation, which has the characteristic unfolding of concoction *in virtue of* actualizing *concoction*'s characteristic capacities. Whereas standard generation *non-accidentally* unfolds in the concoction way, spontaneous generation does so merely *accidentally*. Their 'fundamental' types are thus not the same.

The upshot is that while both processes do have a common feature—unfolding in the concoction way—this is not the feature in virtue of which they belong to their 'fundamental' kinds. This disjunctivist interpretation has certain attractions. First, it may help to preserve an appealing view about causation: that properly causing an effect (including a process) of a certain type requires having the *right* kind of cause—one that has the capacity to do so and will do so if all goes well.[100] As in disjunctivism about perception, the basic insight is that we need not generalize from the bad case to the good one: even if we cannot subjectively distinguish

---

[98] Compare Martin's suggestion that 'the most fundamental kind that the perceptual event is of, the kind in virtue of which the event has the nature that it does, is one which couldn't be instanced in the case of hallucination'; but 'while the perceptual event is of a fundamental kind which could not occur when hallucinating, nonetheless this very same event is also of some other psychological kind or kinds which a causally matching hallucinatory event (i.e. one brought about by the same proximate causal conditions) belongs to' ('Limits', 60).

[99] Alternatively, we might suppose that the fundamental type is just the concoction-unfolding type (leaving putrefaction out of the type, but not requiring that this unfolding be had in virtue of actualizing concoction capacities). The point can still be made that this fundamental type differs from the fundamental type of standard generation, which is the type that *does* have this unfolding in virtue of being actualization of the right capacities. This is closer to Martin's approach, which makes the fundamental type to which hallucinations belong 'indiscriminable from veridical perception'. Veridical perception also has this feature, but in this case, its explanatory potential depends on the explanatory potential of veridical perception and so it is not fundamental ('Limits', 69–70).

[100] For a version of this idea, cf. S. Kelsey, 'The Argument of *Metaphysics* vi 3', *Ancient Philosophy*, 24 (2000), 119–34.

between veridical perception and hallucination, we need not infer (for instance) that mind-independent objects cannot be constituents of veridical perception. Similarly, the fact that both the bad and good cases of animal generation involve a concoction-like unfolding does not require us to generalize from the bad case to the good one: to think that in the good case (like the bad one) this concoction-like unfolding must not be an actualization of certain capacities to do so. Aristotle's fundamental idea may be that even if the final stages of spontaneous generation are sufficient for the production of an oyster, what is doing the real causal 'work' (in virtue of which these stages end in an oyster) is the actualization of a different capacity than the one that does this causal work in standard generation.[101]

Second, this disjunctivist interpretation can preserve the insights of standard accounts of Aristotle's views on spontaneous generation: that spontaneous generation is really quite 'like' standard generation.[102] It is compatible with the disjunctivist approach that spontaneous generation unfolds as concoctions do and can be described accordingly, so long as this is not mistaken for a fact about its fundamental type. Similarly, some disjunctivists about perception and more moderate fellow travellers allow that hallucinations are 'like' veridical perception—perhaps in being subjectively indistinguishable.[103]

With this outline in place, I want to end by sketching the biological facts in virtue of which spontaneous generation counts as having these capacities and characteristic unfoldings, filling out the picture given in Section 3. There, I argued that *Generation of*

---

[101] This move is analogous to moves sometimes made by disjunctivists in response to the objection that any common features of perception and hallucination 'screen off' the uniquely perceptual features from giving an explanation (see Martin, 'Limits', 62–70). See n. 99.

[102] Cf. nn. 41 and 42.

[103] For the more purely epistemological characterization, see Martin, 'Limits', 49–50 and perhaps J. M. Hinton, 'Selections from *Experiences*', in A. Byrne and H. Logue (eds.), *Disjunctivism: Contemporary Readings* [*Contemporary Readings*] (MIT, 2009), 13–32 at 30. For more moderate options (to different degrees), see P. Snowdon, 'Perception, Vision, and Causation', in Byrne and Logue (eds.), *Contemporary Readings*, 33–48 at 41 ff.; M. Johnston, 'The Obscure Object of Hallucination', in Byrne and Logue (eds.), *Contemporary Readings*, 207–70 at 213, 225–6. For an overview of possibilities, see S. Sturgeon, 'Disjunctivism about Visual Experience', in Haddock and Macpherson (eds.), *Disjunctivism*, 112–43 at 117–19.

Animals 3. 11, 762ᵃ8–18 presents the *first* component of spontaneous generation as a process of putrefaction that is also responsible
for *shaping* the testacean: that is, we can now see, as also unfolding
in *concoction*'s characteristic way.[104] In addition, we can now see
that this very passage (762ᵃ8–18) *also* presents this shaping process
as having the characteristic unfolding of *putrefaction*. Putrefaction,
we now know, happens when environmental heat forces out a
body's *proper heat* and *moisture*, leaving behind *a dry and earthy
remainder* (*Meteor.* 4. 1, 379ᵃ23–5). This is, in fact, just what happens at *Generation of Animals* 3. 11, 762ᵃ8–18. What gets separated
off is *moisture:* the 'sweet', which Aristotle associates with nourishing fresh water (3. 11, 761ᵃ32–ᵇ12) and perhaps the rain just mentioned (762ᵃ11–12).[105] As *Meteor.* 4. 1, 379ᵃ23–5 reminds us, natural
moisture follows *natural heat*. And *Generation of Animals* 3. 11's
initial separation also yields a *principle* (762ᵃ13), later conceived of the
part that has soul-*heat* and soul principle (762ᵃ20, cf. 762ᵇ16–17).[106]
Indeed, *Generation of Animals* 4. 1 defines this sort of 'principle'
as the 'part having the principle of the natural heat' (τῷ μορίῳ τῷ
ἔχοντι τὴν τῆς φυσικῆς θερμότητος ἀρχήν, 766ᵃ35–6). This is just to
say that one product of this initial separation is *heat* that was once
natural to the putrefying stuff and that will come to be the principle
of the testacean soul.[107] This too is what happens in putrefaction
(*Meteor.* 4. 1, 379ᵃ23–5). Moreover, what is left behind after the sweet
is separated off is a 'remainder' (περιττεῦον) and 'residue' (περίττωμα,

---

[104] See the next paragraph for details.

[105] That the sweet is the rainwater is also supported by Aristotle's remark that
spontaneously generated eels are 'nourished' by rainwater (τρέφεσθαι ὀμβρίῳ ὕδατι,
HA 6. 16, 570ᵃ11–12).

[106] In line with *History of Animals* 5. 15, 547ᵇ11–13, I thus take the principle
referred to at 762ᵃ13 to be the leading part of the testacean, rather than the soul-
heat/principle it also has. Cf. A. L. Peck (ed. and trans.), *History of Animals*, vol. i
(Loeb, 1965), lxx. On this principle, cf. *Generation of Animals* 3. 11, 762ᵇ31 ff.,
763ᵃ10–12 (the principle requires nourishment!) and 762ᵇ6–9 (and is formed by
environmental heat; cf. n. 118).

[107] Zwier helpfully comments that all spontaneous generation is 'either formed in
putrefying, wet, earthy material heated by the sun (cf. *GA* 3. 11 762ᵃ10–12, 763ᵃ28–
34; *HA* 5. 1, 539ᵃ23–4; 5. 15, 547ᵇ12–14, 18–20, 547ᵇ35–548ᵃ3; 5. 19, 551ᵃ1–2), or in/on
living plants or animals (cf. *GA* 1. 1, 715ᵇ29–30; *HA* 5. 1, 539ᵃ24–5; 5. 19, 551ᵃ6–10;
Meteor. 4. 1, 379ᵇ6–7; 4. 3, 381ᵇ10–13), or in animal excrement (*HA* 5. 19, 551ᵃ5–7),
or in the dead remains of plants and animals (*GA* 2. 1, 715ᵃ25, 716ᵇ5; 4. 11, 762ᵃ11–18;
HA 5. 19, 551ᵃ5). ... Aristotle's thought when speaking of "natural residue" [737ᵃ3–6]
was that some kind of life-principle from the living matter or its remains is present'
('Methodology', 366). This life-principle is the heat forced out in putrefaction.

GA 3. 11, 762ᵃ12–15). Again, this is typical of putrefaction, for 'all putrefying things come to be dry, and its end is earth and dung'.¹⁰⁸ For further support for identifying the products of this process as a heat-containing principle, moisture, and earthy residue, we may recall Aristotle's observation that spontaneous generation happens in lagoons because they contain all the parts required to generate testacea: fluid, *pneuma*, and earth (*GA* 3. 11, 761ᵇ11). What our passage (762ᵃ8–18) does is describe how these are separated out from one another in the required way—by means of a process that unfolds in a way characteristic of *putrefaction*.

Importantly, however, this dried-out, earthy stuff—the sort of thing that putrefaction is famous for producing—also lends its *shape* (μορφήν, *GA* 3. 11, 762ᵃ13) to the developing testacean. That is, it ensures that the materials *of which* it is a remainder—the separated sweet stuff and the principle¹⁰⁹—end up being *shaped* in the way required to produce an organism with a particular shell shape. The remainder itself can therefore be described as 'a residue of what has been concocted' (περίττωμα τοῦ πεφθέντος, 762ᵃ15). That the residue supplies those other materials with a shape is reinforced by Aristotle's observations that putrefied residues are *earthy* (*Meteor.* 4. 1, 379ᵃ22–3), that the key shape-making separation and enclosing takes place in liquid containing *earth* (*GA* 3. 11, 762ᵃ19), and that *earthy* material will eventually harden around other materials into what seems to be a *shell* (*GA* 3. 11, 762ᵃ29–31), which will be of a particular *shape* (*PA* 4. 5). This means that those enclosed materials—likely the sweet and the principle—may eventually end up shaped by the earthy shell that encloses them.¹¹⁰ That is to say, this separating process, which happens as putrefactions do (yielding such a residue), *also* happens as concoctions do. More specifically, it happens as a certain kind of concoction does: it brings something to completion by bringing out an 'underlying shape' (*Meteor.* 4. 2, 379ᵇ26–7) in the matter. This is why it is a residue *of* what has been *concocted* (*GA* 3. 11, 762ᵃ15).¹¹¹

---

¹⁰⁸ *Meteor.* 4. 1, 379ᵃ22–3: ξηρότερα γίγνεται τὰ σηπόμενα πάντα, καὶ τέλος γῆ καὶ κόπρος.

¹⁰⁹ For a similar *separation* of more and less liquid (as the sweet and principle are) components in concoction, see *Meteor.* 4. 3's account of boiling as separating a thicker and a thinner part (380ᵇ20–1, 381ᵃ6–8).

¹¹⁰ Cf. Gotthelf, 'Teleology', 146 and n. 15 on the contents of the enclosure.

¹¹¹ For further details on how this process unfolds like a concoction, see the last paragraph of this section.

So far, we have seen that this process has the characteristic unfolding of putrefaction *and* concoction. However, we should recognize that the concoction unfolding belongs to it only *accidentally*, not in virtue of capacities whose actualization unfolds in the concoction way. We can see this by considering Aristotle's answer to what in spontaneous generation corresponds to the male and female principles found in standard generation (*GA* 3. 11, 762ᵃ35–ᵇ18). The exact details of his argument are difficult. In assessing them, we need to recognize that they concern roughly the same component of spontaneous generation as our first passage.¹¹² The evidence is that the later passage refers to 'that in the *pneuma* of the soul principle that is being enclosed or separated off', which then 'makes a fetation and implants movement' (762ᵇ16–18).¹¹³ This would seem to be the very *separation* (ἀποκρινομένου) of sweet stuff, principle, and remainder as in our earlier passage (762ᵃ12–13).¹¹⁴ The later passage, of course, has a different project: it is concerned not with explaining how putrefaction is involved in spontaneous generation, but rather with how it is *analogous* to standard generation. Its aim is to show that spontaneous generation is *like* a process (standard generation) that is of the *concoction* type (762ᵇ2–9).¹¹⁵

It is with this project—sketching an analogy to standard generation—in mind that Aristotle says that 'that which the heat in animals works up from the nourishment, this the heat of the season in

---

¹¹² This is also the same separating and enclosing we find in the account of the frothy bubble: note ἐμπεριληφθῇ, ἐμπεριλαμβάνεται, 762ᵃ22; περιλαμβανόμενον, 762ᵃ27; περιλαμβανομένου, 762ᵃ31–2.

¹¹³ τὸ δ' ἐναπολαμβανόμενον ἢ ἀποκρινόμενον ἐν τῷ πνεύματι τῆς ψυχικῆς ἀρχῆς κύημα ποιεῖ καὶ κίνησιν ἐντίθησιν.

¹¹⁴ There is a difference between ἐναπολαμβάνεσθαι and περιλαμβάνεσθαι. But the remark that the *pneuma* of the soul principle is ἐναπολαμβανόμενον echoes *Generation of Animals* 2's remark that the *pneuma* is itself enclosed (ἐμπεριλαμβανόμενον) in the *semen* and *foam* (2. 3, 736ᵇ26–7; cf. 737ᵃ9). In any case, ἐναπολαμβάνεσθαι occurs only here in the *Generation of Animals*; all evidence from the *Generation of Animals* therefore suggests it is at least co-referential with περιλαμβάνεσθαι. Elsewhere, Aristotle uses ἐναπολαμβάνειν to highlight that what is enclosed is put *inside* something. See *HA* 6. 37, 580ᵇ11–12; *Phys.* 4. 6, 213ᵃ27; *Meteor.* 2. 8, 366ᵇ10; 3. 3, 372ᵇ30–1; *De caelo* 4. 2, 309ᵃ6. The emphasis of certain uses of περιλαμβάνειν is more on *covering* or *encircling* (*De caelo* 4. 6, 313ᵇ12, 14; *GA* 1. 12, 719ᵇ12–13). This may be why Aristotle adds ἐντὸς to περιλαμβανομένου at *Generation of Animals* 3. 11, 762ᵃ31–2. I am grateful to Jim Lennox for suggesting a possible distinction along these lines.

¹¹⁵ There are two concoctions in standard generation: first the mother concocts her nourishment into residue, then the principle in the father's semen concocts this residue into a fetation. See n. 118.

the environment combines and puts together from sea and earth by *concocting*' (762ᵇ13–16).[116] Importantly, what does this so-called 'concocting' (πέττουσα) is 'the heat of the season in the environment' (ἡ τῆς ὥρας ἐν τῷ περιέχοντι θερμότης, 762ᵇ14–15). Seasonal environmental heat is *Meteorologica* 4's favoured example of the *alien* heat that initiates *putrefaction* (4. 1, 379ᵃ16–18, 379ᵃ11–12). It is the heat whose actuality, when it can overcome another body's natural heat, is *putrefaction*. This reveals that spontaneous generation is really an actualization of the capacities that cause *putrefaction* when applied to materials of this sort. The seasonal heat—*not* the heat of the soul principle that will eventually become the proper heat of the resulting testacean—is the cause whose actualization is the process that yields the shape that ends up being the shape of the testacean. Aristotle is clear that this soul principle is *not* the one that efficiently causes the process of *separation* described at 3. 11, 762ᵃ8–18; its role is simply to 'implant movement and make a fetation' (κύημα ποιεῖ καὶ κίνησιν ἐντίθησιν, 762ᵇ17–18) while the separation is happening.[117]

Nonetheless, as we have seen, this separation unfolds in the way characteristic of *concoction*: it yields an underlying shape that it then lends to the materials of which the shaped material is the residue. This is why Aristotle can characterize the seasonal heat as 'concocting' (πέττουσα, 762ᵇ15), at least when he is emphasizing the analogy to standard generation, as he is here (762ᵃ35–ᵇ18). Aristotle's point in this passage is roughly that the 'concoction' label is appropriate because the process caused by seasonal heat unfolds in much the same way that a process of concoction would in standard generation. But how, exactly, does it resemble standard generation? In standard generation, there are two process of concoction: one that produces female residue and one by which the male acts on the residue. At first glance, it is not obvious which of these is meant to be analogous to the action of the seasonal heat: Aristotle may be saying either that 'the heat in the animal by separating and concocting makes the residue, the principle of the fetation, out of the incoming nourishment' or (dropping the comma)

---

[116] ὅπερ ἡ ἐν τοῖς ζῴοις θερμότης ἐκ τῆς τροφῆς ἀπεργάζεται, τοῦθ' ἡ τῆς ὥρας ἐν τῷ περιέχοντι θερμότης ἐκ θαλάττης καὶ γῆς συγκρίνει πέττουσα καὶ συνίστησιν.

[117] That is, it takes over in the second component of spontaneous generation. See n. 35.

that 'the heat in the animal by separating and concocting out of the incoming nourishment makes the residue into the principle of the fetation' (762ᵇ7–9).[118] One reason to prefer the second possibility is that Aristotle thinks that the seasonal heat is analogous to the *male*'s heat (2. 6, 743ᵃ32–6). The upshot is that the process of putrefaction caused by seasonal heat is analogous to standard generation in that it makes the 'principle' in the sense of the leading part of the organism (cf. 3. 11, 763ᵃ11). That is, this process unfolds in a way that mimics the concocting work normally done by *both* parents: this is why it is said to be 'concocting' (πέττουσα, 762ᵇ15).[119] In saying this, of course, Aristotle is merely highlighting *how* spontaneous generation unfolds, not the proper efficient causes of this unfolding.

6. Concluding remarks

These considerations provide some reasons to believe that Aristotle might be a kind of disjunctivist about animal generation: the 'fundamental' type to which spontaneous generation belongs is *not* the type to which standard generation belongs. While both have the concoction way of unfolding, their fundamental types differ because these unfoldings are differently related to their efficient causes. Only in standard generation does the process have this unfolding in virtue of its proper causes. This result squares with our initial observation that reliably producing testacea makes spontaneous generation similar to standard generation, but also the recognition that putrefying is a destructive process: one that just is not the sort of thing that should produce anything.

   This picture also solves the puzzle about how spontaneous generation is genuinely 'spontaneous': how it happens *rarely* in virtue of being *accidentally caused*. Putrefaction is, at bottom, a destructive process. If a case of putrefaction ever comes to have the features required to produce an organism (a concoction-like way of

---

[118] ἐκ τῆς εἰσιούσης τροφῆς ἡ ἐν τῷ ζῴῳ θερμότης ἀποκρίνουσα καὶ συμπέττουσα ποιεῖ τὸ περίττωμα, τὴν ἀρχὴν τοῦ κυήματος. This relies on the use of ποιεῖ in constructions of the form 'making *x* (into) *y*' (cf. *GA* 2. 6, 743ᵃ21, 743ᵇ1). Less plausibly, we may (with Henry, 'Themistius,' 200 n. 23) take τὴν ἀρχὴν τοῦ κυήματος to be the object, skipping over τὸ περίττωμα.

[119] Scholars have differed in their identification of the product of the process described here. For the view that it is 'something like a female residue', see Gotthelf, 'Teleology', 147. For the view that it is a 'proto-organism equipped with a life principle', see Stavrianeas, 'Spontaneous Generation', 327.

unfolding), it has these features only accidentally. This is like saying that the market-goer's action is properly (non-accidentally) a case of going to court and accidentally one of collecting a debt. For this reason, processes like it happen *rarely*. It is rare for a process of putrefaction to happen in such a way that it can be described as a case of concoction.[120] Importantly, this concoction process is accidentally caused *even though* it has just the right (concoction-like) features to promote the development of a specific kind of testacean. To say that the specific materials involved in spontaneous generation contribute to the form of the testacean is *not* to say what capacity controls their actualization.

There is, of course, a further question of why concoction and putrefaction are Aristotle's preferred types for thinking about these issues. While a full answer is beyond the scope of this paper, it may be useful to note the place in Aristotle's theory that putrefaction and concoction fill. These, as *Meteorologica* 4 presents them, are the types associated with the *active* rather than the *passive* capacities. In focusing on them, Aristotle is highlighting the *efficient causes* of the process, rather than the matter on which it acts. This, of course, is exactly what he promised to do in the *Generation of Animals*: to consider this cause is just to consider the generation of each animal (*GA* 1. 1, 715ᵃ13–15).[121, 122]

Brown University

---

[120] Dudley briefly suggests, without mentioning putrefaction, that '[s]pontaneous generation is an unusual outcome of the sun (the efficient cause) shining on the earth' (J. Dudley, *Aristotle's Concept of Chance: Accidents, Cause, Necessity, and Determinism* (SUNY, 2012), 184). But Dudley's official account makes the rarity of spontaneous generation relative to *all* generations (191–2).

[121] For a very recent account of the scientific details, see Malcolm Wilson's 'Heat, Meteorology, and Spontaneous Generation', in H. Bartoš and C. King (eds.), *Heat, Pneuma, and Soul in Ancient Philosophy and Science* (Cambridge, 2020), 159–181. Wilson develops the interpretation of the theory of *GA* 3. 11 (which he takes to revise that of *Meteorologica* 4. 1 and 4. 11) that allows concoction alone to be responsible for generating the organism, while what putrefies is merely leftover material. He thus takes the source of the concocting heat mentioned at 762a8–18 to be the 'soul-heat' mentioned later, at 762a20. Wilson also offers a fascinating account of the place of spontaneously generated organisms in Aristotle's *scala natura*.

[122] I wish to thank David Charles, Verity Harte, Jim Lennox, and the University of Toronto. Diana Quarantotto and Michael Della Rocca for their astute comments on many versions of this paper. It was also improved greatly as a result of helpful comments from Victor Caston and an anonymous reader at *OSAP*. I am also grateful to audiences at Yale, the University of Florida (where I received helpful comments from Taylor Pincin), Virginia Tech (where I received helpful comments from Patricia Marechal) for their questions and suggestions.

BIBLIOGRAPHY

Ackrill, J., 'Aristotle on Action', *Mind*, 87 (1978), 595–601.

Allen, J., 'Aristotle on Chance as an Accidental Cause' ['Chance'], in Leunissen (ed.), *Critical Guide*, 66–87.

Balme, D. M., 'Development of Biology in Aristotle and Theophrastus: Theory of Spontaneous Generation' ['Development'], *Phronesis*, 7 (1962), 91–104.

Bonello, A., *Aristotle on Spontaneity* [*Spontaneity*], PhD diss., University of Toronto, 2015.

Bonitz, H., *Index Aristotelicus*, 2nd ed. (Akademische Druck, 1955).

Byrne, A. and Logue, H., 'Either/Or', in Haddock and Macpherson (eds.), *Disjunctivism*, 57–94.

Byrne, A. and Logue, H., *Disjunctivism: Contemporary Readings* [*Contemporary Readings*] (MIT, 2009).

Charles, D., 'Aristotle on Agency', *Oxford Handbooks Online* (2017), section IV.1; DOI: 10. 1093/oxfordhb/9780199935314. 013. 6.

Charles, D., 'Aristotle's Processes' ['Processes'], in Leunissen (ed.), *Critical Guide*, 186–205.

Charles, D., 'Processes, Activities, and Actions', in Stout (ed.), *Process*, 20–40.

Connell, S. M., *Aristotle on Female Animals* (Cambridge, 2016).

Coope, U., 'Aristotle on Action', *Proceedings of the Aristotelian Society*, suppl. vol. 81 (2007), 109–38.

Coope, U., 'Change and its Relation to Actuality and Potentiality', in G. Anagnostopoulos (ed.), *A Companion to Aristotle* (Wiley-Blackwell, 2009), 277–91.

Coope, U., 'Commentary on 246ᵃ10–246ᵇ3', in S. Maso, C. Natali, and G. Seel (eds.), *Reading Aristotle:* Physics *VII.3* (Parmenides, 2012), 57–72.

Drossaart Lulofs, H. J. (ed.), *De generatione animalium* (Oxford, 1965).

Dudley, J., *Aristotle's Concept of Chance: Accidents, Cause, Necessity, and Determinism* (SUNY, 2012).

Düring, I., *Aristotle's Chemical Treatise:* Meteorologica, *Book IV,* with introduction and commentary [*Chemical Treatise*] (Elanders, 1944).

Fobes, F. H. (ed.), *Aristotelis* Meteorologicorum *Libri Quattuor* (Harvard, 1919).

Freudenthal, G., *Aristotle's Theory of Material Substance: Heat and Pneuma, Form and Soul* (Clarendon, 1995).

Gill, M. L., 'Aristotle's Theory of Causal Action in *Physics* III 3', *Phronesis*, 25 (1980), 129–47.

Gotthelf, A. 'Teleology and Spontaneous Generation in Aristotle: A Discussion' ['Teleology'] in id., *Teleology, First Principles, and Scientific Method in Aristotle's Biology* (Oxford, 2012), 142–50.

Haddock, A. and Macpherson, F. (eds.), *Disjunctivism: Perception, Action, Knowledge* [*Disjunctivism*] (Oxford, 2008).

Heinaman, R., 'Is Aristotle's Definition of Change Circular?', *Apeiron*, 27 (1994), 25–38.

Henry, D., 'Themistius and Spontaneous Generation in Aristotle's *Metaphysics*' ['Themistius'], *Oxford Studies in Ancient Philosophy*, 24 (2003), 183–207.

Hinton, J. M., 'Selections from *Experiences*', in Byrne and Logue (eds.), *Contemporary Readings*, 13–32.

Hull, D., 'The Conflict Between Spontaneous Generation and Aristotle's *Metaphysics*' ['Conflict'], *Proceedings of the Inter-American Congress of Philosophy*, 7 (1967–8), 245–50.

Johnson, M. R., 'The Medical Background of Aristotle's Theory of Nature and Spontaneity' ['Medical Background'], *Proceedings of the Boston Area Colloquium in Ancient Philosophy*, 27 (2012), 105–52.

Johnston, M., 'The Obscure Object of Hallucination', in Byrne and Logue (eds.), *Contemporary Readings*, 207–70.

Judson, L., 'Chance and "Always or For the Most Part" in Aristotle' ['Chance'], in id. (ed.) *Aristotle's* Physics: *A Collection of Essays* (Clarendon, 1991), 73–99.

Judson, L., 'What Can Happen When You Eat Pungent Food', in N. Avgelis and F. Peonidis (eds.), *Aristotle on Logic, Language and Science* (Sakkoulas, 1998), 185–204.

Kelsey, S. 'The Argument of *Metaphysics* vi 3', *Ancient Philosophy*, 24 (2000), 119–34.

Kelsey, S., '*Physics* 199ª8–12', *Apeiron*, 44 (2011), 1–12.

Kress, E., 'How Things Happen for the Sake of Something: The Dialectical Strategy of Aristotle, *Physics* 2. 8' ['How Things Happen'], *Phronesis*, 64 (2019), 321–47.

Lee, H. D. P. (ed. and trans.), *Aristotle:* Meteorologica (Loeb, 1952).

Lefebvre, D., 'La génération des animaux', in P. Pellegrin (ed.), *Aristote, Œuvres complètes* (Flammarion, 2014).

Lennox, J., 'Aristotle on the Emergence of Material Complexity: *Meteorology* IV and Aristotle's Biology', *HOPOS*, 4 (2014), 272–305.

Lennox, J., 'Teleology, Chance, and Aristotle's Theory of Spontaneous Generation' ['Teleology'], in id. (ed.), *Aristotle's Biology: Studies in the Origins of Life Science* (Cambridge, 2001), 229–49.

Leunissen, M. (ed.), *Aristotle's Physics: A Critical Guide* [*Critical Guide*] (Cambridge, 2015).

Lewis, E. (trans.), *On Aristotle:* Meteorology 4 (Duckworth, 1996),

Lloyd, G. E. R., 'The Master Cook', in id., *Aristotelian Explorations* ['Master Cook'] (Cambridge, 1996), 83–103.

Louis, P., 'La génération spontanée chez Aristote' ['Génération spontanée'], *Revue de Synthèse*, 89 (1968), 293–305.

Marmodoro, A., 'The Union of Cause and Effect in Aristotle: *Physics* III 3', *Oxford Studies in Ancient Philosophy*, 32 (2007), 205–32.

Marmodoro, A., *Aristotle on Perceiving Objects* (Oxford, 2014).

Martin, M. G. F., 'The Limits of Self-Awareness' ['Limits'], *Philosophical Studies*, 120 (2004), 37–89.

Maso, S., Natali, C., and Seel, G. (eds.), *Reading Aristotle: Physics VII.3* (Parmenides, 2012).

Mignucci, M. "'Ὡς ἐπὶ τὸ πολύ" et nécessaire dans la conception aristotél-icienne de la science', in E. Berti (ed.), *Aristotle on Science: The 'Posterior Analytics'*, *Proceedings of the Eighth Symposium Aristotelicum* (Editrice Antenore, 1981), 173–203.

Nielsen, K., 'The Private Parts of Animals: Aristotle on the Teleology of Sexual Difference', *Phronesis*, 53 (2008), 373–405.

Panayides, C., 'Aristotle on Chance and Spontaneous Generation: A Discussion Note', *Filozofia*, 68 (2013), 121–2.

Peck, A. L. (ed. and trans.), *Aristotle:* Generation of Animals [*Generation of Animals*], revised and reprinted (Cambridge, MA, 1963).

Peck, A. L. (ed. and trans.), *History of Animals*, vol. i (Loeb, 1965).

Preus, A., *Science and Philosophy in Aristotle's Biological Works* (Georg Olms, 1975).

Ross, W. D. (ed.), *Aristotelis* Physica (Oxford, 1950).

Snowdon, P., 'Perception, Vision, and Causation', in Byrne and Logue (eds.), *Contemporary Readings*, 33–48.

Stavrianeas, S. 'Spontaneous Generation in Aristotle's Biology' ['Spontaneous Generation'], *Rhizai*, 2 (2008), 303–38.

Steward, H., 'Processes, Continuants, and Individuals', *Mind*, 122 (2013), 781–812.

Stout, R. (ed.), *Process, Action, and Experience* [*Process*] (Oxford, 2018).

Stout, R., 'Ballistic Action', in id. (ed.), *Process*, 210–27.

Stout, R., *Things That Happen Because They Should: A Teleological Approach to Action* (Oxford, 1996).

Sturgeon, S., 'Disjunctivism about Visual Experience', in Haddock and Macpherson (eds.), *Disjunctivism*, 112–43.

Thurot, C. 'Observations critiques sur les *Meteorologica* d'Aristote (suite et fin)', *Revue archéologique,* nouvelle série, 21 (1870), 396–407.

Zwier, K., 'Methodology in Aristotle's Theory of Spontaneous Generation' ['Methodology'], *Journal of the History of Biology* (2018), 51, 355–86.

CICERO'S *TUSCULAN DISPUTATIONS*: A SCEPTICAL READING

J. P. F. WYNNE

1. Introduction

DEATH comes to us all, and harm, pain, or loss almost to all. In large part, when and how they come is beyond our control: it seems that we are weak. When they come, they can destroy our happiness: it seems that we are fragile.[1] When Cicero pondered the blows fortune had dealt him, he would start, 'to dread the weakness and the fragility of the human race' (humani generis imbecillitatem fragilitatemque extimescere, *Tusc.* 5. 3). But he found that philosophy could help him. 'Whose power should we use before yours, [Philosophy,] who have both bestowed on us tranquillity of life, and removed the fear of death?' (cuius ... potius opibus utamur quam tuis, quae et vitae tranquillitatem largita nobis es et terrorem mortis sustulisti?, *Tusc.* 5. 6). I find that the *Tusculan Disputations* are an earnest and coherent, if difficult, attempt to offer the same, philosophical help to others.[2]

---

[1] I take the term *fragilitas* directly from Cicero. But, of course, Cicero's subject in the *Tusculans* has much in common with Martha Nussbaum's in *The Fragility of Goodness* (Cambridge, 2001) and *The Therapy of Desire* (Princeton, 1994). She naturally makes use of *Tusculans* Books 3 and 4 in her account of Stoic therapy, and in chapter 6 of *Therapy* treats Sextus Empiricus' Pyrrhonist approach to life's troubles. But, in *Fragility* or in *Therapy*, Nussbaum does not address my specific subjects here, neither Academic scepticism nor Cicero's project in the *Tusculans* as a whole.

I take the Latin text from M. Pohlenz, M. *Tullius Cicero: Tusculanae Disputationes* [*Tusculans*] (Stuttgart, 1982). Translations are my own, unless otherwise noted (and often modified).

[2] At least to this extent I am in agreement with C. Lévy, *Cicero Academicus: Recherches sur les* Académiques *et sur la philosophie cicéronienne* [*Academicus*] (Rome, 1992); W. Görler, 'Zum Literarischer Charakter und zur Struktur der *Tusculanae disputationes*' ['Charakter'], in W. Görler and C. Catrein (eds.), *Kleine Schriften zur hellenistisch-römischen Philosophie* (Leiden, 2004), 212–39; S. White, 'Cicero and the Therapists' ['Therapists'], in J. Powell (ed.), *Cicero the Philosopher: Twelve Papers* [*Cicero*] (Oxford, 1995), 219–46; M. Schofield, 'Philo and Cicero's *Tusculans*' ['Philo'], in G. Clark and T. Rajak (eds.), *Philosophy and Power in the Graeco-Roman World: Essays in Honour of Miriam Griffin* (Oxford, 2002), 91–107;

J. P. F. Wynne, *Cicero's* Tuscan Disputations: *A Sceptical Reading*. In: Oxford Studies in Ancient Philosophy Volume LVIII. Edited by: Victor Caston, Oxford University Press (2020).
© J. P. F. Wynne.
DOI: 10.1093/oso/9780198858997.003.0006

But to some, the *Tusculans* have a monstrous aspect: they seem both to be a vital organ of Cicero's philosophical corpus, and also not to fit into it. For the *Tusculans* differ in many ways from the other members of the body of philosophical dialogues Cicero wrote between 46 and 44 BCE. Yet we know Cicero thought the *Tusculans* a part of this body. One response is to decide that, although the *Tusculans* make much use of philosophical material, Cicero's final aim in writing them was not philosophical.[3] I shall offer a version

and R. Woolf, *Cicero: The Philosophy of a Roman Sceptic [Cicero]* (London, 2015). But White, while sensitive to the dialogue's sceptical structure along the lines I suggest ('Therapists', 225), is concerned with the Stoic aspects of Cicero's therapeutic project of *Tusculans* 3 and 4. Lévy gives due emphasis to the New Academic, and sceptical, nature of the *Tusculans* (*Academicus*, ch. 3). He strongly defends their shared purpose with the rest of Cicero's philosophical writing. But Lévy's conception of Cicero's New Academic scepticism is different than mine, in particular in his emphasis on the continuity between the New Academy and Platonic ideas. He finds that Cicero in the *Tusculans* recommends, doubtfully, a view of the happy life sympathetic to Platonism, 'an important milestone on the road that leads to Plotinus' ('un jalon important dans la voie qui conduit à Plotin', 494). I agree with A. Douglas, 'Form and Content in the *Tusculan Disputations*' ['Form'], in J. Powell (ed.), *Cicero*, 197–218, when he thinks Cicero is sincere that the *Tusculans* are a *philosophical* comfort, but see below n. 3. I agree with R. Gorman's assessment of the 'moral seriousness or earnestness apparent in the *Tusculans*' (*The Socratic Method in the Dialogues of Cicero [Socratic]* (Stuttgart, 2005), 69) with their 'life-saving propositions' (76). However, although I would not describe suspension of judgement as a negative result, I take exactly the contrary position to Gorman's view that, '[I]n [the *Tusculans*], in spite of Cicero's claim to be arguing in a purely negative fashion against propositions put to him, he establishes no ironic distance between himself and the views he expresses. The object of Cicero's arguments is here not the negative result of ἐποχή but the production of an effective conviction in the mind of his companion, and in his own' (70).

[3] One suggestion is that the *Tusculans* are a response to the *political* circumstances of 45 BCE. I. Gildenhard, *Paideia Romana: Cicero's Tusculan Disputations [Paideia]* (Cambridge, 2007), 276: 'Read as a philosophical treatise, the *Tusculans* will remain a colourless work that bears out authorial incompetence. Read as an effort to reckon intelligently with the realities of tyranny, the dialogue will sparkle and testify to the genius of Cicero's political and literary imagination.' Another is that the *Tusculans* are above all a search for *comfort* wherever it may be found. For example, Douglas, 'Form', does not doubt that *Cicero* saw the purpose of the *Tusculans* as philosophical, but finds them to be 'rhetorized' philosophy' (200) in which Cicero 'turns inwards, to personal problems' (208). Thus 'if the answer could be found in philosophy in general . . . it would be natural to play down so far as possible the differences between the schools . . . or at least not to allow any one school the whole stage, but to seek comfort wherever it might be found' (208). But had this been Cicero's plan, I would not agree with Douglas that Cicero could have counted it as philosophy. He was acutely aware that one could not be both a Stoic and an Epicurean. I would instead have had to adopt the view that Douglas attributes to 'professional philosophers' that, in the *Tusculans*, 'there seems to be that lack of the

of the other answer: even those features of the *Tusculans* that seem at odds with Cicero's philosophical ambitions are, in fact, designed to serve them.[4] In particular, I hope to solve the puzzle that, at first sight, the *Tusculans* seem much *less sceptical* than Cicero's other dialogues of the period would lead us to expect.

More specifically, the two halves of the puzzle I hope to solve are as follows. One half is that Cicero wrote the *Tusculans* as part of a sequence of dialogues he wrote from 46 to 44 BCE, one after another and, at least in part, so as to promote some form of New Academic scepticism. This latter purpose seems clear if we imagine some-body who reads the sequence of works as Cicero describes it in a list of his philosophical writings (see *Div.* 2. 1–3) and in the order in which Cicero wrote them. First, by the *Hortensius*, readers are turned to philosophy, but then, the *Academica*, turns them specif-ically to some form of New Academic scepticism. Next, in *De fini-bus*, they find a treatment of the goals of human life, but according to a sceptical method, where the argument for each position is bal-anced with an argument against. Then they read the *Tusculans*, which set our puzzle. Next come *De natura deorum* and *De divina-tione*. Each of the latter pair is explicitly New Academic in design (*ND* 1. 11–14, 17–18; 3. 95; *Div.* 1. 7; 2. 150). Finally, they read *De fato*, which has the same form as each book of the *Tusculans*. In general, then, the sequence might well seem designed to lead the reader to a philosophically sceptical point of view on many sub-jects. If we look back in the list to the description of *Tusculans*, we find that Cicero gives more space to them than to any other work, and says that they 'laid open matters most necessary for living a happy life' (res ad beate vivendum maxime necessarias aperuerunt, *Div.* 2. 2).[5] Thus Cicero regarded the *Tusculans* not merely as *a*

---

philosophical substance and solidity which can...be found in *Academica* and *De fato*' (213).

[4] I do not deny that the *Tusculans* might *also* have had other goals, nor is anything I say here inconsistent with that thesis. For example, it is at least consistent with what I say that Cicero may have had immediate and practical political goals for writing the *Tusculans* when he did.

[5] When Cicero wrote that the *Tusculans* aperuerunt, 'laid open' matters neces-sary for a happy life, did he mean that they made these matters *apparent* or *proved* them in some way? If so, that would contradict my interpretation in this paper, since such proof would invite or compel assent to the points so proven. But *aperio*, 'open', can mean simply to make accessible, as when one opens a book (Cicero, *Ad Att.* 5. 11. 7 = 104. 7 Shackleton Bailey) or opens one's mind to an audience

part of this seemingly sceptical sequence of writings, but even as a *vital* part.

The other half of the puzzle is that the *Tusculans* can seem not to be the work of a sceptic. In his list, Cicero says, 'the fifth [book of the *Tusculans*] covers the subject which sheds more light than any other on the whole of philosophy. It *teaches* that virtue is sufficient on its own for a happy life.'⁶ More generally, in the *Tusculans*:

a. Cicero, as a character in the drama, gives long, unanswered speeches against five controversial propositions, and

b. Cicero the author chooses these propositions so that the five speeches together seem to commend a coherent, Stoic account of happiness.

Thus, where we would expect scepticism, the *Tusculans* appear instead to teach the reader a Stoic view of the happy life.

I shall argue that this problem is merely apparent. For I think the *Tusculans* continue uninterrupted the sceptical programme of the rest of the sequence of works. My answer to the general problems just posed will be that:

a*. Cicero the speaker argues against the sincere views of his interlocutor, in order to argue him out of those views, and not into any others, and

b*. Cicero the author hopes to argue us not into a Stoic (or any other) idea of happiness, but rather *out* of commonly held, and profoundly troubling, views.

(Cicero, *Orator* 116). In the *Tusculans* themselves, the metaphor is that Cicero will 'open the sources of philosophy' (philosophiae fontis aperiemus) because his superior writing will shed new light on them for Roman readers (*Tusc.* 1. 6). Further, Cicero does not claim that the *Tusculans* make, or can make, readers happy. His own state of mind as he writes them suggests that they are unlikely to make readers happy (*Tusc.* 5. 1–5). Thus, there is no implicit claim that they give the reader what is necessary for happiness. Therefore, when he wrote *aperuerunt*, Cicero meant that the *Tusculans* made accessible and attractive philosophical debate about matters that would be necessary for happiness. This is consistent with my interpretation.

⁶ quintus eum locum complexus est, qui totam philosophiam maxime inlustrat; *docet* enim ad beate vivendum virtutem se ipsa esse contentam (*Div.* 2. 2). The Latin text is from R. Giomini (ed.), M. *Tulli Ciceronis, De divinatione, De fato, Timaeus* (Stuttgart, 1975). My emphasis is added to the translation from Schofield, 'Philo', 100. I use Schofield's translation here because it preserves an ambiguity in the Latin on which a potentially controversial point I make below depends (see Section 3 below).

I shall argue for (*a**) and (*b**) below in Sections 3 and 4, respectively.[7] My solution to the puzzle about scepticism opposes those who do not think that the aim of the *Tusculans* is philosophical. But it also puts me at odds with interpreters who, like me, find that the *Tusculans* have philosophical goals, but who think that the *Tusculans* aim to *teach* some philosophical opinions. Some scholars, for example, suppose that Cicero's scepticism is not as I describe it below in Section 2, but is rather of a sort that permits him to teach opinions.[8] By contrast, I attribute to Cicero the sceptical stance that wisdom requires one to withhold assent from any proposition, and that it would be an abuse of authority to teach somebody to assent to some conclusion. Since in the *Tusculans* Cicero might seem to teach a Stoic view of the happy life, it might appear that the *Tusculans* are a hard case for my interpretation of Cicero's scepticism. One aim of this paper is to show that, on the contrary, the *Tusculans* are a source of strength for my view, because they exhibit the practice and the depth of the more radical strain of Academic scepticism.

---

[7] Although my conception of Cicero's scepticism in the dialogue is more austere, in many ways I am in agreement with chapter 6 of Woolf, *Cicero*, where he argues that in the *Tusculans*, 'above all [Cicero's] attitude is sceptical in both the philosophical and more colloquial senses of the term' (201). The predecessor to whom I am closest is Görler, 'Charakter'. I agree with Görler that the *Tusculans* are serious philosophical writing, and that their *propositum* structure is meant to do the sceptical job that speeches for and against do in Cicero's other sceptical dialogues. I also agree that the interlocutor is no mere 'fall-guy' but rather a sincere speaker whose contributions Cicero wants us to take seriously. But I do not accept Görler's claim (234–5) that Cicero's goal is to gain, and to suggest to us, more modest versions of the 'higher' (höheren) philosophical theses for which Marcus argues. The root of this disagreement lies, I think, in my further disagreement with Görler's view, published elsewhere, that Cicero is a 'mitigated' rather than a Clitomachean sceptic (compare W. Görler, 'Cicero's Philosophical Stance in the *Lucullus*' ['Stance'], in B. Inwood and J. Mansfeld (eds.), *Assent and Argument* (Leiden, 1997), 36–57 with my Section 2 below). Meanwhile, Görler's intriguing suggestion that the interlocutor represents Cicero's *own* doubts about these theses, so that the *Tusculans* are a soliloquy (Selbstgespräch, 'Charakter', 235), perhaps could be consistent with my view that the interlocutor is an everyman, if an everyman could represent Cicero in these matters.

[8] For example, Görler, 'Charakter' and Schofield, 'Philo' read the *Tusculans* in light of the 'mitigated' scepticism of Philo of Larissa, which permits the formation of provisional opinions about the truth. M. Graver says that Cicero's scepticism 'requires of him only that he study the views of others and accede to those which appear most plausible.' If 'accede' does not imply 'assent', I could agree. But she also says that Cicero 'recommends' the Stoic view of the emotions to his readers, which I dispute (*Cicero on the Emotions* [*Emotions*] (Chicago, 2002), xii).

I now touch on some other puzzles about the *Tusculans* germane to this paper.

Among Cicero's dialogues, one distinction of the *Tusculans* is that their setting is minimal. The conversations are stripped of almost all narrative. Cicero's friends are anonymous. (To deal with the last point, I adopt the following nomenclature. The character labelled 'M.' in our modern editions, Cicero's own character, I shall call 'Marcus'. Cicero the author, and his authorial voice, I shall call 'Cicero'. The interlocutor labelled 'A.' I too shall call 'A.'.[9])

A second distinction is that the *Tusculans* have seemed more 'rhetorical' than their peers.[10] All the dialogues are rhetorical achievements, of course. In the *Tusculans* in particular, Cicero aims to show by example that his superior rhetorical skills can illuminate and make more appealing properly philosophical argument. Not only are the two philosophical and rhetorical aspects of argument not exclusive, Cicero's view is that they perfect one another (*Tusc.* 1. 7).[11] But in the *Tusculans* it sometimes seems that Cicero aims at rhetorical persuasion *rather than* philosophical argument. Cicero even seems to remark on the point, calling the sort of conversation we witness 'the rhetorical exercise of my old age' (senilis declamatio, 1. 7; 2. 26). Yet the other dialogues of 46–44 BCE plainly, and confessedly, aim at philosophical argument.

---

[9] Who is A.? In each book, he is one of the group of Cicero's *familiares* that attends the conversations of the *Tusculans* (1. 7). More than that we can seek to conclude only from his speeches. It is hard to say whether A. is the same person on all five days. On the one hand, the A. of Books 1 and 2 is the same person, and the A. of Books 3 and 4 is the same person. We see continuity in A.'s attitudes from one book to another, which Marcus exploits in order to base later arguments on those of earlier days (2. 10, 67; 4. 8; 5. 15). At no point is A. wholly uninitiated in philosophy: even in Books 1 and 2, Marcus assumes his interlocutor to be familiar with technical terms like the Greek ἀξίωμα ('proposition', 1. 14), presumably because this A. has attended many philosophy classes in Athens (2. 26) and has read at least Plato's *Phaedo* a number of times (1. 24). The A. of Book 5 has read with some degree of understanding at least Book 4 of Cicero's *De finibus*, and is so familiar with Stoic arguments as to be jaded about them (5. 13–14). But A. also develops over the five days. Despite his education and interest, the A. of Books 1 and 2 resembles a hapless beginner at philosophical conversation (1. 11–14; 2. 14). But the A. of Book 5 is much surer on his feet. He dismisses Marcus' first responses with ease, and justifiable contempt (5. 12), and has a definite position on virtue and happiness that drives his questions (see my Section 3 below). Perhaps it is hard to imagine that one character would have matured so much in five days.

[10] Douglas, 'Form'; 197–205, Görler, '*Charakter*', 212–17, 239; Schofield, 'Philo', 107.

[11] My thanks to an anonymous reviewer for *Oxford Studies* for stressing this point.

Third, Marcus in the *Tusculans* seems to practise something like 'eclecticism': he takes what is best from each school (it seems) in order to make his case. But in the other dialogues of this sequence, Cicero assigns the defence of only one school's position to each speaker, so that no single character seems 'eclectic'.

I think that my reading of the *Tusculans* incidentally helps to explain the three distinctive qualities I have just mentioned, as I shall note below (Section 3).

Before I argue for my sceptical interpretation of the *Tusculans*, I must specify precisely what kind of scepticism I attribute to Cicero. This I shall do in the next section.

2. Hasdrubalic scepticism

We learn from Cicero's *Academica* that Academic scepticism had a complex history. Different Academics took up significantly different sceptical stances. Thus, in order to argue that the *Tusculans* is a work of Academic scepticism, I must say what sort of Academic scepticism Cicero has in mind. Now, everything I say here is subject to scholarly controversy.[12] But my focus is to interpret the *Tusculans*. So I have space only to say what I think about Cicero's scepticism, citing the strongest pieces of evidence.

Cicero took as his most immediate predecessor in the sceptical tradition another non-Greek philosopher. It is perhaps a sign of his intellectual independence from his Roman peers that he chose, of all people, a Carthaginian. This was Hasdrubal, who left his native Carthage for Athens, where he became a follower of Carneades, and took the Greek name Clitomachus, by which he has been best known both to Cicero and to ourselves. It is my view that Cicero writes his late sequence of dialogues as a *Clitomachean*, or shall we say as a *Hasdrubalic*, sceptic. Although he takes much else from his own teacher, Philo of Larissa, he favours Clitomachus' interpretation of Academic scepticism, not Philo's.

---

[12] Some sharply different recent views of Cicero's scepticism are Lévy, *Academicus*; W. Görler, 'Stance'; and H. Thorsrud, *Ancient Scepticism* (Berkeley, 2009), 84–101 and id., 'Arcesilaus and Carneades', in R. Bett (ed.), *The Cambridge Companion to Ancient Scepticism* (Cambridge, 2010), 58–80 at 76–80.

So then, what was Clitomachus' scepticism like? I aim to capture Cicero's Clitomachus here, and not necessarily the historical man. Thus I do not try to account for the evidence outside Cicero. I shall engage in paraphrase and reorder some of the data from the *Academica*.

Clitomachus' dispute with Philo was, or had its start in, a dispute about how to interpret their Academic master Carneades. According to Cicero, Clitomachus interpreted Carneades to have intended that:

1. any of our impressions might be false (*Acad.* 2. 40, 83), which implies that there are no cataleptic impressions.

Next Clitomachus takes to heart a second premise, shared with the Stoics, that:

2. we should never take to be true, or 'assent to', an impression that might be false (*Acad.* 2. 66–8).

Clitomachus drew the obvious conclusion, that we should never assent, that we should never take our views to be true. Of course he faced a particularly acute version of the 'inactivity objection': how *can* we act if we don't believe that anything is true? He answered with the following:

3. Instead of taking any impression to be true, we can follow impressions that seem to us for now to be plausible (*probabilis*) or like the truth (*veri similis, Acad.* 2. 103–5).

Accordingly, in the *Tusculans*, Cicero will often say that an Academic investigator, while leaving others' judgement free, looks among the arguments for what seems most plausible or like the truth, at least for the present (*Tusc.* 1. 17; 2. 5; 4. 7; 5. 33).

Now in the *Academica*, Cicero claims to follow Clitomachus (*Acad.* 2. 78), and I think he gives us some of his reasons for this attraction. He says that he loves the truth. Like any Academic, his ideal is discovery, and in the *Tusculans* he imagines contemplative happiness, in either this life (1. 44–5) or the next (5. 68–72). But such happiness for now is no more than a hope (1. 82; 5. 2). For Cicero loves the truth in such a way that he has the following intuition about the ethics of belief: 'Just as I judge that this is most beautiful—to see the truth—just so it is most vicious to accept falsehoods in place of truths' (sed ut hoc pulcherrimum esse iudico, vera videre, sic pro veris probare falsa turpissimum est, *Acad.* 2. 66 Plasberg). Cicero finds plausible the arguments for (1), so that to take *any* impression to be true would seem to him to risk accepting a falsehood in place of truth. On the principle from *Acad.* 2. 66 just given, that would be to risk the greatest vice in return for a chance at beauty. Thus Cicero also favours Clitomachus' (2) and (3) (*Acad.* 2. 68, 78, 104–5). Cicero, then, passionately desires the truth, but in such a way that, lacking the truth, he cannot risk falling for its counterfeits. It seems to him that one should never take any impression to be true.[13]

Cicero sometimes explains his attraction to Academic scepticism with respect to the faults that other schools display but it avoids. Two important examples are:

temeritas: 'rashness', taking to be true what might be false (e.g. *Acad.* 2. 108, 128; *ND* 1. 1; *Div.* 1. 4), and

arrogantia: the willingness to induce a listener rashly to take one's own opinions to be true (e.g. *Div.* 2. 1; cf. *Acad.* 2. 7–10).

With these points in mind, it seems to me not only that Cicero represented himself as a follower of Clitomachus in the *Academica*, but also that he wrote all his dialogues in the sequence from the *Hortensius* to *De fato* from this point of view (*Div.* 2. 1–3, see Section 1). For in the dialogues that present arguments on both sides of issue, i.e. in all the dialogues of our sequence except the *Tusculans* and *De fato*, Cicero the author hides his own view by balancing the speeches he presents. He thus encourages the reader to avoid *temeritas*, but avoids *arrogantia* on his own part. But Cicero allows us to glimpse how things seem to 'Marcus', his avatar in the drama. This dramatizes the Clitomachean who, rather than assent, can follow what seems most like the truth to himself on each occasion (e.g. *ND* 3. 95; *Div.* 2. 150). The result, then, is that the dialogues help us to see, after thorough and responsible investigation, what view (if any) seems most plausible or most like the truth to us. But also, and more importantly to Cicero, they help us not to take any view to be true.

---

[13] For more detail on my interpretation of Cicero's scepticism, see J. Wynne, 'Cicero', in D. Machuca and B. Reed (eds.), *Skepticism: From Antiquity to the Present* (New York, 2018), 93–101.

Now that we can view them from a Clitomachean perspective, I turn to the *Tusculans* themselves. I have reminded the reader that Clitomachus was born Hasdrubal not only for the curiosity of the fact. For another Punic perspective on Clitomachus is that he lived from about 187 to about 110 BCE. This means that he was about forty years old at the time of the Romans' destruction of Carthage in 146 BCE.[14] Now, the worst of what every schoolchild used to know about this sack has turned out to be a modern invention. No fields were ploughed with salt. But, on any account, it was a desperate thing. Very many Carthaginians were killed or were taken into slavery. The material fabric of the city was much damaged.[15] Whatever the Romans intended, we know that they largely succeeded in deleting Punic Carthage and its culture from our historical record. Imagine the impact of this news on Clitomachus, safely removed to Athens for a number of years. It is poignant for a moment to think of Clitomachus' scepticism as 'Hasdrubalic' scepticism. In such circumstances, could this philosophy yield any wisdom, for Clitomachus himself or for others?

You might think that it could not. It offered him no firm opinion on which to found a consolation of the sort a Stoic could find. Now, perhaps the negative character of Clitomachus' scepticism, and his resulting *lack* of opinions, could produce detachment and tranquillity in the Pyrrhonist manner. But that is far from clear, especially when we reflect that Clitomachus could find himself following what seemed plausible to him: it probably seemed plausible to him that something overwhelmingly bad had happened. Meanwhile, Clitomachus' avoidance of the exercise of authority, so that others could arrive at their own views, might seem to keep him from consoling anybody else. By his own principles, he could not set out

---

[14] Besides Cicero, the ancient sources for Clitomachus' life are Diogenes Laertius 4. 67 and the Herculaneum papyrus *Index Academicorum*. His story is best told by W. Görler, 'Die Akademie zwischen Karneades und Philon', in H. Flashar (ed.), *Grundriß der Geschichte der Philosophie*, Bd 4. 2 (Basel, 1994), 898–914.

[15] A concise debate on the myths around the sack, which incidentally surveys the ancient sources and makes clear the scale of the violence that *did* happen, is R. Ridley, 'To Be Taken With a Pinch of Salt: The Destruction of Carthage', *Classical Philology*, 81 (1986), 140–6; S. Stevens, 'A Legend of the Destruction of Carthage', *Classical Philology*, 83 (1988), 39–41; P. Visonà, 'Passing the Salt: On the Destruction of Carthage Again', *Classical Philology*, 83 (1988), 41–2; and B. Warmington, 'The Destruction of Carthage: A *retractatio*', *Classical Philology*, 83 (1988), 308–10.

philosophically to convince the survivors that all was well, or that grief was the wrong response. Clitomachean scepticism seems, at first, to be helpless in the face of what befell Clitomachus.

But Cicero tells us otherwise. In book 3 of the *Tusculans*, in a reflection on the fading of grief over time, Marcus says:

[T1] legimus librum Clitomachi, quem ille eversa Karthagine misit consolandi causa ad captivos, cives suos; in eo est disputatio scripta Carneadis, quam se ait in commentarium rettulisse. cum ita positum esset, videri fore in aegritudine sapientem patria capta, quae Carneades contra dixerit, scripta sunt. tanta igitur calamitatis praesentis adhibetur a philosopho medicina, quanta inveteratae ne desideratur quidem, nec, si aliquot annis post idem ille liber captivis missus esset, volneribus mederetur, sed cicatricibus. (*Tusc.* 3. 54)

There is a book by Clitomachus, which he addressed to his fellow Carthaginians after that city was destroyed, to console them in their captivity. I have read it. It contains a disputation by Carneades which Clitomachus says he took down in his notes. The opinion stated as the thesis is that the wise person would be grieved if his homeland were to be conquered in war. Then are recorded Carneades's arguments in the negative. Here we see the philosopher applying strong medicine in a case where the disaster is still present. Had it been long in the past, however, no such strong medicine would have been needed or even wanted. If he had addressed that same book to the captives some years afterward, he would have been tending to scars, not wounds. (trans. Graver, modified)

What should we make of Clitomachus' book? First, its goal is clear: to console, to give strong medicine in the aftermath of a disaster. Second, Clitomachus pursued this goal without ever arguing for any point in his own voice. He puts the arguments in the mouth of Carneades. Not just that, but he also reports a *particular occasion* on which Carneades spoke *against a particular thesis*. This latter point is important, because it means that Clitomachus gave his reader no reason to conclude that Carneades *preferred* to give the arguments in the book, much less that they were Carneades' own, unprompted views. For on another particular occasion, when the contrary thesis was given, Carneades would have argued the other side. Thus these arguments, although from Carneades' mouth, lack Carneades' endorsement.

Now, you may say, this was a clever literary dodge, but surely it did not obscure what was really going on: Clitomachus wanted to give arguments not only *against* the proposition that the wise person would grieve if his homeland were conquered in war, but even *for* the proposition that the wise person would *not* so grieve. The latter must be the form Carneades' arguments took, and it would seem the stronger medicine for Clitomachus to dispense to his wounded friends. After all, if Clitomachus had really wished to leave the judgement of his readers intact, he could have followed this book with another full of arguments that grief was, indeed, the wise response. So, despite the literary fig leaf, you might conclude that, *in extremis*, Clitomachus threw his authority behind a saving thesis, after all.

But that would be too hasty. For consider the state of mind of Clitomachus' addressees. In captivity or exile[16] after the sack of their city, there must have crowded in upon them strong impressions that even a wise person would grieve at evils of this number and magnitude. Thus Clitomachus did not *need* to supply arguments *for* the thesis that the wise would grieve—his readers were already burdened with all too many reasons for, and causes of, assent to it. Where philosophy could help was with the many and surprisingly compelling arguments one could give to the contrary. When he had brought the two influences into some sort of balance, Clitomachus' countrymen might be freed from the rash *opinion* that grief was the right response. This would salve their grief, because they would no longer be committed, headlong and inflexibly, to the truth of the idea that their grief was wise. But the gift of this salve is wholly compatible with Clitomachus' principles. For Carneades' response to a particular thesis, on a particular occasion, not only lacks his or Clitomachus' endorsement of any argument, it also reflects the structure of Clitomachus' own situation and objectives. Clitomachus merely answered a chorus of Carthaginians asserting, sincerely and with fresh reason, that their grief was wise.

I think that Clitomachus' book for the Carthaginians, as reported in the *Tusculans*, is the right model to understand what Cicero did, five times over, when he wrote the *Tusculans* themselves.[17] In the

---

[16] Depending on how many survivors there were, on their circumstances, and on the likelihood that they would receive and wish to read a philosophical text in Greek, we might wonder who Clitomachus expected his readers to be. Perhaps the book was addressed to the captured Carthaginians, but was primarily for the benefit of Greek readers.

[17] I do not mean that Cicero intended this anecdote, unmarked in Marcus' treatment of the fading of grief, as a sort of hidden key to the *Tusculans*. I think it is

guise of Marcus, Cicero takes the role of Carneades, the speaker against theses proposed by his audience. As with Carneades in Clitomachus' book, this aspect of the drama shows us that Marcus does not endorse the outcome of his arguments. For if A. had proposed a different thesis, Marcus would have argued against that instead. Meanwhile, Cicero as author also takes the role of Clitomachus, the author who reports Carneades' conversations. A sort of consolation is offered to Marcus' audience, and to Cicero's readers, but the offering is Clitomachean scepticism.

I must argue for this point at two levels. First, I shall argue that what *Marcus* does, within the drama, is sceptical in the way I suggest (Section 3). Second, I shall argue that what *Cicero* does, in orchestrating the drama, is sceptical in the same way (Section 4).

Last in this section, I should answer the question, what if I am wrong that Cicero is a Clitomachean sceptic? How much of my argument in this paper could stand? Much of it could, provided that Cicero is an Academic sceptic of *some* sort. For example, suppose that he is a 'mitigated' sceptic, for whom the upshot of Academic scrutiny of some question is provisional assent to the truth of an answer which, so far as the one who assents can tell, might be false. Then, in my view, Cicero in the *Tusculans* would hope not to recommend this or that opinion, but rather to take our heartfelt opinions, and to render them merely provisional.

3. Marcus in the *Tusculans*: a sceptical reading

I begin this section with a passage from the start of the second book of *De finibus*, in which Marcus describes some styles of philosophical conversation.

[T2] is enim percontando atque interrogando elicere solebat eorum opiniones quibuscum disserebat, ut ad ea quae ii respondissent si quid videretur diceret. qui mos cum a posterioribus non esset retentus, Arcesilas eum revocavit instituitque ut ii qui se audire vellent non de se quaererent, sed ipsi dicerent quid sentirent; quod cum dixissent, ille contra. sed eum qui audiebant, quoad poterant, defendebant

simply a bit of luck for us that he happened to think his model for the *Tusculans* was also a good example for Marcus to describe in that connection. (My thanks to Catherine Steel for calling my attention to the importance of these points.)

sententiam suam. apud ceteros autem philosophos qui quaesivit
aliquid tacet; quod quidem iam fit etiam in Academia. ubi enim is
qui audire vult ita dixit: 'Voluptas mihi videtur esse summum
bonum', perpetua oratione contra disputatur, ut facile intellegi possit eos qui aliquid sibi videri dicant non ipsos in ea sententia esse sed
audire velle contraria. (*Fin.* 2. 2)

Socrates' own technique was to investigate his interlocutors by
questioning them. Once he had elicited their opinions in this way, he
would then respond to them, if something occurred to him. This
method was abandoned by his successors, but Arcesilaus revived it
and laid it down that those who wanted to hear him speak should not
ask him questions but rather state their own view. When they had
spoken, he would speak against them. Now Arcesilaus' audiences
would defend their position as best they could. But the practice with
other philosophers is that a member of the audience states a view,
and then is silent. This is in fact what happens even in the Academy.
One who wants to listen says, 'It seems to me that pleasure is the
highest good.' The philosopher then puts the contrary position in a
continuous discourse. Evidently, then, the one who declared that
such-and-such seemed so to him, did not really hold that view, but
wanted to hear the opposing arguments.[18]

Now, my purpose here is not to reconstruct the history of some
Socratic and Academic teaching methods, if in fact that is possible
from this passage. Two points are what matter to me: first, Marcus
in *De finibus* says that there was a sceptical Academic practice of
speaking against a thesis proposed by a volunteer from the audience. In Arcesilaus' case, the teacher's motivation might well be
the avoidance of the appearance that he endorsed the arguments he
would give. Rather than answer a yes-or-no question, in which case
he would have his choice of answers, Arcesilaus argued against a
particular and unpredictable thesis. Second, Marcus implies that it
is *decadent* to submit a proposition you do not believe *in order to*
hear your teacher dismiss it. Thus he implies that it is better to put
up *what you really think* for refutation. Marcus says this, I presume, because it seems to him that a skilled Academic will be able
to give you surprisingly good arguments against any belief you
hold—arguments that might be so good that they will oblige you to
relinquish the belief. That being so, however uncomfortable it may

[18] The Latin text is from L. D. Reynolds' edition (ed.), *M. Tulli Ciceronis De finibus bonorum et malorum, Libri quinque* (Oxford, 1998). Translation from J. Annas and R. Woolf, *Cicero: On Moral Ends* (Cambridge, 2001), modified.

be to hear your beliefs called into question by an able critic, you ought to try it.

Now let us look at some remains of the preface to *De fato*. Here Cicero explicitly enshrines a form of dialogue that seems to mirror the teaching practice I have just mentioned. He also explicitly contrasts this with the speech-on-either-side dialogues:

[T3] quod autem in aliis libris feci, qui sunt de natura deorum, itemque in iis, quos de divinatione edidi, ut in utramque partem perpetua explicaretur oratio, quo facilius id a quoque probaretur, quod cuique maxime probabile videretur, id in hac disputatione de fato casus quidam ne facerem impedivit. (*De fato* 1 Giomini)

A chance occurrence prevented me from doing, in this discussion about fate, what I have done in my other books which are concerned with the nature of the gods, and likewise in those which I published on divination; that is, that a continuous speech should be set out on each side, so that each person should more easily recommend what seemed most plausible to each.

HIRT. sed quoniam rhetorica mihi vestra sunt nota teque in iis et audivimus saepe et audiemus, atque hanc Academicorum contra propositum disputandi consuetudinem indicant te suscepisse Tusculanae disputationes, ponere aliquid, ad quod audiam, si tibi non est molestum, volo. (*De fato* 4)

HIRT. But since I am familiar with your [= Marcus'] rhetoric and have often both heard and will hear you practising it, and since your *Tusculan Disputations* show that you have adopted the Academic practice of arguing against something proposed (*propositum*), I would like, if you don't mind, to propose something on which I can hear you.[19]

Due to a lacuna, we do not know whether Hirtius followed the invidious practice of putting up a thesis he wanted to hear knocked down. But we learn from what survives that the form of *De fato*, and thus the identical form of the *Tusculans*, is inspired by a method of the general sort Cicero described in [T2].

With this background in hand, I turn to *Tusculans* 1. Let us look at the end of Cicero's preface, his introduction to the first conversation, in relation to the *propositum* ('proposition') method.

[T4] ponere iubebam, de quo quis audire vellet; ad id aut sedens aut ambulans disputabam. itaque dierum quinque scholas, ut Graeci

---

[19] Translations from R. Sharples, *Cicero: On Fate (De Fato) and Boethius: The Consolation of Philosophy (Philosophiae Consolationis) IV. 5–7, V* (Warminster, 1991), modified.

appellant, in totidem libros contuli. fiebat autem ita ut, cum is qui audire vellet dixisset, quid sibi videretur, tum ego contra dicerem. haec est enim, ut scis, vetus et Socratica ratio contra alterius opinionem disserendi. nam ita facillime, quid veri simillimum esset, inveniri posse Socrates arbitrabatur. (*Tusc.* 1. 7–8)

I asked anyone to put forward a proposition he wanted to hear about, and then debated it, either sitting or walking around. I have recorded these five days of 'lectures', as the Greeks call them, in the same number of books. What happened was that when the man who wanted to listen had said what seemed so to him, I would speak against it. As you know, this is the old Socratic method, consisting in arguing against another person's opinion. For Socrates thought that was the easiest way of finding out what was most like the truth.[20]

Cicero gives a motivation that he traces to Socrates, but which is nevertheless thoroughly Clitomachean. This is, finding out what seems most like the truth. The method is the *Tusculans'* version of the practice of giving speeches on either side, so that readers may lose their opinions. Their judgement is left intact to see which side might strike them as more like the truth at any time, and they can act on this basis if they wish. I suggest this works in the same way as Clitomachus' consolatory book. For A. is already convinced of the *propositum* he puts forward, so that Marcus' job is to provide the balance for whatever convinced A. of the *propositum*. This allows A., and probably other participants in the conversation, to discover what seems most like the truth to them, freed from the undue influence of whatever has been weighing on their minds up to now. Marcus' endorsement of his arguments is not implied because, again, he does not know what case he will argue until he is prompted with the *propositum*. On another day, he might have argued the opposite.

Thus understood, Marcus' job is as follows. When A. asserts a *propositum*, that *p* seems so to him, Marcus does not try to teach

[20] Translation from A. Douglas, *Cicero:* Tusculan Disputations *I* (Warminster, 1985), modified. Gildenhard says (*Paideia*, 20–1; note also his references on the point) that there is a *contradiction* between the first formulation in this passage (ponere iubebam, de quo quis audire vellet) and the second (cum is qui audire vellet dixisset, quid sibi videretur, tum ego contra dicerem). His basis for saying this is that the first formulation describes one kind of extempore exercise, while the second describes another. But I do not see the contradiction: 'proposing a topic on which Cicero may speak' could well apply to reporting a belief against which Cicero may speak. Even if we have here strict formulations of two different kinds of declamatory procedures, the latter can be a species of the former.

A. that not-*p* is true, or even that not-*p* is plausible. Rather, he aims
to persuade A. *not* to take *p* to be true. For example, when A. says
that he believes that death is an evil, Marcus does not try to teach
A. that death is not an evil, but rather to persuade him not to take
it to be true that death is an evil.

If Cicero writes the *Tusculans* with some amount of psychological realism, we should not expect to find that Marcus has too
neat a success in this enterprise. For it is psychologically implausible that somebody could just drop beliefs as primal and tangled
into the psyche as A.'s *proposita*, merely because he has heard one
afternoon's worth of philosophical arguments against them. We
might think of Lucretius, Seneca, or Epictetus: although all three
take themselves to offer sound arguments for vital truths, none
supposes that his listeners will really change their mind after just
one hearing—even if they find themslves rationally to be persuaded
by the arguments. Rather, all three envisage a long process of mull-
ing the new ideas, overcoming one's worse instincts, and so on.
Similarly, it is no surprise if, within the dramatic time of the dialogue, A., or even Marcus himself, continues to find conviction on
one side or another of the disputes. Nevertheless, there is textual
evidence for my interpretation in the *interest* both Marcus and
A. take in A.'s reactions to Marcus' arguments, and especially in
the way they phrase these reactions: has A. *ceased* to believe his
proposita? Let us look at some examples.

In Book 1, A.'s *propositum* is that 'death seems to me to be an
evil' (malum mihi videtur esse mors, *Tusc.* 1. 9). In 1. 111, Marcus
finishes his speech by conceding that, in part, he has been concerned to hack out his *own* opinion that death is bad for the dead.
A. replies that Marcus need not worry: he has nevertheless helped
A., too, not to be troubled by death. The ultimate result is: 'But by
your whole discourse certainly the task was completed, that I did
not take death to be among the evils' (omni autem oratione illud
certe perfectum est, ut mortem non ducerem in malis, 1. 112). That
is, A. reassures Marcus that Marcus has induced A. to cease to believe
the *propositum*—not that Marcus has convinced him to believe that
death is not an evil.

In Book 2, A.'s gives his *propositum* as: 'I judge that pain is the
greatest of all evils' (dolorem existimo maximum malorum omnium,
Tusc. 2. 14). He quickly retreats from this to the more respectable
claim that it is *an* evil, albeit not the greatest. At the end of his

ensuing speech, Marcus asks after the result: 'but perhaps you
remain in your view?' (sed tu fortasse in sententia permanes?, 2. 67).
Again, Marcus is interested in whether or not A. has dropped his
opinion, not whether A. has acquired a new one. A. responds:
'Certainly not. I hope that in two days I have been freed from fear
of two things which I feared above all' (minime vero, meque biduo
duarum rerum, quas maxime timebam, spero liberatum metu, 2. 67).
Not only is A., like Marcus, interested specifically in the *removal* of
his opinion, he regards this as a basis for hope that, since he no
longer thinks pain is an evil, he will no longer fear it. Further, A.'s
phrasing—'two things which I feared above all'—shows that his initial statement of the *propositum*, although quickly dropped, was in
fact an opinion that mattered to him. Embarrassing though it was to
admit, A. was indeed somebody who regarded pain as the worst
thing in the world, and who feared it, alongside death, above all.
Marcus has helped A. rationally to drop this opinion, and thus
A. hopes to be freed from the associated fear.

Books 3 and 4 form a unit, in which Marcus argues against the
conviction that it is impossible even for the wise person to be free
from emotion in general, and from distress in particular. At the end
of Book 4, Marcus reflects on the achievements of these two days,
and their connection with the subjects of Books 1 and 2. What his
Stoic arguments of Books 3 and 4 have established, he says, is that
emotions are caused by our opinions, and are thus that they are
under our rational and voluntary control (4. 82). The Stoics' rem-
edy, of course, is to shed our mere opinions by replacing them with
knowledge, which, they promise, will yield no troubling emotions,
but rather joy. But for Marcus, philosophy's promise is not the
acquisition of such knowledge.

[T5] sed et aegritudinis et reliquorum animi morborum una sanatio est,
omnis opinabilis esse et voluntarios ea reque suscipi, quod ita rectum esse videatur. hunc errorem quasi radicem malorum omnium
stirpitus philosophia se extracturam pollicetur. demus igitur nos
huic excolendos patiamurque nos sanari. his enim malis insidenti-
bus non modo beati, sed ne sani quidem esse possumus. aut igitur
negemus quicquam ratione confici, cum contra nihil sine ratione
recte fieri possit, aut, cum philosophia ex rationum conlatione constet, ab ea, si et boni et beati volumus esse, omnia adiumenta et aux-
ilia petamus bene beateque vivendi. (*Tusc.* 4. 83–4)

But there is one method to cure both distress and the other diseases of
the soul: to show that they are a matter of belief and are voluntary,

and that we contract them because we think it right to do so. It is this error which philosophy promises to pull out, since it is, as it were, the root of all evils. Let us therefore hand ourselves over to philosophy and let ourselves be healed. For as long as these ills remain we cannot attain to happiness, nor even to health. Let us therefore either deny that reason can do anything—when in fact nothing can be done rightly without reason—or, since philosophy consists of comparing reasoned arguments, let us seek from it every form of assistance, so that we may live both happily and well, if such is indeed our wish. (trans. Graver, modified)

What philosophy promises is the *removal* of an error and some mere opinions, but not, so far as Marcus says, the addition of knowledge. It is this process of removal which offers the only (but apparently still uncertain) hope of freedom from troubling emotions, and thus of health and happiness. Now, this is the climax of Marcus' speech to A., so it is spoken not as an earnest guide to the *Tusculans*, but rather in Marcus' sceptical role: by this rousing call to grant that emotions are rational and voluntary, he hopes to convince A. to drop the opinion that even a wise person cannot lack emotions. Nevertheless, it seems to me that the passage captures the scope of the sceptical medicine Marcus has on offer. It confirms Cicero's answer to the question with which he began his preface to Book 3: if there is a medicine for the body, why is there no medicine for the soul? Philosophy seems to be that medicine, but, even after the Stoicism of Marcus' speeches in Books 3 and 4, philosophy is not described in a specifically dogmatic way: it *consists of the comparison* of reasoned arguments (ex rationum conlatione constet) and promises to *uproot erroneous opinions*. Not only is this description not specifically dogmatic, it emphasises those aspects of philosophy that the sceptic in particular values.

In Book 5, we hear some of A.'s reactions to Marcus' arguments. A.'s initial position is to deny that virtue is sufficient for happiness (*Tusc.* 5. 12). He is soon ready to grant to Marcus a result of the previous days' discussions of the emotions, that the virtuous person lacks emotion, and that this would imply that virtue is sufficient for happiness. He says that the discussion is 'almost' over (5. 18). But, while this suggests that Marcus may well succeed in releasing A. from his *propositum* (cf. 5. 32), Marcus tells A. that the quick concession is too hasty (5. 18). Later we learn more of A.'s position. He assents to the biconditional that virtue is the only good if and only if virtue is sufficient for happiness (5. 21). Together with his initial position, this would imply that A. holds that virtue is not the only good, and presumably that vice is not the only evil. Accordingly, he will variously challenge M. over whether the virtuous person's happiness can survive torture (5. 73), or how a Peripatetic could consistently claim that there are goods and evils other than virtue or vice, and that virtue is sufficient for happiness (5. 21, 82). That is to say, he wishes to hear Marcus' arguments against the biconditional to which he, A., declared his assent, perhaps because he hopes to withdraw his assent. But this is the last we hear of A.'s state of mind. Book 5 ends neither with A.'s attitudes, nor with a general reminder of scepticism as at the end of Book 4. But I do not think this means that the project of Book 5 is any less sceptical. For, in Section 4 below, I will argue that in Book 5 Cicero shifts our focus to his own reaction to the five days at Tusculum.

There is also textual evidence that, unlike the modern students described in [T2] and perhaps unlike Hirtius in *De fato* after [T3], A. asserts what he really believes. For one example, as we have seen, A. describes death and pain as his two greatest fears after he has been freed of them at the end of Book 2 (*Tusc.* 2. 67). For another, at the start of Book 5, A. gets especially worked up at Marcus' first moves. Marcus says, 'Can you then either fail to call unhappy one who lives badly, or deny that one who (as you admit) lives well, lives happily?' (potes igitur aut, qui male vivat, non eum miserum dicere aut, quem bene fateare, eum negare beate vivere?, 5. 12). A. says, 'Why couldn't I? Even under torture, it is possible to live rightly, honourably, and reputably ... These qualities too are thrown onto the rack ...' (quidni possim? nam etiam in tormentis recte honeste laudabiliter et ob eam rem bene vivi potest ...; haec etiam in eculeum coiciuntur ... 5. 12–13). A. seems laudably aware of the intuitive strengths of his position, and *irate* about the Stoic alternative—he appears to be sincere.

To finish my case for a sceptical reading of Marcus in the *Tusculans*, I remark that it helps us to understand two of the other three oddities I mentioned (Section 1).

The first is the impression that the dialogue leaves on some readers that, rather than putting rhetoric into the service of philosophy, Cicero makes arguments that are rhetorical *rather than* philosophical. On this score, it helps to see that Marcus' task is to bring about a change of attitude in his listener, not to prove the truth any thesis. But Marcus' reasons for undertaking this task are philosophical: Clitomachean scepticism.

The second problem my reading helps to clear up is Marcus' apparent eclecticism. On this score, we can see why, given his task, Marcus can use and combine weighty arguments from different philosophers. Even if all he did was pile up many different arguments against the *propositum*, he would do something much like what Sextus Empiricus does on either side of a question in *Adversus Mathematicos*. It would no more make Marcus an 'eclectic' than it does Sextus.

Now, there are some obvious textual objections to my position on Marcus' scepticism in the *Tusculans*. I should like to deal with those objections now.

The first objection draws on the quotation from *De divinatione* I cited in Section 1 above (*Div.* 2. 2 Giomini). Does not Cicero say there that the fifth book of the *Tusculans* teaches (docet) that virtue is sufficient for happiness? I answer that Cicero does *not* say this. For the subject of 'It teaches' (docet) is the same as the antecedent of 'which sheds more light' (qui inlustrat). But two words could be that antecedent: 'liber' (book) or 'locus' (subject). Thus I may understand the sentence as follows: the book contains the *subject* (locus), which teaches that virtue is sufficient for happiness, but the *book* does not teach that virtue is sufficient for happiness. In the same way, for example, *De divinatione* contains in Quintus' speech in Book 1 the *locus*, which teaches that divination really works. But neither *De divinatione* as a whole, nor its first book, teaches that divination really works.

Not only is it possible that 'locus' is the subject of 'docet', it is more likely than that 'liber' is the subject. For if 'liber' is the subject, then Cicero's description of his own book is inaccurate. For the fifth book of the *Tusculans* does *not teach* that virtue is sufficient for happiness. In its opening sentences, Cicero tells us that the book is *about* the sufficiency of virtue, a view that is hard to approve, such that we must work hard in order for it to be easier to approve (5. 1). In the rest of the preface, Cicero as author evidently hopes that virtue is sufficient for happiness, but he fears that it is not (5. 2). He regards his doubt about the matter in the face of adversity as a 'fault' (culpa, 5. 5). But he does not claim that virtue is or is not sufficient for happiness. He *is* in doubt (5. 3). Therefore, the *book*, framed by the preface, does not teach one answer or the other. But the rest of the book consists mostly of Marcus' arguments against A.'s denial that virtue is sufficient for happiness. Thus the book *contains* the arguments for a conclusion that it does not teach, that virtue is sufficient for happiness. Therefore, if 'locus' is the subject of 'docet', then Cicero's description of his own book is accurate.[21]

The second objection comes from the fifth book of the *Tusculans*, where Marcus has argued that the Peripatetics' view of happiness is *inconsistent*, since they claim that poverty, loneliness, and pain are evils, but also that the wise man, subject to these evils, will always be happy (*Tusc.* 5. 31). A. rejoins as follows:

[T6] A. Adducis me, ut tibi adsentiar. sed tua quoque videne desideretur constantia.

  M. Quonam modo?

  A. Quia legi tuum nuper quartum de finibus; in eo mihi videbare contra Catonem disserens hoc velle ostendere—quod mihi quidem probatur—inter Zenonem et Peripateticos nihil praeter verborum novitatem interesse. quod si ita est, quid est causae quin, si Zenonis rationi consentaneum sit satis magnam vim in virtute esse ad beate vivendum, liceat idem Peripateticis dicere? rem enim opinor spectari oportere, non verba.

  M. Tu quidem tabellis obsignatis agis mecum et testificaris, quid dixerim aliquando aut scripserim. cum aliis isto modo, qui legibus impositis disputant: nos in diem vivimus; quodcumque nostros animos probabilitate percussit, id dicimus, itaque soli sumus liberi. (*Tusc.* 5. 32–3, with speakers' names added)

  A. You persuade me to agree with you. But perhaps you too are lacking in consistency.

  M. In what way do you mean?

  A. Because I recently read the fourth book of your *De finibus*. In it I thought that in your discourse against Cato you wanted to demonstrate, what I approve of, that there is no difference between Zeno and the Peripatetics except verbal innovations. If that is so, what reason is there why, if it is consistent with Zeno's thinking that there is enough power in virtue for living happily, the Peripatetics should not be allowed to say the same thing? I think that substance should be attended to, not mere words.

  M. You are taking proceedings against me with documents signed and sealed, and putting into evidence what I have said or written

---

[21] Further, in the list of the books of the *Tusculans* in *De divinatione*, Cicero says that each of the first four books is *about* the thesis under debate, not that it teaches or argues for it. We readers expect a parallel description of Book 5. If 'liber' is the subject of 'docet', we do not have a parallel description, because the book teaches the thesis under debate, but if 'locus' is the subject, we have a parallel, because the book merely contains the arguments for the thesis which it is about (*Div.* 2. 2).

some time or other. You do that to others who discuss with rules laid down. We live from day to day. Whatever strikes our minds as plausible, we say, so that we alone are free.[22]

This passage raises the objection that A. seems to think that Marcus *asserts* both what he wrote for the Marcus of *De finibus* Book 4, and what he has said in his speech in *Tusculans* Book 5. If so, then A. disagrees with my claim that Marcus does not assert the arguments of *Tusculans* 5. Thus, if you think that A. is a better judge of Marcus than I am, you might conclude that I am wrong. My answer is that A. has misunderstood what Marcus does. He is aware that Marcus' job is persuasion, but perceives a lack of persuasiveness in what seems to him to be an inconsistency among Marcus' pronouncements at different times. Marcus points out that consistency is not his goal, even among his own views from one time to another. Consistency in his arguments against others certainly cannot be expected. He explains how such a sceptic might give plausible arguments: whatever strikes him as plausible, he says. This does not mean he accepts it, or asserts it, as his own view. Marcus agrees with me, and is a better judge of himself than is A.

A third objection stems from one among a number of metaphors that Marcus uses to describe his activity in the *Tusculans*, especially in his prefaces. He says:

[T7] cultura autem animi philosophia est; haec extrahit vitia radicitus et praeparat animos ad satus accipiendos eaque mandat is et, ut ita dicam, serit, quae adulta fructus uberrimos ferant. agamus igitur, ut coepimus. dic, si vis, de quo disputari velis. (*Tusc.* 2. 13)

Now the cultivation of the soul is philosophy. It tears out vices by the roots and prepares the souls to receive the sowings, and commits to them and so to speak sows those seeds which might bear the most abundant crops on coming to maturity. So let us go on as we have begun. Tell me please what you want to have discussed. (trans. Douglas, modified)

---

[22] Translation from A. Douglas, *Cicero:* Tusculan Disputations *II & V* [*II & V*] (Warminster, 1990), modified. You might see a problem for my interpretation in 'Whatever strikes our mind as plausible, we say ...'. For it might suggest that Cicero says only what strikes him as plausible, in the sense that he only speaks his current *views*. But that cannot be the right reading of this phrase. Carneadean speakers, whether followers of Philo or of Clitomachus, evidently spoke for or against views indiscriminately. Thus they must have been ready to speak against conclusions that at the time they found more plausible, or to give arguments that they found less plausible. This phrase, then, must describe how Cicero, though a sceptic, can find arguments that are plausible to his listeners: he says what he finds plausible, but not necessarily what he finds *most* plausible at the time.

This metaphor suggests that there are three stages to philosophy's cultivation of the soul, all of which, the context further suggests, will be found in the discussion in *Tusculans* Book 2. The stages are, first, the uprooting of the vices, second, the preparation of the soul, and, third, the sowing of seeds which might bear fruit. The first two stages are easy to make sense of in sceptical terms. Tearing out the vices is the expulsion of opinions from the soul. (In 1. 111, Marcus says that he emphasizes his arguments against the possibility of punishment after death, because 'I wished this opinion hacked out of me down to the roots' (hanc excutere opinionem mihimet volui radicitus)).[23] To prepare the soil is to equip the soul with the armoury of arguments necessary to avoid the formation of new, rash opinions. But what about sowing seeds? It goes a step beyond the use of the weeding metaphor in [T5]. Does it not sound like an attempt to replace the old weeds with new plants—that is, to *teach* some opinions? I answer that it is important to examine the metaphor closely. Marcus will not replace the old weeds with new *plants*—that is, with fully developed opinions. He certainly will not transplant crops from his field to his audience's, or whatever the metaphor for teaching his own opinions would be. Rather, he will broadcast *seeds*, the remnants of the fruit of old plants, potential sources of ideas he has from the tradition, which he hopes will mature in well-prepared soil. The speeches in the *Tusculans*, and indeed in the other dialogues of our sequence, are the scattering of these many arguments. They are intended to relieve A. of his opinions. Some might strike the well-prepared listener as like the truth.

A fourth objection concerns the following passage in Marcus' conclusion to his speech in Book 4.[24] I translate more literally here, in order to exhibit the strength of the objection.

[T8]   sed cognita iam causa perturbationum, quae omnes oriuntur ex iudiciis opinionum et voluntatibus, sit iam huius disputationis modus. scire autem nos oportet cognitis, quoad possunt ab homine cognosci, bonorum et malorum finibus nihil a philosophia posse aut maius aut utilius optari quam haec, quae a nobis hoc quadriduo disputata sunt. (*Tusc.* 4. 82)

But now that we have grasped the cause of emotions, all of which arise from judgements of opinion and volitions, let us set now set a limit

---

[23] Gorman, *Socratic*, 70 takes this remark to be evidence that Marcus endorses his own arguments. But it shows no such thing: Marcus says he wants to lose an opinion, not to gain a new one.

[24] I thank an anonymous reviewer for *Oxford Studies* for pressing this objection.

to this discussion. But when the ends of goods and evils have been grasped, so far as they can be grasped by a human being, we should know that we can hope for nothing greater or more useful from philosophy that these things which we have discussed in these four days.

The verb I have translated 'grasp' (cognosco), is usually Cicero's term of art for a cognitive grasp (κατάληψις) in Stoicism, or an equivalently secure epistemic state in other systems of thought. Clitomachus, and Cicero as a follower of Clitomachus, would agree that such a grasp on some proposition would warrant or even require assent to its truth. Their scepticism arises when they find themselves to have no such grasp of any proposition. Thus, you might object to my interpretation on the basis of this passage, first because Marcus says here that he and A. have achieved a cognitive grasp on the cause of emotions sufficiently good to warrant or even to require assent as to its truth, and second because this passage leads into the rest of the conclusion to Book 4, part of which I quoted above in support of my interpretation.

I answer, first, that we should note that the phrase in question is a play on words: 'causam cognoscere' ('to get to know the case') was an idiom in legal practice meaning to investigate a case.[25] Thus in addition to the meaning I have given it above, the phrase means that it is time for Marcus to stop his speech, because he and A. have now studied the case of emotions. Second, Marcus sometimes speaks hyperbolically about his results in the course of his speeches, in order to make the rhetorically strongest case to A. For example, in Book 1, he says that it is easy to talk about burial of the dead 'especially when those things have been grasped' (is praesertim cognitis), namely, what he has just said about the cessation of sensation at death (*Tusc.* 1. 102). But in Book 1, it is explicit that Marcus does not himself endorse the claim that sensation ends at death. Thus 'grasped' in that passage is hyperbolic. For another example of hyperbole, we can look to our passage itself. When Marcus says that 'the ends of goods and evils been grasped, so far as they can be grasped by a human being', how far is that? In Book 5, Marcus will make an argument that whatever the end of goods may be, virtue is sufficient for happiness (*Tusc.* 5. 84–120). He will remark on his sceptical freedom from dogma on the question (*Tusc.* 5. 33–4, 83). Certainly, then, the ends of goods and evils have not

---

[25] *OLD* s.v. *cognosco* 4a; Lewis and Short, s.v. *cognosco* III.A; Dougan and Henry ad loc.

been grasped so as to warrant or require assent. Similarly, when Marcus says that the cause of emotions has been grasped, he means to suggest to A. only that he has made a good case.

A fifth objection, due to Robert Gorman (*Socratic*, 72–3) is that the atmosphere of the *Tusculans* is *co-operative*. As we have seen, A. is sometimes pleased to be talked out of his opinions. Marcus sees no problem in asking A. not to be contrary, and A. complies without demur (2. 15). Thus, you might say, A. did not really hold the views he states, for if he had, he would have fought for them. But I answer that it is possible both sincerely and deeply to believe that p, and to wish not to believe that p. There are those who both sincerely and deeply believe that there is no loving God, and wish to believe that there is a loving God. Or you might sincerely believe that your dog is dying, and wish not to believe that your dog is dying, because you wish to discover that he is not dying, or to learn that his symptoms leave room for reasonable hope. Similarly, A. might both sincerely believe (for instance) that his destiny, death, is an evil, and wish not to believe that death is an evil. Thus he might co-operate with Marcus in the attempt to remove his own deeply seated, and sincere, opinions.

4. Cicero and the *Tusculans*: a sceptical reading

Suppose you grant me my contention in the last section, that Marcus in the *Tusculans* proceeds along Clitomachean lines. I think you might still, and reasonably, take issue with my thesis in the following way: I have argued that *inside the drama*, Marcus acts out a sceptical practice. But (you might say) this falls well short of a sensitive reading of the dialogue as a whole. For while Marcus has to respond to whatever A. happens to propose, *Cicero chooses A.'s propositions*. Thus *Cicero* brings it about that Marcus argues that death is not an evil (Book 1), that pain is not the greatest evil (Book 2), that a wise man feels no distress (Book 3) and can lack all passions (Book 4), and that virtue is sufficient for a happy life (Book 5). These topics lead, one from another, into a coherent and Stoic answer to the spectre of human fragility.

In answer to this challenge, I shall argue first that the *Tusculans* do *not* commend a Stoic world-view.[26]

---

[26] Here I am in allegiance with Woolf, *Cicero*, chapter 6, which readers should consult for a subtle and much more detailed treatment of the complexities of the positive positions, Stoic and otherwise, that Cicero recruits against A.'s *proposita*.

Certainly, the five theses for which Marcus argues, the five neg-
ations of A.'s *proposita*, are all Stoic. Further, among the dogmatic
Hellenistic schools, the theses for which he argues in Books 3 and 4
are *distinctively* Stoic,[27] and therefore, of the schools, only a Stoic
could assent to these two, or indeed to the conjunction of all five.
Further, it is undeniable that, for the most part, the theoretical
basis, and many of the arguments, for Marcus' theses in Books 3
and 4 are Stoic.[28] But Marcus' arguments in each of Books 1, 2, and
5 are conceived so that his respective attacks on A.'s *proposita* are
well supported *whether or not Stoicism is correct*. Not only that, but
Marcus, when arguing against A., sometimes even dismisses the
importance of Stoicism, or says that the Stoics are incorrect. In
order to see these points, let us look at the structure of the argument in each of Books 1, 2, and 5.

In Book 1, Marcus argues by disjunction. Either the soul is mortal, or it is not mortal. If the soul is not mortal, then death is not
bad—indeed, he argues, it is good. If the soul is mortal, then death
is not bad. Therefore, death is not bad. Now beside the two horns
of the dilemma a third, and perhaps relevantly different, option
might be that the soul lives through what we usually call death, and
for a long time, but is not immortal. Marcus says that this is a Stoic
view. But he does not consider it worth following up: 'Surely

---

[27] If the conclusion of Marcus' argument in Book 2 were that pain is not an evil,
that too would be distinctively Stoic. But his conclusion (*Tusc.* 2. 66) is strictly a
reply to A.'s initial, and very quickly rejected, *propositum*, that pain is the greatest
evil. For, the disjunction that *either* pain is a small evil, *or* it is no evil, refutes the
contention that pain is the *greatest* evil. It does not refute the contention that pain is
an evil. Marcus' speech in Book 2 is an *expansion* of his very quick refutation of A.'s
initial *propositum* ('I see clearly, but I'd like more,' says A. (video plane sed plus
desidero, 2. 15)), not an argument for the further conclusion that pain is not an evil.

[28] But these arguments are often so chosen as to make them as useful as possible
to other schools, or at least to Peripatetics and Antiocheans. Most notably, in Book
4, Marcus opposes emotion not on the basis of the Stoic theory of value, that only
virtue is good or only vice bad, but rather on the basis that emotion would be a
mistaken response even if conventional goods and evils *are* good or bad (*Tusc.* 4.
59–62). Moreover, Marcus gives as the 'source' of his Stoic taxonomy of the passions what seems to be a decidedly *anti*-Chrysippean division of the soul into
rational and non-rational parts (4. 10–11). I suspect that this is indeed an anti-
Chrysippean psychology, because I think Marcus gives it in order to hold on to the
Platonic (or Pythagorean) account of the soul which A. found most helpful in con-
quering the fear of death in Book 1 (1. 20, 24–5, 39, 80). If so, then even the Stoicism
of Book 4 flows from a questionably Stoic, and anti-Chrysippean, 'source'. But the
passage is difficult. Graver's notes in *Emotions* attempt a reconciliation: the passage
is Cicero's misguidedly colourful way to sketch a Stoic distinction between normative and non-normative reason.

there's no reason not to dismiss our friends, the Stoics?' (num quid igitur est causae, quin amicos nostros Stoicos dimittamus?, *Tusc.* 1. 78). A. concurs easily. And indeed, Stoic views of the soul receive very little other attention in Book 1.

In Book 2, Marcus argues against the proposition that pain is the greatest evil (*Tusc.* 2. 14). His strategy is to show that pain is easily overcome not only by virtue, but even by enthusiasm or mere opinion (2. 66), so that it is either no evil at all, or a small one. In the course of this argument, he takes up the distinctively Stoic view that pain is not only a lesser evil, but even no evil at all. Pithily, he *rejects* it:

[T9] 'dum nihil bonum nisi quod honestum, nihil malum nisi quod turpe'—optare hoc quidem est, non docere; illud et melius et verius, omnia quae natura aspernetur in malis esse, quae adsciscat, in bonis. (*Tusc.* 2. 30)

[The Stoics say,] 'Nothing is good but what is virtuous, nothing is bad but what is vicious.' *That* is wishful thinking, not demonstration. This is both better and more true: that everything of a sort that nature rejects, is an evil; everything of a sort that nature admits, is a good. (trans. Douglas, modified)

Thus Marcus supports his thesis, that pain is not the greatest evil, primarily with the *anti-Stoic* contention that it is a small evil.

In Book 5, Marcus contends that virtue is sufficient for a happy life. He treats the Stoic and Peripatetic accounts of the matter as worthwhile. If the Stoics are right, virtue alone is good, so that it is sufficient for happiness. If the Peripatetics are right, virtue is overwhelmingly good, so that (says Marcus) it is sufficient for happiness.[29] Thus, on any worthwhile account of the matter, virtue is sufficient for happiness (*Tusc.* 5. 119–20). As for unworthy thinkers, even Epicurus *asserts* that the virtuous man is always happy, although Marcus finds this inconsistent with Epicurus' other views (5. 31, 75, 119). In Book 5, then, Marcus proceeds as he did in Book 1: whether or not the relevant Stoic views are correct, his thesis is well supported.

Now that we have surveyed the arguments of Books 1, 2, and 5, let us return to the question of whether the *Tusculans* aim to persuade the reader of a Stoic view of happiness. It seems to me that if that were the *Tusculans*' aim, Cicero would have taken a very strange approach to their composition. For he would have asked

---

[29] This latter inference, he says, he is free to draw as an Academic sceptic, whatever the various dogmatic schools themselves may think (*Tusc.* 5. 82–3).

the reader to accept three of his five theses for reasons that are not necessarily Stoic, some of which explicitly are not Stoic (if the reader chooses a non-Stoic disjunct in Books 1 or 5), and some of which even explicitly contradict Stoicism (those in Book 2). If the reader accepted not only the theses, but also the arguments (which presumably they should), they would be left not with a thoroughly Stoic philosophy, but rather with a concoction of dissonant philosophical views. Thus, if the *Tusculans* were intended to persuade the reader of a view about human happiness, that view is not Stoic philosophy, which is to say it is not Stoicism. At most, the view it teaches would be five bare propositions of which only the Stoics would approve, but on a basis that they would think confused, and rightly so. I doubt that this was Cicero's goal.

What, then, is Cicero up to? I submit that his method makes sense if his goal is not to persuade the reader to accept all, or to any, of Marcus' theses, but rather to persuade the reader to cease to believe A.'s *proposita*. For if readers do not assent to the theses, then they have no need to accept all, or any, of Marcus' arguments, and thus the consistency or otherwise of those arguments with one other, or with the whole set of theses, does not matter to them. Thus I think we should see the purpose of the dialogue as a generalization of the sort of principle I suggested with Clitomachus' consolation. Clitomachus wanted to help his readers with their belief that it was wise to grieve the loss of Carthage. He could also rely on them to have this belief, so that he did not need to give the arguments in its favour to ensure balance. What if Cicero thinks he can rely not just on somebody like A., but also on his readers, to believe the *Tusculans' proposita*? Then his plan could be to free his readers from something they already believe to be true. But why would Cicero think that his readers agree with A. about the *proposita*?

One reason he might think so stems from the world in which the dialogues were both written and set. Cicero was severely bereaved at the death of his beloved daughter, Tullia.[30] Meanwhile, in the drama, Brutus, the addressee, has just left Cicero's house, and Cicero entertains his other, anonymous houseguests with five days of his rhetorical and philosophical exercises. Whether some precise dates are intended for these days, and if so which dates, is

---

[30] See S. Treggiari, *Terentia, Tullia and Publilia: The Women of Cicero's Family* (London, 2007), 135–8.

controversial.[31] But at any rate it is the summer of 45 BCE, and Caesar's arrival home from Munda is in the air. Cicero and friends may well contemplate a future where pain, violence, loss, and death could be their lot. Thus A.'s preoccupations with the threat of fragility, and how to deal with it, are understandable. Marcus aims to help A., by liberating him from his greatest fears through the removal of the opinions behind those fears. Cicero's first readers, meanwhile, lived a few months later, at a similar level in Roman society, and at a period of Caesar's dictatorship not much less threatening.

Although this interpretation is attractive, and probably played a part in Cicero's thinking,[32] the dialogue's setting, and characterization, seems to me to be too spare for a purely historical answer to my question to be altogether convincing. I would prefer to rest my case on something much more general. For all the *proposita* of the *Tusculans* have the following pair of characteristics.

First, all the *proposita* are very plausible, and very widely held. Indeed, we might even guess that most people, in most times and places, believe most or all of them. Of course, some are more often disputed than others. The most controversial is perhaps the first, that death is an evil. We often hear people claim not to believe this. But even so we might wonder. If they do not think death is bad, why do they go so far out of their way to avoid it?

Second, all the *proposita* in the *Tusculans* are *troubling* things to believe. If you, a mortal who love mortals, think that death is bad, then you inevitably face fear. If you believe that death and pain are bad, and that it is wise to respond to the threat of such things with fear, or to their reality with distress, you add the disturbance caused by these beliefs to the evils you confront. If you believe that your happiness can be smashed by blows such as these, which are far beyond your control, then you will never feel safe. Cicero wants to argue you out such beliefs. Maybe the world can break you, who are weak, but philosophy can help you not to anticipate the world's work by breaking yourself from the inside.

Cicero's purposes in the *Tusculans* are best seen in Book 5, to which I now return. Although, as I said above, we do not hear A.'s

---

[31] For the problem of the dramatic date of the *Tusculans*, see Gildenhard, *Paideia*, 279–81.

[32] In the still more uncertain times after Caesar's assassination, both Atticus and Cicero did in fact look back to the *Tusculans* for comfort (*Ad Att.* 15. 2. 4, 15. 4. 2 = 379. 4, 381. 2 Shackleton Bailey).

last reaction, Book 5 is in a way the most thoroughly sceptical part of the *Tusculans*. For we are reminded several times that Marcus, Cicero a little while ago, is an Academic sceptic (5. 11, 33–34, 82–3). He ends the book with a promise to his friends to write up their five afternoons of philosophical discussion:

[T10] ... quantum ceteris profuturi simus, non facile dixerim, nostris quidem acerbissimis doloribus variisque et undique circumfusis
molestiis alia nulla potuit inveniri levatio. (*Tusc.* 5. 121)

How much I shall benefit others I could not easily say. For my own
most bitter pains and varied troubles which have surrounded me on all
sides, no other relief could have been found. (trans. Douglas, modified)

In this final sentence, Marcus turns the reader's attention to his *own* reaction. He turns us back to the start of the book, and a little forward in time, to where Cicero showed us what sort of relief, in the event, he has found in writing up his dialogues. The quotations about fragility in the face of disaster with which I began this paper come from that examination of Cicero's own state of mind. So too do his fear that virtue is not sufficient for happiness, his doubt whether it is, and his self-reproach for this fear and doubt (5. 3–4). Cruel experience urges that the arguments of the books he has already written might be wrong:

[T11] vereor enim ne natura, cum corpora nobis infirma dedisset isque et
morbos insanabilis et dolores intolerabilis adiunxisset, animos
quoque dederit et corporum doloribus congruentis et separatim
suis angoribus et molestiis implicatos. (*Tusc.* 5. 3)

I am afraid that after giving us weak bodies, and adding to them
incurable diseases and unendurable pains, nature has given us as well
souls which both respond to physical pains and, apart from that, are
tangled up their own agonies and troubles. (trans. Douglas, modified)

Cicero himself feels the force of the *proposita*, even after he has given all the speeches of the *Tusculans* and written them up for our benefit. While he hopes that the *proposita* are false, he has not found sufficient reason in philosophy to deny them. What he found there is relief from sufficient reason to assent to them. He remains a follower of Clitomachus.

I suggest, then, that Cicero chooses his set of *proposita* because they seem to be (1) beliefs we tend to have because we are con-stantly assaulted by good reasons to retain them, yet against which philosophy can provide some surprisingly good arguments, and (2) beliefs by which we are severely troubled. Perhaps this is *why* the setting of the dialogue is so sparse (cf. Section 1 above): it is intended to address universal concerns, not only Cicero's, so that A. is more the everyman than other speakers in Cicero's dialogues. Further, this is likely why Cicero freely chose the *propositum* form for the *Tusculans*, but not for the other dialogues of his later sequence.[33] Each object of counter-argument is not only a philosophical thesis, but also a trouble common to us all. Sad to say, we do not need Cicero to establish that any of them is plausible.[34, 35]

University of Utah

[33] He chose the *propositum* form for *De fato*, but not freely. I accept the reason that he gave in [T3]: unexpectedly, he was busy, which constrained him to write in a shorter form.

[34] I disavow what might seem to be a natural extension of my argument. This is the conclusion that Cicero, or Clitomachus, or Carneades, proposed tranquillity—freedom from trouble—as the *goal* either of Academic philosophy, or of life. This conclusion might seem tempting on two counts. First, I hope to have shown that in the *Tusculans*, Cicero uses New Academic arguments in order to relieve the reader of troubling opinions. Elsewhere he called this 'la[ying] open matters most necessary for living a happy life' (res ad beate vivendum maxime necessarias aperuerunt, *Div.* 2. 2, cf. n. 6 above). In the *Tusculans* themselves, he says that philosophy has given us 'tranquillity of life' (5. 6, quoted at the start of this paper). Thus it might seem that Cicero thinks this sort of sceptical inquiry is directed at a goal, happiness, which might seem to be, or to require, tranquillity. Second, Sextus Empiricus says that tranquillity is a goal of Pyrrhonist sceptics (*PH* 1. 25–30). This helps to make it plausible that Clitomachean scepticism might have had such a goal. But I do not think this is right. Carneades argued for a highest good, but it is clear that he did so only to counter his dogmatic opponents (*Acad.* 2. 131, *Fin.* 5. 20). In any case, tranquillity was not the goal he mentioned. Further, in the *Academica*, there is no other hint that Clitomachean scepticism has any goal beyond itself, that is to say, beyond the suspension of judgement, which the Academic finds is the way to maintain our rational integrity in an epistemically helpless predicament. Even so, there is no reason that Cicero, or Clitomachus, should not have observed that humanity seems fragile and troubled, and that suspension of judgement on certain matters seems likely to help us to be less troubled. These matters are those that seem to be, and that are said to be, most necessary for happiness. The palliation of profound distress is the goal of the *Tusculans*, not of Academic scepticism, nor of human life.

[35] I would like to thank audiences at the 2014 Cornell conference on 'Cicero's Philosophy' and a 2016 meeting of the work in progress group of the Chicago Area Consortium in Ancient Greek and Roman Philosophy. I recall gratefully helpful comments at those meetings or on a draft from Catherine Steel, Margaret Graver, Raphael Woolf, Charles Brittain, Jed Atkins, David Ebrey, Dhananjay Jagannathan, Agnes Callard, Rachel Barney, and Tad Brennan. Principally, I would like to thank the editor and two anonymous readers for *Oxford Studies*, who have improved the paper substantially. All errors remain my own.

BIBLIOGRAPHY

Annas, J. and Woolf, R., *Cicero:* On Moral Ends (Cambridge, 2001).

Douglas, A., *Cicero:* Tusculan Disputations *I* (Warminster, 1985).

Douglas, A., *Cicero:* Tusculan Disputations *II & V [II & V]* (Warminster, 1990).

Douglas, A., 'Form and Content in the *Tusculan Disputations*' ['Form'], in J. Powell (ed.), *Cicero the Philosopher: Twelve Papers* (Oxford, 1995), 197–218.

Gildenhard, I., *Paideia Romana: Cicero's* Tusculan Disputations *[Paideia]* (Cambridge, 2007).

Giomini, R. (ed.), *M.* Tulli Ciceronis, De divinatione, De fato, Timaeus (Stuttgart, 1975).

Görler, W., 'Die Akademie zwischen Karneades und Philon', in H. Flashar (ed.), *Grundriß der Geschichte der Philosophie*, Bd 4. 2 (Basel, 1994), 898–914.

Görler, W., 'Cicero's Philosophical Stance in the *Lucullus*' ['Stance'], in B. Inwood and J. Mansfeld (eds.), *Assent and Argument* (Leiden, 1997), 36–57.

Görler, W., 'Zum Literarischer Charakter und zur Struktur der *Tusculanae disputationes*' ['Charakter'], in W. Görler and C. Catrein (eds.), *Kleine Schriften zur hellenistisch-römischen Philosophie* (Leiden, 2004), 212–39.

Gorman, R., *The Socratic Method in the Dialogues of Cicero [Socratic]* (Stuttgart, 2005).

Graver, M., *Cicero on the Emotions [Emotions]* (Chicago, 2002).

Lévy, C., *Cicero Academicus: Recherches sur les* Académiques *et sur la philosophie cicéronienne [Academicus]* (Rome, 1992).

Nussbaum, M., *The Therapy of Desire* (Princeton, 1994).

Nussbaum, M., *The Fragility of Goodness* (Cambridge, 2001).

Pohlenz, M. (ed.), *M.* Tullius Cicero, Tusculanae Disputationes *[Tusculans]* (Stuttgart, 1982).

Powell, J. (ed.), *Cicero the Philosopher: Twelve Papers* [Cicero] (Oxford, 1995).

Reynolds, L. D. (ed.), *M.* Tulli Ciceronis De finibus bonorum et malorum, Libri quinque (Oxford, 1998).

Ridley, R., 'To Be Taken With a Pinch of Salt: The Destruction of Carthage', *Classical Philology*, 81 (1986), 140–6.

Schofield, M., 'Philo and Cicero's *Tusculans*' ['Philo'], in G. Clark and T. Rajak (eds.), *Philosophy and Power in the Graeco-Roman World: Essays in Honour of Miriam Griffin* (Oxford, 2002), 91–107.

Sharples, R., *Cicero:* On Fate (De Fato) *and Boethius:* The Consolation of Philosophy (Philosophiae Consolationis) *IV. 5–7, V* (Warminster, 1991).

Stevens, S., 'A Legend of the Destruction of Carthage', *Classical Philology*, 83 (1988), 39–41.

Thorsrud, H., *Ancient Scepticism* (Berkeley, 2009).

Thorsrud, H., 'Arcesilaus and Carneades', in R. Bett (ed.), *The Cambridge Companion to Ancient Scepticism* (Cambridge, 2010), 58–80.

Treggiari, S., *Terentia, Tullia and Publilia: The Women of Cicero's Family* (London, 2007).

Visonà, P., 'Passing the Salt: On the Destruction of Carthage Again', *Classical Philology*, 83 (1988), 41–2.

Warmington, B., 'The Destruction of Carthage: A *retractatio*', *Classical Philology*, 83 (1988), 308–10.

White, S. 'Cicero and the Therapists' ['Therapists'], in J. Powell (ed.), *Cicero the Philosopher: Twelve Papers* [*Cicero*] (Oxford, 1995), 219–46.

Woolf, R., *Cicero: The Philosophy of a Roman Sceptic* [*Cicero*] (London, 2015).

Wynne, J., 'Cicero', in D. Machuca and B. Reed (eds.), *Skepticism: From Antiquity to the Present* (New York, 2018), 93–101.

SEXTUS EMPIRICUS ON
RELIGIOUS DOGMATISM

MÁTÉ VERES

In the third book of his *Outlines of Pyrrhonism*, Sextus Empiricus
presents an ambitious case for withholding assent from any account
of the conception, existence, and providential activity of god (*PH*
3. 3–12).[1] The parallel discussion in the first book of *Against the
Physicists*—which, by an accident of transmission, has become
widely known as Book 9 of *Adversus Mathematicos*—breaks down
into a section on the origin of the concept of god (*M* 9. 14–48) and
a broad-ranging survey of the opposition between theists and atheists which motivates suspension of judgement about the existence
of god (*M* 9. 50–191). Sextus adds in both works the caveat that his
polemic against dogmatic theology does not amount to a rejection
of religious cult; in fact, Pyrrhonians will engage in the relevant
practices of their respective communities without breaching their
suspensive policy (*PH* 3. 2, *M* 9. 49).

It has been argued, however, that Pyrrhonists will have trouble
acquiescing in the religious practices of their compatriots, since
those practices depend on beliefs that are supposedly eliminated by
suspension of judgement.[2] According to this objection, unless
Sceptics abandon their suspensive stance, the Sceptic's religious
behaviour will be inescapably disingenuous. As a way out of this
predicament, some interpreters have suggested that the sort of

---

[1] In the relevant cultural and philosophical context, the singular 'god' and the
plural 'gods' are more or less interchangeable.

[2] In the words of R. Bett, '*Against the Physicists* on Gods (*M* IX. 13–194)'
['Gods'], in K. Algra and K. Ierodiakonou (eds.), *Sextus Empiricus and Ancient
Physics, Proceedings of the 2007 Symposium Hellenisticum* (Cambridge, 2015), 33–73
at 65–6: 'Sextus does not, in the end, have an acceptable story to tell about the relation between his approach to everyday religion and his sceptical discussions about
God.' See also R. Bett, 'Sextus Empiricus' ['Sextus'] in G. Oppy and N. Trakakis
(eds.), *The History of Western Philosophy of Religion*, vol. i: Ancient Philosophy of
Religion (Durham, 2009), 173–85 at 174, 178, 182–3; R. Ziemińska, 'Scepticism
and Religious Belief: The Case of Sextus Empiricus' ['Case'], in D. Łukasiewicz
and R. Pouivet (eds.), *The Right to Believe: Perspectives in Religious Epistemology*
(Frankfurt, 2011), 149–60 at 154–9.

Máté Veres, *Sextus Empiricus on Religious Dogmatism*. In: Oxford Studies in Ancient Philosophy
Volume LVIII. Edited by: Victor Caston, Oxford University Press (2020).
© Máté Veres.
DOI: 10.1093/oso/9780198858997.003.0007

religion that Sextus was familiar with did not require the kind of belief that is subjected to Sceptical examination.[3] This, however, acquits Sextus of the charge of insincerity at the price of taking religious behaviour to be a culturally contingent exception to, rather than a standard case of, Pyrrhonian conduct.

Another worry concerns the fixity of Sextus' philosophical agenda. The argument in *PH* 3 concludes that, if one goes by what dogmatic philosophers have to say, one will be forced to think that god is inconceivable. By contrast, the first part of the *M* 9 section on theology argues not for suspension of judgement across the board, but only for the more modest claim that several noteworthy explanations of the emergence of religious belief are unsatisfactory. Insofar as this is the case, *M* 9 fails to live up to the standard set by *PH* 3, a failure due either to authorial incompetence or to a difference in philosophical objective.[4] If that is the case, then the two discussions cannot be read as successful examples of the same philosophical outlook.

In this paper, I argue for a comprehensive reading of Sextus' take on religious matters that responds to these worries. In the first half of the paper, I present the two caveats as formulating a uniform agenda concerning theology (Section 1) which is further consistent with the Pyrrhonian stance as presented in *PH* 1 (Section 2). I show not only that Sextan Sceptics are able to engage in ordinary religious practices, but also that they can do so whether or not their cultural environment takes these practices to depend on holding dogmatic beliefs. In the second half of the paper, I argue by way of a detailed analysis that both *PH* 3 and *M* 9 are intended to motivate suspension of judgement about highly specific dogmatic tenets, and while their sources and targets might change, their intended

---

[3] For the most developed version of this reading, see J. Annas, 'Ancient Scepticism and Ancient Religion' ['Religion'], in B. Morison and K. Ierodiakonou (eds.), *Episteme, etc.: Essays in Honour of Jonathan Barnes* (Oxford, 2012), 74–89. For gestures towards a similar reading, see also L. Couloubaritsis, 'Réflexions de Sextus Empiricus sur les dieux (*Adv. Math.*, IX)', *Kernos*, 2 (1989), 37–52 at 45, 51–2; S. Knuuttila and J. Sihvola, 'Ancient Scepticism and Philosophy of Religion', in J. Sihvola (ed.), *Ancient Scepticism and the Sceptical Tradition* (Helsinki, 2000), 125–44; J. Sihvola, 'The Autonomy of Religion in Ancient Philosophy', in V. Hirvonen, T. J. Holopainen, and M. Tuominen (eds.), *Mind and Modality: Studies in the History of Philosophy in Honour of Simo Knuuttila* (Leiden, 2006), 87–99.

[4] Bett, 'Gods', 46: 'But the inconceivability of God does not follow from what he has just argued; from the fact that no good explanation has been given of how we came to have a conception of God, it does not follow that there is not or cannot be any such conception.'

outcome remains the same. The argument in *PH* 3, often understood as a sort of 'master argument' aimed at disarming a broad theistic consensus, depends in fact on peculiar commitments concerning the nature of inquiry (Section 3). The conceptual section of *M* 9 incorporates explicitly dogmatic—and quite plausibly Epicurean—material in order to argue for suspension of judgement about yet another issue, namely, the question of the natural or conventional origin of the concept of god (Section 4).

These results are significant for at least two reasons. First, even though an influential line of interpretation defends the possibility of a Pyrrhonian way of life, such a reading has not yet been spelled out in the religious case, nor has it been defended against the specific objections that arise in this domain.[5] In fact, none of the available discussions of Sextus on religion proceeds along these lines. Second, in order to evaluate properly Sextus' arguments against dogmatic theology, one needs to have in place a detailed analysis of the arguments with a particular focus on the dogmatic positions targeted by them. By providing such an analysis, I throw light both on Sextus' Sceptical methodology and on the inter-dogmatic polemics on which he exercises it.[6]

1. The caveats

Having rounded up his series of counter-arguments against the logical part of dogmatic philosophy in *PH* 2, Sextus transitions to natural philosophy by announcing that he will first look at candidates

[5] For the generic defence, see M. Frede, 'The Sceptic's Beliefs' ['Beliefs'], in M. F. Burnyeat and M. Frede (eds.), *The Original Sceptics: A Controversy* (Indianapolis, 1997), 1–24; and M. Frede, 'The Sceptic's Two Kinds of Assent and the Question of the Possibility of Knowledge', in Burnyeat and Frede (eds.), *Original Sceptics*, 127–52; with notable variations in T. Brennan, *Ethics and Epistemology in Sextus Empiricus* (London, 1999), and K. M. Vogt, *Skepsis und Lebenspraxis: Das pyrrhonische Leben ohne Meinungen* [*Lebenspraxis*] (Freiburg, 2015), 129–72.

[6] In addition, such a case study will allow for more detailed comparisons with Cicero's *De natura deorum* than are currently available. This, however, lies beyond the confines of the present paper. On the Academic credentials of Cicero's position, see C. Lévy, *Cicero Academicus: Recherches sur les Académiques et sur la philosophie cicéronienne* (Rome, 1992), 557–88; J. G. DeFilippo, 'Cicero vs Cotta in *De Natura Deorum*', *Ancient Philosophy*, 20 (2000), 169–87; J. P. F. Wynne, 'Learned and Wise: Cotta the Sceptic in Cicero's *De natura deorum*', *Oxford Studies in Ancient Philosophy*, 47 (2014), 245–73; and D. Sedley, 'Carneades' Theological Arguments' ['Carneades'], in P. Kalligas, C. Balla, E. Baziotopolou, and V. Karasmanis (eds.), *Plato's Academy: Its Workings and its History* (Cambridge, 2020), 220–41.

for first principles (ἀρξώμεθα δὲ ἀπὸ τοῦ περὶ ἀρχῶν λόγου) and, more specifically, at causes that actively bring about change (τῶν δραστικῶν, *PH* 3. 1).[7] This in turn leads him directly to the conception and existence of god, a topic he introduces with the following remark:

[T1]   οὐκοῦν ἐπεὶ θεὸν εἶναι δραστικώτατον αἴτιον οἱ πλείους ἀπεφήναντο, πρότερον περὶ θεοῦ σκοπήσωμεν, ἐκεῖνο προειπόντες, ὅτι τῷ μὲν βίῳ κατακολουθοῦντες ἀδοξάστως φαμὲν εἶναι θεοὺς καὶ σέβομεν θεοὺς καὶ προνοεῖν αὐτοὺς φαμεν, πρὸς δὲ τὴν προπέτειαν τῶν δογματικῶν τάδε λέγομεν. (*PH* 3. 2)

Since the majority have asserted that god is a most active cause, let us first consider god, remarking by way of preface that, following ordinary life without dogmatic opinions,3 we say that there are gods and we are pious towards the gods and say that they are provident: it is against the rashness of the Dogmatists that we make the following points.[8]

In this passage, Sextus qualifies his procedure in a number of ways. First, he sets out a binary opposition between ordinary life (βίος) and dogmatic rashness (προπέτεια). Second, he states that Pyrrhonians argue against theological tenets as specimens of the latter, while aligning themselves with the former by doing and saying what their local customs and laws prescribe. One might initially suppose that Sextus takes the domain of ordinary life, or at least this particular aspect of that domain, to be immune to Sceptical argumentation. The Pyrrhonian stance would then amount to an affirmation of ordinary life with an added combative element: unlike non-philosophers, Pyrrhonians respond to the challenge of dogmatic revisionism—the attempt to correct or discard popular conceptions

---

[7] See also the transition to the next section 'On the active cause' (περὶ τοῦ ἐνεργητικοῦ αἰτίου, *PH* 3. 13). *M* 9 starts from a similar distinction between active (δραστήριος) and material (ὑλικός) principles, followed up by a survey of thinkers from Homer to the Stoics, whom Sextus takes to have observed it (9. 4–11). As M. Frede points out ('The Original Notion of Cause', in M. Frede (ed.) *Essays in Ancient Philosophy* (Oxford, 1987), 125–50 at 126–7), Sextus' presentation reflects a post-Aristotelian, and plausibly Stoic, notion of cause; see also R. J. Hankinson, *The Sceptics* (London, 1995), 213. Cf. an unattributed dogmatic tenet at *M* 9. 199: 'If there is a god, there is cause; for god administers the universe. But there is a god, according to the common conceptions of human beings; therefore there is cause' (εἰ ἔστι θεός, ἔστιν αἴτιον· οὗτος γὰρ ἦν ὁ τὰ ὅλα διοικῶν. ἔστι δέ γε κατὰ τὰς κοινὰς ἐννοίας τῶν ἀνθρώπων θεός· ἔστιν ἄρα αἴτιον); and *M* 9. 11.

[8] Here and in what follows, I quote *PH* from the translation of J. Annas and J. Barnes, *Sextus Empiricus, Outlines of Pyrrhonism [Outlines]* (Cambridge, 2000), with occasional modifications. For the Greek, see H. Mutschmann (ed.), *Sexti Empirici Opera*, vol. i (Leipzig, 1912).

on the basis of philosophical considerations—with vigorous counter-arguments.

A similar reflection on the Pyrrhonian agenda can be found in the parallel discussion in *M* 9, offering a slightly different picture:

[T2] τάχα γὰρ ἀσφαλέστερος παρὰ τοὺς ὡς ἑτέρως φιλοσοφοῦντας εὑρεθήσεται ὁ σκεπτικός, κατὰ μὲν τὰ πάτρια ἔθη καὶ τοὺς νόμους λέγων εἶναι θεοὺς καὶ πᾶν τὸ εἰς τὴν τούτων θρῃσκείαν καὶ εὐσέβειαν συντεῖνον ποιῶν, τὸ δ' ὅσον ἐπὶ τῇ φιλοσόφῳ ζητήσει μηδὲν προπετευόμενος. *M* 9. 49

For perhaps the Sceptic will be found to be safer than those who do philosophy in another way; in line with his ancestral customs and laws, he says that there are gods and does everything that tends to worship of and reverence towards them, but as far as philosophical investigation is concerned, he makes no rash moves.[9]

In this passage, the contrast is not drawn between ordinary life and philosophical dogmatism. Rather, Sextus positions himself within the philosophical community, as the follower of a specific kind of philosophy which supposedly makes him 'safer' than those who are of a different philosophical persuasion.[10] The alleged safety of his position is linked either to the fact that Sceptics lack rash commitments, or to the fact that they live by following the customs and laws of the land, or to a combination of the two.[11]

On the incomplete reading of [T1] offered above, it would seem that Sextus envisions different agendas in his two caveats. The Sceptics in [T2] conform to popular religion out of concern for their safety, while the Sceptics in [T1] seemingly have no qualms about ordinary life and resist philosophical revision as a matter of principle.[12] Importantly, however, [T2] puts emphasis on the fact that

---

[9] Here and in what follows I quote *M* 9 from the translation of R. Bett, *Sextus Empiricus, Against the Physicists* (Cambridge, 2012), with occasional modifications. For the Greek, see H. Mutschmann (ed.), *Sexti Empirici Opera*, vol. ii (Leipzig, 1914).

[10] On Sextus' notion of philosophical inquiry, one which eminently applies to the Pyrrhonist position, see M. Veres, 'Keep Calm and Carry On: Sextus Empiricus on the Origins of Pyrrhonism', *History of Philosophy and Logical Analysis*, 23 (2020), 100–22.

[11] In Section 2.3, I provide a detailed discussion of the relevant notion of safety.

[12] As implied, perhaps, by K. Algra, 'Stoic Philosophical Theology and Graeco-Roman Religion', in R. Salles (ed.), *God and Cosmos in Stoicism* (Oxford, 2009), 224–52 at 228 n. 14, according to whom Sceptics take themselves to have shown 'the epistemological impossibility of a rational alternative [to tradition]'. Cf. J. Mansfeld, 'Theology', in K. Algra, J. Barnes, J. Mansfeld, and M. Schofield (eds.), *The Cambridge History of Hellenistic Philosophy* (Cambridge, 1997), 452–78, who claims at 477 that Sceptics 'reject' philosophical theology.

Pyrrhonians do not subscribe to ordinary cult without further ado but only insofar as it is possible to do so *adoxastōs*, without holding dogmatic opinions. The qualification distinguishes Sceptics not only from non-Sceptical philosophers but also from non-philosophers who never set foot in philosophy and in whose way of life Pyrrhonians claim to participate.[13]

It is possible, then, to read the two caveats as amounting to different statements of the same position.[14] Situated in between laymen and philosophers, Sextans are dissenters from both camps. On the one hand, they investigate matters of philosophy—in this case, tenets of philosophical theology—but refuse to commit themselves to any claim on the basis of preceding inquiry. On the other hand, in the absence of guidance from philosophy, they engage in practices they are otherwise familiar with—in this case, those sanctioned by local traditions, customs, and laws—not as zealots of ordinary life but only insofar as it is possible without doctrinal commitments. While [T2] expresses the latter point in terms of resisting rashness (προπέτεια), [T1] qualifies the Sceptic's action and speech as being without premature doxastic commitments (i.e. as being carried out ἀδοξάστως).[15]

A further advantage of such a consolidated reading is that it fits well with the overall Sextan position as described in *PH* 1.

---

[13] In terms of syntax, ἀδοξάστως in [T1] could go either with βίῳ κατακολουθοῦντες or with φαμεν, allowing for difference of emphasis as to whether or not ordinary life itself lacks illicit *dogmata* (see J. Barnes, 'Pyrrhonism, Belief, and Causation', in id., *Proof, Knowledge, and Scepticism, Essays in Ancient Philosophy III* (Oxford, 2014), 417–511 at 448 n. 113 and 459 n. 150, who prefers the former construal). One might argue that φαμεν is enclitic and should not start a new clause, but the alternative construal is also possible. (Accentuation is a feature of later manuscripts only.)

[14] One could resist a unified reading by appealing to a reconstructed trajectory of Sextus' intellectual development with a corresponding chronology of his works (see, most notably, Bett's ongoing quest to revise and replace the chronology proposed by Janáček; for a critical overview, see K. Algra and K. Ierodiakonou, 'Introduction' in eid. (eds.), *Sextus Empiricus and Ancient Physics, Proceedings of the 2007 Symposium Hellenisticum* (Cambridge, 2015), 1–32 at 5–7). I shall proceed on the assumption that, if a consistent reading is possible, such considerations are philosophically irrelevant.

[15] The term *adoxastōs* as applied to the Sceptic is unique to *PH* (see 1. 15, 23, 226, 231; 2. 13, 102, 246, 254, 258; 3. 151, 235, with K. Janáček, *Sextus Empiricus' Sceptical Methods* (Prague, 1972), 61–2 and J. Barnes, 'The Beliefs of a Pyrrhonist' ['Beliefs'], in Burnyeat and Frede (eds.), *Original Sceptics*, 58–91 at 78 n. 77). As G. Fine, 'Sceptical *Dogmata*: Outlines of Pyrrhonism I 13', *Méthexis*, 13 (2000), 81–105 at 100 n. 65, points out, it is equivalent to the claim in *PH* 1. 13 that the Sceptic lacks illicit *dogmata*; cf. A. Bailey, *Sextus Empiricus and Pyrrhonean Scepticism [Sextus]* (Oxford, 2002) at 188–93.

According to that account, philosophical inquiry originated with the desire of outstanding individuals to eliminate their intellectual disturbance by way of arriving at reason-based decisions about the truth and falsity of conflicting appearances. In their quest for the truth, some inquirers have realized that every presently available argument is matched by an equally convincing counter-argument. In response to this recognition, they have suspended their judgement about all matters of inquiry and, much to their surprise, doing so has brought them into an unexpected state of intellectual tranquillity (*PH* 1. 12, 26, 29).

The Sceptics' subsequent inquiry consists in the exercise of their capacity to set out such oppositions in order to maintain their suspensive state of mind as well as to bring about the same condition in their fellow inquirers (*PH* 1. 8–11; 3. 280–1). With this purpose in mind, Sceptics target a comprehensive account of dogmatic or 'so-called' philosophy in order to motivate suspension of judgement about each and every one of its tenets (*PH* 1. 6, 18; 2. 1; 3. 1; *M* 7. 1–23). The encounter with theological claims figures in Sextus' discussion of theology understood as a part of natural philosophy, and his caveats remind the reader to understand his arguments as nothing more than carefully selected remedies for particular specimens of dogmatic belief.[16]

2. Conformism or hypocrisy?

According to Sextus' account of Pyrrhonism, suspension of judgement leaves intact the possibility of a life based on what appears to

---

[16] In *M* 9, Sextus further qualifies his project as bringing about *aporia* concerning theology in order to disprove two claims: first, that philosophy is the pursuit of wisdom (ἐπιτήδευσις σοφίας) and, second, that wisdom is the knowledge of divine and human affairs (ἐπιστήμη θείων τε καὶ ἀνθρωπίνων πραγμάτων, *M* 9. 13). This is another indication that the rejection of religious dogmatism is part of his ongoing struggle against the dogmatic understanding of philosophy. For an argument that the definition of wisdom referred to in this passage is peculiarly Stoic, see R. Brouwer, *The Stoic Sage: The Early Stoics on Wisdom, Sagehood and Socrates* (Cambridge, 2014), 8–41. Surprisingly, D. Obbink, *Philodemus, On Piety, Part i: Critical Text with Commentary* [*Philodemus*] (Oxford, 1996), 4 takes the passage to express a Sceptical requirement, even though Sextus claims that it is the dogmatists who think it a necessity to provide a theological account: 'The argument concerning gods seems absolutely necessary to those who do philosophy dogmatically' (ὁ περὶ θεῶν λόγος πάνυ ἀναγκαιότατος εἶναι δοκεῖ τοῖς δογματικῶς φιλοσοφοῦσιν, *M* 9. 13).

one to be the case. On any given matter of inquiry, Sceptics suspend their judgement due to the availability of opposing accounts, but might nevertheless retain an appearance that they do not consider rationally preferable to any other alternative. As it turns out, appearances of religious significance are prime examples of one type of the available appearances:

[T3] τοῖς φαινομένοις οὖν προσέχοντες κατὰ τὴν βιωτικὴν τήρησιν ἀδοξάστως βιοῦμεν, ἐπεὶ μὴ δυνάμεθα ἀνενέργητοι παντάπασιν εἶναι. ἔοικε δὲ αὕτη ἡ βιωτικὴ τήρησις τετραμερὴς εἶναι καὶ τὸ μέν τι ἔχειν ἐν ὑφηγήσει φύσεως, τὸ δὲ ἐν ἀνάγκῃ παθῶν, τὸ δὲ ἐν παραδόσει νόμων τε καὶ ἐθῶν, τὸ δὲ ἐν διδασκαλίᾳ τεχνῶν, . . . ἐθῶν δὲ καὶ νόμων παραδόσει καθ' ἣν τὸ μὲν εὐσεβεῖν παραλαμβάνομεν βιωτικῶς ὡς ἀγαθὸν τὸ δὲ ἀσεβεῖν ὡς φαῦλον . . . ταῦτα δὲ πάντα φαμὲν ἀδοξάστως. (PH 1. 23–4)

Thus, attending to what is apparent, we live in accordance with everyday observances, without holding dogmatic opinions—for we are not able to be utterly inactive. These everyday observances seem to be fourfold, and to consist in guidance by nature, necessitation by feelings, handing down of laws and customs, and teaching of kinds of expertise. . . . By the handing down of customs and laws, we accept, from an everyday point of view, that piety is good and impiety is bad. . . . And we say all this without holding dogmatic opinions.[17]

This in itself suggests that insofar as Sceptics receive appearances concerning piety and impiety as part of transmitted customs and laws, they will be able to act on the basis of such appearances.[18] Nevertheless, a number of readers seem to believe that the position

---

[17] The terms εὐσεβεῖν and ἀσεβεῖν ('piety' and 'impiety' above) might refer to pious practice rather than to pious thought, in which case one should translate 'acting piously' and 'acting impiously' (M. C. Nussbaum, *The Therapy of Desire: Theory and Practice in Hellenistic Ethics* (Princeton, 1994), 292–3 with n. 18; M. F. Burnyeat, 'Can the Sceptic Live His Scepticism?', in Burnyeat and Frede (eds.), *Original Sceptics*, 25–57 at 36 n. 26; Barnes, 'Beliefs', 81–2). Sextus occasionally reports on allegations of impiety in this vein: see *M* 9. 62 (the deification of kings) and 128 (the Pythagorean ban on eating meat); *PH* 3. 221 (human sacrifice). In the context of the present argument, however, it is specific doxastic commitments that seem to invite allegations of impiety: see *PH* 3. 12–13 (with Section 3.3 below), and *M* 9. 192.

[18] This implies that Sceptics brought up in a predominantly secular society will hardly receive such appearances, unless they belong to a religious-minded minority. Sextus has, understandably, little to say about possible cases of conflict, but see his answer to a similar dilemma in *M* 11. 165–6: faced with a tragic dilemma, the Sceptic will be able to act one way or another, though their course of action will be determined by non-philosophical considerations.

implies either the crime of dogmatic conformism[19] or the blunder of proposing a life of hypocrisy and pretence.[20] One's preference for one horn of the dilemma or the other will correspond to their view as to the content of the Sceptic's religious appearances, i.e. whether they are of the form 'It appears to me that there are gods', in which case one is hardly a hypocrite, or of the form 'It appears to me that I should follow others in acting as if there were gods', which does not suggest confidence regarding the correctness of the relevant societal standards.[21]

In the next sections, I discuss these charges and argue first, that the Sextan Pyrrhonist is not a dogmatic conformist (Section 2.1); second, that the question of hypocrisy is philosophically irrelevant (Section 2.2); and third, that here as elsewhere Sextus is primarily concerned with showing that Pyrrhonism is preferable to dogmatism for reasons of intellectual tranquillity (Section 2.3).

[19] On Sextus' failure to employ his oppositional capacity against received views, see Bett, 'Sextus', 183; Bett, 'Gods', 60–2 with n. 60; cf. the measured remarks in Barnes, 'Beliefs', 84–6. For outright conformist readings of the Sextan position, see P. Hallie, 'Classical Scepticism—A Polemical Introduction', in P. Hallie (ed.), *Sextus Empiricus: Selections from the Major Writings on Scepticism, Man and God* (Cambridge, 1985), 3–29 at 8, 29; A. Drozdek, 'Sceptics and a Religious Instinct', *Minerva*, 18 (2005), 93–108 at 107.

[20] The first horn of the dilemma is a variant of the familiar charge of inaction (ἀπραξία) or inactivity (ἀνενεργησία) which calls into question the viability of a Sceptical life. By the time one gets to the second horn, the opponent has already conceded viability, only to move on to implicating the Sceptic in an unappealing, undesirable, or reprehensible way of life. On this, see G. Striker, 'Sceptical Strategies', in Schofield, Burnyeat, and Barnes (eds.), *Doubt and Dogmatism*, 54–83; K. M. Vogt, 'Scepticism and Action', in R. Bett (ed.), *The Cambridge Companion to Ancient Scepticism* (Cambridge, 2010), 165–80; F. Grgić, 'Skepticism and Everyday Life', in D. Machuca (ed.), *New Essays on Ancient Pyrrhonism* (Boston, 2011), 69–90; and F. Grgić, '*Apraxia*, Appearances, and Beliefs', *Croatian Journal of Philosophy*, 16 (2016), 441–58.

[21] For a clear formulation of the former option, see M. L. McPherran, '*Ataraxia* and *eudaimonia* in Ancient Pyrrhonism: Is the Skeptic Really Happy?', *Proceedings of the Boston Area Colloquium in Ancient Philosophy*, 5 (1989), 135–71 at 164: 'Hence, just as one will find the world colored after rejecting naïve realism, so one might still find the world endowed with the blessings of the gods after rejecting naïve theology'; on the latter, see S. Marchand, 'Religion et piété sceptiques selon Sextus Empiricus' ['Piété'], in A.-I. Bouton-Touboulic and C. Lévy (eds.), *Scepticisme et religion: Constantes et évolutions, de la philosophie hellénistique à la philosophie médiévale* (Turnhout, 2016), 103–17 at 115: 'For a Sceptic, to say that there is providence is to refer to a social consensus according to which this type of attitude is better than another, to refer to a group of actions *as if there were providence*' ('Pour un sceptique, dire qu'il y a une providence, c'est renvoyer au consensus social selon lequel ce type d'attitude est meilleur qu'un autre, c'est renvoyer à un ensemble d'actions *comme s'il y avait une providence*', emphasis in the original).

2.1. *Dogmatic conformism*

Since Sextus regularly includes ordinary views among the cases of
oppositions that motivate suspension of judgement, the charge of
dogmatic conformism is easily avoided.[22] According to the Tenth
Mode of suspension, the diversity of persuasions, customs, laws,
mythical beliefs, and dogmatic suppositions militates against
accepting any of them as correct (*PH* 1. 145). He goes on record
that the same predicament applies to religious opinion, since some
deny the existence of gods, while 'most of the dogmatists, and the
common preconception of ordinary life, say that there is [a god]'
(καὶ εἶναι μὲν οἱ πλείους τῶν δογματικῶν καὶ ἡ κοινὴ τοῦ βίου πρόληψις,
M 9. 50). He does not fail to register disagreements within the theistic camp either: 'Of those who believe in gods, some believe in
the traditional gods, others in those invented by the dogmatic
schools' (καὶ τῶν εἶναι θεοὺς ἀποφηναμένων οἱ μὲν τοὺς πατρίους
νομίζουσι θεούς, οἱ δὲ τοὺς ἐν ταῖς δογματικαῖς αἱρέσεσιν ἀναπλασσομέ-
νους, *PH* 3. 218),[23] and even ordinary believers have incompatible
views about the divine (*M* 9. 191).

Insofar as he makes this case, Sextus cannot charitably be taken
to endorse the truth or even the plausibility of the religious tenets
with which he happens to have been brought up. Given the disagreement, Sceptics suspend their judgement about all views
involved (*PH* 1. 6, *M* 9. 191–2) or, to use a different terminology,
they say that one is no more the case than the other (*M* 9. 50). They
do not come to accept any view as true or false, hence they do not
come into outright conflict with the customs and laws of their community; in fact, they would be more likely to get into trouble if they
had to give reasons for not acting in the way everyone else around
them does. Their return to ordinary life is facilitated not by a new-
found belief in its correctness, but rather by the need to act in a way
that is compatible with suspensive tranquillity, as described in [T3].

---

[22] As pointed out by Bett, 'Gods', 56–9; cf. H. Thorsrud, 'Sextus Empiricus on
Skeptical Piety' ['Piety'], in D. E. Machuca (ed.), *New Essays on Ancient Pyrrhonism*
(Leiden, 2011), 91–111 at 98–101. For a rebuttal of dogmatic conformist readings,
see V. Tsouna-McKirahan, 'Conservatism and Pyrrhonian Skepticism', *Syllecta
Classica*, 6 (1996), 69–86, esp. 76; see also Bett, 'Sextus', 181–2.

[23] In Sextus, the verb ἀναπλάσσω often refers to alleged philosophical fictions,
including dogmatic aetiologies of religious belief (see *M* 9. 14, 16, 17, 33, 42), the
indicative sign (*PH* 2. 102; *M* 8. 158), 'the generic human being' (*M* 7. 222), and
things by nature to be chosen or avoided (*M* 11. 157).

2.2. *Hypocrisy*

Sceptics are thus exonerated from the charge of unwilling dogmatism, but they might still be vulnerable to the second horn of the dilemma. Their opponent might be inclined either to take their word that they follow an appearance concerning piety while falling short of genuine belief, or to accuse them of not even having such an appearance in the first place. Readers of Sextus routinely cast doubt on the intellectual integrity of his position along these lines in order to discredit the proposed way of life either as being a life of thoughtless assimilation to the masses or as promoting actions that do not match one's beliefs or, to be precise, the lack thereof.[24]

Two notable attempts have been made to rebut the charge of hypocrisy. First, some have claimed that Pyrrhonian suspension might in fact pave the way for genuine piety. On this reading, Sextus identifies the conviction that pious affective states should be grounded in corresponding pious beliefs as the main obstacle to genuine religious sentiment, and hence recommends the elimination of the former in order to achieve the latter.[25] However, this suggestion attributes to Sextus a religious motive that is at odds with his overall philosophical project. He cannot and does not promote Scepticism on the basis that it brings one closer to a religious state of mind, and were he to do so, he would have to be committed

---

[24] For representatives of this charge, see B. Mates, *The Skeptic Way: Sextus Empiricus' Outlines of Pyrrhonism* [*Skeptic Way*] (Oxford, 1996), 289: 'So the Pyrrhonist will say this although he does not believe it. It is possible that he makes the statement merely as a report of his own present *pathos*, short for "It seems to me that there are gods". But from the tenor of the discussion here and elsewhere I suspect that it does not even *seem* to him that there are gods, and that he only says such things in order to avoid trouble'; and Bailey, *Sextus*, 193: 'If the Pyrrhonist does not have the belief that a divine being exists, then his participation in religious worship would seem to be little more than a piece of hypocrisy and dissimulation. Nevertheless Sextus is apparently not prepared to acknowledge the existence of this deeper disquiet.... Sextus' discussion indicates that these reassuring statements really amount to nothing more than the claim that the Pyrrhonist can be relied upon, in the right cultural setting, to perform the characteristic actions associated with religious believers.'

[25] Thorsrud, 'Piety', 109–10: '... if firm assertion and dogmatic belief about the gods interfere with, or detract from, one's reverent affective states, i.e. firm belief about the gods leads us unwittingly to impiety, then ... skeptical argument could indeed serve religious ends.... By eliminating both ordinary and philosophical religious belief, the skeptic may be seen as clearing the impediments to genuinely reverent affective states, rather than clearing the way for their dogmatic attendants.'

to an underlying theory of genuine reverence incompatible with his philosophical position.[26]

A much more promising case has been made for giving due consideration to the understanding of piety that was predominant in Sextus' time and place. In formulating his position, Sextus could have drawn on a feature of ancient Greek religion, namely, that it required orthopraxy, i.e. correct action, rather than orthodoxy, i.e. sharing the relevant beliefs associated with those particular acts.[27] In such a context, the participation of Pyrrhonians in religious activities could hardly have seemed disingenuous. Along these lines, Julia Annas has suggested a distinction between theological and religious beliefs, where only the former are subjected to Sceptical examination.[28] On this reading, pagan Greek believers who have successfully purged themselves of theological beliefs might nevertheless continue to act on the basis of religious beliefs, since the latter do not necessarily imply the former (Annas, 'Religion', 82–3).

The difference between theological and religious belief could be spelled out either in terms of content or in terms of one's attitude towards the very same content. If theological beliefs differ from religious beliefs with regard to their content, then the former will turn out to be universal in scope, making a statement about the divine as such, while the latter will be culturally specific and localized

---

[26] Indeed, Thorsrud's reading seems motivated by perceived analogies with Reformed Epistemology; while it notably differs from fideistic readings, it is based on a similar misreading of the Sextan project. On Scepticism and fideism, see F. Caujolle-Zaslawsky, 'L'interprétation du scepticisme comme philosophie du doute religieux: Analyse d'un malentendu', *Revue de Théologie et de Philosophie*, 27 (1977), 81–112 at 97–104; T. Penelhum, 'Skepticism and Fideism', in M. F. Burnyeat (ed.), *The Skeptical Tradition* (Berkeley, 1983), 287–318; T. Penelhum, 'Sceptics, Believers, and Historical Mistakes', *Synthese*, 67 (1986), 131–46; and Bett, 'Gods', 53, 64–5.

[27] For a critical discussion of the oft-repeated claim of pagan Greek orthopraxy, see R. Parker, *On Greek Religion* (Ithaca, 2011), 1–39.

[28] Annas, 'Religion', 76–83. For critical remarks, see Bett, 'Gods', 57–9, Thorsrud, 'Piety', 94–103, and E. Spinelli, 'Le dieu est la cause la plus active: Sextus Empiricus contre la théologie dogmatique' ['Dieu'], in A.-I. Bouton-Touboulic and C. Lévy (eds.), *Scepticisme et religion: Constantes et évolutions, de la philosophie hellénistique à la philosophie médiévale* (Turnhout, 2016), 89–102 at 93–4. Alternatively, one could understand the claim that religious practice enjoys a degree of autonomy from doxastic commitments as the claim that religious believers do not or perhaps even should not share in any beliefs. This is clearly not what is meant here.

beliefs relative to a given divinity or religious tradition. It is in this spirit that Annas sets local beliefs concerning the cult of Athena in opposition to beliefs introduced in philosophical theories of the divine (Annas, 'Religion', 78–9).[29] The main problem with this reading is that Sextus, as we have seen, takes ordinary beliefs to be subject to Sceptical investigation.

If instead religious beliefs differ from theological beliefs with regard to one's attitude towards the very same proposition, be it universal or local in scope, then the contrast will be drawn in the following way. On the one hand, some beliefs are accepted on the basis of reasons and arguments brought forward in investigation and are taken to establish something as true. On the other hand, some beliefs are acquired due to cultural transmission, legal provision, or indoctrination. The resulting distinction seems to match quite clearly the stance outlined in the Sextan caveats, but is ultimately equivalent to the distinction between dogmatic opinion and appearance, a contrast which is not in any way unique to the case of religion.[30] If this is the proposed reading, then there is no need to introduce topic-specific terminology, such as Annas' distinction between theological and religious beliefs, to account for Sextus' position concerning religion.

Thus we are back to the question of whether religious practice rooted in what appears to one to be the case is to be considered

---

[29] This might also be understood in terms of Bett's claim that, in this context, an earlier form of Pyrrhonism surfaces in Sextus, one that does not take relativized affirmations to be dogmatic (Bett, 'Sextus', 178, see also 183–5). It does not follow, however, that Sextus cannot and does not accommodate the earlier material into his distinct position; and one might *ceteris paribus* prefer a reading that does not call Sextus' philosophical coherence into question.

[30] On this reading, Annas' proposal would amount to a Fredean reading of Pyrrhonian belief: 'For we can imagine someone who has been raised by Stoics and who has thus the Stoic concept of God. As a sceptic, he no longer believes that the Stoic proofs of God's existence entail their conclusion; since, however, his belief was not induced by these arguments, nothing about his belief need change even when the arguments no longer carry conviction' (Frede, 'Beliefs', 23; see also B. Morison, 'The Logical Structure of the Sceptic's Opposition', *Oxford Studies in Ancient Philosophy*, 40 (2011), 265–95 at 266). One complication derives from Frede's idiosyncratic terminology, as he distinguishes between two kinds of belief, one concerning what seems to be the case and another concerning what *really* is the case; on any charitable reading, the former will turn out to be equivalent to the appearances and the latter will amount to dogmatic opinions. One reason to prefer appearance-talk is that having beliefs and opinions of either kind arguably involves some commitment to their being true, while appearances can be followed without any such commitment.

disingenuous. The answer to that question is, however, philosophically neither here nor there. Disingenuity is relative to standards which might vary significantly from one cultural setting to another: a Pyrrhonist might or might not come into conflict with non-suspensive observers of a given religious tradition. More importantly, Pyrrhonism is motivated by the concern for intellectual tranquillity with regard to any given matter of inquiry, not by the search for adequate grounds for living an authentic religious or, for that matter, irreligious lifestyle. As a consequence, whether or not the charge of hypocrisy happens to stand, it poses no threat to the philosophical credibility of Sextan Pyrrhonism.

2.3. Safety

A further argument in favour of Sceptical hypocrisy might go along the following lines. It comes fairly naturally to connect Sextus' insistence on the safety of his position to the discomfort arising from the charge of insincerity. On this reading, Sextus is aware of the obnoxious implications of his stance and recommends religious conformism out of concern for safety from social opprobrium and possible persecution.[31] If this were correct, then it would seem that Sextus was after all concerned with external safety rather than with intellectual safety, i.e. with the approval of his fellow citizens, rather than with the avoidance of dogmatic opinions and the connected achievement of suspensive tranquillity.

---

[31] Bett, 'Gods', 55: 'But the care Sextus takes, in both works, to remind the reader of his conventional piety at the start of his discussions of God's existence makes it look as if he sees a possibility that these discussions will be read in the wrong way, as constituting an attack on ordinary religion.' See also 39, 53–6; Bett, 'Sextus': 182–3, as well as D. Sedley, 'Epicurus' Theological Innatism' ['Innatism'], in J. Fish and K. Sanders (eds.), *Epicurus and the Epicurean Tradition* (Cambridge, 2011), 29–52 at 50 n. 59: 'the Sceptic is likely to be playing "safer" than other philosophers, since despite his self-restraint regarding the philosophical question whether there are gods he follows local convention in *saying* that the gods exist and in taking a full part in their worship' (emphasis in the original). See also 53–6, and Bett, 'Sextus': 182–3. As D. Sedley, 'The Atheist Underground', in V. Harte and M. Lane (eds.), *Politeia in Greek and Roman Philosophy* (Cambridge, 2013), 329–48 at 335–41 points out, 'in classical Athens, and no doubt well beyond', it must have been quite dangerous to be seen as an atheist. On the atheistic potential of Sceptical arguments, see T. Whitmarsh, *Battling the Gods: The Struggle against Religion in Ancient Greece* (New York, 2015), 156–73.

In order to evaluate this claim, it is worth recalling that the appeal to safety in [T2] was made in connection with the contrast between Pyrrhonism and dogmatic kinds of philosophy. According to the text, the former is preferable to the latter either because of suspension of judgement and the resulting lack of dogmatic opinions, or because of its conformist streak, or due to a combination of the two.[32] From among these options, conformism alone cannot quite do the job. If safety were a question of compliance with customs, then dogmatists were just as safe as Pyrrhonians claim to be, since—despite their criticism of various tenets of religious cult—they univocally encouraged their followers to participate in religious life.[33] Furthermore, if one were to assume that Sextus' main concern was the avoidance of harassment for the anti-religious potential of his philosophical stance, one would have to find it somewhat surprising that he openly announces his intention to evade persecution by pretence—even if, in the absence of information about Sextus' audience, this objection carries relatively little weight.

At any rate, the Sceptics' claim to be better off than dogmatists must have something to do with their refusal to commit to dogmatic opinions. The question, then, is whether the element of conformism still has a role to play.[34] On a minimal reading, the suggestion would amount to the following. The Sceptic refuses to give rash assent to dogmatic proposals, and hence remains in a state of intellectual safety, safe from error or from intellectual perturbations, and is completely indifferent to the societal overtones of this stance.

---

[32] Thorsrud, 'Piety', 91 fails to notice this: 'It is surprising that Sextus does not say he will be safer as a result of suspending judgement, rather than as a result of participating in orthodox religious practice; for the skeptic's tranquillity depends, in general, not on his behaviour but rather the fact that he has suspended judgement.'

[33] On the conformist consensus, see G. Betegh, 'Greek Philosophy and Religion', in M.-L. Gill and P. Pellegrin (ed.), *A Companion to Ancient Philosophy* (Oxford, 2009), 625–39 at 625–9. Compare the argument in *M* 11. 188–200 that whenever their cherished 'art of living' would recommend non-conformist deeds, including deeds of piety, dogmatists refrain from endorsing this outcome. For the claim that Sextus' presentation is unreliable, see K. M. Vogt, *Law, Reason, and the Cosmic City: Political Philosophy in the Early Stoa* (Oxford, 2008), 34–40.

[34] The conformist reading might receive some support from the linguistic point that, according to Sextus' formulation, it is not Sceptics' position or procedure that is safeguarded, but rather Sceptics themselves are safer (ἀσφαλέστεροι). However, it is possible to read it as a somewhat clumsy formulation of the claim that, as a result of not committing themselves rashly, Sceptics will find *themselves* in a safer intellectual position.

As we shall see in the remaining sections, Sextus does make the case that the present pool of arguments on any given theological tenet leads to suspension of judgement.

A brief overview of Sextus' use of the adjective ἀσφαλής is consistent with this understanding, even if the evidence is hardly overwhelming. In his discussion of dogmatic claims, no technical sense emerges over and above a vague sense of safety from error (*M* 2. 52; 3. 1; 7. 151; 8. 374). On the few occasions that he employs it with reference to the Pyrrhonian position, it appears in conjunction with suspension of judgement. Pyrrhonians safely suspend judgement about sign-inference and about demonstration (*M* 8. 298, 300); in fact, recognizing that assent to the conclusion of the argument that there is no demonstration would be self-refuting, they give the safe answer by explaining that they do not form a dogmatic opinion in this respect either (*M* 8. 472–3).[35] None of this suggests that Sextus is driven by non-philosophical concerns.

In the religious context, however, he goes on to add a further point. Dogmatists not only make an intellectual mistake, endorsing the conclusion of arguments despite the availability of equally persuasive arguments to the contrary, but also insist on dragging us into their mistaken position. Their position, furthermore, involves rashly accepted views that go against the standards of piety recognized in their society. This is especially the case with regard to their claims concerning divine providence, which inescapably lead them to endorse impious claims.[36] In other words, if anyone should be afraid of disapproval, it is those who assent to such problematic claims, not those who suspend judgement and thereby avoid coming into conflict with ordinary cult.[37] In the following two sections,

---

[35] On the self-refutation argument, see M. L. McPherran, 'Skeptical Homeopathy and Self-Refutation', *Phronesis*, 32 (1987), 290–328; and L. Castagnoli, *Ancient Self-Refutation: The Logic and History of the Self-Refutation Argument from Democritus to Augustine* (Cambridge, 2010), 251–307.

[36] See discussion of [T9] below, as well as the transitional remark in *PH* 3. 13: 'Lest the dogmatists attempt to slander us because they are at a loss to produce substantive arguments against us, we shall raise more general puzzles about active causes…' (ἵνα δὲ μὴ καὶ ἡμᾶς βλασφημεῖν ἐπιχειρήσωσιν οἱ δογματικοὶ δι' ἀπορίαν τοῦ πραγματικῶς ἡμῖν ἀντιλέγειν, κοινότερον περὶ τοῦ ἐνεργητικοῦ αἰτίου διαπορήσομεν…).

[37] This might even serve as an advertisement for the Pyrrhonian position among those concerned with divine punishment: if you adopt this stance, you will not only avoid forming problematic beliefs but also conform to religious practice. Hence, when it comes to human or, possibly, divine punishment, Scepticism is the safest bet, though not of the Pascalian sort. (I thank Katja Vogt for pushing me on this.)

I shall show that a careful analysis of Sextus' arguments against dogmatic theology supports this general understanding.

3. The 'master argument' in *PH* 3. 3–12

The *PH* 3 chapter on theology breaks down into three parts, each offering its interim conclusion. Sextus considers, first, the way one might conceive of gods (3. 2–5), then proofs for their existence (3. 6–8), and finally the question whether they exercise providential care (3. 9–12). He argues that if one goes by what dogmatists have to say, one will have to come to conclusions that are invariably detrimental to the prospects of theology: that god cannot be conceived of (ἀνεννόητος, 3. 5), that it cannot be apprehended on the basis of a proof whether there is a god (ἀκατάληπτον ἔσται εἰ ἔστι θεός, 3. 9), and that a consideration of providence will also make it impossible to apprehend whether there is a god (καὶ διὰ ταῦτα ἄρα ἀκατάληπτόν ἐστιν εἰ ἔστι θεός, 3. 11).

Taken together, the three sub-arguments are meant collectively to establish that the presently available dogmatic arguments fail to bring about knowledge of the divine. The first and second argument jointly show, in the spirit of the Two Modes (*PH* 1. 178–9), that one can apprehend god neither in itself nor by way of a proof. The third argument elaborates on that conclusion by adding that one cannot learn of god through divine acts of providence and that no firm assertion about divine providence can be upheld. Sextus repeatedly insists, however, that these conclusions follow only insofar as the dogmatic arguments under discussion are concerned.[38] This is consistent with the caveat in [T1], as the rejection of firm assertions of natural philosophy still allows for the Sceptic's non-assertive utterances about divine providence.

Marchand, 'Piété', 109–17 argues that Sextus' objective is to distance the Pyrrhonian position from the seemingly similar stance of the Epicureans, claiming that Sceptics will be even safer than their Epicurean colleagues. On the Epicurean notion of 'safety' or ἀσφάλεια as connected to hiding one's true beliefs about the gods in order to avoid harm, see Obbink, *Philodemus*, 377–89, 491–7, 509–13, and 575–6.

[38] On the meaning of ὅσον ἐπὶ τῷ λόγῳ, ὅσον ἐπὶ τοῖς δογματικοῖς, and related expressions, see especially J. Brunschwig, 'The ὅσον ἐπὶ τῷ λόγῳ formula in Sextus Empiricus', in id. (ed.), *Papers in Hellenistic Philosophy* (Cambridge, 1994), 244–58, but cf. Janáček, *Methods*, 13–20 and Frede, 'Beliefs', 11–12.

3.1. *The concept of god* (*PH 3. 3–6*)

As a first step, Sextus will argue that no suggestion as to the correct conception of god has been successfully vindicated in the debate. His main strategy is to set out a case of disagreement among the relevant philosophical proposals in order to show that none of them is evidently the correct one. This conclusion in turn amounts to the refutation of a prominent strategy in Hellenistic philosophy, endorsed by Epicureans and to some extent Stoics, which aims to establish the universally shared preconception (πρόληψις) of god as the basis for infallible judgements concerning divine existence as well as the truth and falsity of further theological claims.

Sextus gets the argument going by claiming that dogmatic philosophers disagree over the proper way to conceive of god in three respects. Conceiving of something, he tells us, requires that we conceive of it as possessing a certain substance (οὐσία), a certain form (εἶδος), and a certain place (ποῦ). Unfortunately, dogmatists disagree about god on each count. As for divine substance, some say that god is of a corporeal nature, others that god is incorporeal; as for their outward shape, some take gods to be anthropomorphic, others not; and as for the divine whereabouts, some say that god does not occupy a place, while others maintain the opposite, but even those belonging in the latter group disagree whether the divinity resides within or outside the cosmos (*PH 3. 2–3*).[39]

In the dialectical situation envisaged by Sextus, dogmatic philosophers urge ordinary believers to take them up on their offer of a revised notion (ἔννοια) of god, claiming it to be rationally preferable to any other available conception. Given their disparate views on the subject, however, they cannot offer guidance as to the particular conception that is in fact superior to the alternatives, as a result of which one can only suspend one's judgement as far as the philosophical arguments are concerned:

---

[39] The list of headings under which Sextus subsumes the relevant cases of disagreement might reflect a specifically Sceptical concern for engineering disagreement among the dogmatists, perhaps on the basis of doxographical accounts pointing to issues on which accounts typically tend to diverge. Compare Cicero describing three questions about which 'not only the uneducated, but the educated disagree' (non solum indocti sed etiam docti dissentiunt, *ND* 1. 5): it is easy to match his 'regarding the form of the gods' (de figuris deorum) with εἶδος, and 'regarding their locations' (de locis) with ποῦ, but instead of οὐσία, he speaks 'about their conduct of life' (de actione vitae, 1. 2).

[T4] πῶς δυνησόμεθα ἔννοιαν θεοῦ λαμβάνειν μήτε οὐσίαν ἔχοντες αὐτοῦ ὁμολο-
γουμένην μήτε εἶδος μήτε τόπον ἐν ᾧ εἴη; πρότερον γὰρ ἐκεῖνοι ὁμολο-
γησάτωσάν τε καὶ συμφωνησάτωσαν, ὅτι τοιόσδε ἐστὶν ὁ θεός, εἶτα ἡμῖν
αὐτὸν ὑποτυπωσάμενοι οὕτως ἀξιούτωσαν ἡμᾶς ἔννοιαν θεοῦ λαμβάνειν. ἐς
ὅσον δὲ ἀνεπικρίτως διαφωνοῦσιν, τί νοήσομεν ἡμεῖς ὁμολογουμένως παρ'
αὐτῶν οὐκ ἔχομεν. (*PH* 3. 3)

How shall we be able to apprehend a conception of god if we possess
neither an agreed substance for god nor a form nor a place in which
god is? Let them first agree and form a consensus that god is of
such-and-such a kind; and only then, having given us an outline
account, let them require us to apprehend a conception of god. To
the extent that they remain in undecidable dispute, we have no
agreement from them as to what conception we should have.

At this point, Sextus introduces a possible dogmatic response.
According to an unnamed opponent, acknowledging that people
disagree endlessly about particular attributes of god does not hin-
der our access to a satisfactory notion of god. One could simply
skirt the controversy and focus on two essential characteristics that
everyone would agree belong to anything that is to count as a divine
entity:

[T5] ἀλλ' ἄφθαρτόν τι, φασί, καὶ μακάριον ἐννοήσας, τὸν θεὸν εἶναι τοῦτο νόμιζε.
(*PH* 3. 4)

But, they say, conceive of something indestructible and blessed, and
hold god to be that thing.

The proposed notion focuses on exactly the characteristics that
Epicurus was eager to attribute to a criterial notion of the divine.[40]
As Cicero reports in his *De Natura Deorum*, Epicurus introduced a
novel argument for the existence of god, namely, that every human
being with properly functioning mental faculties is in possession of
an innate preconception (πρόληψις, *notio*) of god as an indestructible and blessed living being.[41] Given further tenets of Epicurean
epistemology, the universal availability of this preconception is

[40] See *Ep. Men.* 123 = LS 23 B1: 'First, think of god as an imperishable and
blessed creature, as the common idea of god is in outline' (πρῶτον μὲν τὸν θεὸν ζῷον
ἄφθαρτον καὶ μακάριον νομίζων, ὡς ἡ κοινὴ τοῦ θεοῦ νόησις ὑπεγράφη); and *KD* 1 = LS
23 G: 'That which is blessed and imperishable neither suffers nor inflicts trouble'
(τὸ μακάριον καὶ ἄφθαρτον οὔτε αὐτὸ πράγματα ἔχει οὔτε ἄλλῳ παρέχει).

[41] It is true, as an anonymous reader suggests, that the *consensus omnium* argument already appears in Plato's *Laws*, 10. 886 A. However, the Epicurean claim
seems to point not only to common consensus but also to a sort of concept that

taken to guarantee not only that it is a correct description of the
divine but also that there is something in reality that corresponds
to it.[42] Importantly, the argument is introduced by Velleius, the
Epicurean interlocutor in Cicero's dialogue, in response to the endless disagreement dominating Greek theology prior to Epicurus'
arrival at this extraordinary insight.[43] Thus the dogmatic rejoinder
introduced in [T5] shows affinity with the Epicurean proposal in
terms of both content and dialectical setup.

The subsequent Epicurean move would be to secure agreement
on this minimal notion and argue that further views about the
divine are incompatible with it. Most notably, Epicureans would
claim that providential care cannot be reconciled with the perfect
life of leisure that the gods supposedly lead. It is at this point that
Stoics, who relied on a similar strategy, would disagree: their formulation of the notion of god insists not only on divine providence
($\pi\rho o\nu o\eta\tau\iota\kappa\grave{o}\nu$ $\kappa\acute{o}\sigma\mu o\upsilon$ $\tau\epsilon$ $\kappa\alpha\grave{\iota}$ $\tau\hat{\omega}\nu$ $\grave{\epsilon}\nu$ $\kappa\acute{o}\sigma\mu\omega$) but also on the rejection of
divine anthropomorphism ($\mu\grave{\eta}$ $\epsilon\hat{\iota}\nu\alpha\iota$ $\mu\acute{\epsilon}\nu\tau o\iota$ $\grave{\alpha}\nu\theta\rho\omega\pi\acute{o}\mu o\rho\phi o\nu$, D.L. 7. 147),

---

comes with an existential implication; at any rate, the Ciceronian report attributes
the alleged discovery to Epicurus.

[42] *ND* 1. 45 = LS 23 E3: '[we have such a preconception] that we think the gods
blessed and immortal. For as well as giving us a delineation of the gods themselves,
nature has also engraved on our minds the view of them as everlasting and blessed'
(... hanc igitur habemus, ut deos beatos et immortales putemus. quae enim nobis
natura informationem ipsorum deorum dedit, eadem insculpsit in mentibus ut eos
aeternos et beatos haberemus). Opinions concerning the Ciceronian testimony
diverge. Sedley, 'Innatism' defends its faithfulness to Epicurus' position, including
the existential implication, while V. Tsouna, 'Epicurean Preconceptions' ['Preconceptions'], *Phronesis*, 61 (2016), 160–221 at 174–85 takes it to be an elaboration
or 'free commentary' on it, perhaps attributable to later Epicureans. On common
consensus, see also D. Obbink, 'What All Men Believe Must Be True: Common
Conceptions and *consensio omnium* in Aristotle and Hellenistic Philosophy', *Oxford
Studies in Ancient Philosophy*, 10 (1992), 193–231, and G. Boys-Stones, 'Ancient
Philosophy of Religion: An Introduction', in G. Oppy and N. Trakakis (eds.), *The
History of Western Philosophy of Religion, vol. i: Ancient Philosophy of Religion*
(Durham, 2009), 1–22 at 6–13.

[43] Velleius spends nearly two-thirds of his exposition on doxography (Cicero,
ND 1. 18–42), only to summarize Epicurean theology in a considerably shorter and
rather more confusing span of passages (1. 43–56). According to R. McKirahan,
'Epicurean Doxography in Cicero, *De Natura Deorum* Book I', in G. Giannantoni
and M. Gigante (eds.), *Epicureismo greco e romano*, vol. ii (Naples, 1996), 865–78 at
867–8, this reflects Cicero's evaluation of Epicureanism as being unreasonably hos-
tile and uncharitable towards other philosophical options, 'marked by a tone of
smugness, intolerance and disrespect', giving the appearance of a school of thought
which is 'partisan, polemical and *prima facie* preposterous'.

another feature that was involved in the original controversy in [T4].[44]

Sextus is aware of these controversies, and he goes on to set out a further case of disagreement with regard to the question whether the blessed (τὸ μακάριον) would take care of the things subordinated to it or rather would renounce any other related activities (*PH* 3. 5).[45] At this point, having implicated the dogmatists in unresolved disagreement on two consecutive levels, he could move on to the next stage of his argument. Instead of doing so, however, he offers another objection to the [T5] proposal. He appeals to a methodological principle, in virtue of which any successful theological account would have to settle the question of divine substance before moving on to the question of divine attributes:

[T6] τοῦτο δέ ἐστιν εὔηθες· ὥσπερ <γὰρ> ὁ μὴ εἰδὼς τὸν Δίωνα οὐδὲ τὰ συμβεβηκότα αὐτῷ ὡς Δίωνι δύναται νοεῖν, οὕτως ἐπεὶ οὐκ ἴσμεν τὴν οὐσίαν τοῦ θεοῦ, οὐδὲ τὰ συμβεβηκότα αὐτῷ μαθεῖν τε καὶ ἐννοῆσαι δυνησόμεθα. (*PH* 3. 4)

But this is silly: just as, if you do not know Dio, you cannot think of his attributes as attributes of Dio, so, since we do not know the substance of god, we shall not be able to learn and to conceive of his attributes.

The problem with this rather interesting objection is that it is far from clear which, if any, dogmatic interlocutors would be committed to the principle on which it relies. A distant Platonic relative is familiar from Plato's *Meno*, where the question is raised of whether

[44] For the suggestion that Sextus in [T5] has the Stoics as well as the Epicureans in mind, see Annas and Barnes, *Outlines*, 144; Spinelli, 'Dieu', 96–7. A further possible objection against this attribution could come from the Stoics' unwillingness to label god imperishable (ἄφθαρτος). Long, 'Gods', 285–8 has argued, on the basis of Plutarch's report in *De stoicorum repugnantiis*, 1051 F–1052 A, that indestructibility would not belong to the criterial notion of the divine, as only Zeus can be correctly described as indestructible, while other divine entities are subject to the conflagration. This proposal has been rejected by K. Algra, 'Eternity and the Concept of God in Early Stoicism', in C. G. Steel, G. van Riel, C. Macé, and L. van Campe (eds.), *Platonic Ideas and Concept Formation in Ancient and Medieval Thought* (Leuven, 2004), 173–90 at 179–85, who argues that one should not mistake Plutarch's polemical inference for the actual Stoic account. See also D. L. 7. 134, where god as the active principle (τὸ ποιοῦν) is described not only as the everlasting demiurge (ἀίδιον ὄντα διὰ πάσης αὐτῆς δημιουργεῖν ἕκαστα) but also as being without generation and destruction (ἀγενήτους καὶ ἀφθάρτους). See also Hankinson, *The Sceptics*, 218.

[45] It is puzzling that he does not make a similar move concerning indestructibility, since he has at his disposal Carneadean material for the conclusion that the possibility of divine disintegration follows from various dogmatic tenets (*M* 9. 139–80).

one can know what a thing is like without first coming to know what it is (ὃ δὲ μὴ οἶδα τί ἐστιν, πῶς ἂν ὁποῖόν γέ τι εἰδείην, 71 B 3–4).[46] Irrespective of whether the Platonic Socrates is ultimately committed to this nonchalantly introduced principle of inquiry, it seems to have become a preoccupation of Hellenistic epistemologists to provide an account that successfully answers to it.[47] The comparison throws light, however, on an important difference. In the course of a few paragraphs, Sextus employed the term *ousia* in two different senses. In [T4], where corporeal and incorporeal conceptions of god were concerned, he used it in the sense of underlying matter, while here in [T6] it refers to the definitional essence, the 'what it is' of the thing under investigation. Hence even a successful case of disagreement about the former might not warrant the claim that we have no access to the definitional essence sought in the latter. Sextus could perhaps reply that the question of corporeality is relevant for the definitional question, and it will have to feature in the correct differentia of god; yet the connection is not entirely obvious, and even if he does not viciously conflate the two senses, the flow of his argument is less continuous than would be desirable.

Alternatively, one could resort to the idea that the main target of Sextus' discussion is some version of the Epicurean position. He does regularly attribute a similar tenet to Epicurus, namely, that philosophical inquiry must begin from a properly fixed conception of the thing investigated, since it is impossible to investigate or to raise difficulties without a preconception already in place (οὔτε ζητεῖν ἔστιν οὔτε ἀπορεῖν ἄνευ προλήψεως, *M* 11. 21).[48] It is possible

---

[46] D. T. Runia, 'The Beginnings of the End: Philo of Alexandria and Hellenistic Theology', in D. Frede and A. Laks (eds.), *Traditions of Theology: Studies in Hellenistic Theology, its Background and Aftermath* (Leiden, 2002), 281–316 at 281 points to a similar passage in Aristotle, *Posterior Analytics* 2. 1, 89ᵇ34–5: 'And knowing that it is, we seek what it is, such as "what is a god?", or "what is a man?"' (γνόντες δὲ ὅτι ἔστι, τί ἐστι ζητοῦμεν, οἷον τί οὖν ἐστι θεός, ἢ τί ἐστιν ἄνθρωπος). This, however, lays out a different argumentative strategy: starting out from a confident belief that something exists, one inquires into its proper definitional essence. For a reading that brings Aristotle's account of inquiry in line with the *Meno* claim, see D. Bronstein, *Aristotle on Knowledge and Learning* (Oxford, 2016), esp. 74–130.

[47] As shown convincingly by G. Fine, *The Possibility of Inquiry: Meno's Paradox from Socrates to Sextus* (Oxford, 2014), Peripatetics, Stoics, and Epicureans consciously responded to the *Meno*'s paradox of inquiry. Besides Sextus, see the evidence of Plutarch fr. 215c–f Sandbach.

[48] See also *M* 1. 57; 2. 1; 8. 300–1, 337–6a; 9. 12; 10. 6; cf. *PH* 2. 228.

that Sextus dialectically appropriates this principle in order to show that Epicureans wishing to bypass theological disagreement by the [T5] move disregard their own methodological strictures. If indeed he is pitting an Epicurean assumption against Epicurus, then the worry concerning the discontinuity of Sextus' argument is removed at the price of raising the question whether one can conflate the notion of *ousia* in the sense of definitional essence with that of Epicurean *prolēpsis*.[49]

3.2. *Existential arguments (*PH *3. 6–9)*

In the next section, Sextus argues that any putative proof of divine existence is bound to fail. Somewhat surprisingly, he makes no mention here of the widespread disagreement between theists and atheists.[50] Rather, he connects the need for proof with the outcome of the conceptual section: given the epistemic predicament that results from considering the available philosophical arguments, the existence of the divine appears non-evident and in need of a proof (ἄδηλον ἡμῖν εἶναι δοκεῖν καὶ ἀποδείξεως δεόμενον, *PH* 3. 6). As it turns out, however, no successful proof of divine existence is available.

[49] It is possible that Sextus applies an argument form that works better elsewhere. Compare his counter-argument to the definition of things good, bad, and indifferent by nature (*PH* 3. 169–78, *M* 11. 21–41, cf. *PH* 3. 169–78), the very context in which the Epicurean principle quoted above is introduced. The discussion starts from dogmatic disagreement (11. 31–4), which would not obtain if a successful account of natural value were available. In response, dogmatists argue for an underlying agreement concerning attributes of the good, say, that it is what is choiceworthy or what benefits. Sextus has none of it, as these specify not the good itself but rather its attributes, and there is endless disagreement about what these attributes pick out (11. 35–9; similarly with bad being what harms, 40–1). On this argument, see R. Bett, *Sextus Empiricus, Against the Ethicists* (Oxford, 1997), 77–9 with Appendix A.

[50] He does employ the oppositional method in *M* 9. 50–191 which, as Algra and Ierodiakonou, 'Introduction', 19 point out, is the only neat application of that method in *M* 9. In this lengthy section, Sextus makes use of a rich collection of doxographical material to show that the case for and against has been made with equal persuasive force, so that one should not rashly commit oneself to either view (*M* 9. 50, 59). On these passages, see C. Vick, 'Karneades' Kritik der Theologie bei Cicero und Sextus Empiricus', *Hermes*, 37 (1902), 228–48; P. Couissin, 'Les sorites de Carnéade contre le polythéisme', *Revue des Études Grecques*, 54 (1941), 43–57; M. F. Burnyeat, 'Gods and Heaps', in M. Schofield and M. C. Nussbaum (eds.), *Language and Logos: Studies in Ancient Greek Philosophy Presented to G.E.L. Owen* (Cambridge, 1982), 315–38; Long, 'Gods'; J. Warren, 'What God Didn't Know: Sextus Empiricus *AM* 9. 162–6', in D. E. Machuca (ed.), *New Essays on Ancient Pyrrhonism* (Leiden/Boston, 2011), 126–41; and D. Sedley, 'Carneades'.

One question concerns the relationship between the two interim conclusions. On the most straightforward reading, Sextus is building a cumulative case against dogmatic theology along a Gorgianic structure, making two distinct cases for suspension of judgement: one cannot come to a resolution about the conception of god, but even if one could, one would still have to refrain from any view concerning divine existence. Alternatively, one could think that Sextus does not object to forming a conception of god insofar as one does so without passing judgement on whether anything corresponds to that conception in reality.[51] That would amount to the rejection of the existential implication of having a concept, very much along the lines of the transition from conception (ἐπίνοια) to existence (ὕπαρξις) in *M* 9. 49 (right before [T2]).[52]

Furthermore, Sextus' argument against the possibility of proving god's existence presupposes a peculiar theory of proof. A crucial

---

[51] These two interpretations correspond to slightly different readings of the transitional remark in *PH* 3. 6: ἵνα δὲ καὶ ἐπινοῆται ὁ θεός, ἐπέχειν ἀνάγκη περὶ τοῦ πότερον ἔστιν ἢ οὐκ ἔστιν, ὅσον ἐπὶ τοῖς δογματικοῖς. It is more natural to read the Greek as a purpose clause, even if its meaning is philosophically awkward: the claim would then be that, *in order to* form a conception of god, one must first suspend judgement about god's existence; cf. the renderings of R. G. Bury, *Sextus Empiricus, Outlines of Pyrrhonism* (Cambridge, MA/London, 1933); J. Grenier and G. Goron, *Œuvres choisies de Sextus Empiricus: Contre les physiciens; Contre les moralistes; Hypotyposes pyrrhoniennes* (Paris, 1948); M. Hossenfelder, *Sextus Empiricus, Grundriß der pyrrhonischen Skepsis* (Frankfurt a.M., 1968). On the second, more plausible reading, one takes notice of the καί and effectively substitutes ἐάν for ἵνα: *even if* god were conceivable, one would still have to suspend judgement about god's existence: see Annas and Barnes, *Outlines*; P. Pellegrin, *Sextus Empiricus, Esquisses pyrrhoniennes* (Paris, 1997). A third possibility was suggested to me by Charles Brittain. One could emend ἐπέχειν to ἐπικρίνειν and translate: 'In order to conceive of god, it is necessary to come to a judgement about whether or not god exists, as far as the dogmatists are concerned.' Thus the *PH* 3 discussion acquires structural unity: we are considering god as an active cause, and only an existing god can have causal effects by which one could come to know of it, hence one has to judge that god exists before arguing for a particular conception (which does not mean that one has to *argue* that god exists, only that one has to endorse divine existence). Unfortunately, this reading has no basis in the MSS, nor is it supported by the Latin tradition; thus one would have to assume an error in the archetype of our transmitted text. I thank Roland Wittwer for discussion on this point.

[52] But cf. M. Schofield, 'Preconception, Argument, and God', in Schofield, Burnyeat, and Barnes (eds.), *Doubt and Dogmatism*, 283–308 at 289–305 on Sextus' alleged 'epistemological confusion' as to whether a preconception comes with an existential implication. Compare also Cotta's attack on Stoic theology, separating conceptual and existential issues without any obvious analogue in Balbus' exposition (*ND* 3. 17 with M. Dragona-Monachou, *The Stoic Arguments for the Existence and Providence of the Gods* [*Arguments*] (Athens, 1976), 72).

assumption of this theory is that what is proved is conceived of in relation to what proves (τὸ ἀποδεικνυόμενον πρὸς τῷ ἀποδεικνύντι νοεῖται), so much so that the two are apprehended together (συγκαταλαμβάνω, *PH* 3. 7). In effect, this amounts to saying that the two have the same epistemic status as a result of being apprehended simultaneously and with the same sort of cognitive grasp. Furthermore, Sextus takes it to be the case that the premisses of a proof are either pre-evident (πρόδηλος) or non-evident (ἄδηλος), the distinction being exclusive and exhaustive.[53] Given these two features of proof—that is, the distinction between evident and non-evident premisses and the principle of co-apprehension—Sextus can reject the possibility of proof in a few simple steps. On this view, evident premisses will have to lead to an evident conclusion, while non-evident premisses will be conjoined with a non-evident conclusion. Since an evident conclusion is ruled out from the start, the remaining option is to claim that divine existence is proved by something non-evident, in which case the alleged proof is no proof at all. At this point, one must either give up or fall into infinite regress (*PH* 3. 7–8).

In other words, a successful proof is taken by Sextus to be such that a mere perusal of the available evidence would give us an evident conclusion, about which no further reasonable disagreement would be possible. This might strike his reader as highly implausible, in response to which Sextus will support his exposé by referring the reader to his previous examination of dogmatic theories of proof (ἀπόδειξις). In that context, Sextus has argued that dogmatists have failed to provide a coherent and convincing account of proof.[54] The reason for this is that they conceive of proof as a kind of sign (σημεῖον), namely, as an indicative (ἐνδεικτικόν) sign, which concludes to something by nature (φύσει) non-evident by way of something pre-evident. Hence the notion of proof inherits various difficulties associated with the account of sign-inference: it requires

[53] On the dogmatic distinction between evident and non-evident, see *PH* 2. 97–9, *M* 8. 144–7. Sextus relies on this distinction only dialectically; see J. Allen, *Inference from Signs: Ancient Debates about the Nature of Evidence* (Oxford, 2001), 87–9, 97–106.

[54] See *PH* 2. 134–92 (esp. 134–43) and *M* 8. 300–481 (esp. 300–15, 411–23). For analysis, see J. Brunschwig, 'Proof Defined', in Schofield, Burnyeat, and Barnes (eds.), *Doubt and Dogmatism*, 125–60, with J. Barnes, 'Proof Destroyed', in Schofield, Burnyeat, and Barnes (eds.), *Doubt and Dogmatism*, 161–81 at 173–81, who argues that Sextus exposes a real problem in the Stoic theory.

a case of asymmetry where the facts, it seems, can only ever be symmetrical.[55]

As his conclusion indicates, Sextus takes himself at this point to have covered both possible strategies of recognizing divine existence, that of self-evidence and that of proof:

[T7]   οὐκ ἄρα ἐξ ἑτέρου δύναται ἀποδείκνυσθαι τὸ εἶναι θεόν. εἰ δὲ μήτε ἐξ ἑαυτοῦ ἐστι πρόδηλον μήτε ἐξ ἑτέρου ἀποδείκνυται, ἀκατάληπτον ἔσται εἰ ἔστι θεός. (*PH* 3. 8–9)

The existence of a god, therefore, cannot be proved from anything else. But if it is neither pre-evident from itself nor proved from something else, then it will be inapprehensible whether or not there is a god.

3.3. *Providential arguments (PH 3. 9–12)*

Having arrived at the assessment that dogmatic accounts of the conception and the existence of god lead to suspension of judgement, Sextus could easily draw the *PH* 3 discussion to a close. Instead of doing so, he indicates that claims about divine existence are as a rule accompanied by affirmative or negative claims about divine providence, hence a Sceptic should devote some attention to the latter as well. In the course of this final section, he considers all three logical possibilities concerning god's providence, namely, that it provides for everything, or for some things, or for nothing at all, only to find them all unacceptable.[56]

He formulates the point in terms of two divine characteristics: god's will (βούλησις) and power (δύναμις) to provide. Four possible combinations arise, the first of which is that god is both willing and

---

[55] A sign is conceived of in relation to what it signifies (*PH* 2. 165, 175, 179; and *M* 8. 335, 387, 462), hence the two are co-apprehended (*PH* 2. 116–20, 125; *M* 8. 165–6, 168–70, 174–5; see also 'argument' at *PH* 2. 169 and 'proof' at *PH* 2. 179, cf. *M* 8. 394). However, the sign is also revelatory of what it signifies, with the implication that the one is apprehended before the other. On sign and proof in Sextus and Stoicism, see Allen, *Inference*, 87–146 and 170–84. M. Duncombe, 'Relativity against Dogmatism in Sextus Empiricus', in id. *Ancient Relativity: Plato, Aristotle, Stoics, and Sceptics* (Oxford, 2020), 226–45, argues that, on the view operative in Sextus' discussion, one cannot conceive of a relative without conceiving of its correlative, the two being separate entities. Furthermore, Sextus takes this to imply that knowing one implies knowing the other (epistemic symmetry) and that one exists only when the other exists (existential symmetry).

[56] For the sake of convenience, I use the verb 'provide' as a shorthand for 'to exercise providential care'. This is a somewhat archaic but correct use of the English term.

able to provide for everything in the cosmos. If this were the case, Sextus adds, there would be no evil in the world; yet they say that everything is full of evil, and hence they cannot maintain that god exercises universal providence (ἀλλ' εἰ μὲν πάντων προυνόει, οὐκ ἦν ἄν ... οὔτε κακία ἐν τῷ κόσμῳ· κακίας δὲ πάντα μεστὰ εἶναι λέγουσιν· οὐκ ἄρα πάντων προνοεῖν λεχθήσεται ὁ θεός, *PH* 3. 9–10). Sextus' argument is not as strong as it might initially seem. In order to avoid the conflict, one could just as well renounce the rather strong claim that everything is full of evil, or qualify it by providing an explanation of the presence of evil that is compatible with divine providence.

The creationist cosmology proposed in Plato's *Timaeus* might offer two plausible lines of defence. On the one hand, one could argue that the inherent properties of matter set a boundary on what the demiurge can achieve (48 A, 75 A–B), which is compatible with the claim that the demiurge brings about the best possible configuration. On the other hand, the demiurge might not be responsible for the shortcomings of creation, since they have quite conscientiously given over various tasks to the lesser gods with a view to the betterment of the whole (41 A ff.). Furthermore, one might be committed to the further claim that the presence of evil is either necessary or the result of subpar human activities.[57] By contrast, the claim that everything is full of evil is reminiscent of an Epicurean assessment of the state of the world, amounting to a criticism of creationist cosmologies.[58]

At any rate, we are left with three further options: a deficit either of divine will, or of divine power, or of both. Sextus makes short shrift of all three suggestions:

[T8] εἰ δὲ βούλεται μέν, οὐ δύναται δέ, ἀσθενέστερός ἐστι τῆς αἰτίας δι' ἣν οὐ δύναται προνοεῖν ὧν οὐ προνοεῖ· ἔστι δὲ παρὰ τὴν θεοῦ ἐπίνοιαν τὸ ἀσθενέστερον εἶναί τινος αὐτόν. εἰ δὲ δύναται μὲν πάντων προνοεῖν, οὐ βούλεται δέ, βάσκανος ἂν εἶναι νομισθείη. εἰ δὲ οὔτε βούλεται οὔτε δύναται, καὶ βάσκανός ἐστι καὶ ἀσθενής, ὅπερ λέγειν περὶ θεοῦ ἀσεβούντων ἐστίν. (*PH* 3. 10–11)

---

[57] On the necessity of evil, see Gellius 7. 1. 1–13 = *SVF* 2. 1169–70, going back to Plato, *Theaetetus* 176 A. On the bad human soul, cf. *Timaeus* 42 D–E; *Laws* 10. 896 C–897 B. See also the third theological pattern (τύπος) in *Republic* 2, 379 C 2–7, and the rejection of divine responsibility for suffering due to human decisions in the myth of Er (10, 617 E).

[58] See especially Lucretius, *DRN* 2. 167–81; 5. 187–234. On the Stoics as the intended target of Sextus' argument, see Annas and Barnes, '*Outlines*', 145 n. 15; Spinelli, 'Dieu', 100 n. 36.

If it wants to but cannot, it is weaker than the cause in virtue of which it cannot provide for the things for which it does not provide; but it is contrary to the concept of god that a god should be weaker than anything.[59] If it can provide for all but does not want to, it will be thought to be malign. If it neither wants to nor can, it is both malign and weak—and only the impious would say this about god.

The only remaining option, then, is to maintain that god does not provide for anything. Importantly, this is not the preferred conclusion of the argument; rather, Sextus rejects this as being an impious proposition. Readers who fail to recognize that the actual conclusion of the argument is that none of the possible stances on providence is acceptable go on to claim rather quickly that Sextus takes over an Epicurean argument lock, stock, and barrel. However, even if there were an Epicurean blueprint for the previous stages of the providential discussion, it is clearly abandoned by the point where Sextus states his conclusion, which would be unacceptable for Epicurus.[60]

Sextus' remark that the denial of providence constitutes impiety might indicate unease at being unable to refute the Epicurean position convincingly. In response, Epicurus would simply reject the impiety charge on the basis of his reinterpretation of piety, insisting that it is impious to attach properties to the notion of god that are incompatible with its essence as stated in [T5], the most notable instance being the attribution of providential activity to god.[61]

---

[59] Cf. *M* 9. 44: god, besides being imperishable and blessed, is also said to possess the most power in the world (πλείστην δύναμιν ἐν τῷ κόσμῳ). Sextus' response might perhaps have something to do with understanding god as an active cause, that is, as bringing about change unimpeded by other factors that enter a causal explanation.

[60] This is missed by Ziemińska, 'Case', 153–4; Hankinson, *The Sceptics*, 214, who claims that 'Sextus' argument does not touch the disengaged divinities of Aristotle or the Epicureans'; and partly by E. Spinelli, 'Senza teodicea: critiche epicuree e argomentazioni pirroniane', in D. De Sanctis, E. Spinelli, M. Tulli, and F. Verde (eds.), *Questioni epicuree* (Sankt Augustin, 2015), 213–34 at 225–8, who speaks of a 'Santa Alleanza' between Epicurean anti-providentialism and Pyrrhonian anti-dogmatism, though he corrects himself in 226 n. 56. No version of the argument is found in the extant Epicurus, but Lactantius attributes to him an argument in this spirit (*De ira Dei* 13. 19–22). For discussion, see T. O'Keefe, *Epicureanism* (Durham, 2010), 48. Sextus is aware that Epicurus denied providence (*PH* 1. 155; 3. 219) and reports allegations of Epicurus' atheism (*M* 9. 58).

[61] Epicurus, *Ep. Men.* 123–4 = LS 23 B3: 'The impious man is not he who denies the gods of the many, but he who attaches to gods the beliefs of the many about them' (ἀσεβὴς δὲ οὐχ ὁ τοὺς τῶν πολλῶν θεοὺς ἀναιρῶν, ἀλλ' ὁ τὰς τῶν πολλῶν δόξας θεοῖς

In an attempt to strengthen his hand, Sextus ties the discussion back to the question of apprehending the existence of god:

[T9] οὐκ ἄρα προνοεῖ τῶν ἐν κόσμῳ ὁ θεός. εἰ δὲ οὐδενὸς πρόνοιαν ποιεῖται οὐδὲ ἔστιν αὐτοῦ ἔργον οὐδὲ ἀποτέλεσμα, οὐχ ἕξει τις εἰπεῖν, πόθεν καταλαμβάνεται ὅτι ἔστι θεός, εἴγε μήτε ἐξ ἑαυτοῦ φαίνεται μήτε δι' ἀποτελεσμάτων τινῶν καταλαμβάνεται. καὶ διὰ ταῦτα ἄρα ἀκατάληπτόν ἐστιν εἰ ἔστι θεός. (*PH* 3. 11)

God, therefore, does not provide for the things in the world. But if god provides for nothing and has no function and no effect, we will not be able to say how it is apprehended that there is a god, since it is neither apparent from itself nor apprehended by way of any effects. For this reason too, then, it is inapprehensible whether there is a god.

As it happens, Epicureans would have an answer to this objection, too. As Sextus is well aware, thinkers in the atomist tradition formulated a theory of divine images (εἴδωλα or *simulacra*, *M* 9. 19, 25, 42–3), claiming that humans come to know of gods due to the images that the gods emit as a matter of physical regularity. Alternatively, some readers suggest that the Epicurean knowledge of the divine is grounded in the innate preconception that all human beings possess.[62] On either interpretation, it simply does not follow that the lack of providential activity rules out apprehension of the existence of god.

In addition, one might find it rather puzzling that, according to Sextus, all pronouncements on divine providence are unacceptable. This outcome is especially problematic in light of his claim in [T1] that Sceptics will say that gods exist and that they are provident.[63] Rather than disallowing any and every possible take on this question, Sextus could have appealed to opposing views concerning providence, as he does at *PH* 1. 151, and claim only to suspend judgement on the matter. One might think that he backed himself into a corner by choosing to work with the actual *PH* 3 argument instead.[64]

προσάπτων. οὐ γὰρ προλήψεις εἰσὶν ἀλλ' ὑπολήψεις ψευδεῖς αἱ τῶν πολλῶν ὑπὲρ θεῶν ἀποφάσεις).

[62] For a defence of this view, see Sedley, 'Innatism'. See also my Section 4.

[63] Providence is not mentioned in [T2], as there is no corresponding discussion in *M* 9. Sextus' aim is not to provide a definitive list of utterances acceptable for a Pyrrhonian, but rather to insist that his arguments against dogmatic views do not result in a definite denial of the relevant claims about god.

[64] Bett, 'Sextus', 175 tries to save Sextus from embarrassment by claiming that either he aims at dogmatic self-refutation, which in itself does not explain away the

In order to see one's way out, one has to pay attention to the terminology used by Sextus. He finds fault only with those statements that are made 'affirmatively' (διαβεβαιωτικῶς)—that is, with the aim of establishing something as true. By contrast, the Sceptic's utterances are made in the characteristically Sceptical manner of non-assertion: they report on how things appear to the Sceptic without taking a stand on what is true or rational to believe.[65] Since the Sceptic's utterance does not aim at establishing the relevant claim as true, it does not actually come into conflict with the outcome of the philosophical discussion. It is in this spirit that Sextus concludes his *PH* 3 treatment of theology:

[T10] ἐκ δὲ τούτων ἐπιλογιζόμεθα, ὅτι ἴσως ἀσεβεῖν ἀναγκάζονται οἱ διαβεβαιωτικῶς λέγοντες εἶναι θεόν· πάντων μὲν γὰρ αὐτὸν προνοεῖν λέγοντες κακῶν αἴτιον τὸν θεὸν εἶναι φήσουσιν, τινῶν δὲ ἢ καὶ μηδενὸς προνοεῖν αὐτὸν λέγοντες ἤτοι βάσκανον τὸν θεὸν ἢ ἀσθενῆ λέγειν ἀναγκασθήσονται, ταῦτα δέ ἐστιν ἀσεβούντων προδήλως. (*PH* 3. 12)

From this we deduce that those who firmly state that there is a god are bound to be impious: if they say that god provides for everything, they will say that god is a cause of evil; and if they say that god provides for some things or even for none at all, they will be bound to say either that god is malign or that god is weak—and clearly anyone who says this is impious.

4. Religious aetiology in *M* 9. 14–48

At the outset of the *M* 9 discussion of theology, Sextus declares his intention to work his way through the difficulties (διαπορῶμεν) concerning active and passive principles in two consecutive steps (*M* 9. 12). First, he will make the case that the arguments for and against the existence of god, understood as an active cause, balance each other out (9. 50–193). Second, he will present arguments for the non-existence of active and passive principles in general (9. 195–330).

tension with [T1], or provides one pair of a set of oppositions, where the opposing claim—that there is providence—would be included in both sides.

[65] This is Sextus' interpretation of the old Pyrrhonian claim to speechlessness (ἀφασία, see *PH* 1. 192–3). On the development of this idea from Pyrrho's falling silent to Sextus' manner of speaking without dogmatic commitments, see J. Brunschwig, 'L'aphasie pyrrhonienne', in C. Lévy and L. Pernot (eds.), *Dire l'évidence: Philosophie et rhétorique antiques* (Paris, 1997), 297–320. Vogt, *Lebenspraxis*, 97 points out that the Sceptic's utterance is parasitic on the non-Sceptical use of language.

He describes the former section as inquiry of a 'more dogmatic' or 'quasi-dogmatic' nature (σκεπτόμενοι ... οἷον δογματικῶς), in contrast to the latter, which he labels 'more aporetic in spirit' (ἀπορητικώτερον, *M* 9. 12). Given that 'aporetic' is an acceptable designation for the Sceptic (*PH* 1. 7), while 'dogmatic' functions as its antonym, the description has understandably puzzled some interpreters.[66]

However, a brief consideration of Sextus' authorial method and his use of the relevant terms elsewhere sheds light on the probable meaning of these qualifications. In order to bring his interlocutor to suspend judgement on a given matter of inquiry, Sextus will either point out that the dogmatists themselves have made the case on both sides with equal persuasive force, or he will resort to arguments developed by earlier Sceptical thinkers in order to counterbalance a given dogmatic proposal. A programmatic statement of this method figures in his discussion of the criterion, where Sextus indicates that he will first look at the various dogmatic accounts of the criterion and only then will see whether anything corresponds to them in reality.[67]

The clearest example of this distinction appears in Sextus' discussion of dogmatic musicology, where he claims that one can argue for suspension of judgement using either 'more dogmatic' or 'aporetic' arguments. In the former case, he uses Epicurean arguments for the uselessness of musical knowledge as a counterweight to the mainstream view that said knowledge is useful in one's

---

[66] Bett, 'Gods', 41 writes that ' "*inquiring*... sort of dogmatically" has the feel of an oxymoron'; see also R. Bett, 'La double "schizophrénie" d'*Adversus Mathematicos* I–VI, et son origine historique', in J. Delattre (ed.), *Sur le Contre les professeurs de Sextus Empiricus* (Lille, 2006), 17–34, and R. Bett, 'A Sceptic Looks at Art (But Not Very Closely): Sextus Empiricus on Music', *International Journal for the Study of Skepticism*, 3 (2013), 155–81 at 162–3 with n. 11. M. J. White, 'Cause: *M* 9. 195–330', in K. Algra and K. Ierodiakonou (eds.), *Sextus Empiricus and Ancient Physics*, *Proceedings of the 2007 Symposium Hellenisticum* (Cambridge, 2015), 74–104 at 76 rightly points out that the aporetic section 'will have wider and deeper sceptical implications concerning causation, in general—not just the sort of active causal principle represented by god or the deities', but that is not in itself a satisfactory explanation of the contrast.

[67] *M* 7. 28; cf. 7. 1. On this passage, see J. Brunschwig, 'Sextus Empiricus on the κριτήριον: The Sceptic as Conceptual Legatee', in id. (ed.), *Papers in Hellenistic Philosophy* (Cambridge, 1994), 230–43 at 232–3, cf. F. Grgić, 'Sextus Empiricus on the Possibility of Inquiry', *Pacific Philosophical Quarterly*, 89 (2008), 436–59 at 442. On the two kinds of argumentation, see Algra and Ierodiakonou, 'Introduction', 22–5, esp. 23 n. 55.

search for wisdom. In the latter case, he employs arguments to the effect that nothing real corresponds to the core notions of dogmatic musicology (6. 4–5).[68] If one reads Sextus' remarks along these lines, it becomes clear that the section on god is 'quasi-dogmatic' in the sense that it uses theological arguments of dogmatic origin for a specifically Sceptical purpose.

The material concerning divine existence probably derives, at least in part, from an Academic source, as a later reference to Clitomachus indicates (*M* 9. 182).[69] This is consistent not only with Sextus' view of Academics as unwilling dogmatists, but also with his methodological remarks in the beginning of the treatise. According to Sextus, Clitomachus and the 'rest of the Academic chorus' (οἱ περὶ τὸν Κλειτόμαχον καὶ ὁ λοιπὸς τῶν Ἀκαδημαϊκῶν χορός) have made dangerous concessions to the views of their interlocutors and have thereby acquired dogmatic opinions.[70] By contrast, he takes the aporetic method of doing away with (ἀναιρεῖν) the very foundations of dogmatic theology to be strongly preferable (9. 1–2, cf. *PH* 3. 1), a claim which does not stop him from recounting the Academic arguments in detail.

The discussion is prefaced, however, by a section on the origin of the concept of god (*M* 9. 14–48), which argues that none of the available accounts of the emergence of the concept of god succeeds at the task. Despite the fact that Sextus' somewhat clumsy introduction does not explicitly say so, this section probably exemplifies the 'quasi-dogmatic' investigation as well. To begin with, it offers a survey of some ten historical proposals concerning the origin of the concept of god, ranging from Presocratic theories to those put forward by recent Stoics (9. 14–28). Furthermore, the refutation of these aetiological accounts derives from a dogmatic, and likely

---

[68] In *M* 6. 4, he refers back to a similar distinction between arguments against grammar. The proem to *M* 1–6 situates his procedure in the background of a wider contrast between Epicurean and Pyrrhonian approaches to the liberal arts (*M* 1. 1–7).

[69] M. Schofield, 'Aenesidemus: Pyrrhonist and Heraclitean', in A. M. Ioppolo and D. Sedley (eds.), *Pyrrhonists, Patricians, Platonizers. Hellenistic Philosophy in the Period 155–86 BC*, Tenth Symposium Hellenisticum (Naples, 2007), 269–338 at 289; Algra and Ierodiakonou, 'Introduction', 12–13, 30.

[70] Sextus refers to such a dialectical concession with the term συγχώρησις (cf. *PH* 1. 168, 173 on arguing κατὰ συγχώρησιν). His point might go back to Aenesidemus, who made similar accusations against his erstwhile Academic colleagues, using the verb συμφέρεσθαι to describe their mistake (Photius, *Bibl.* 212, 169^b36–170^a17). On the dogmatism of the Academics, see also *PH* 1. 3, 229–30.

Epicurean, context, where they were used to establish the natural origin of the concept of god.

Sextus formulates two types of refutations. On the one hand, he indicates that the availability of different explanations in itself indicates that one should suspend judgement about the truth of each and every one of them.[71] On the other hand, he nevertheless offers individual refutations, many of which amount to saying that the alleged answer merely pushes the question back a step. For example, those who argue that a select group of individuals deceived the rest of humanity into believing in gods have to answer how the deceivers themselves have acquired the concept in the first place. Similarly, those who propose that kings or heroes were treated as gods by their fellow humans still have to explain where the concept of a god came from; and those who argue that dream-images were mistaken for divine apparitions have to explain why these were not taken to be apparitions of extraordinary human beings, rather than of gods (*M* 9. 30–1, 34).

In a further twist, Sextus includes an appeal to the fundamental conceptual unity that underlies religious diversity around the world. Proponents of the theory that belief in gods was instigated by deceitful masterminds might try to argue that various nations and communities distant in place and time happened to have their own lawgivers and inventors initiating their very own religious traditions (9. 32). In response to this proposal, Sextus points to the alleged homogeneity of all religious conceptions:

[T11] ὅπερ ἐστὶν εὔηθες· κοινὴν γὰρ πάλιν πρόληψιν ἔχουσι πάντες ἄνθρωποι περὶ θεοῦ, καθ' ἣν μακάριόν τί ἐστι ζῷον καὶ ἄφθαρτον καὶ τέλειον ἐν εὐδαιμονίᾳ καὶ παντὸς κακοῦ ἀνεπίδεκτον, τελέως δέ ἐστιν ἄλογον τὸ κατὰ τύχην πάντας τοῖς αὐτοῖς ἐπιβάλλειν ἰδιώμασιν, ἀλλὰ μὴ φυσικῶς οὕτως ἐκκινεῖσθαι. (*M* 9. 33)

---

[71] *M* 9. 29: 'But we do not think they need counterargument; for the variety of their assertions puts a seal on their ignorance of the entire truth—while there can be many ways of conceiving god, the one among them that is true is not apprehended.' (οὐκ οἰόμεθα δὲ αὐτὰ χρείαν ἔχειν ἀντιρρήσεως· τὸ γὰρ πολύτροπον τῆς ἀποφάσεως τὴν ἀγνωσίαν τοῦ παντὸς ἀληθοῦς ἐπισφραγίζεται, πολλῶν μὲν δυναμένων εἶναι τρόπων τῆς τοῦ θεοῦ νοήσεως, τοῦ δὲ ἐν αὐτοῖς ἀληθοῦς μὴ καταλαμβανομένου.) According to J. Barnes, 'Pyrrhonism, Belief, and Causation', in H. Temporini and W. Haase (eds.), *Aufstieg und Niedergang der Römischen Welt* II. 36. 4 (Berlin, 1990), 2608–95 at 2666, this is a possible jibe at the Epicurean theory of multiple explanations. This is an attractive proposal. However, I suggest below that the relevant accounts might be those that an Epicurean *rejects*. At any rate, a simple Sceptical reading on which disagreement indicates the lack of apprehension is sufficient in the present context.

This is silly; for all humans, on the contrary, have a common preconception about god, according to which god is a blessed and imperishable animal, perfect in happiness and not receptive of anything bad,
and it is completely unreasonable that everyone intuited the same
peculiarities at random, and were not incited in this way naturally.

At first sight, this argument is rather striking. If one were to take it
at face value, one would have to say that Sextus commits himself to
a dogmatic view concerning the concept of god.[72] In order to dispel
this impression, one first has to recognize that the conception of
god invoked by Sextus is exactly the Epicurean conception that
made a crucial appearance in the conceptual section of *PH* 3.[73]
Having come to this realization, one might come to notice another
feature of the [T11] move, namely, that it supports the innate or
natural origin of the concept of god by reducing alternative proposals to contradiction.

This argumentative strategy is quite similar to the Epicurean
line taken against linguistic conventionalism. Epicureans would
claim that it is absurd to suggest that language is a human invention, since doing so would presuppose that the inventor is already
in possession of the preconception of the usefulness of language.
However, that preconception can only derive from having previously experienced the use of language, which in turn implies that
language already exists. Furthermore, even if one were to concede
that some individual could have invented language, it would be
impossible for that individual to communicate their discovery to
their fellow humans, since the latter would lack the relevant linguistic capacity.[74]

The analogy seems to suggest that the aetiological discussion in
M 9, or at least a significant part of it, derives from an Epicurean
source that supported the claim that all humans by nature possess
a preconception of god. The most obvious objection to this proposal

---

[72] Mates, *Skeptic Way*, 290 thinks that Sextus contradicts himself, as his argument in *PH* 3. 3–5 discredits the conception he takes for granted here. Similar mis-
understandings might arise whenever scholars fail to differentiate between Sextus'
account of his own position and his dialectical arguments against dogmatic proposals; see e.g. Thorsrud, 'Piety', 101 n. 4 with regard to *M* 9. 123–5.

[73] In the words of Sedley, 'Innatism', 44 n. 42, this argument is of 'unmistakeably
Epicurean origin'.

[74] For the argument, see Lucretius, *DRN* 5. 1041–55, with S. Everson, 'Epicurus
on Mind and Language', in id. (ed.), *Language,* Companions to Ancient Thought,
vol. iii (Cambridge, 1994), 74–108 at 92.

is that the accounts rejected by Sextus include the atomist claim that humans first formed a conception of god as a result of the dream-images they have received while asleep. This suggestion is met by the very same response as the others, as Sextus asks why these humans have formed the concept of god rather than that of an extraordinary human being (*M* 9. 19, 25, 42–3). This seems to fly in the face of the suggestion that Sextus relies on Epicurean material here.

There are at least two ways in which one can explain this objection away. First, one could stipulate an intermediate source, be it Academic or aporetic, which inserted these passages into the text in order to show that Epicurus' preferred account is vulnerable to his specious objection. Second—and this seems more plausible—it is perhaps a mistake to identify the theory of dream-images as Epicurus' preferred account concerning the correct preconception of god, rather than as his explanation of the origin of superstitious beliefs.[75] In this case, the present section could derive from an Epicurean source, once again calling for the recognition of an innate preconception of god.

Thus, a good case can be made that Sextus seized upon a set of Epicurean arguments against the conventional origin of the preconception of god, and repurposed them in order to bring about suspension of judgement on yet another topic of dogmatic speculation, or perhaps to block the innatist inference from the conception to the existence of god in a different way than he does in *PH* 3. At any rate, Sextus has a standing interest to show that the arguments that Epicureans took to vindicate their position were in fact only good enough to counterbalance the arguments of their opponents.

Importantly, this suggestion helps us respond to the worry concerning the fixity of Sextus' philosophical agenda. As the worry goes, the conceptual arguments in *PH* 3 and the existential discussion in *M* 9 make a comprehensive case for suspension of judgement about their subject matter, while the introductory section in the latter treatise seems more modest in its aims. It merely belabours the point that none of the presently available aetiological

---

[75] See also Lucretius, *DRN* 4. 722–822, 962–1036; 5. 1168–82. Tsouna, 'Preconceptions', 182–5 argues for the error theory, but see Obbink, *Philodemus*, 306–7 for a straightforward reading.

accounts succeeds at explaining the historical emergence of religious belief. Given this apparent disanalogy, one might hesitate to attribute the same overall design to Sextus' two explorations of dogmatic theology.[76] Now we can see, however, that this worry stems from a misunderstanding. The conceptual discussions of *PH* 3 and *M* 9 target slightly different dogmatic strategies. The former argues that, given the dogmatic disagreement, one cannot settle on any of the proposed notions of the divine. The latter takes aim at a position that argued against the conventional origin of the concept of god as a way of showing that our innate conception of the divine guarantees that something corresponds to it in reality.

Pyrrhonian therapy needs to address all forms of dogmatism. Some dogmatists have taken their departure from considerations of pious speech, others have engaged in conceptual analysis, yet others have constructed arguments on the basis of observable features of the universe, and some have proposed explanations of the origins of religious belief. Insofar as dogmatic theology encompasses such a variety of approaches, the rigorous Pyrrhonian has to offer remedies against all of them. At the end of the day, by showing that the arguments for and against the conventional origin of the concept of god balance each other out, Sextus does not confuse his Pyrrhonian project but rather brings it to bear on yet another topic of contention.

5. Conclusion

In this paper, I argued for a comprehensive interpretation of Sextus Empiricus' treatment of religious dogmatism as a straightforward application of Sextan Pyrrhonism. In both *PH* 3 and *M* 9, the reader is invited to suspend judgement about particular tenets

---

[76] Bett, 'Gods', 46–7: 'A non-sceptical account of how our conception of God arose, as in Aëtius, would lead naturally into that transition [from conception to existence], and so would an argument, as in *PH* 3, to the effect that there is *no* clear conception of God. But an argument that there is no good explanation for why we have the conception that we have does not.' Hankinson, *The Sceptics*, 214 sees no problem, and takes the entire section from 9. 13 up until 9. 74 to be 'a doxography of comparative theology' introduced in order 'to reinforce the point of *PH* 3. 2–5 that there is no commonly-shared conception of the divine'.

formulated in the context of philosophical investigation, and is provided with a wide array of counter-arguments in order to motivate this response to dogmatic philosophizing. Notwithstanding their differences and their respective philosophical acumen, these arguments serve the same philosophical purpose.

Furthermore, I have argued that the Sceptic's reliance on the appearances does not commit them to the truth of traditional or customary views, as they merely follow them without forming the opinion that these appearances correctly represent the divine. The Sceptic's motivation for doing so derives primarily from the desire to be safe from premature assent, and only then—if at all—from the desire to avoid conflict with the surrounding culture. Whether or not such a stance is considered to be disingenuous will be very much in the eye of the non-Sceptical beholder.

It would require further argumentation to establish, first, that Sextus' treatment of matters of religious significance is representative of his stance concerning all possible matters of inquiry, and second, that it is a viable position to take in the first place. At any rate, the case study developed in this paper provides reason enough to trust the prospects of a generic interpretation formulated along these lines.[77]

Eötvös Loránd University, Budapest
Central European University, Budapest

BIBLIOGRAPHY

Algra, K., 'Eternity and the Concept of God in Early Stoicism', in C. G. Steel, G. van Riel, C. Macé, and L. van Campe (eds.), *Platonic Ideas and Concept Formation in Ancient and Medieval Thought* (Leuven, 2004), 173–90.

[77] I would like to thank the editor, Victor Caston, and my anonymous readers, as well as audiences at Fordham University, the Institute of Classical Studies, University of London, the University of Hamburg, the University of Geneva, and the University of Tübingen. I am especially grateful to Gábor Betegh, István Bodnár, Tad Brennan, Charles Brittain, Gail Fine, David Sedley, Shaul Tor, Justin Vlasits, Katja Vogt, and Ramona Winter for comments on earlier drafts. I thank Matthew Duncombe for allowing me to consult his (then) unpublished manuscript. My work was supported by the DFG-2311 project and by the Swiss Government Excellence programme.

Algra, K., 'Stoic Philosophical Theology and Graeco-Roman Religion', in R. Salles (ed.), *God and Cosmos in Stoicism* (Oxford, 2009), 224–52.

Algra, K. and Ierodiakonou, K., 'Introduction', in eid. (eds.), *Sextus Empiricus and Ancient Physics, Proceedings of the 2007 Symposium Hellenisticum* (Cambridge, 2015), 1–32.

Allen, J., *Inference from Signs: Ancient Debates about the Nature of Evidence* [*Inference*] (Oxford, 2001).

Annas, J., 'Ancient Scepticism and Ancient Religion' ['Religion'], in B. Morison and K. Ierodiakonou (eds.), *Episteme, etc.: Essays in Honour of Jonathan Barnes* (Oxford, 2012), 74–89.

Annas, J. and Barnes, J., *Sextus Empiricus, Outlines of Pyrrhonism* [*Outlines*] (Cambridge, 2000).

Bailey, A., *Sextus Empiricus and Pyrrhonean Scepticism* [*Sextus*] (Oxford, 2002).

Barnes, J., 'Pyrrhonism, Belief, and Causation', in H. Temporini and W. Haase (eds.), *Aufstieg und Niedergang der römischen Welt* II. 36. 4 (Berlin, 1990), 2608–95.

Barnes, J., 'Pyrrhonism, Belief, and Causation', in id., *Proof, Knowledge, and Scepticism: Essays in Ancient Philosophy III* (Oxford, 2014), 417–511.

Barnes, J., 'Proof Destroyed', in Schofield, Burnyeat, and Barnes (eds.), *Doubt and Dogmatism*, 161–81.

Barnes, J., 'The Beliefs of a Pyrrhonist' ['Beliefs'], in Burnyeat and Frede (eds.), *Original Sceptics*, 58–91.

Betegh, G., 'Greek Philosophy and Religion', in M. L. Gill and P. Pellegrin (eds.), *A Companion to Ancient Philosophy* (Oxford, 2009), 625–39.

Bett, R., *Sextus Empiricus, Against the Ethicists* (Oxford, 1997).

Bett, R., 'La double "schizophrénie" d'*Adversus Mathematicos* I–VI, et son origine historique', in J. Delattre (ed.), *Sur le Contre les professeurs de Sextus Empiricus* (Lille, 2006), 17–34.

Bett, R., 'Sextus Empiricus', in G. Oppy and N. Trakakis (eds.), *The History of Western Philosophy of Religion,* vol. i: Ancient Philosophy of Religion (Durham, 2009), 173–85.

Bett, R., *Sextus Empiricus, Against the Physicists* (Cambridge 2012).

Bett, R., 'A Sceptic Looks at Art (But Not Very Closely): Sextus Empiricus on Music', *International Journal for the Study of Skepticism*, 3 (2013), 155–81.

Bett, R., '*Against the Physicists* on Gods (*M* IX.13–194)' ['Gods'], in K. Algra and K. Ierodiakonou (eds.), *Sextus Empiricus and Ancient Physics, Proceedings of the 2007 Symposium Hellenisticum* (Cambridge, 2015), 33–73.

Boys-Stones, G., 'Ancient Philosophy of Religion: An Introduction', in G. Oppy and N. Trakakis (eds.), *The History of Western Philosophy of Religion,* vol. i: Ancient Philosophy of Religion (Durham, 2009), 1–22.

Brennan, T., *Ethics and Epistemology in Sextus Empiricus* (London, 1999).

Bronstein, D., *Aristotle on Knowledge and Learning* (Oxford, 2016).

Brouwer, R., *The Stoic Sage: The Early Stoics on Wisdom, Sagehood and Socrates* (Cambridge, 2014).

Brunschwig, J., 'Sextus Empiricus on the κριτήριον: The Sceptic as Conceptual Legatee', in id. (ed.), *Papers in Hellenistic Philosophy* (Cambridge, 1994), 230–43.

Brunschwig, J., 'The ὅσον ἐπὶ τῷ λόγῳ Formula in Sextus Empiricus', in id. (ed.) *Papers in Hellenistic Philosophy* (Cambridge, 1994), 244–58.

Brunschwig, J., 'L'aphasie pyrrhonienne', in C. Lévy and L. Pernot (eds.), *Dire l'évidence: Philosophie et rhétorique antiques* (Paris, 1997), 297–320.

Brunschwig, J., 'Proof Defined', in Schofield, Burnyeat, and Barnes (eds.), *Doubt and Dogmatism*, 125–60.

Burnyeat, M. F., 'Gods and Heaps', in M. Schofield and M. C. Nussbaum (eds.), *Language and Logos: Studies in Ancient Greek Philosophy Presented to G.E.L. Owen* (Cambridge, 1982), 315–38.

Burnyeat, M. F., 'Can the Sceptic Live his Scepticism?', in Burnyeat and Frede (eds.), *Original Sceptics*, 25–57.

Burnyeat, M. F., and Frede, M. (eds.), *The Original Sceptics: A Controversy* [*Original Sceptics*] (Indianapolis, 1997).

Bury, R. G., Sextus Empiricus, *Outlines of Pyrrhonism* (Cambridge, 1933).

Castagnoli, L., *Ancient Self-Refutation: The Logic and History of the Self-Refutation Argument from Democritus to Augustine* (Cambridge, 2010).

Caujolle-Zaslawsky, F., 'L'interprétation du scepticisme comme philosophie du doute religieux: Analyse d'un malentendu', *Revue de Théologie et de Philosophie*, 27 (1977), 81–112.

Couissin, P., 'Les sorites de Carnéade contre le polythéisme', *Revue des Études Grecques*, 54 (1941), 43–57.

Couloubaritsis, L., 'Réflexions de Sextus Empiricus sur les dieux (*Adv. Math.*, IX)', *Kernos*, 2 (1989), 37–52.

DeFilippo, J. G., 'Cicero vs Cotta in *De natura deorum*', *Ancient Philosophy*, 20 (2000), 169–87.

Dragona-Monachou, M., *The Stoic Arguments for the Existence and Providence of the Gods* [*Arguments*] (Athens, 1976).

Drozdek, A., 'Sceptics and a Religious Instinct', *Minerva*: 18 (2005), 93–108.

Duncombe, M., 'Relativity against Dogmatism in Sextus Empiricus', in id. (ed.) *Ancient Relativity: Plato, Aristotle, Stoics, and Sceptics* (Oxford, 2020), 226–45.

Everson, S., 'Epicurus on Mind and Language', in id. (ed.), *Language*, Companions to Ancient Thought, vol. iii (Cambridge, 1994), 74–108.

Fine, G., 'Sceptical *dogmata: Outlines of Pyrrhonism* I 13', *Méthexis*, 13 (2000), 81–105.

Fine, G., *The Possibility of Inquiry: Meno's Paradox from Socrates to Sextus* (Oxford, 2014).

Frede, M., 'The Original Notion of Cause', in id. (ed.), *Essays in Ancient Philosophy* (Oxford, 1987), 125–50.

Frede, M., 'The Sceptic's Beliefs' ['Beliefs'], in Burnyeat and Frede (eds.), *Original Sceptics*, 1–24.

Frede, M., 'The Sceptic's Two Kinds of Assent and the Question of the Possibility of Knowledge', in Burnyeat and Frede (eds.), *Original Sceptics*, 127–52.

Grenier, J. and Goron, G., *Œuvres choisies de Sextus Empiricus: Contre les physiciens; Contre les moralistes; Hypotyposes pyrrhoniennes* (Paris, 1948).

Grgić, F., 'Sextus Empiricus on the Possibility of Inquiry', *Pacific Philosophical Quarterly*, 89 (2008), 436–59.

Grgić, F., 'Skepticism and Everyday Life' in D. Machuca (ed.), *New Essays on Ancient Pyrrhonism* (Boston, 2011), 69–90.

Grgić, F., '*Apraxia*, Appearances, and Beliefs', *Croatian Journal of Philosophy*, 16 (2016), 441–58.

Hallie, P., 'Classical Scepticism—A Polemical Introduction', in P. Hallie (ed.), *Sextus Empiricus: Selections from the Major Writings on Scepticism, Man and God* (Cambridge, 1985), 3–29.

Hankinson, R. J., *The Sceptics* (London, 1995).

Hossenfelder, M., *Sextus Empiricus,* Grundriß der pyrrhonischen Skepsis (Frankfurt am Main: 1968).

Janáček, K., *Sextus Empiricus' Sceptical Methods* [*Methods*] (Prague, 1972).

Knuuttila, S. and Sihvola, J., 'Ancient Scepticism and Philosophy of Religion', in J. Sihvola (ed.), *Ancient Scepticism and the Sceptical Tradition* (Helsinki, 2000), 125–44.

Lévy, C., *Cicero Academicus: Recherches sur les* Académiques *et sur la philosophie cicéronienne* (Rome, 1992).

Long, A. A., 'Scepticism about Gods in Hellenistic Philosophy' ['Gods'], in A. A. Long (ed.), *From Epicurus to Epictetus: Studies in Hellenistic and Roman Philosophy* (Oxford, 2006), 114–27.

Long, A. A. and Sedley, D. N. (eds.), *The Hellenistic Philosophers*, 2 vols. (Cambridge, 1987).

Mansfeld, J., 'Theology', in K. Algra, J. Barnes, J. Mansfeld, and M. Schofield (eds.), *The Cambridge History of Hellenistic Philosophy* (Cambridge, 1997), 452–78.

Marchand, S., 'Religion et piété sceptiques selon Sextus Empiricus' ['Piété'], in A.-I. Bouton-Touboulic and C. Lévy (eds.), *Scepticisme et religion: Constantes et évolutions, de la philosophie hellénistique à la philosophie médiévale* (Turnhout, 2016), 103–17.

Mates, B., *The Skeptic Way: Sextus Empiricus' Outlines of Pyrrhonism* [*Skeptic Way*] (Oxford, 1996).

McKirahan, R., 'Epicurean Doxography in Cicero, *De Natura Deorum* Book I', in G. Giannantoni and M. Gigante (eds.), *Epicureismo greco e romano*, vol. ii (Naples, 1996), 865–78.

McPherran, M. L., 'Skeptical Homeopathy and Self-Refutation', *Phronesis*, 32 (1987), 290–328.

McPherran, M. L., '*Ataraxia* and *eudaimonia* in Ancient Pyrrhonism: Is the Skeptic Really Happy?', *Proceedings of the Boston Area Colloquium in Ancient Philosophy*, 5 (1989), 135–71.

Morison, B., 'The Logical Structure of the Sceptic's Opposition', *Oxford Studies in Ancient Philosophy*, 40 (2011), 265–95.

Mutschmann, H. (ed.), *Sexti Empirici Opera*, vols. i–ii (Leipzig, 1912–14).

Nussbaum, M. C., *The Therapy of Desire: Theory and Practice in Hellenistic Ethics* (Princeton, 1994).

O'Keefe, T., *Epicureanism* (Durham, 2010).

Obbink, D., ' "What all men believe must be true": Common Conceptions and *consensio omnium* in Aristotle and Hellenistic Philosophy', *Oxford Studies in Ancient Philosophy*, 10 (1992), 193–231.

Obbink, D., *Philodemus* On Piety, Part i: Critical Text with Commentary [*Philodemus*] (Oxford, 1996).

Parker, R., *On Greek Religion* (Ithaca, 2011).

Pellegrin, P., Sextus Empiricus, *Esquisses pyrrhoniennes* (Paris, 1997).

Penelhum, T., 'Skepticism and Fideism', in M. F. Burnyeat (ed.), *The Skeptical Tradition* (Berkeley, 1983), 287–318.

Penelhum, T., 'Sceptics, Believers, and Historical Mistakes', *Synthese*, 67 (1986), 131–46.

Runia, D. T., 'The Beginnings of the End: Philo of Alexandria and Hellenistic Theology' in D. Frede and A. Laks (eds.), *Traditions of Theology: Studies in Hellenistic Theology, its Background and Aftermath* (Leiden, 2002), 281–316.

Schofield, M., 'Aenesidemus: Pyrrhonist and Heraclitean', in A. M. Ioppolo and D. Sedley (eds.), *Pyrrhonists, Patricians, Platonizers. Hellenistic Philosophy in the Period 155–86 BC*, Tenth Symposium Hellenisticum (Naples, 2007), 269–338.

Schofield, M., 'Preconception, Argument, and God', in Schofield, Burnyeat, and Barnes (eds.), *Doubt and Dogmatism*, 283–308.

Schofield, M., Burnyeat, M. F., and Barnes, J. (eds.), *Doubt and Dogmatism: Studies in Hellenistic Epistemology* (Oxford, 1980).

Sedley, D., 'Epicurus' Theological Innatism' ['Innatism'], in J. Fish and K. Sanders (eds.), *Epicurus and the Epicurean Tradition* (Cambridge, 2011), 29–52.

Sedley, D., 'The Atheist Underground', in V. Harte and M. Lane (eds.), *Politeia in Greek and Roman Philosophy* (Cambridge, 2013), 329–48.

Sedley, D., 'Carneades' Theological Arguments' ['Carneades'], in P. Kalligas, C. Balla, E. Baziotopolou, and V. Karasmanis (eds.), *Plato's Academy: Its Workings and its History* (Cambridge, 2020), 220–41.

Sihvola, J., 'The Autonomy of Religion in Ancient Philosophy', in V. Hirvonen, T. J. Holopainen, and M. Tuominen (eds.), *Mind and Modality: Studies in the History of Philosophy in Honour of Simo Knuuttila* (Leiden, 2006), 87–99.

Spinelli, E., 'Senza teodicea: critiche epicuree e argomentazioni pirroniane', in D. De Sanctis, E. Spinelli, M. Tulli, and F. Verde (eds.), *Questioni epicuree* (Sankt Augustin, 2015), 213–34.

Spinelli, E., 'Le dieu est la cause la plus active: Sextus Empiricus contre la théologie dogmatique' ['Dieu'], in A.-I. Bouton-Touboulic and C. Lévy (eds.), *Scepticisme et religion: Constantes et évolutions, de la philosophie hellénistique à la philosophie médiévale* (Turnhout, 2016), 89–102.

Striker, G., 'Sceptical Strategies', in Schofield, Burnyeat, and Barnes (eds.), *Doubt and Dogmatism*, 54–83.

Thorsrud, H., 'Sextus Empiricus on Skeptical Piety' ['Piety'], in D. E. Machuca (ed.), *New Essays on Ancient Pyrrhonism* (Leiden, 2011), 91–111.

Tsouna, V., 'Epicurean Preconceptions', *Phronesis*, 61 (2016), 160–221.

Tsouna-McKirahan, V., 'Conservatism and Pyrrhonian Skepticism', *Syllecta Classica*, 6 (1996), 69–86.

Veres, M., 'Keep Calm and Carry On: Sextus Empiricus on the Origins of Pyrrhonism', *History of Philosophy and Logical Analysis,* 23 (2020), 100–22.

Vick, C., 'Karneades' Kritik der Theologie bei Cicero und Sextus Empiricus', *Hermes*, 37 (1902), 228–48.

Vogt, K. M., *Law, Reason, and the Cosmic City: Political Philosophy in the Early Stoa* (Oxford, 2008).

Vogt, K. M., 'Scepticism and Action', in R. Bett (ed.), *The Cambridge Companion to Ancient Scepticism* (Cambridge, 2010), 165–80.

Vogt, K. M., *Skepsis und Lebenspraxis: Das pyrrhonische Leben ohne Meinungen* [*Lebenspraxis*] (Freiburg, 2015).

Warren, J., 'What God Didn't Know: Sextus Empiricus *AM* 9. 162–6', in D. E. Machuca (ed.), *New Essays on Ancient Pyrrhonism* (Leiden, 2011), 126–41.

White, M. J., 'Cause: *M* 9. 195–330', in K. Algra and K. Ierodiakonou (eds.), *Sextus Empiricus and Ancient Physics, Proceedings of the 2007 Symposium Hellenisticum* (Cambridge, 2015), 74–104.

Whitmarsh, T., *Battling the Gods: The Struggle against Religion in Ancient Greece* (New York, 2015).

Wynne, J. P. F., 'Learned and Wise: Cotta the Sceptic in Cicero's *De Natura Deorum*', *Oxford Studies in Ancient Philosophy*, 47 (2014), 245–73.

Ziemińska, R., 'Scepticism and Religious Belief: The Case of Sextus Empiricus', in D. Łukasiewicz and R. Pouivet (eds.), *The Right to Believe: Perspectives in Religious Epistemology* (Frankfurt, 2011), 149–60.

ANCIENT PHILOSOPHY, ANCIENT HISTORY

A Discussion of M. T. Griffin, *Politics and Philosophy at Rome: Collected Papers*, edited by Catalina Balmaceda. Oxford University Press, Oxford, 2018. pp. xvi + 775.

JONATHAN BARNES

MIRIAM GRIFFIN's collected papers were written over half a century. They run to fifty items, and occupy more than 700 large and close-packed pages. Five of the fifty have not hitherto been published, and a dozen or more of them appeared in relatively esoteric places. Some of them are wide in scope, some investigate a detailed text or topic. Some are written for a large public, a few for fellow-specialists. Several of the pieces are classics, and familiar; some of them are classics, and unfamiliar.

MG (as I shall call her[1]) writes with erudition, lucidity, and sanity—the last, being a rare virtue among historians of antiquity, may be illustrated. Cicero reports that when Lucius Gellius Poplicola passed through Athens in 93 on his way to govern the province of Asia, he summoned the philosophers of the city together, and urged them to settle their differences, offering himself as arbiter of the case (*Leg.* 1. 53). A learned historian has suggested that Gellius was making a serious proposal. Cicero thought that Gellius was joking. MG:

I cling to Cicero's interpretation of this incident as a deliberate joke, rejecting the rather owlish notion that it has to do with the political friction between the philosophical schools in Athens that led up to the tyranny of Athenion. (349; cf. 428 n. 19)[2]

Or again, on Seneca's most readable work:

---

[1] I am too old-fashioned to refer to ladies by a bare surname; it would be impertinent to refer to her here as 'Miriam'; and neither 'Miriam Griffin' nor 'Dr Griffin' nor 'Mrs Griffin' is appealing. If 'MG' hints at something sprightly and elegant, so much the better.

[2] All page references are to *Politics and Philosophy at Rome* (= *PPR*) unless otherwise stated.

Jonathan Barnes, *Ancient Philosophy, Ancient History: A Discussion of M. T. Griffin*, Politics and Philosophy at Rome: Collected Papers. In: Oxford Studies in Ancient Philosophy Volume LVIII. Edited by: Victor Caston, Oxford University Press (2020). © Jonathan Barnes. DOI: 10.1093/oso/9780198858997.003.0008

Many scholars have thought that the *Apocolocyntosis* has a serious political aim, that by attacking Claudius' deification Seneca either made an
attack on Agrippina ... or on Britannicus ... The mistake is to take a work
in which almost nothing is serious too seriously. (392)

Several of the papers in *PPR* are entertaining, and scarcely one
is tedious. Most are enlightening, and some are peerless. What a
collection.

I

The project of assembling the volume was suggested to the Oxford
University Press by Catalina Balmaceda, who was a graduate student of MG and is now a Professor of Ancient History at the
Catholic University in Santiago; and it is she who has edited the
volume, no light task: the scholarly world owes her a double debt—
a debt which the following observations do not reduce.

The editor has added English translations where the original
text gave only Latin (or Greek). She has created a consolidated
bibliography. She has compiled a list of abbreviations, and two
indexes. The papers, all of them reset, have been arranged in a way
which 'helps to give the whole collection a greater coherence, creat-
ing a unity which is more than the simple sum of its parts' (ix).
The translations are useful (though they are not consistently done),
and so too is the bibliography. The list of abbreviations is meagre,
and the Subject Index is rather thin. The Index of Persons and
Deities is full but vexatious (if you look up Cicero, you will find,
under Tullius, twenty-one lines beginning: 'Chapter 1, 27, 28,
29,...'). There is no *index locorum*, a distressing absence. Nor—a
mild vexation—is the pagination of the original publication noted.
Nor have the different styles of reference used in the text and the
notes been homogenized. It may be conjectured that the editor felt
time's chariot at her shoulder, and was determined that the volume
should be presented to Miriam and not *in memoriam*. She succeeded.
But it was a close-run thing, and the running cut a few corners.

The book has a charming dust-jacket. Inside, it is less pleasing:
the font is small, and the font used in the footnotes requires a mag-
nifying glass or an arc lamp; the margins are minimalist; and the
pages are crammed—and for that reason disagreeable to read. And

the book is heavy—at least, it weighs heavy on my ancient knees. No doubt the publisher will explain that large fonts and wide margins cost money, that two medium volumes cost more than twice as much as one large, that financial considerations must (alas and alack) trump aesthetics. But that hypothetical explanation will not pass.

The editor remarks that 'one of the goals of this collection is to make these results available to the widest possible audience' (ix—what, I wonder, were the other goals?). If that was the editor's goal, it was not the publisher's; for *PPR* will set you back $155 (a snip at $122 from Amazon), and that is a sum which only libraries and a handful of scholars will be ready to pay. It is a shame—I had almost said, a scandal—that the Oxford University Press, whose 'mission' (the word is theirs) is 'to make the best scholarship and research available to as many people as we can' and which in its Annual Report for 2018/2019 declared a profit (after tax) of 88.2 million pounds sterling, has chosen to price this shining example of the best scholarship and research beyond the reach of any interested graduate student. It is curious to reflect that had the Press last year sold all its academic books at cost price, its profit would have been more than 85 million pounds.

Let it be hoped that a second edition of *PPR* will be produced: two volumes, legible print, spacious margins, improved indexes, etc. etc., and all at no more than the price of a bottle of decent champagne.

The editor has arranged the papers into three groups, under the rubrics 'Roman History', 'Roman Historiography', and 'Philosophy and Politics', the third group containing exactly half the papers and occupying more than half the pages. Each group begins with a general piece, the remaining items turning up in order of their publication. Perhaps such an arrangement gives the book a unity and a coherence: certainly it has some curious consequences. Thus—to take a trifling example—Chapters 23 and 25 are about Sir Ronald Syme, MG's 'mentor and friend'. They are separated by a squib (on exaggerated mourning) which is in effect a pendant to Chapter 18—a chapter which partners with Chapter 15. Less trivially, in Part III, where the protagonists are Cicero and Seneca and the younger Pliny, the first scenes put Seneca on stage; then Cicero comes forward; then Seneca is back, with Pliny; then Cicero–Seneca–Pliny–Seneca; and in Chapter 47 the trio appear together. To be sure,

there is no order which is the right order, and there is no order at
which no one will grumble. But some orders are odder than others.

It should also be said that there are repetitions and overlappings.
Thus in Part II Chapter 18 repeats most of the contents of Chapter
15—though in a different and more relaxed style. And the several
papers in Part III which are given to Seneca's *De clementia* have
many claims and contentions in common—and several paragraphs
which are verbatim the same.

Readers of *OSAP* will no doubt be most enthused by Part III of
PPR. But the divisions between the parts are porous; so that, for
example, the last part of Chapter 15, 'The Senate's Story' and a
section of Chapter 19, 'Pliny's *Letters*', should be read alongside
Chapter 30, 'Philosophy, Cato, and Roman Suicide'. And Chapter
17, '*Iure plectimur*: The Roman Critique of Roman Imperialism',
might as well be in Part III as in Part II. One or two of the historical chapters are technical and esoteric (I worked hard to enjoy
Chapter 2, 'The "Leges Iudiciariae" of the Pre-Sullan Era'); but
almost all of them are open to amateurs. Chapter 1, 'Cicero and
Rome', is an unbeatable introduction to its subject, and the same
may be said of Chapter 4 on Julius Caesar. Chapter 16, 'Pliny and
Tacitus', is a warm double portrait. And the twin papers in
Chapters 15 and 18 ('The Senate's Story' and 'Writing History:
the Senate vs. Tacitus') argue compellingly that of the two surviving accounts of the death of Germanicus Caesar and its aftermath,
one of them an inscription recording the decisions of the Senate
and the other the several pages in the *Annals* which Tacitus gave to
the affair, it is not the dry, official, bureaucratic and contemporary
report but the coruscating narrative composed a century or so after
the event which is closer to the historical truth.

II

Part III of *PPR* addresses, and answers, the question to which its
rubric points. In the opening paper, the question is put like this:
'What effect did philosophy have on the conduct of Roman statesmen who were exposed to philosophical lectures in Rome and
abroad, and who, for whatever motives, frequently had a philosophical companion in their entourage?' (347). The question concerns Rome, not the world at large—and Rome here is, as often as

not, the city rather than the nation or the empire. It concerns the conduct of statesmen, and more particularly the political conduct— the political decisions and the political actions—of the Roman ruling classes. In a few cases the statesmen were themselves philosophers; but in most cases any philosophical effect on Roman statesmen will have been made by friends or companions of their mature years, or by the lectures they had attended and the books they had read as young men.

The question was not new when MG posed it: on the contrary, as she rather glumly observes, 'the relation of philosophy to Roman politics is a vast subject, and there are many books on it' (421). Many indeed—many more in the thirty-odd years since that sentence was first published. The vast majority of those historians who discussed the matter had worked, implicitly, on the basis of three assumptions: first, that philosophy is primarily a matter of *doctrines*; secondly, that the sort of philosophy pertinent to the question is the third of the three parts into which ancient philosophy was customarily divided, the moral or ethical part; and thirdly, that of the several schools of philosophy which advertised their wares in the forum, it is the Stoic school which has the chief claim to have worked upon the Roman mind.

Those were not outrageous assumptions. The prominence of Stoicism at Rome seemed to be an empirical fact—a fact sometimes explained by the notion that there was an intrinsic affinity between the austere ethics of the Stoa and the severe *mos maiorum* of the Romans. Again, that it is ethics (which includes political philosophy) rather than physics or logic, which made, or might have made, a mark upon a Roman statesman, appears self-evident: ethics, after all, is the part of philosophy which bears upon action. As for doctrines, ancient schools of philosophy were generally identified or defined by their doctrines (you were a Stoic if you believed this, a Platonist if you believed that); and ancient historians of philosophy took their subject to be the history of philosophical opinions or δόξαι—they were, in the modern jargon, doxographers.

That being so, the question of Part III was in effect understood to amount to this: what influence, if any, did Stoic ethical doctrines have on Roman political activity? Did Blossius of Cumae, who taught Tiberius Gracchus his Stoicism, encourage, or even cause, that turbulent tribune to propose his radical and revolutionary measures? Did the solid Stoic beliefs of Cato, who unlike the gods voted for the losing cause, determine him to fall on his sword once there was no hope left of saving the Republic? When Pliny went out to govern Bithynia, were his reflections on Christianity and its discontents influenced by his years with those profound and pre-eminent thinkers, Euphrates and Artemidorus?

The questions are difficult—not least (but not only) because of the nature of the evidence. How much is known about Blossius? Virtually nothing.[3] What can be ascertained of Cato's thoughts after the battle of Thapsus? There are stories; but they are romantic—and perhaps largely romance. As for Pliny, he was writing from the East to his Emperor in Rome, and it might be supposed that in situations of that sort writers do not always reveal their inmost convictions. But the difficulty of the question did not lead histor-ians to a judicious scepticism: answers were proposed—in the one sense by the imaginative and cavalier among them, in the other by the roundheaded realists.

One strong argument on the side of realism was this: in antiquity, philosophers, and students of philosophy, were celebrated for say-ing one thing and doing another, for professing this or that noble doctrine and then performing that or this shady action. It was not only the enemies of philosophy who made the charge: it was fre-quently in the mouths of the philosophers themselves. Epictetus for example, speaks of 'those who take up the teachings of the philosophers only to talk about them' (τοὺς μέχρι λόγου μόνον ἀναλαμβάνοντας τὰ τῶν φιλοσόφων, *Diss.* 2. 19. 1); they philosophize 'without acting—they go only as far as talking' (ἄνευ τοῦ πράττειν, μέχρι τοῦ λέγειν, *apud* Gellius 17. 19. 1); they are 'lions at school, and foxes abroad' (ἐν σχολῇ λέοντες, ἔξω δ' ἀλώπεκες, *Diss.* 4. 5. 37).[4] And a dozen more texts in the *Dissertationes*—which may be matched from a dozen other authors.[5] The refrain is, I guess, still heard—I recall how some of my ex-colleagues were surprised, and even aghast, to learn that their students urged one thing in their philosophy essays and quite another in the Junior Common Room. So too in antiquity: Quintus subscribed to the Stoic paradox that only the wise man is rich, and devoted his life to his bank account.

---

[3] There is scarcely a page on him in *DPhA*: M. Ducos, 'Blossius de Cumes', in R. Goulet (ed.), *Dictionnaire des philosophes antiques*, 7 vols. and suppl. (Paris, 1994–2018), vol. ii. 116–17.

[4] All translations are mine.

[5] See J. Barnes, *Logic and the Imperial Stoa [Logic]* (Leiden, 1997), 39–42.

Sextus the Epicurean, whose motto was 'Pleasure' and 'Live in Obscurity' (λάθε βιώσας), exhausted himself in the pursuit of public office and public honours.

Many such men are hypocrites: they say what they don't believe—in order to impress their superiors, or to disguise their vices, or simply because that is what they are like. But for many of those whom Epictetus and his fellows castigate, the word 'Humean' is more appropriate than 'hypocrite'. In the gloom of the study they are led to embrace to profess this or that depressing doctrine; but at the backgammon table cheerfulness will keep breaking in. The Latin for 'Humean' is 'Aurelian':

> For some, doctrines on certain subjects were kept in a separate compartment of one's mind. Thus C. Aurelius Cotta, an adherent of the sceptical Academy, is made to say in the *De Natura Deorum* that, as a Cotta and a pontiff, he upholds the traditional lore and the belief in providence and divination without proof. (427)

Cotta was not a hypocrite: rather, he believed things under his pontifical hat which he didn't believe under his Academical bonnet.[6] I know many Aurelians. No doubt I am one myself.

Syme, the *novus Tacitus*, cared little for philosophy: 'he regarded all philosophy as mere "doctrine"' (*PPR*, vii). Not just as doctrine: as mere doctrine. A claim to philosophy was a mask, a veil, a veneer. Fine words which buttered foul parsnips, noble affirmations which concealed an ignoble lust for power—or perhaps nothing worse than cultivated murmurings which graced a dinner-table and ornamented a polite *conversazione*. Pliny in his letters was pleased to refer to his philosophical teachers, and to recount their *bons mots*. Did the *bons mots* affect his actions? According to Syme, his letters 'betray no influence from any lessons imparted by Euphrates or by Artemidorus' (615, quoting from Syme's 'A Political Group').[7] Were Caesar's murderers moved by philosophical principle? Syme writes:

> It is all too easy to label the assassins as fanatic adepts of Greek theories ... Yet it is in no way evident that the nature of Brutus would have

---

[6] But see below, p. 290.
[7] R. Syme, 'A Political Group', in A. R. Birley (ed.), *Ronald Syme, Roman Papers*, vol. vii [*Roman Papers*] (Oxford, 1991), 568–87 at 573.

been very different had he never opened a book of Stoic or Academic philosophy.[8]

A philosophical reader will niggle at that second sentence; but it is Symean rhetoric. What Syme means is that Brutus would have acted as he did had he never known anything about philosophy. (It is a question what evidence Syme might have discovered, or might have thought he had discovered, for that metaphysical observation.)

MG did not dismiss Symean realism out of hand. But she did not believe that the philosophical utterances of Roman statesmen were normally masks or veils or veneers. And she did not accept the three implicit assumptions which had formed the background of many a discussion of the great question. The Stoa may indeed have been the most prominent of the schools in Rome during a certain period of decades; but it was never the only school—and of course, as Galen for one insisted, you could philosophize without bawling allegiance to any school at all. Again, ethics is not the only part of ancient philosophy with a practical application: on the contrary, physics—or at least some part of physics—bears directly upon action; and logic is concerned with deliberation about action no less than with theoretical thought. Thirdly, and most importantly, philosophy is not merely doctrine (let alone merely mere doctrine); and whatever the doxographers may suggest, schools of philosophy are not defined by bodies of doctrine (if they were, then sceptical Pyrrhonism could not constitute a philosophical school). Any philosophy, whether or not it sets down propositions which are to be believed, will set out terms and concepts by means of which its philosophical propositions may be formulated, and will furnish methods of argument by which such propositions may be examined, and proved, and found wanting.

MG's answer to the question of Part III, then, is this: *philosophy* had an influence on Roman statesmen, but philosophical *doctrines* did not. In the Prologue to *PPR*, she says this:

The overlap between philosophy and politics has been the principal focus of academic interest throughout my career. This is not to say that I do not credit the Roman philosophers writing in Latin with any intellectual originality, but that I write as a historian, interested in how their thinking

---

[8] R. Syme, *The Roman Revolution* (Oxford, 1939), 57.

relates to their historical circumstances and to their actions. Long study of the subject has convinced me that philosophical doctrines did not dictate those actions, but rather provided the vocabulary and argumentative skill to make and justify the decisions that gave rise to them. (viii)

That view she had first expressed, in a particular form, in *Seneca*:

His works show clearly that, although late Stoicism was too complex to provide its adherents with definite directives, it did give them a rich supply of terms and arguments to use in analysing different courses and weighing the alternatives.[9]

Neither directives nor doctrines, but expressions and arguments.

The theme, with some minor variations, runs though most of Part III of *PHP*; but it is in Chapter 26, 'Philosophy, Politics, and Politicians'—to my mind, the most starry chapter in the star-studded book—that the view is most elaborated. A number of alleged cases of the influence of philosophical doctrine on Roman politics are considered; and the conclusion is severe: 'those attempts to establish connections between philosophical doctrines and particular policies and decisions fail' (359). Then:

What kind of connection between philosophy and politics can we reasonably expect? Perhaps we should look more to the language in which choices are analysed and justifications framed when we are seeking to understand the role that philosophy played in the life of Roman statesmen. (360)

And the following paragraph opens like this:

It was not just for intellectual exercise that Cicero in March 49, when he was trying to decide whether or not to join Pompey in the East, was debating in Greek and in Latin a series of philosophical θέσεις on tyranny. (360)

A couple of letters prove the point.[10]

A final quotation, from 'Intellectual Developments of the Ciceronian Age', written for the new *Cambridge Ancient History* and appearing in *PPR* as Chapter 32:

Unconvincing attempts to make firm connexions between intellectual concerns and political activity have only confused the issue ... It is more profitable to concentrate on the subtler contributions made by intellectual

---

[9] M. T. Griffin, *Seneca: A Philosopher in Politics* [*Seneca*] (Oxford, 1976), 366.
[10] See below, p. 299.

developments in Roman life, namely, the provision of tools of thought and expression. (459)

What has confused the issue was the implicit assumption that philosophy is essentially a matter of doctrine. Once that assumption is abandoned, the truth may emerge.

Why does MG think that doctrine is irrelevant to the case? Not—certainly not primarily—because the profession of a doctrine may be hypocritical or Aurelian. Rather, those historians who suppose that doctrines might, or ought to, influence political action:

> ...misconstrue the nature of the doctrines of the Hellenistic schools, expecting them to offer unambiguous directives on political issues when, in fact, their *dogmata* were very general. In order to apply them to particular situations, much casuistical skill was necessary, and the history of the schools showed that different philosophers had applied them differently. (428)

It is the nature of the doctrines, not the imbecility of those who profess them, which makes their political application impossible.

It may be added that general doctrines always allow for exceptions, so that they do not give a fixed and certain answer to any particular question; and further, that even where a doctrine seems unambiguous and determinate, it is always open to interpretation. It is the Christian philosophers who provide the most diverting examples of that second addendum. Jesus Christ declared that

> it is easier for a camel to go through the eye of a needle, than for a rich man to enter into the kingdom of God. (Mark 10:25)

The disciples were amazed, as well they might have been, and asked, 'Who then can be saved?' (10:26). Clement of Alexandria had the answer. In his sermon 'Which Rich Man is Saved?', he explains that by 'rich', Jesus did not mean 'loaded with dosh': he meant 'loaded with sin'.

There is a further point: it is normally superfluous to invoke philosophical doctrine in explanation of political action—things are clear enough without it. Any historian who reflects on Cato's self-slaughter will naturally take note of his Stoical allegiance and recall that the Stoa, like every other school of philosophy, had its doctrine of suicide, explaining if and when a man might top himself. But having noted the fact, the historian will recall how Cato spent his final night on the planet: he read not Chrysippus' *Use of Reason* but Plato's *Phaedo*, and he read it twice. (Or at least, that's how the story goes.) And next the historian will observe, with many an historical instance, that Cato was following a well-established Roman custom which owed nothing to any Greek theorizing. That is quite enough to explain Cato's deed. He acted, no doubt, according to Stoic views—but he did not act on his Stoic convictions. Those convictions were doubtless genuine, but they were idle. Cato's Stoic doctrines revolved like wheels in the clockwork of his mind: they had no particular effect upon the motions of his hands. 'Philosophy', as MG puts it, 'helped to provide *the etiquette and style* for suicide' (417, emphasis in the original).

Pliny's letters provide later examples of Roman self-slaughter, and they 'reflect the emphasis which philosophy placed on rational decisions about suicide: reason was to govern both the decision and the performance of the act' (291—the word 'performance' is carefully chosen). A letter to Catilius Severus reflects upon the suicide of Titius Aristo:

Nam impetus quodam et instinctu procurrere ad mortem commune cum multis, deliberare vero et causas eius expendere, utque suaserit ratio, vitae mortisque consilium vel suscipere vel ponere ingentis est animi. (1. 22. 10 Mynors)

For it is common to many to anticipate death on impulse and by instinct; but to deliberate, and to weigh its causes, and to accept or reject the decision of life and death as reason may persuade, that is the mark of a great mind.

A great mind acts upon reason, and if the great mind is of a Stoical bent, it is Stoic reasoning and not Stoic doctrine which determines his act.[11]

But it is by reference to Cicero that MG's position is most frequently illustrated and best supported. So, for example, in a long letter to his friend Gaius Matius, written shortly after the assassination of Caesar, there is this:

sed te, hominem doctissimum, non fugit, si Caesar rex fuerit, quod mihi quidem videtur, in utramque partem de tuo officio disputari posse, vel in eam qua ego soleo uti, laudandam esse fidem et humanitatem tuam qui amicum etiam mortuum diligas, vel in eam qua non nulli utuntur,

---

[11] See Griffin, *PPR*, 261–2; and A. N. Sherwin-White, *The Letters of Pliny* (Oxford, 1966), 136–8.

libertatem patriae vitae amici anteponendam. (*Ad fam.* 11. 27. 8
Shackleton Bailey)

It does not escape you, who are a most learned man, that if Caesar was a
king (which seems to me to be the case), it can be argued on both sides [*in
utramque partem ... disputari posse*] as to your duty: on the one hand, which
I myself incline to plead, praise should be given to your loyalty and
humanity for caring for a friend even after he is dead, and on the other
hand, which not a few men plead, the liberty of one's country should be
put before the life of one's friend.

What should Matius do? Philosophy gives no answer; but it suggests a way of coming to an answer: argue the case on both sides, *in
utramque partem*, as the Academic philosophers enjoined (and as
the Stoics had practised before them).[12]

MG's view suggests—though MG herself does not—that the
part of philosophy most pertinent to Roman politics was not ethics
but logic. And it is diverting to recall that Galen, in his *De optima
doctrina*, claims that all a philosophical teacher need offer his pupils
is 'the probative method': learn what sorts of things proofs are,
practise their construction and their criticism, and the rest you can
do for yourself—method is all. (It should be added that Galen's
essay is directed precisely against the Academic notion that argument *in utramque partem* is the best way of teaching.) To be sure,
most of the illustrative examples which MG produces concern
moral or political problems. But it does not follow that most of the
examples draw upon aspects of moral philosophy.

III

There is no doubt but that the search for the influence of philosophical doctrine on practical politics has been largely fruitless, nor
that the search for the influence of philosophical concepts and
philosophical methods discovers peaches. But there are—of course
there are—points on which objections, or at least questions, may be
raised. Here are three of them.

First, consider the sources on which MG largely draws. They
are the letters of Roman bigwigs: Cicero and his friends, Seneca,

---

[12] See Griffin, *PPR*, 429—and for Matius the whole of Chapter 36, 'From
Aristotle to Atticus: Cicero and Matius on Friendship'.

Pliny—and, a little apart from the others, in Chapter 49, 'The Prince and his Tutor', Fronto and Marcus Aurelius. The Ciceronian correspondence is far the richest treasury (two of the best chapters in *PPR* are 33, 'Philosophical Badinage in Cicero's Letters to his Friends', and 36, 'From Aristotle to Atticus: Cicero and Matius on Friendship'). Cicero's letters were written by a philosopher, and they are, most of them, *pièces d'occasion*, showing (as the old saw has it) his soul to his friends—as MG puts it, 'we can see that philosophy had entered his marrow' (460).

Pliny's letters too—with the exception of Book 10, the official correspondence with Trajan—were *pièces d'occasion*; but they were not written by a philosopher, and they were selected and polished for publication. In Chapter 43, 'The Younger Pliny's Debt to Moral Philosophy', MG disputes her mentor's claim that the letters 'betray no influence from any lessons imparted by Euphrates or by Artemidorus'. She is right inasmuch as the letters contain frequent references, some of them explicit, to the teachings of the philosophers. But Syme was not unaware of that fact: his sceptical ghost allows that Pliny *expresses* himself in philosophical terms, but wants reasons to believe that Pliny also *thought* in philosophical terms: perhaps those philosophical sentences are ornamental flourishes rather than revelations of philosophical marrow?

Seneca is a different case. He was, to be sure, a philosopher (though a less gifted philosopher than Cicero); but his letters, whether or not they were ever posted to Lucilius, are letters in form only: they are philosophical essays, or perhaps (as some have argued) a course of philosophical instruction, wrapped up in epistolary form. They do not discover Seneca's soul in the way in which Cicero's letters discover his.

Those differences make a difference. The case for Cicero is indisputable: they prove that, whether or not Cicero acted on his philosophical beliefs, he did frequently think philosophically about problems of a political or a moral nature. Seneca's *Epistulae morales* may properly be said to contain more philosophy per square page than do the letters of Cicero. But the particular cases with which Seneca illustrates his moral reflections are *exempla* rather than examples: they are intended to picture how Lucilius ought, or ought not, to behave rather than how Seneca, or anyone else, has behaved under the influence of philosophical notions. And as for Pliny, the case is less clear. I don't mean that Pliny and Seneca are irrelevant to MG's thesis; but they need, I think, to be treated with different pairs of kid gloves.

The second question concerns the sort of influence that philosophy *did* have on political action—the non-doctrinal influence, so to speak. In what exactly did it consist and how did it manifest itself? According to the Prologue to *PPR*, there are two kinds or aspects of non-doctrinal influence: philosophy 'provided the vocabulary and argumentative skill to make and justify decisions' (viii); and other texts, all of them previously cited, say the same thing in slightly different ways—philosophy offers 'a rich supply of terms and arguments',[13] it offers 'the language in which choices are analysed and justifications framed' (360), it gives the philosophical politician 'language and justification', or 'tools of thought and expression' (459).

The argumentative skill is evident in the case of Cicero. In particular, he had adopted from the Academics the idea of *in utramque* argumentation, which he practised sedulously in his back garden and applied self-consciously in his political and ethical inquiries. But there is nothing quite like that in Pliny—or in Seneca. Pliny, to be sure, insists that great men apply reason and deliberation in practical no less than in theoretical matters; but it scarcely took philosophy to teach him such an easy lesson (easy to learn, hard to put into practice); and in any event, there is no indication in his letters that he took from philosophy any specific advice on *how* to deliberate, and *how* to apply reason to matters of practical concern.

The case of Seneca is more perplexing. As a matter of course he knew Stoic logic, and as a matter of fact he held some parts of it in contempt. A particular disdain was reserved for Zeno's celebrated syllogisms. Consider this: 'No evil is glorious: death is glorious: so death is no evil' (nullum malum gloriosum est; mors autem gloriosa est; mors ergo non est malum, *Ep.* 82. 9). What a futility, how useless—it will never persuade anyone that death is not a thing to be feared. And more generally, let Lucilius fly logical disputations, for they are all no good (*Ep.* 102. 20). Let him abandon all such melancholy futilities, such 'melancholy triflings' (tristes ineptiae, 113. 26). That is severe; but too much may not be made of it—after all, Cicero, who was no enemy to logic, had derided Zeno's 'trivial deductions' (ratiunculae, *Tusc.* 2. 29). And in *Ep.* 113 Seneca

---

[13] Griffin, *Seneca*, 366.

implicitly allows that not all parts of logic are 'triflings' (ineptiae); for elsewhere he explicitly says, of logical textbooks, 'I do not forbid you to read these things—so long as you bring whatever you read to bear upon ethics' (haec, Lucili virorum optime, quominus legas non deterreo, dummodo quidquid legeris ad mores statim referas, *Ep.* 89. 18); and in *Ep.* 102 he indicates that not all logic is a matter of disputations: he states that 'certain logical matters are mixed in with morals' (quaedam ... moralibus rationalia inmixta sunt, 4), and he claims that he has treated that part of logic which is correct and 'pertinent to ethics' (ad mores spectant, 5).[14] But what those salutary parts of logic may be, and how they are mixed in with morals, Seneca does not say.

So much for argumentative skill: what of the other part of the thing, which the Prologue calls vocabulary? That is a strangely elusive item. Take, for example, the word *honestus* or 'honourable', which turns up whenever a Latin text ventures into moral philosophy. It is used a number of times in Pliny's letters: is it to be inferred that Pliny was influenced by philosophical vocabulary, and that Syme was wrong when he asserted that the letters 'betray no influence from any lessons imparted by Euphrates or by Artemidorus'?[15] Of course not: *honestus* was an ordinary Latin adjective, not a toy of the philosophers.

Porphyry somewhere says that philosophers, like other scientists, make discoveries and then need names for them: either they invent a new name or they give a new sense to an old one—he is talking of Aristotle's use of κατηγορεῖν, which is an example of the latter case. If we are looking for philosophical vocabulary, then, we must be on the *qui vive* for philosophical neologisms and for philosophical senses of familiar words. (In fact, ancient philosophers rarely went in for neologism: if they needed a new name, they generally borrowed an old one.) In itself, the presence of *honestus* in Pliny's letters shows nothing: the question concerns not the occurrence of that word but its occurrence in a philosophical sense (or perhaps in a Stoic sense, or in an Aristotelian sense, ...).

But the search for such occurrences in Pliny's letters, or indeed in any Latin text, is vain—not because it is difficult to distinguish a philosophical sense from an ordinary sense of *honestus* but because

---

[14] On all this, see Barnes, *Logic*, 12–23.
[15] R. Syme, *Roman Papers*, 573.

there is no philosophical sense to distinguish. Philosophers who use the word do so because they want to say something about what is honourable and noble—that is to say, about the quality to which the word, in its ordinary sense, alludes. And that is what they ineluctably *will* say something about, unless they note, explicitly or implicitly, that are using the word in a new sense, to mean, say, 'honest'. (It is a Stoic paradox that only the wise are rich. The paradox uses the words 'wise' and 'rich' in their ordinary senses—otherwise there is nothing paradoxical.)

It may be said that what is in play is not the adjective *honestus* but the noun *honestum*, which is the Latin for τὸ καλόν). The *OLD* gives the noun as a separate head-word, before the adjective, and surely it is a specifically philosophical term? But the *OLD* gives *bonum* and *malum* as head-words separate from the adjectives, and no one will suppose that they are specifically philosophical—the old and resolutely unphilosophical Cato was pleased to use *bonum publicum* and *malum publicum*. More generally, the nominalization of Latin adjectives was not a peculiarly philosophical operation.[16]

There are, of course, philosophical sentences which use the word *honestus*—for example, the sentence 'nothing is advantageous unless it is honourable' (nihil utile nisi honestum); and although the word *honestus* does not there have a philosophical *sense*, it may be said to have a philosophical *use*. Suppose that one of Pliny's letters were to contain the sentence 'nothing is advantageous unless it is honourable': that would indeed betray the influence of philosophy—not because it contains a philosophical word, or a word used in a philosophical sense, but because it expresses a philosophical thought. Surely *that* can't be what MG means; for she explicitly wants to distinguish the influence of vocabulary from the influence of doctrine. True—but doctrine may influence you in more ways than one: it may affect your actions, and it may affect your thoughts about actions. It is the former influence, not the latter, which MG denies.

Septimus has read Aristotle's *Ethics*, and he has been struck by 'the doctrine of the mean': he doesn't *accept* the doctrine (he is sceptical of its truth), nor does it determine him to do this rather than that. But when he comes to wonder what he ought to do with

---

[16] See e.g. R. Kühner, *Ausführliche Grammatik der lateinischen Sprache*, 2. Aufl., neugearbeitet von C. Stegmann (Hannover, 1912–14), vol. ii.1, §61.3.

his vast wealth, he finds it useful to think in terms of the doctrine. The doctrine reminds him that there are two faults to avoid, the fault of excess and the fault of deficiency, that there are excesses and deficiencies along various dimensions: he mustn't give too little or too much, to too many or to too few, too rarely or too often, ... The doctrine, to put it crudely, doesn't tell him *what* to think: it tells him *how* to think.

The third of the three questions concerns philosophical doctrine. There is something initially disquieting about MG's account of the thing. For if she is right, then it seems that doctrines can have no practical influence whatsoever: if their generality and fluidity and indeterminacy make them unfit for political application, then they surely make them unfit for application of any sort. And that seems to be a paradox worthy of the Stoics themselves. But perhaps it is not as odd as it looks. Consider again the doctrine of the mean. It may be formulated as a thesis stating that any moral virtue is intermediate between two opposite vices, a vice of deficiency and a vice of excess. So formulated, it evidently cannot direct or determine any particular path of action. Then take a practical formulation: 'Neither too much nor too little.' That too offers no particular directives, as Aristotle himself remarks:

Ἐπεὶ δὲ τυγχάνομεν πρότερον εἰρηκότες ὅτι δεῖ τὸ μέσον αἱρεῖσθαι, μὴ τὴν ὑπερβολὴν μηδὲ τὴν ἔλλειψιν, τὸ δὲ μέσον ἐστὶν ὡς ὁ λόγος ὁ ὀρθὸς λέγει, τοῦτο διέλωμεν ... ἔστι δὲ τὸ μὲν εἰπεῖν οὕτως ἀληθὲς μέν, οὐθὲν δὲ σαφές· καὶ γὰρ ἐν ταῖς ἄλλαις ἐπιμελείαις, περὶ ὅσας ἐστὶν ἐπιστήμη, τοῦτ᾽ ἀληθὲς μὲν εἰπεῖν, ὅτι οὔτε πλείω οὔτε ἐλάττω δεῖ πονεῖν οὐδὲ ῥᾳθυμεῖν, ἀλλὰ τὰ μέσα καὶ ὡς ὁ ὀρθὸς λόγος· τοῦτο δὲ μόνον ἔχων ἄν τις οὐδὲν ἂν εἰδείη πλέον, οἷον ποῖα δεῖ προσφέρεσθαι πρὸς τὸ σῶμα, εἴ τις εἴπειεν ὅτι ὅσα ἡ ἰατρικὴ κελεύει καὶ ὡς ὁ ταύτην ἔχων. (*EE* 5. 1 = *NE* 6. 1, 1138ᵇ18–32)

Since we have said earlier that one should choose the intermediate and not the excess nor the deficiency, and that the intermediate is what is said by correct reasoning, let us discuss this ... To say that is true but perfectly unilluminating: for also in other pursuits which are objects of knowledge it is true to say that one should neither exert oneself nor relax too much or too little but to an intermediate extent and as correct reasoning says. But someone who grasped that alone would be none the wiser—for example, he wouldn't know what to apply to his body if someone were to say, 'Whatever medicine and the medical men prescribe.'

MG's view of philosophical doctrines is a generalization of Aristotle's view of the doctrine of the mean.

In any event, MG herself does once or twice appear to allow that doctrine had a political pay-off. Lucius Calpurnius Piso, the Epicurean patron of Philodemus and one of the few members of the cast of Syme's *Roman Revolution* who is not odious, was the object of one of Cicero's more spectacular pieces of invective. MG:

> Cicero's speech *In Pisonem* suggests that L. Calpurnius Piso used his Epicureanism to explain why he had not asked the senate to grant him a triumph when he returned home from his governorship of Macedonia. According to Cicero ... he said that he had never desired a triumph, calling men who did *idiotae*, that is, philosophically ignorant. (361)

And again:

> Cicero attributes to L. Calpurnius Piso Epicurean reasons for not seeking a triumph (*In Pis.* 55 ff.) and to Manlius Torquatus an Epicurean justification for the pursuit of glory and renown (*Fin.* I. 34–6). (429; cf. 554–5)

The Epicurean reasons that Piso offered for his actions, whether they were genuine reasons or (as Cicero claimed) a pious sham, did not consist in matters of vocabulary or exhibitions of argumentative skill: Piso claimed that his Epicurean *beliefs* determined him not to ask for a triumph.

Perhaps it is not a coincidence that Syme too seems to admit that Piso applied his philosophical opinions to his political life:

> The mild and humane doctrines of the Epicureans ... might still be of more use to the Commonwealth than the more elevated principles that were professed, and sometimes followed, with such robust conviction. (135–6)

But that is Syme in Gibbonian vein, and it is not plain what he means us to make of it.

There is no echo of Syme in Chapter 43, 'The Younger Pliny's Debt to Moral Philosophy'. There MG states that 'Pliny is ... explicit about the relevance of philosophical doctrine to just conduct', and that (in one particular letter) 'what Pliny had in mind was the Stoic conception of justice, taken over from Aristotle' (616). MG does not say that philosophy thereby provided Pliny with 'etiquette and style' (a phrase she uses of Cato's philosophical suicide at 417): rather she indicates—although she does not explicitly state—that Pliny offers a few exceptions to the general rule that doctrine did not influence action.

It is worth looking more closely at another passage in *PPR*. In Chapter 31, 'Philosophy for Statesmen', there is this:

> Attempts to explain particular policies pursued by Roman statesmen in terms of their adherence to a particular philosophical sect have not been very successful ... Perhaps we should look more to the language and justification when we are trying to understand the role played in the thought and conduct of Roman statesmen. Thus it is moving to see Cicero, in March of 49, when he was trying to decide whether or not to join Pompey in the East writing to his friends in terms of the *honestum* and the *utile* (*Fam.* 4. 2; 5. 19). (428)

The pertinent part of *Ad fam.* 5. 19, to Mescinius Rufus, is this:

> iudici, quod intellego te, id quod omnes fortes ac boni viri facere debent, nihil putare utile esse nisi quod rectum honestumque sit ... Est enim res profecto maxima. Quid rectum sit apparet; quid expediat obscurum est, ita tamen ut, si nos ii sumus qui esse debemus, id est studio digni ac litteris nostris, dubitare non possimus quin ea maxime conducant quae sunt rectissima. (1–2 Shackleton Bailey)

> I know that you think as all strong and upright men ought to think: you deem that nothing is advantageous if it is not right and honourable [*nihil ... utile esse nisi quod rectum honestumque sit*] ... The present matter is certainly of the greatest moment. What is right is evident: what is advantageous is obscure—save that if we are what we ought to be, that is to say, worthy of our studies and our writings, then we cannot doubt that whatever is most right is most in our interest [*ea maxime conducant quae sunt rectissima*].

The pertinent part of *Ad fam.* 4. 2, to Sulpicius Rufus, is virtually the same, save that (first) Cicero does not there say what it is that we ought to be (namely, worthy of what they have thought and written), and (secondly), instead of 'whatever is most right is most in our interest' he writes 'nothing is expedient which is not right and honourable' (nihil ... expedire nisi quod rectum honestumque sit).

MG comments (429) that Cicero 'is thinking in terms of the Stoic doctrine that nothing could be *utile* which was not *honestum*': true—but he is saying more than that, namely that we should accept the doctrine. 'Philosophy provided the moral vocabulary and the concepts with which to analyse moral problems': true—but philosophy provided more than the vocabulary. 'But it was Cicero who had to decide what was in this, as in any other particular, case': true—but here at least the *honestum* is evident to him, and there can be no doubt what we should do. The practical conclusion is reached like this: (1) It is honourable to do X (evident truth). (2) It is not evident that it is expedient to do X. (3) But whatever is honourable is expedient (philosophical doctrine). (4) Therefore it is both honourable and expedient to do X. (5) Therefore we should do X.[17]

It may be objected that that interpretation of Cicero's argument cannot be right; for Cicero was an Academic philosopher, and Academic philosophers do not have doctrines. The objection misfires: it misrepresents the Academic philosophy—or rather, it misrepresents Cicero's version of the Academic philosophy (of which, notoriously, there were several versions). It is universally agreed that there are no Academic doctrines. There are (say) Epicurean doctrines inasmuch as there are certain philosophical propositions that every Epicurean must accept. There are no Academic doctrines inasmuch as there are no philosophical propositions that every Academic must accept. To be an Academic you must follow certain philosophical methods of reasoning, but that does not require you to accept any particular philosophical propositions. It does not follow that no one who is an Academic can accept any philosophical proposition. (There are no propositions you must accept: it does not follow that you must accept no propositions.) And so—as Cicero likes to put it—the Academy alone leaves you free to adopt whatever philosophical propositions may commend themselves to your reason (and to adopt no proposition which does not so commend itself). As an Academic you may, at one extreme, be an out-and-out sceptic (if your reason commends no philosophical proposition), or at the other extreme you may be a Peripatetic (if your reason commends all and only the propositions that Peripatetics champion). That is why Cicero likes the New Academy— and why any philosopher worth the name must like it.

The doctrine that whatever is honourable is expedient does not determine any answer to the question 'Should Cicero join Pompey in the East?': it is not itself a directive, and it does not imply any particular directive. Nevertheless, the doctrine plays an essential part in an argument which concludes to a directive; and in that way

---

[17] The pertinent doctrine is perhaps properly expressed as an equivalence: X is expedient if and only if X is honourable. Cicero gives two different conditional versions of it. The version in *Ad fam.* 4. 2, repeated in *Ad fam.* 5. 19, is the wrong way round: the second version in 5. 19 is the right way round, but it uses superlatives.

it may have an influence on action. So too with the doctrine of the mean, and so too (no doubt) with any number of other philosophical doctrines. It is true that doctrines cannot *determine* actions: it does not follow, and it is not true, that doctrines cannot *influence* actions. Whether on any given an occasion a doctrine does in fact influence an action is, of course, quite another question.

What is the upshot? Nothing, alas, very thrilling. MG's general thesis states that philosophy influenced Roman politics not by providing doctrines but by offering a vocabulary and some argumentative skills. The several papers in *PPR* suggest somewhat different particular forms of the thesis—something neither remarkable nor lamentable. The best form of the thesis might look something like this: Philosophy offered argumentative skills—it offered them to anyone in any walk of life, and some Roman politicians at least took up the offer. Philosophy offered a vocabulary, which Roman politicians used often enough; but its expressions were almost all part of ordinary Latin, and they took a philosophical colouring only in the context of philosophical theorizing. Philosophy offered doctrines. Some politicians subscribed to certain doctrines, and in some cases followed a course of action which those doctrines, in conjunction with other matter, recommended. But, so far as the meagre evidence goes, the influence of philosophical doctrine on Roman political life—or, come to that, on anything else—was slight.

That, I think, is true—and it was all to change when the Christian philosophy came to dominate the Roman Empire.

IV

'Miriam Griffin has played a central rôle in shaping the study of Roman philosophy today ... The essays in this volume demonstrate not only the skill and energy needed to bridge historical and philosophical research, but also, and more importantly, the innovative results of combining these areas, traditionally treated apart.' So the editor (ix). The first sentence is incontestable: the second required a gloss. For in truth, the essays collected in *PPR* show little sign of philosophical research—and MG would have laughed at (did more than once laugh at) the suggestion that by trade she was a philosopher, or even half a philosopher. The editor might better have said, and doubtless means, that the essays combine work in (political) history with work in (the history of) philosophy. MG was as much at ease on the left bank, among historians of philosophy (witness, say, Chapter 37 on 'The Composition of the *Academica*') as she was on the right bank, among the political historians (witness, say, Chapter 2 on 'The "Leges Iudiciariae" of the Pre-Sullan Era'); and she could indeed bridge the dry gulch which separates the two banks (witness, say, Chapter 26, the nonpareil 'Philosophy, Politics, and Politicians at Rome'). MG was as well versed in ancient philosophy as any of those scholars who bear the quaint appellation of ancient philosopher. (An ancient philosopher is no more a kind of philosopher than a fake Leonardo is a kind of Leonardo.) So if MG is not to be classed as a philosopher, she is to be classed as an ancient philosopher—as a historian of ancient philosophy.

But what sort of historian of philosophy? For as Michael Frede insisted in the Nellie Wallace lectures, which he gave in Oxford some thirty years ago, more than one kind of practice has sailed under the flag of 'history of philosophy'.[18] In particular, Frede distinguished two such practices, one of which he called 'philosophical doxography' and the other 'historical history of philosophy': the former sort, he claimed was what most *soi-disant* ancient philosophers indulged in, whether they knew it or not, while the latter sort was relatively unpractised.[19]

What Frede calls philosophical doxography may be characterized like this:[20] doxographers attempt to reconstruct those views and arguments of past philosophers which have a contemporary resonance; they do so with the intention of contributing to the contemporary discussion; and they treat the philosophers of the past

---

[18] *The Historiography of Philosophy* is under contract with OUP. For the moment, see his review of J. J. E. Gracia, *Philosophy and its History: Issues in Philosophical Historiography*, in *Philosophy and Phenomenological Research*, 54 (1994), 233–6); 'The Study of Ancient Philosophy', in id., *Essays in Ancient Philosophy* (Oxford, 1987), ix–xxvii; id., 'The History of Philosophy as a Discipline', *Journal of Philosophy*, 85 (1988), 666–72; id., 'Doxographie, historiographie philosophique et historiographie historique de la philosophie', *Revue de métaphysique et de morale*, 97 (1992), 311–25.

[19] Frede doesn't claim that these two are the only practices which have gone, or might go, under the title 'history of philosophy'. Indeed, the lectures begin by distinguishing among three practices, one of which he finds to be uninteresting—and to have fallen into desuetude.

[20] It should be noted that in Frede's mouth, the word 'doxography' is not pejorative.

as though they were colleagues, and they read Cicero's *De fato* as though it were hot from the Clarendon Press. Philosophical doxography, Frede thinks, may be called historical inasmuch as it deals with the past—but only a Pickwick will call it history.

Although Frede claimed that most of his colleagues who worked on past philosophers were doxographers, I don't think I have ever met very many doxographers myself. It is true that my tutor Dick Hare suggested that I read the *Meno* as though it had been published in a supplement to *Mind*, and it is true that I said the same thing to my own pupils. We suggested that the *Meno* should be read as a contribution to present philosophy rather than to past history, and the obedient pupils read it with the aim of a Fredean doxographer. But they were not Fredean doxographers: they were not required to *reconstruct* past thoughts—the thoughts were there on the page, waiting to be read. What they thought Plato had said was often inaccurate, or partial, or cuckoo. No matter, provided that the *Meno* had caused them to ruminate.

If you want to learn some logic, it is a good idea to read *Methods of Logic*, say, or *Beginning Logic*. You don't read them to find out what Quine really meant or what Lemmon actually thought (who gives a hoot about that?): you read them to learn logic. If you want to learn something about fate and freedom, it is a good idea to read, *inter alia*, Cicero, or Alexander. You don't read them to discover what Cicero really meant or what Alexander actually thought (though to be sure some people do give more than a hoot about that): you read them to help you on a philosophical inquiry.

Semi-doxography of that sort is, I think, a Good Thing. But semi-doxographers court intellectual danger. Reading the *De fato* might rouse an interest not in fate and freedom but in ... Cicero's *De fato*. That interest once aroused, the *apparatus criticus* will be scanned and the text of the essay subjected to philological scrutiny, the pages of *SVF* will be turned and Cicero's account of Chrysippus' position will be measured against other surviving accounts, the role of Carneades, to whose Academy Cicero bore allegiance, will be given particular attention, and the various theses and arguments which make up the text will be reconstructed and assessed with historical rigour and exegetical subtlety. And so it seems semi-doxographers have become full Fredean doxographers. But although they may continue to believe that they are making a contribution to the timeless discipline of Dame Philosophy, and may even (*experto crede*) add a few philosophical flourishes to their books and articles, they are almost certainly deceiving themselves, for the truth is that their elegant reconstructions of the thoughts of the past are unlikely to offer more than the occasional footnote to the works of their philosophical colleagues. They have changed from being semi-doxographers of one sort to semi-doxographers of another sort.

Scholars who work on Galen's *De methodo medendi* neither intend nor expect that their work will contribute to contemporary discussion of the best way to treat alopecia (perhaps a *pomade* roast hedgehog?) or priapism (cold bandages, not amputation). Scholars who labour over Galen's *Institutio logica* do not aim at the improvement of modern logic (perhaps 'It's not the case that both *P* and *Q*' isn't a negated conjunction). What goes for Galen's *Institutio logica* goes for Aristotle's *Prior Analytics*—and for any other work of ancient philosophy, and for most works of past philosophy.

What of MG's work on Cicero and Seneca et al.? Plainly, it is neither doxography nor semi-doxography: it has no philosophical aim, and it is not concerned to reconstruct the thoughts of those eminent old men.

The historical history of philosophy with which Frede contrasts philosophical doxography is, as its name doubly suggests, a sort of history: it collects a certain sort of past fact; it offers explanations of those facts; and it weaves the explanations into a narrative. The facts—the 'basic facts'—are facts about what Frede calls philosophical views, the most important of which are philosophical beliefs. Views are viewings, and beliefs are believings: they are states of mind. One basic fact for a historian of ancient philosophy is the fact that in March 49 Cicero held the belief that only honourable actions are expedient. The basic facts concern not only the holding of beliefs but also the adopting and rejecting of them—and indeed the having, or the taking up, or the putting down of any intellectual attitude towards a philosophical proposition. They also include the expression, in private or in public, of such attitudes. So another basic fact for a historian of ancient philosophy is the fact that in March 49 Cicero wrote to two of his acquaintances that only the honourable is expedient.

In general, a philosophical historian's basic facts might be expressly, artificially, in formulas of the form:

Such-and-such a person at such-and-such a time (or for such-and-such a period) takes such-and-such an attitude towards such-and-such a proposition.

Say:

at *t, x* has *A* that *P*.

Given that '*P*' is a philosophical proposition, *any* true formula of that form expresses a basic fact: *x* may or may not be a philosopher, the attitude *A* may or may not be insane. The basic facts concern past events or states of affairs. They are typical historical facts. They are not philosophical facts.

Historical historians of philosophy explain the facts they have assembled—they look for truths of the form:

Because *Q*, at *t, x* has *A* that *P*.

Any sentence which gives such an explanation—any concrete case of '*Q*'—is likely to be long and complicated. Some its elements are likely to be basic facts, either basic facts about *x* or basic facts about someone else ('Because at *t*, x** had *A** that *P**'); but there is in principle no limit on the sort of fact which may be an element of *Q*.

Some of the basic facts which are elements of *Q* may advert to reasons that *x* had or gave at *t* for having *A* that *P*; but a historian does not offer them as *x*'s reasons: Cicero may have said, 'Determinism excludes responsibility because it implies necessity', the historian will say, 'Because at *t* Cicero thought that determinism implied necessity, at *t** he asserted that determinism excludes responsibility.' Here is one of the points at which doxography and historical history differ: a doxographer is interested in *x*'s reasons for having, at *t, A* that *P*, and a historian is concerned to explain why, at *t, x* had *A* that *P*.

Events and states of affairs have effects as well as causes. When there is a basic fact among the causes of another basic fact, the second is an effect of the first. That being so, basic facts will, as it were, chain together—or rather, they will intermesh. And the history of philosophy which the historical historian is writing is a description of that intermeshing.

Frede thought that few historians went in for historical history of philosophy. But numbers of historians of philosophy have practised an impure version of the enterprise. They have taken as their basic facts not the attitudes of individuals at particular times towards philosophical propositions but rather the propositions themselves. The German for that sort of thing is '*Begriffsgeschichte*', and a German might, for example, relate how the conception of truth had changed or developed: at first truth was conceived of as a sort of openness or evidence, and later it was conceived of as a correspondence with or adequacy to reality or the world; and the historian will tell you when the change took place, and why it did. Or—less unpromisingly—a historian of logic may recount the story of wholly hypothetical syllogisms in antiquity: they started out as (in effect) caterpillars of the form 'If *Fa* then *Ga*; if *Ga* then *Ha*: so if *Fa* then *Ga*', and they ended up, after a few intermediate stages, as the familiar modern butterfly: if *P* then *Q*; if *Q* then *R*; so if *P* then *R*. And the historian undertakes to explain how and why things developed in that way.

Impure historical history differs from the pure thing in two respects: first, it does not (save incidentally) consider dated attitudes to philosophical propositions; and secondly, its explanatory suggestions are philosophical. It is, so to speak, philosophical historical history of philosophy. It is in one respect an easier enterprise than the pure version: the philosophical historian is not overwhelmed by the quantity of basic facts. It is also a more elusive enterprise; for the explanations it offers are largely speculative.

MG did not engage in *Begriffsgeschichte*, nor was she a historical historian of philosophy: she was not concerned, save incidentally, with the ways in which Stoic philosophy developed, from Zeno to Seneca; and she did not inquire into the causes of Cicero's philosophical attitudes. But she might be classified—by someone with a Varronian penchant for classification—as a partial historical historian of philosophy. Her basic facts are the basic facts of a historical historian—what Cicero said there and then, what Pliny wrote then and there; and if she is concerned not with their causes she is concerned with their effects—and in particular with their effects on public life.[21]

Ceaulmont

---

[21] The author would like to note that the editor has made two sorts of alterations to the author's English without the latter's approval.

BIBLIOGRAPHY

Barnes, J., *Logic and the Imperial Stoa* [*Logic*] (Leiden, 1997).

Ducos, M., 'Blossius de Cumes', in R. Goulet (ed.), *Dictionnaire des philosophes antiques*, 7 vols. with a suppl. vol. (Paris, 1994–2018), vol. ii. 116–17.

Frede, M., 'The Study of Ancient Philosophy', in id., *Essays in Ancient Philosophy* (Oxford, 1987), ix–xxvii.

Frede, M., 'The History of Philosophy as a Discipline', *Journal of Philosophy*, 85 (1988), 666–72.

Frede, M., 'Doxographie, historiographie philosophique et historiographie historique de la philosophie', *Revue de métaphysique et de morale*, 97 (1992), 311–25.

Frede, M., review of J. J. E. Gracia, *Philosophy and its History: Issues in Philosophical Historiography*, in *Philosophy and Phenomenological Research*, 54 (1994), 233–6.

Griffin, M. T., *Seneca: A Philosopher in Politics* [*Seneca*] (Oxford, 1976).

Kühner, R., *Ausführliche Grammatik der lateinischen Sprache*, 2. Aufl., neugearbeitet von C. Stegmann (Hannover, 1912–14), 2 vols.

Sherwin-White, A. N., *The Letters of Pliny* (Oxford, 1966).

Syme, R., *The Roman Revolution* (Oxford, 1939).

Syme, R., 'A Political Group', in A. R. Birley (ed.), *Ronald Syme, Roman Papers*, vol. vii [*Roman Papers*] (Oxford, 1991), 568–87.

INDEX LOCORUM

Sophocles
Tragicorum Graecorum fragmenta, ed.
  Nauck

[Themistius]
In Aristotelis Analyticorum posteriorum
  paraphrasis, ed. Wallies
In Aristotelis Analyticorum priorum
  librum I paraphrasis, ed. Wallies

Thucydides

Xenophon
Memorabilia

Notes for Contributors to Oxford Studies in Ancient Philosophy

1. Articles should be submitted with double line-spacing throughout. At the stage of initial (but not final) submission footnotes may be given in small type at the foot of the page. Page dimensions should be A4 or standard American quarto (8½ × 11″), and ample margins (minimum 1¼″ or 32 mm) should be left.

2. Submissions should be made as an **anonymized** PDF file attached to an e-mail sent to the Editor. Authors are asked to supply an accurate word-count (*a*) for the main text, and (*b*) for the notes. The e-mail which serves as a covering letter should come from the address to be used for correspondence on the submission. A postal address should also be provided. If necessary, arrangements for alternative means of submission may be made with the Editor. Authors should note that the version first submitted will be the one adjudicated; unsolicited revised versions cannot be accepted during the adjudication process. *The remaining instructions apply to the final version sent for publication, and need not be rigidly adhered to in a first submission.*

3. In the finalized version, the text should be double-spaced and in the same typesize throughout, **including displayed quotations and notes**. Notes should be numbered consecutively, and may be supplied as either footnotes or endnotes. Any acknowledgements should be placed in a final note attached to the last word of the article. Wherever possible, references to primary sources should be built into the text.

4. **Use of Greek and Latin.** Relatively familiar Greek terms such as *psuchē* and *polis* (but not whole phrases and sentences) may be used in transliteration or likewise a few, isolated terms where translation would be prejudicial. Wherever possible, Greek and Latin should not be used in the main text of an article in ways which would impede comprehension by those without knowledge of the languages; for example, where appropriate, the original texts should be accompanied by a translation. For further details or instructions, please consult the Editor. Greek must be supplied in an accurate form, with all diacritics in place. Please indicate whether the Greek is in a Unicode font or if not, the software used to input it (e.g. GreekKeys, Linguist's Software) to facilitate file conversion.

5. For citations of Greek and Latin authors, house style should be followed. This can be checked in any recent issue of *OSAP* with the help of the Index Locorum. The most exact reference possible should normally be employed, especially if a text is quoted or discussed in detail: for example, line references for Plato (not just Stephanus page and letter) and Aristotle (not just Bekker page and column).

6. In references to books, the first time the book is referred to give the initial(s) and surname of the author (first names are not usually required), and the place and date of publication; where you are abbreviating the title in subsequent citations, give the abbreviation in square brackets, thus:

> T. Brickhouse and N. Smith, *Socrates on Trial* [*Trial*] (Princeton, 1981), 91–4.

Give the volume-number and date of periodicals, and include the full page-extent of articles (including chapters of books):

> D. W. Graham, 'Symmetry in the Empedoclean Cycle' ['Symmetry'], *Classical Quarterly*, NS 38 (1988), 297–312 at 301–4.

> G. Vlastos, 'A Metaphysical Paradox' ['Metaphysical'], in G. Vlastos, *Platonic Studies,* 2nd edn. (Princeton, 1981), 43–57 at 52.

Where the same book or article is referred to on subsequent occasions, usually the most convenient style will be an abbreviated reference:

> Brickhouse and Smith, *Trial,* 28–9.

Do *not* use the author-and-date style of reference.

7. Authors are asked to supply *in addition,* at the end of the article, a full list of the bibliographical entries cited, alphabetically ordered by (first) author's surname. Except that the author's surname should come first, these entries should be identical in form to the first occurrence of each in the article, including where appropriate the indication of abbreviated title:

> Graham, D. W., 'Symmetry in the Empedoclean Cycle' ['Symmetry'], *Classical Quarterly*, NS 38 (1988), 297–312.

8. If there are any unusual conventions contributors are encouraged to include a covering note for the copy-editor and/or printer. Please say whether you are using single and double quotation marks for different purposes (otherwise the Press will employ its standard single quotation marks throughout, using double only for quotations within quotations).

9. Authors should send a copy of the final version of their paper in electronic form by attachment to an e-mail. The final version should be provided as a Microsoft Word file (or Rich Text Format file), accompanied by a note of the system (**not just the font**) used for producing Greek characters (see point 4 above). This file must be accompanied by a second file, a copy in PDF format of the final version, to which it must correspond **exactly**. If necessary, arrangements for alternative means of submission may be made with the Editor. With final submission authors should also send, in a separate file, a brief abstract and a list of approximately ten keywords.